Grammar and Writing 6

Student Edition

Second Edition

Christie Curtis

Mary Hake

Houghton Mifflin Harcourt Publishers, Inc.

Grammar and Writing 6

Second Edition

Student Edition

Copyright © 2014 by Houghton Mifflin Harcourt Publishing Company and Mary E. Hake and Christie Curtis

This edition is based on the work titled *Grammar and Writing 6* © 2006 by Mary E. Hake and Christie Curtis and originally published by Hake Publishing.

Printed in the U.S.A.

ISBN 978-0-544-04426-5

12 2266 23 22 21

4500817250 B C D E F G

Contents

Introduction

Welcome to a language arts program created for easy reading and instruction. Behind this program is a team of dedicated teachers who care about your success and want to present incremental teaching material in a simple format.

This program consists of a series of **daily lessons**, **review sets**, and **tests** that are carefully sequenced to develop a variety of skills and concepts. We include lessons on capitalization, punctuation, parts of speech, sentence structure, spelling rules, and correct word usage, all with a focus on improving your writing.

To increase your understanding, you will learn to diagram sentences. Diagramming a sentence, like doing a puzzle, exercises your brain and helps you to see the structure of the sentence and the function of its parts. Knowing how to diagram an English sentence will make your future study of foreign languages much easier. It will also help you with correct word usage and punctuation as you write.

Because of the incremental nature of this program, **it is essential that the lessons be taught in order, that all review sets are completed, and that no lessons are skipped.**

In addition to the daily lessons, the program includes a series of **writing lessons**. These are designed to guide you through the process of composing a complete essay. Also included are weekly **dictations** for practice in spelling and punctuation. You will also be asked to keep a journal; the program contains suggested **journal topics**.

Before you start your lesson, you need not wait for teacher instruction because you know how to begin each day:

MONDAY—Find your weekly dictation in the appendix and copy it to practice for your Friday test.

TUESDAY, WEDNESDAY, THURSDAY—Find your journal topic in the appendix and begin writing.

FRIDAY—Look over your dictation to prepare for your dictation test.

Mastery of the English language is one of the most valuable tools you can possess. It is our hope that this program provides you with a strong foundation not only for future language arts studies but also for a lifetime of satisfying and successful writing.

Best wishes!

Four Types of Sentences

Dictation or Journal Entry

Vocabulary:

Punctual means "on time; not late." The *punctual* students were in their seats when the bell rang.

Considerate means "thoughtful of others; kind." A *considerate* person listens when others are speaking.

A group of words that expresses a complete thought is called a sentence. A capital letter begins each sentence. There are **four types of sentences.**

Declarative

A **declarative sentence** makes a statement and ends with a period:

A team of teachers devised this language arts series.

Practice helps us to remember new concepts.

Review is an important learning tool.

Interrogative

An **interrogative sentence** asks a question and ends with a question mark:

Have you devised a plan for building the clubhouse?

Do you have any brothers or sisters?

Does his father speak Chinese?

Imperative

An **imperative sentence** expresses a command or a request and ends with a period:

Do your homework.

Think before you speak.

Please believe me.

Exclamatory

An **exclamatory sentence** shows excitement or strong feeling and ends with an exclamation point:

Help!

I can't wait until Saturday!

What fun it is to learn new things!

Example Tell whether the following sentences are declarative, interrogative, imperative, or exclamatory.

(a) How was your vacation?

(b) Hard work builds strength.

(c) Mow the lawn before you wash the car.

(d) I'm drowning!

Solution (a) This is an **interrogative** sentence because it asks a question and ends with a question mark.

(b) This sentence makes a statement and ends with a period. It is **declarative.**

(c) This sentence commands you to do something, and it ends with a period. Therefore, it is **imperative.**

(d) This sentence ends with an exclamation point and shows strong feeling. We recognize the **exclamatory** sentence.

✓ **Practice** Identify the sentence type. Write "declarative," "interrogative," "imperative," or "exclamatory."

a. Please read *Oliver Twist*.

b. *Oliver Twist* is a novel written by Charles Dickens.

c. Are you familiar with Charles Dickens?

d. Hurrah! I finished *Oliver Twist*!

e. Make each day count.

Replace each blank with the correct vocabulary word.

f. If you arrive on time, you are _____.

g. If you act kindly toward other people, you are _____.

Replace each blank with the correct word to complete sentences 1–10.

1. A _____ sentence makes a statement.

2. An _____ sentence asks a question.

3. An _____ sentence expresses a command or request.

4. An _____ sentence shows strong feeling.

5. Declarative and imperative sentences end with a _____.

6. A group of words that expresses a complete thought is called a _____.

7. A sentence expresses a complete _____.

8. A sentence begins with a _____ letter.

9. An interrogative sentence ends with a _____ mark.

10. An exclamatory sentence ends with an _____ point.

Tell whether sentences 11–24 are declarative, interrogative, exclamatory, or imperative.

11. Slava doesn't have any pets.

12. Do you have any pets?

13. Please don't bring me any lizards.

14. What an unusual reptile you have!

15. It was a wonderful day!

16. Kim is usually punctual.

17. Feed the rabbit before you leave.

18. Did you lock the door?

19. Critics consider Charles Dickens one of the greatest English novelists.

20. Have you read any novels by Charles Dickens?

21. Please be quiet.

22. Wow! Poor Oliver was so hungry!

23. Did you know that your uncle always wanted to climb Mt. Everest?

24. *Oliver Twist* shocked the British public into having more compassion for their poor and homeless.

For 25 and 26, replace each blank with the correct vocabulary word.

25. The _____ teacher started class on time.

26. The _____ boy helped his little brother tie his shoes.

27. Unscramble these words to make a declarative sentence:

    likes   the   me   dog

28. Unscramble these words to make an interrogative sentence:

    considerate   you   are

29. Unscramble these words to make an exclamatory sentence:

    is   exciting   this

30. Unscramble these words to make an imperative sentence:

    to   be   try   punctual

Simple Subjects • Simple Predicates

A sentence has two main parts: (1) the subject and (2) the predicate. The subject is the part that tells who or what the sentence is about. The predicate is the part that tells something about the subject. The sentences below have been divided into their two main parts—subjects and predicates.

COMPLETE SUBJECT	COMPLETE PREDICATE
A moral person	treats others fairly.
Queen Esther	saved her people.
The jiggly jellyfish	slid off my dish.
Geometry	is fun.

The complete (whole) subject or predicate may consist of a single word or many words. However, a subject or predicate consisting of many words always has an essential part that we call the *simple subject* or *simple predicate.*

Simple Subject The main word or words in a sentence that tell <u>who or what</u> is doing or being something is called the **simple subject.** In the sentence below, *John* is the simple subject because it tells <u>who</u> played the piano.

Red-headed *John* played the piano all night.

In the sentences below, we have italicized the simple subjects.

A moral *person* treats others fairly.

Queen Esther saved her people.

The jiggly *jellyfish* slid off my dish.

Geometry is fun.

Example 1 What is the simple subject of the following sentence?

The basketball player shoots baskets every day.

Solution   Who or what shoots baskets? The basketball player does, so **player** is the simple subject. (The word "basketball" tells what kind of player.)

Simple Predicate   The **simple predicate** is the verb. A verb <u>expresses action</u> or being. In the sentence below, "told" is the simple predicate <u>because</u> it tells what Tom did.

Tom <u>told</u> me a joke.

We have underlined the simple predicates of the sentences below.

> ACTION: A moral *person* <u>treats</u> others fairly.
>
> ACTION: *Queen Esther* <u>saved</u> her people.
>
> ACTION: The jiggly *jellyfish* <u>slid</u> off my dish.
>
> BEING: *Geometry* <u>is</u> fun.

Notice that sometimes the simple predicate contains more than one word, as in these sentences:

A *thief* <u>had stolen</u> the jewels.

Mom <u>will be waiting</u> at the airport.

You <u>should have come</u> sooner.

Example 2   Give the simple predicate of the sentence below.

The basketball player shoots baskets every day.

Solution   We examine the sentence and discover that the player "shoots." Therefore, **shoots** is the simple predicate.

Sometimes the order of the subject and predicate is reversed as in the sentences below.

Now <u>comes</u> the *fun.*

Over the fence <u>came</u> my neighbor's *dog.*

Example 3   Give the simple subject and the simple predicate of this sentence:

(At the end of the rainbow) sat a pot of gold.

Solution   We remember that sometimes the predicate comes before the subject. The simple subject of this sentence is **pot.** What did the pot do? It "sat." The simple predicate is **sat.** Do not be confused by the word "rainbow." It is not the subject. "At the end of the rainbow" tells where the pot sat.

Split Predicate In interrogative sentences, we usually find parts of the predicate split by the subject, as in this sentence:

Did *you* see me?

In the sentence above, the simple subject is *you*, and the simple predicate is <u>did see</u>.

Example 4 Give the simple predicate of this sentence:

Has Buckeye finished the job?

Solution The subject *Buckeye* <u>has finished</u>. Therefore, the simple predicate is **has finished.**

√ **Practice** For a–d, write the simple subject of each sentence.

a. The expiration date made the coupon invalid.

b. One character (in *The Secret Garden*) believed himself an invalid.

c. Mary's honest answer demonstrates her high morals.

d. Dickon, a character in *The Secret Garden,* had a sibling named Martha.

For e–g, write the simple predicate of each sentence.

e. Will Dickon succeed?

f. Courageous people inspire us.

g. Dickon devised a way to talk to his beloved animals.

For h and i, replace each blank with the correct vocabulary word.

h. The word *moral* refers to a concern for right and _____.

i. One who does not care about right conduct is not _____.

More Practice See "More Practice Lesson 2" in Student Workbook.

√ **Review Set 2** Replace each blank with the correct word to complete sentences 1–5.

Numbers in parentheses indicate the lesson in which the concept was introduced.

1. The main word in a sentence that tells who or what is
(2) doing something is called the simple _____.

2. The simple subject of a sentence tells _____ or
(2) _____ is doing something.

3. The simple _____ is the verb.
(2)

4. A verb expresses _____ or being.
(2)

(2) **5.** A complete _____ has a subject and a predicate.

Write the simple subject of sentences 6–14.

6. Were the leaves changing colors?
(2)

7. Up in the tree sat three squirrels.
(2)

8. The boy looked longingly out the window.
(2)

9. Freddy studied Hebrew.
(2)

10. Beth speaks Spanish.
(2)

11. Dr. Monty can straighten your teeth.
(2)

12. Have you traveled to China?
(2)

13. She is writing poetry.
(2)

14. Have you read the directions?
(2)

15–23. Write the simple predicate of sentences 6–14.
(2)

24. Unscramble these words to make a declarative sentence:
(1)   has   high   Frank   morals

25. Unscramble these words to make an interrogative sentence:
(1)   considerate   he   is

26. Unscramble these words to make an exclamatory sentence:
(1)   keys   my   lost   I

27. Unscramble these words to make an imperative sentence:
(1)   vegetables   eat   your

For 28–30, replace each blank with the correct vocabulary word.

28. The police must have high _____ standards.
(2)

29. They must also be _____, or "on time."
(1)

(1) **30.** You are _____ if you care about others.

Identifying Complete Sentences, Fragments, and Run-on Sentences

> **Dictation or Journal Entry**
> **Vocabulary:**
> *Reliable* means "trustworthy." The teacher chose a *reliable* student to collect the money.
>
> *Respectful* means "courteous and polite." Judy is *respectful* toward her parents.

Complete Sentences

A **complete sentence** expresses a complete thought. It has both a subject and a predicate. The following are **complete sentences**.

A sibling is a brother or a sister.

Who devised this language arts book?

Please clean your room today.

Notice that the sentence above, "Please clean your room today," does not appear to have a subject. It is an imperative sentence, a command. The subject *you* is understood.

(You) please clean your room today.

Fragments

A piece of a sentence is called a **fragment.** When a sentence fragment fails to tell us who or what is doing the action, it is missing the subject. The following sentence fragments are missing subjects.

Opened the book. (who?)

Jumping over the fence. (who or what?)

If we identify the subject, and we do not know what the subject is being or doing, the expression is missing a verb. The sentence fragments below are missing verbs.

The doctor at the hospital. (did or was what?)

The student with the notebook. (did or was what?)

If the subject or verb is missing, we identify the expression as a **fragment.** Other errors that result in fragments are leaving out punctuation marks or using the *to* form and *ing* form of the verb.

FRAGMENTS	COMPLETE SENTENCES
The girl walking her dog.	The girl walked her dog.
	The girl walking her dog smiled at me.

Jenny to make her bed.

Mom asked Jenny to make her bed.

Jenny wanted to make her bed.

Run-on Sentences A sentence is complete only if it expresses a complete thought. A **run-on sentence** is defined as two complete thoughts written or spoken as one sentence without proper punctuation or connecting words, as shown below.

The invalid devised a plan to go to the market he should stay home until he recovers. (Run-on)

Placing a comma where a period should be results in a run-on sentence.

The invalid devised a plan to go to the market, he should stay home until he recovers. (Run-on)

If we join sentences with *and*'s, *and so*'s, or *but*'s, and omit the joining words or punctuation, we have a run-on sentence.

RUN-ON SENTENCE:
Some people have only one sibling other people have two but some people have three.

COMPLETE SENTENCE:
Some people have only one sibling, and other people have two, but some people have three.

Example Tell whether each of the following is a complete sentence, sentence fragment, or run-on sentence.
(a) Exercise makes us feel better it is fun too.

(b) The doctor wearing a white coat.

(c) Water is good for our health.

(d) To play after the rain.

Solution (a) This expression is two complete thoughts without punctuation. Therefore it is a **run-on sentence.** (Corrected: Exercise makes us feel better. It is fun too.)

(b) This expression is missing part of the verb, so it is a **sentence fragment.** [Corrected: The doctor wearing a white coat smiled. (or) The doctor is wearing a white coat.]

(c) **Complete sentence.**

(d) This expression uses the *to* form of the verb, and it lacks a subject. It is not a complete thought. It is a **sentence fragment.** [Corrected: I want to play after the rain. (or) I will play after the rain.]

✓**Practice** For a–d, tell whether each expression is a sentence fragment, run-on sentence, or complete sentence.

  a. At the beginning of *Romeo and Juliet.*

  b. Romeo is the boyfriend of Juliet their families hate one another.

  c. Thinking Romeo is dead.

  d. Romeo drinks poison because he thinks Juliet is dead Juliet wakes up and stabs herself.

Replace each blank with the correct vocabulary word.

  e. A person who can be trusted is _____.

  f. If you are courteous and polite, you are _____.

More Practice Tell whether each sentence is a complete sentence, a sentence fragment, or a run-on sentence.

  1. Michelangelo painted.

  2. A great Renaissance artist from Italy.

  3. For two years, Michelangelo lay on his back on top of high scaffolds he painted the ceiling of the Vatican's Sistine Chapel in Rome.

  4. His paintings of the Creation, Adam and Eve, and the Flood.

5. He also made sculptures of the ancient Biblical leaders David and Moses.

6. He lived from 1475 to 1564 some people say he was the greatest.

√ **Review Set 3** Replace each blank with the correct word to complete sentences 1–6.

1. A complete sentence has both a _____ and a
(3)   _____.

2. A complete sentence expresses a _____ thought.
(3,1)

3. A piece of a sentence is called a _____.
(3)

4. When a fragment fails to tell who or what is doing the
(3, 2)   action, it is missing the _____.

5. If we identify the subject, and it is not being or doing
(3, 2)   anything, the expression is missing a _____.

6. More than one complete thought written as one sentence
(3)   is called a _____ sentence.

7. Which sentence is imperative? Choose *A* or *B*.
(1)
   A. Please be respectful toward your friends.

   B. Are you a reliable friend?

For 8–10, write whether the expression is a complete sentence or a sentence fragment.

8. To walk over the bridge and through the park.
(3)

9. Bryon ran.
(3)

10. Tom is flying to New York.
(3)

For 11 and 12, write whether each sentence is a complete sentence or a run-on sentence.

11. I'm late you're early.
(3)

12. Johnny created the Web site.
(3)

Write the simple subject of sentences 13–16.

13. George Washington crossed the Delaware on Christmas
(2) night, 1776.

14. During the fall, Kurt picked a bushel of apples.
(2)

15. Soltera shared her lunch.
(2)

16. After dinner, they went for a walk.
(2)

Choose the best word to complete sentences 17–20.

17. We can trust a (rich, popular, reliable) person.
(3)

18. Courteous and polite Dr. Noodleman is (snoopy,
(3) respectful, irritable) toward his patients.

19. We hope that our politicians are (happy, moral, thirsty)
(2) leaders.

20. If you finish your homework on time, you are (smart,
(1) perplexed, punctual).

Write the simple predicate of sentences 21–24.

21. Do peacocks live at the arboretum?
(2)

22. Beth planted bulbs in the fall.
(2)

23. On Tuesday, Dr. Curtis saw twelve patients.
(2)

24. The nurse gives flu shots.
(2)

25–28. Write the simple subject of sentences 21–24.
(2)

29. Which sentence is complete? Choose *A* or *B*.
(3)
    A. To fly in a helicopter over a volcano.

    B. Sergio smiled.

30. Which is a complete sentence? Choose *A* or *B*.
(3)
    A. Having always been considerate

    B. A considerate person thinks of others first.

Correcting Sentence Fragments and Run-on Sentences

> **Dictation or Journal Entry**
> **Vocabulary:**
> The prefix *homo-* means "the same." *Homonyms* ("same name") are words that are spelled and pronounced alike but differ in meaning. "Peck" (a measure) and "peck" (to strike with the beak) are *homonyms.* *Homophones* ("same sound") are words that sound the same but differ in spelling and meaning. "Hare" and "hair" are *homophones.*

Correcting Fragments   We can correct sentence fragments by adding subjects, verbs, and punctuation marks.

Example 1   Correct this sentence fragment: Howled all night long.

Solution   There is more than one right answer. We add a subject to tell who or what howled all night long.

> **My *dog* <u>howled</u> all night long.**
>
> **A *wolf* <u>howled</u> all night long.**

Example 2   Correct this sentence fragment: The cheerleaders' routine

Solution   There are different ways to correct this sentence fragment. We can add an action verb telling "what the cheerleaders' routine did."

> **The cheerleaders' *routine* <u>won</u> first place.**

We can also add a being verb to tell "what the cheerleaders' routine was."

> **The cheerleaders' *routine* <u>was</u> outstanding.**

Correcting Run-ons   We correct run-on sentences by adding punctuation, and by removing unnecessary words.

Example 3   Correct this run-on sentence:

> James needs to wash and dry the dishes he should also mow the lawn.

Solution   We add a period and capital letter to make two complete sentences.

> **James needs to wash and dry the dishes. He should also mow the lawn.**

√Practice

For a and b, rewrite and correct each run-on sentence. There is more than one correct answer.

a. George Orwell uses animals for the main characters in his book *Animal Farm* it reveals how people gain power over other people

b. George Orwell was an English writer born in 1903 he witnessed the rise of Hitler

For c and d, rewrite and correct each sentence fragment. There is more than one correct answer.

c. One animal character a boar named Old Major

d. Bluebell, Jessie, and Pincher three dog characters

For e–i, replace each blank with the correct vocabulary word.

e. The prefix _____ means "the same."

f. Words that are pronounced and spelled alike but have different meanings are called _____.

g. Words that sound the same but have different spellings and meanings are called _____.

h. The words *dice* (number cubes) and *dice* (to cut) are _____.

i. The words *cent, sent,* and *scent* are _____.

√ More Practice

For 1–5, correct each sentence fragment. There is more than one correct answer.

1. Wrote a poem about promises.

2. To read poems by Robert Frost.

3. Can write poetry.

4. If you try.

5. An English poet named William Wordsworth.

For 6–10, correct each run-on sentence. There is more than one correct answer.

6. *Procrastination* means "putting things off" don't procrastinate.

7. I procrastinated I didn't do my work.

8. I'll do it tomorrow I won't procrastinate.

9. Procrastination steals time don't do it.

10. Stop procrastinating do your work.

Review Set 4   Write the simple subject of sentences 1–3.

1. The jet landed in Philadelphia.
(2)

2. After noon, the weather became stormy.
(2)

3. Turbo caught the ball in his mouth.
(2)

4–6. For 4–6, write the simple predicate of sentences 1–3.
(2)

For 7–10, correct each sentence fragment by making a complete sentence. There is more than one correct answer.

7. Took his suit to the dry cleaner.
(4)

8. The lady wearing a green cape.
(4)

9. Will eat dinner in half an hour.
(4)

10. Juan, the ingenious web master.
(4)

For 11–14, correct each run-on sentence.

11. The colonel carried quarters he had ten.
(4)

12. He recognized the dilemma then he made a decision.
(4)

13. Nancy will fly to Tucson she has a roundtrip ticket.
(4)

14. Her ticket is expensive it costs two hundred dollars.
(4)

15. Unscramble these words to make a declarative sentence:
(1)

sound   homophones   alike

16. Unscramble these words to make an interrogative
(1) sentence:

ready you are

17. Unscramble these words to make an exclamatory
(1) sentence:

car this no has gas

18. Unscramble these words to make an imperative sentence:
(1)
your waste don't time

For 19–22, tell whether each expression is a complete
sentence, a sentence fragment, or a run-on sentence.

19. The diver on the high diving platform.
(3)

20. Snickered, gasped, and vaulted the fence.
(3)

21. Tim snores.
(3)

22. I'm not late I'm on time.
(3)

For 23–28, choose the best word to complete each sentence.

23. "Phil" and "fill" are homophones. However, "bat," a
(4) mammal, and "bat," to hit a ball, are (homonyms,
homogenized, homophones).

24. Webster's Dictionary is a (fallacious, unusual, reliable)
(3) source of word definitions.

25. Dad trusts Jenny to keep her word because she is
(3) (understanding, reliable, pretty).

26. Fong and Danny treat others with courtesy because they
(3) are (handsome, reasonable, respectful).

27. The (purposeful, punctual, moral) employee starts work
(1) on time.

28. Ilbea spoke softly to be (afraid, considerate, aware) of her
(1) sleeping sister.

For 29 and 30, tell which sentence is complete. Write *A* or *B*.

29. A. To play soccer or to ride bikes.
(3) B. Emily spoke.

30. A. Is Christopher singing?
(3) B. Running around the track.

Action Verbs

Action Verbs   A sentence is made up of a subject and a verb. The verb tells what the subject is or does. An **action verb** describes what the subject does, did, or will do. *Marched* is an action verb in the sentence below. It tells what Colonel Iturbide did.

In 1821, Colonel Iturbide <u>marched</u> into Mexico City.

Sometimes a sentence has more than one action verb. In the sentence below, *proclaimed* and *oppressed* are two action verbs telling what Colonel Iturbide did.

Colonel Iturbide <u>proclaimed</u> himself "emperor" of Mexico and <u>oppressed</u> his people.

Example 1   Identify each action verb in these sentences.

(a) We study Mexican history in the sixth grade.

(b) Historians write about Colonel Augustin de Iturbide.

(c) The Mexican people suffered under Iturbide's oppressive and corrupt rule.

(d) The Mexican people overthrew Iturbide and declared their country a republic.

Solution   (a) The action verb **study** tells what "we" do.

(b) The action verb **write** tells what "historians" do.

(c) The action verb **suffered** tells what "the Mexican people" did.

(d) **Overthrew** and **declared** are action verbs telling what "the Mexican people" did.

Improving Our Writing Using descriptive and precise action verbs can make our writing more vivid or colorful. Look at the following example.

The parrot <u>talked</u> loudly.

Perhaps the parrot <u>screeched</u> loudly,

or maybe it <u>squawked</u> loudly.

We notice that the verbs <u>screeched</u> and <u>squawked</u> excite the reader and may be more descriptive. We try to choose words with the most accurate meaning.

Example 2 Replace the action verb in this sentence with one that might be more precise or descriptive. Consider the different possibilities.

Herbert <u>went</u> to school.

Solution Our answers will vary. We do not know how Herbert went to school, but here are some possibilities:

Herbert **drove** to school.

Herbert **raced** to school.

Herbert **sauntered** to school,

or he may have **hurried, jogged,** or **dashed** to school.

Of course, when we write, we use the action verb with the truest, most precise meaning.

√ **Practice** Write the action verbs in sentences a–g.

a. Santa Anna ruled Mexico from the 1830s to the 1850s.

b. Historians remember Santa Anna for his vanity, dishonesty, and poor leadership of Mexico.

c. Mexico lost half of its territory to the United States due to the poor leadership of Santa Anna.

d. U.S. settlers declared Texas to be independent of Mexico in 1836.

e. Santa Anna defeated the Texan rebels at the Alamo in 1836.

f. The United States and Mexico fought a war over Texas.

g. The United States won the war.

For h and i, replace the action verb with one that might be more accurate or interesting. Use your imagination. There are many possibilities.

h. The teacher <u>talked</u> softly.

i. The clown <u>came</u> into the circus tent.

For j–m, replace each blank with *waist* or *waste*.

j. Most belts fit around one's _____.

k. The chest, or that part of the body just above the _____, varies in size on different individuals.

l. Sewage is _____ that requires treatment at special plants before it can be released into the ocean.

m. Hikers sometimes cause hillsides to erode or _____ away.

√**Review Set 5** Write the action verb in sentences 1–5.

1. Frozen wind stung his face like a horrid insect.
(2, 5)

2. Laughter erupted from the crowd.
(2, 5)

3. The United States proclaimed the Statue of Liberty a
(2, 5) national monument in 1924.

4. The Statue of Liberty stands at the entrance to New York
(2, 5) Harbor.

5. Immigrants entered the United States through Ellis
(2, 5) Island.

For 6–10, replace the action verb in each sentence with one that might be more accurate or descriptive. There are many possibilities.

6. The doctor <u>went</u> to the hospital.
(5)

7. The Hoven's horse, Lady, <u>walked</u> home.
(5)

8. The Statue of Liberty <u>holds</u> a torch in her right hand.
(5)

(5) **9.** The boy <u>came</u> home.

10. I <u>went</u> into the ditch.
(5)

Choose the best word to complete sentences 11–14.

11. Words with the same pronunciation but different
(4) spellings and meanings are called (homonyms, homophones).

12. Words with the same pronunciation and the same
(4) spelling but with different meanings are called (homonyms, homophones).

13. *Waist* and *waste* are (homonyms, homophones).
(4)

14. *Bear* (an animal) and *bear* (to carry) are (homonyms,
(4) homophones).

For 15–17, correct each fragment by making a complete sentence. Answers will vary.

15. Measured the waist of his pants.
(3, 4)

16. The waste of natural resources.
(3, 4)

17. Carlos, a respectful student.
(3, 4)

For 18–20, correct each run-on sentence. Answers may vary.

18. Izumi is reliable she is also punctual.
(3, 4)

19. Fernando will travel to Spain then he will go to Portugal.
(3, 4)

20. Jakapan enjoys basketball he also enjoys soccer and
(3, 4) baseball.

For 21–23, tell whether the expression is a fragment, run-on, or complete sentence.

21. Located on Liberty Island.
(3)

22. The Statue of Liberty, a national monument, consists of
(3) two small islands, Liberty Island and Ellis Island.

23. The Statue of Liberty depicts a woman with the chains of
(3) tyranny at her feet a torch in her right hand her left hand holds a tablet with the date of the independence of the United States.

24. Write the simple subject of this sentence:

(2)

A French sculptor designed the Statue of Liberty.

25. Write the simple predicate of this sentence:

(2)

Grover Cleveland dedicated the Statue of Liberty on October 28, 1886.

26. Replace the blank with the correct word: A _____

(3) sentence has a subject and a predicate.

27. Unscramble these words to make an exclamatory

(1, 3) sentence:

boring this is

28. Unscramble these words to make an interrogative

(1, 3) sentence:

moral a does story this have

29. Unscramble these words to make an imperative sentence:

(1, 3)

considerate others be of times all at

30. Unscramble these words to make a declarative sentence:

(1, 3)

spiked crown a is wearing the Statue of Liberty

LESSON 6

Capitalizing Proper Nouns

Dictation or Journal Entry

Vocabulary:

Integrity is a noun and means "honesty" and "moral soundness." We try to choose friends who have _integrity_. _Honor,_ a synonym (a word with a similar meaning) for integrity, means "honesty and fairness in one's beliefs and actions." We remember George Washington as a man of _honor_. _Antonyms_ (opposites) of _honor_ and _integrity_ are _dishonor_ and _dishonesty_. Please do not allow _dishonesty_ to bring _dishonor_ to your family name.

Proper Nouns

We remember that a noun is a name word—a person, place, or thing. A noun may be common or proper. A _common noun_ does not name a specific person, place, or thing. A **proper noun** does name a specific person, place, or thing and requires a capital letter.

Common noun—dog;   **Proper noun—Snoopy**

We capitalize every proper noun.

COMMON NOUN	PROPER NOUN
country	United States
lake	Lake Tahoe
day	Sunday
month	December
girl	Anne Frank
book	_Charlotte's Web_

Common Nouns Within Proper Nouns

When a common noun such as "lake," "river," "mountain," "street," or "school" is a part of a proper noun, we capitalize it, as in the examples below.

COMMON NOUN	PROPER NOUN
street	Broadway Street
school	Jefferson Junior High School
ocean	Pacific Ocean
river	Nile River
island	Hawaiian Islands
building	Empire State Building

Small Words Within Proper Nouns

When the following small words are parts of a proper noun, we do not capitalize them unless they are the initial or final word:

a, an, and, at, but, by, for, from,

if, in, into, of, on, the, to, with

Notice the examples below.

> *James and the Giant Peach*
> Proctor and Gamble Company
> Gulf of Mexico
> House of Representatives
> Alexander the Great

Example Capitalize letters as needed in these sentences.

(a) The main character is anne frank.

(b) Did you read *the call of the wild* last summer?

(c) Is christmas island located in the indian ocean?

(d) The british still honor their queen.

Solution (a) We capitalize **Anne Frank** because it names a specific person.

(b) ***The Call** of the **Wild*** is a book title. The small words *of* and *the* are not capitalized because they are not initial or final words.

(c) **Christmas Island** is a specific island and needs capital letters. Also, the **Indian Ocean** is a specific ocean.

(d) ***British*** is capitalized because it names a group of people from a specific country.

✓ Practice Rewrite sentences a–f, and capitalize proper nouns.

a. My parents named my sibling jennifer.

b. Juliet devised a way to be with romeo.

c. *The secret garden* portrays one character as an invalid.

d. The morale of america went down with the depreciation of the u.s. dollar.

e. We attended arroyo high school in el monte, california.

f. The nile river is the longest river in the world.

For g–k, replace each blank with the correct vocabulary word.

g. A person with honor or _____ does not lie or cheat.

h. Integrity means "_____ soundness."

i. A synonym for integrity is _____.

j. An antonym for honor is _____.

k. Dishonesty may result in a reputation of _____.

More Practice See "More Practice Lesson 6" in Student Workbook.

✓ **Review Set 6** Write and capitalize each proper noun from sentences 1–10.

1. mexico lies west of florida.
(6)

2. henry resides near mount shasta.
(6)

3. esther's house is located on geburah street.
(6)

4. The cabrillo monument is located on point loma.
(6)

5. Most people enjoy the month of december.
(6)

6. Working people look forward to fridays.
(6)

7. Please, laura, take me to josie's house.
(6)

8. Funny uncle jerod cut his hair very short.
(6)

9. *time magazine* remains a popular choice.
(6)

10. *A christmas carol* features an old miser named ebenezer
(6) scrooge.

Choose the correct word to complete sentences 11 and 12.

11. A moral person has honor and (dishonest, integrity).
(6)

12. To be reliable, one must not be (honorable, dishonest).
(6)

Write the action verb from sentences 13 and 14.

13. Mary Lenox lives with her uncle in England.
(2, 5)

14. Ben Weatherstaff assists Mary with her garden.
(2, 5)

For 15 and 16, replace the verb with a more interesting one.

15. Mary <u>goes</u> to the garden daily.
(5)

(5) **16.** The flowers <u>grow</u> under the care of Ben and Mary.

For 17–20, tell whether the sentence is interrogative, declarative, exclamatory, or imperative.

17. What is your waist size?
(1)

18. Please don't waste time.
(1)

19. *Too*, *to*, and *two* are homophones.
(1)

20. Ouch! The lump on my head is still sensitive to touch!
(1)

Write the simple subject of 21 and 22.

21. Bessie Coleman dreamed of flying an airplane.
(2)

22. Another name for Bessie is "Daredevil of the Sky."
(2)

Write the simple predicate of 23 and 24.

23. Bessie's brothers served in World War I.
(2, 5)

24. Bessie's brother John filled her head with fantastic stories
(2, 5) about courageous female aviators.

For 25–27, tell whether the expression is a sentence fragment, run-on sentence, or complete sentence.

25. Rejected from flying schools because of her gender and
(3) the color of her skin.

26. Bessie's dream seemed impossible her friends
(3) encouraged her not to give up.

27. A man named Mr. Abbott found an aviation school for
(3) Bessie in Paris, France.

For 28–30, correct each sentence fragment or run-on sentence.

28. Learned French and earned money for the trip.
(3, 4)

29. On November 16, 1920, Bessie Coleman set sail on the
(3, 4) *S. S. Imperator* it departed from New York City for Paris.

30. Bessie Coleman received her international pilot's license
(3, 4) she became the first black pilot.

LESSON 7

Present and Past Tense of Regular Verbs

Dictation or Journal Entry

Vocabulary:
The common prefix *geo-* refers to the earth. *Geology* is the scientific study of the origin and structure of the earth. In a *geology* course, one learns the different types of rocks. *Geography* is also a science, but it studies the surface of the earth—its natural features. Map reading is part of the *geography* course.

Verb tense refers to time. Verbs tell us not only what action is occurring but also when it is occurring. The form of a verb, or the verb tense, shows when the action takes place. Three simple verb tenses are present, past, and future. In this lesson, we will talk about the present and past tense of regular verbs. There are many irregular verb forms that we will learn later.

Present Tense

The **present tense** refers to action that is happening now. We add an *s* when the subject is singular, except when the pronoun is *I* or *you*.

PLURAL SUBJECTS AND PRONOUNS *I* AND *YOU*	SINGULAR SUBJECTS
Dogs bark.	The dog barks.
We skate.	Cheri skates.
I pick.	He picks.
We dance.	She dances.
They yawn.	Boomer yawns.
You listen.	Tom listens.
Joel and Jenny call.	Mom calls.

When a verb ends in *s, x, z, ch,* or *sh,* we add *es* when the subject is singular.

PLURAL SUBJECTS AND PRONOUNS *I* AND *YOU*	SINGULAR SUBJECTS
We brush.	Robert brushes.
Bees buzz.	A bee buzzes.
Crackers crunch.	The cracker crunches.
Snakes hiss.	A snake hisses.
Employees box the items.	John boxes the items.

When a verb ends in a consonant and a *y*, we change the *y* to *i* and add *es* for the singular form.

PLURAL SUBJECTS AND PRONOUNS *I* AND *YOU*	SINGULAR SUBJECTS
I <u>fry</u> potatoes.	He <u>fries</u> potatoes.
They <u>empty</u> the trash.	Harold <u>empties</u> the trash.

Example 1   Replace each blank with the singular present tense form of the verb.

(a) You <u>deny</u>. He _____.

(b) Birds <u>fly</u>. A pigeon _____.

(c) Babies <u>cry</u>. A baby _____.

(d) Sodas <u>fizz</u>. One soda _____.

(e) They <u>miss</u>. She _____.

Solution   (a) **denies** (Since the verb ends in *y*, we change the *y* to *i* and add *es*.)

(b) **flies** (Since the verb ends in *y*, we change the *y* to *i* and add *es*.)

(c) **cries** (Since the verb ends in *y*, we change the *y* to *i* and add *es*.)

(d) **fizzes** (The verb ends in *z*, so we add *es*.)

(e) **misses** (The verb ends in *s*, so we add *es*.)

Past Tense   The **past tense** shows action that has already occurred. To form the past tense of regular verbs, we add *ed*.

walk—walked

work—worked

When a one-syllable verb ends in a single consonant, we double the consonant and add *ed*.

tip—tipped

bat—batted

When a verb ends in *e*, we drop the *e* and add *ed*.

rake—raked

love—loved

When the verb ends in *y*, we change the *y* to *i* and add *ed*.

cry—cried

rely—relied

Example 2 Write the past tense form of each verb.

    (a) slip   (b) care   (c) try

    (d) chat   (e) study   (f) move

Solution (a) **slipped** (Since this is a short verb ending in a consonant, we double the consonant and add *ed*.)

(b) **cared** (The verb ends in *e*, so we drop the *e* and add *ed*.)

(c) **tried** (The verb ends in *y*, so we change the *y* to *i* and add *ed*.)

(d) **chatted** (Since this is a short verb ending in a consonant, we double the consonant and add *ed*.)

(e) **studied** (The verb ends in *y*, so we change the *y* to *i* and add *ed*.)

(f) **moved** (The verb ends in *e*, so we drop the *e* and add *ed*.)

Errors to Avoid Do not use the present tense form for the past tense.

NO: Yesterday she <u>calls</u> him twice.
YES: Yesterday she <u>called</u> him twice.

NO: Last night I <u>look</u> everywhere.
YES: Last night I <u>looked</u> everywhere.

NO: A week ago Sam <u>tries</u> to find me.
YES: A week ago Sam <u>tried</u> to find me.

Do not shift from past to present in the same phrase.

NO: She <u>walked</u> out and <u>follows</u> her dog.
YES: She <u>walked</u> out and <u>followed</u> her dog.

NO: The captain <u>deserted</u> his troops and <u>shows</u> up later to apologize.

YES: The captain <u>deserted</u> his troops and <u>showed</u> up later to apologize.

Example 3 Choose the correct form of the verb to complete each sentence.

(a) Larry cleaned the kitchen and (mops, mopped) the floor.

(b) Last night the puppy (barks, barked) for several hours.

Solution (a) Larry cleaned the kitchen and **mopped** the floor.

(b) Last night the puppy **barked** for several hours.

√**Practice** For a–c, replace each blank with the correct vocabulary word.

a. We studied igneous, sedimentary, and metamorphic rocks in our _____ class.

b. The prefix *geo-* means "_____."

c. The science of the earth's surface is _____.

For d–g, replace each blank with the singular present tense form of the underlined verb.

d. José and Sal <u>wash</u>. Mom _____.

e. Selby and Sarah <u>wish</u>. Thad _____.

f. People <u>comply</u>. The man _____.

g. We <u>try</u>. He _____.

For h–o, write the past tense form of each verb.

h. mop **i.** cry **j.** nap **k.** race

l. rely **m.** bake **n.** sip **o.** drop

For p and q, choose the correct verb form.

p. Yesterday my parrot (pecks, pecked) a hole in his cage.

q. He escaped and then (talks, talked) to the dog.

Review Set 7 For 1–10, choose a word from the following list that matches the definition.

punctual   considerate   respectful   reliable   moral
homonyms   homophones   integrity   waist   waste

1. trustworthy
(3)

2. on time
(1)

3. honesty
(6)

4. useless material
(5)

5. thoughtful of others
(1)

6. courteous; polite
(3)

7. concerned with matters of right and wrong
(2)

8. the part of the body just above the hips
(5)

9. words with the same pronunciation but different
(4) spellings and meanings

10. words that are spelled and pronounced alike but have
(4) different meanings

For 11–13, replace each blank with the singular present tense form of the verb.

11. You reply. She _____.
(5, 7)

12. Bees buzz. The bee _____.
(5, 7)

13. Dogs scratch. One dog _____.
(5, 7)

For 14–16, replace each blank with the past tense form of the verb.

14. Yesterday the two friends (talk) _____ on the phone.
(7)

15. The salesperson (rap) _____ on the door.
(7)

16. The mayor (try) _____ to clean up the city.
(7)

For 17–19, write each proper noun that requires capitalization.

17. Tourists enjoy visiting niagara falls.
(6)

18. *oliver twist* and *david copperfield* are classics by charles
(6) dickens.

(6) **19.** Surfers enjoy the waves of the pacific ocean.

20. Write the action verb in this sentence: Whales breach in
(5, 7) the cold Atlantic Ocean.

21. Choose a more descriptive verb for this sentence: Freed
(5, 7) from the leash at last, the dog <u>went</u> down the street.

22. Make a complete sentence from this fragment: A person
(4, 3) of integrity.

23. Rewrite and correct this run-on sentence: Before painting
(4, 3) a room, you must wash the walls you should also sand
the woodwork.

For 24–26, write whether each expression is a sentence
fragment, run-on sentence, or complete sentence.

24. On June 16, 1902, Barbara McClintock was born in
(3) Hartford, Connecticut.

25. Opposed Barbara's wish to go to college.
(3)

26. Barbara was so determined to get an education that she
(3) worked for money and studied on weekends she found a
college called the Cornell School of Agriculture.

27. Write the simple subject of this sentence: Barbara
(2) enrolled in college to study biology.

28. Write the simple predicate of this sentence: Later,
(2) Barbara requested further study in genetics.

For 29 and 30, tell whether the sentence is declarative,
interrogative, imperative, or exclamatory.

29. Did you know that Barbara's request was denied because
(1) she was a woman?

30. That did not stop her!
(1)

Concrete, Abstract, and Collective Nouns

Dictation or Journal Entry

Vocabulary:

The homophones *course* and *coarse* are pronounced the same but have different meanings. *Coarse* means "rough, vulgar, or crude." The thieves used *coarse* language. A *course* is a path or direction taken. The cross-country *course* consisted of several hills and valleys. *Course* can also mean a class or series of study. The English *course* taught the students all about nouns.

We know that a noun is a person, place, or thing. We group nouns into these classes: common, proper, concrete, abstract, and collective.

We have learned the difference between common and proper nouns. In this lesson, we will learn the difference between concrete and abstract nouns. We will also learn to recognize collective nouns.

Concrete Nouns

A **concrete noun** names a person, place, or thing. It may be either common or proper.

CONCRETE COMMON	CONCRETE PROPER
piano	Steinway
teacher	Mr. Garza
town	Temple City

Abstract Nouns

An **abstract noun** names something that cannot be seen or touched. It names something that you can think about. An abstract noun can be common or proper as well.

ABSTRACT COMMON NOUNS	ABSTRACT PROPER NOUNS
religion	Judaism
philosophy	Platonism
holiday	Memorial Day
nationality	German
language	Latin
day	Tuesday

Example 1   Tell whether each noun is concrete or abstract.

(a) Hinduism   (b) faith

(c) Pacific Ocean   (d) truth

(e) chair   (f) patriotism

Solution   (a) **abstract** (Hinduism is a religion.)

(b) **abstract** (We can only *think* about faith.)

(c) **concrete**   (d) **abstract**

(e) **concrete**   (f) **abstract**

Collective   A collective noun names a collection of persons, places,
Nouns   animals, or things. We list a few examples below.

PERSONS: team, tribe, class, congregation, family, chorus

ANIMALS: flock, herd, school (fish), litter

PLACES: Latin America, Europe, United States

THINGS: batch, bunch, assortment, collection, multitude

Example 2   Write the collective noun from each sentence.

(a) The coarse behavior of the unruly team appeared
prodigiously stupid to the spectators.

(b) The captain charted the ship's course for the crew.

(c) The United States sent desperately needed medical
supplies to the war-torn country.

(d) The Red Cross aids victims affected by earthquakes,
hurricanes, and other major catastrophes.

Solution   (a) **team**   (b) **crew**

(c) **United States**   (d) **Red Cross**

Practice   For a–c, replace each blank with *coarse* or *course*.

a. Is the bicycle _____ easy to follow?

b. The history _____ explains the beginnings of the
Industrial Revolution.

c. Profanity makes one seem _____.

For d–g, tell whether each noun is abstract or concrete.
  d. newspaper   **e.** beauty

  f. Mount Wilson   **g.** thought

For h and i, write the collective noun that you find in each sentence.
  h. The audience applauded loudly after James played the piano.

  i. The committee met for several hours to discuss the problem.

More Practice

For 1–12, tell whether each noun is abstract or concrete.
  1. integrity   **2.** bread   **3.** knuckle   **4.** hope

  5. cup   **6.** compassion **7.** patience   **8.** soda

  9. cheese   **10.** ear   **11.** tea   **12.** joy

Write each collective noun that you find in sentences 13–15.
  13. He sold his collection and donated the money to his team.

  14. The squawking flock of parrots devoured a whole bunch of grapes.

  15. The president gave the family permission to develop an assortment of new products.

√ **Review Set 8**

  1. Write the concrete nouns from this list: excellence, leg, *(8)* Judaism, truck.

  2. Write the abstract nouns from this list: roses, book, *(8)* kindness, liberty.

  3. Write the collective nouns from this list: club, member, *(8)* team, moon, herd, United Kingdom, Central America.

For 4–9, choose the best word to complete each sentence.
  (8) **4.** The sandpaper felt (course, coarse) rather than fine.

5. The driver's education (course, coarse) remained a
⁽⁸⁾ popular choice for high-school students.

6. The golf (course, coarse) consisted of eighteen holes.
⁽⁸⁾

7. The pirates used (course, coarse) language to appear
⁽⁸⁾ rough and crude.

8. People who tell lies may gain a reputation of (honor,
⁽⁶⁾ integrity, dishonor).

9. The bully was not (resentful, respectful, reliable) toward
⁽³⁾ his fellow students.

For 10–12, replace each blank with the singular present tense form of the verb.

10. You study. Ellen _____.
^(5, 7)

11. Snakes hiss. A snake _____.
^(5, 7)

12. Parrots screech. A parrot _____.
^(5, 7)

For 13–15, replace each blank with the past tense form of the verb.

13. The umpire insisted that the pitcher (balk) _____.
^(5, 7)

14. The foolish cat (trap) _____ himself on the roof.
^(5, 7)

15. Marissa (fry) _____ the bacon too crisply.
^(5, 7)

For 16–19, write each proper noun that requires capitalization.

16. barbara mcClintock began an intense study of cells.
⁽⁶⁾

17. At the cornell school of agriculture, barbara studied the
⁽⁶⁾ genetic patterns of maize, a kind of colorful corn.

18. In 1941, barbara found a permanent job at cold spring
⁽⁶⁾ harbor, a research facility near new york city.

19. In 1981, at age seventy-nine, barbara mcClintock received
  (6) a nobel prize for her research on genes.

20. Write the action verb in this sentence:
  (5, 7)
  The dolphins swam to the ocean's surface.

21. Write a more descriptive verb for this sentence:
  (5, 7)
  A bottle-nosed dolphin <u>went</u> through the water.

22. Make a complete sentence from this fragment:
  (4, 3)
  Dolphins interest.

23. Correct this run-on sentence:
  (4, 3)
  It takes only a fraction of a second for dolphins to
  exhale and inhale they surface only to breathe.

For 24–26, tell whether each group of words is a sentence
fragment, run-on sentence, or complete sentence.

24. Dolphins travel in groups all the dolphins in a group
  (3) usually belong to one family.

25. Dolphins travel together, hunt together, and play
  (3) together.

26. Close to surfers riding waves.
  (3)

27. Write the simple subject of this sentence:
  (2)
  Surfers often see dolphins.

28. Write the simple predicate of this sentence:
  (2, 7)
  Dolphins measure between five and eight feet.

For 29 and 30, tell whether the sentence is interrogative,
exclamatory, imperative, or declarative.

29. Do dolphins ever stop in the water and stay very still?
  (1)

30. Yes, dolphins "float" while they wait for another of their
  (1) group to catch up.

Dictation or Journal Entry

Vocabulary:
Synonyms are words with similar meanings. *Willpower* and *self-discipline* are synonyms. *Willpower* is the "ability to control oneself." When running a marathon, it takes *willpower* to complete all twenty-six miles. *Self-discipline* is the "ability to train oneself, often for improvement." Plato, a famous philosopher, equated *self-discipline* with the ability to balance reason, passion, and appetite.

Helping Verbs We know that every predicate contains a verb. Sometimes, the verb is more than one word in the sentence. The main verb may have one or more **helping verbs.** The main verb shows the action; the helping verbs do not show action, but they help to form the verb tense.

> You <u>might have read</u> many good books.

In the sentence above, "read" is the main verb, and "might" and "have" are helping verbs. "Might have read" is called a verb phrase.

Memorize these common helping verbs:

> *is, am, are, was, were, be, being, been,*
>
> *has, have, had, may, might, must,*
>
> *can, could, do, does, did,*
>
> *shall, will, should, would*

3 Bs
3 Hs
3 Ds
2 Cs
2 Ss
4 hs
3 ms

Example Write the entire verb phrase and underline the helping verbs in these sentences.

(a) Benito Juárez should be remembered for opposing Santa Anna.

(b) Juárez could have behaved like Santa Anna.

(c) Instead, Juárez must have acted honestly and sincerely.

(d) Unlike Santa Anna, Juárez had come from a poor family.

Solution (a) **<u>should</u> <u>be</u> remembered** ("Should" and "be" are helping verbs for the main verb "remembered.")

(b) **<u>could</u> <u>have</u> behaved**

(c) **<u>must</u> <u>have</u> acted**

(d) **<u>had</u> come**

Practice   **a.** Study the helping verbs listed in this lesson. Memorize them one line at a time. Practice saying them *in order* (perhaps to your teacher or a friend). Then write as many as you can from memory.

For sentences b–e, write the entire verb phrase and underline the helping verbs.

b. Benito Juárez had fought for the Mexican people.

c. Has Juárez helped the poor people?

d. Juárez might have gained more respect than any of Mexico's past leaders.

e. Benito Juárez must have shared more of Mexico's wealth with the needy.

For f–h, replace each blank with *willpower* or *self-discipline.*

f. A synonym for *willpower* is _____.

g. A person on a diet needs self-discipline, or _____, to avoid high-calorie foods.

h. Exercising every day requires willpower, or _____.

More Practice   See "More Practice Lesson 9" in Student Workbook.

Review Set 9   **1.** Write from memory the common helping verbs listed in
(9)   this lesson. Check your list by referring to the lesson.

For 2–8, write the simple subject. Then write the entire verb phrase and underline the helping verbs. (Example: Julita <u>will have been</u> working)

2. The plane should have landed an hour ago.
(2, 9)

3. Shall I wait for you?
(2, 9)

4. He must have worked all day.
(2, 9)

5. Did Juárez help poor people?
(2, 9)

(2, 9) **6.** Do you remember the helping verbs?

7. Have you memorized them?
(2, 9)

8. James might draw a polygon.
(2, 9)

For 9–11, tell whether the expression is a complete sentence, a sentence fragment, or a run-on sentence.

9. Please finish your math.
(3)

10. To arrive in Miami before midnight.
(3)

11. Rabbi Cohen had tremendous courage he never gave up.
(3)

For 12–14, make a complete sentence from each sentence fragment. Answers will vary.

12. Gracie and Lucy a funny pair.
(3, 4)

13. To laugh while watching TV.
(3, 4)

14. Each fisherman on the pier at Oceanside.
(3, 4)

For 15–16, correct each run-on sentence.

15. We shall stay he will arrive.
(3, 4)

16. I gathered my books I left for school.
(3, 4)

For 17–20, tell whether the noun is concrete or abstract.

17. Mrs. Wang
(8)

18. honesty
(8)

19. Red Sea
(8)

20. geometry
(8)

21. Write the two collective nouns from this list:
(8)

group   birds   committee   houses

22. Unscramble these words to make an interrogative
(1, 3) sentence:

time   waste   they   do

23. Unscramble these words to make an imperative sentence:
(1, 3)

geography   study   book   your

Choose the best word to complete sentences 24–30.

24. Willard was tempted to lie, but he didn't because he had
(6) (tonsils, integrity, artichokes).

25. The sandpaper was (course, coarse) and scratchy.
(8)

26. They walked around the golf (course, coarse).
(8)

27. We can learn about rocks and minerals in a (geometry,
(7) geology, graphic art) class.

28. The words *rose*, past tense of *rise*, and *rose*, the flower,
(4) are (homonyms, flowers, antonyms).

29. Malia sent a thank-you note to be (considerate,
(1) concerned, considerable).

30. Although the car was old, it was (respectful, reliable,
(3) ruthless) because it never broke down.

Singular, Plural, Compound, and Possessive Nouns • Noun Gender

Dictation or Journal Entry

Vocabulary:
Let's learn the difference between the words *lay* and *lie*. *Lay* means "to place" something. We can *lay* our books on our desks. *Lie* means "to recline." The golden retriever *lies* in the sun to get warm.

Singular or Plural

Nouns are either singular or plural. A **singular noun** names only one person, place, or thing. A **plural noun** names more than one person, place, or thing.

SINGULAR NOUNS	PLURAL NOUNS
skirt	skirts
church	churches
whiff	whiffs
potato	potatoes

Example 1 Tell whether each noun is singular or plural.

(a) box   (b) brushes   (c) ships

(d) smile   (e) cookies   (f) holiday

Solution (a) **singular**   (b) **plural**   (c) **plural**

(d) **singular**   (e) **plural**   (f) **singular**

Compound

A noun made up of two or more words is a **compound noun.** Sometimes we write a compound noun as one word:

volleyball, pathway, toothpaste

Often we write compound nouns as two words:

high school, nail polish, strip mining

Other compound nouns are hyphenated:

mother-in-law, great-great-grandfather, ex-president

There is no pattern for determining whether to spell a compound noun as one word, two separate words, or one hyphenated word. We must use the dictionary.

Example 2 Write the compound nouns from this list:

horses	maid of honor
sister-in-law	pumpkin

Solution The compound nouns from the list above are **sister-in-law** and **maid of honor.**

Possessive A **possessive noun** tells "who" or "what" owns something. Possessive nouns can be either singular or plural. The possessive form of nouns have an apostrophe and an *s* added to them:

a *woman's* shoe	the *tree's* leaves
the *girl's* dress	the *child's* name
somebody's paper	a *fox's* tail
nobody's business	a *man's* clothes

Usually only an apostrophe is added to plural nouns when they end with the letter *s*:

the *girls'* race	the *boys'* bicycles
the *horses'* saddles	the *doctors'* theories
the *Rivases'* address	the *teachers'* lunches

Example 3 Write the possessive noun from each sentence.

(a) Please help me find the ladies' room.

(b) The children's favorite game was "hide-and-seek."

(c) Beth's comb had lost several teeth.

(d) My friend's gift of love touched the hearts of many.

Solution   (a) **ladies'**   (b) **children's** (c) **Beth's**   (d) **friend's**

Noun Gender We also group nouns according to gender. In English there are four **genders:** Masculine, feminine, indefinite (either sex), and neuter (no sex). Below are examples of each gender of nouns.

MASCULINE	FEMININE	INDEFINITE	NEUTER
father	mother	parent	flower
brother	sister	sibling	car
boar	sow	pig	pencil
buck	doe	deer	biscuit

Example 4   Tell whether each noun is masculine, feminine, indefinite, or neuter.

(a) key   (b) aunt   (c) boy   (d) baby

Solution   (a) **neuter**   (b) **feminine**   (c) **masculine** (d) **indefinite**

✓**Practice**   For a–d, tell whether each noun is singular or plural.

a. strawberries   **b.** magazine

c. Mars   **d.** parents

e. Write the compound nouns from this list:

father-in-law   chuck wagon

headlight   water

For f–i, write the possessive noun from each sentence.

f. Lucius's car slid on the icy road.

g. The neighbor could hear Sam's whistle.

h. The four dancers' routine required coordination and grace.

i. The menu listed quiche as one of the choices for the women's luncheon.

For j–m, tell whether each noun is masculine, feminine, indefinite, or neuter.

j. ram   **k.** grandma   **l.** child   **m.** wax

For n–q, replace each blank with either *lie* or *lay.*

n. The server will _____ a knife, a spoon, and a fork next to each plate.

o. You will get sunburned if you _____ in the sun too long.

p. The word that means "to recline" is _____.

q. The word _____ means "to place" something.

More Practice See "Silly Story #1" in Student Workbook.

Review Set 10 For 1–4, tell whether the noun is singular or plural.

1. dolphin   **2.** pencils   **3.** sleeves   **4.** bench
(10)   *(10)*   *(10)*   *(10)*

5. Write the two compound nouns from this list:
(10)

peanut butter   bread

bicycle   attorney at law

Write each possessive noun from sentences 6 and 7.

6. Barbara McClintock's determination challenges every
(10) scientist.

7. My sister-in-law's advice helps me make good decisions
(10) in life.

For 8–11, tell whether a noun is feminine, masculine, indefinite, or neuter.

8. advisor   **9.** godmother **10.** buggy   **11.** dolphin
(10)   *(10)*   *(10)*   *(10)*

12. From memory, write the common helping verbs listed in
(9) Lesson 9.

For 13–14, write the simple subject. Then, write the entire verb phrase and underline the helping verbs. (Example: Julita <u>will have been</u> working.)

13. Bottle-nosed dolphins can communicate with each other.
(2, 9)

14. Do you know the meaning of "echolocation"?
(2, 9)

For 15–17, tell whether the expression is a complete sentence, a sentence fragment, or a run-on sentence.

15. Dolphins social animals.
(3)

16. "Echolocation" helps dolphins determine the distance to
(3) and size of an object.

17. Dolphins make squeaks or whistles a special organ inside
(3) their head helps them focus on the sound as the noise
bounces back.

18. Make a complete sentence from this sentence fragment:
(3, 4)
Surfers, swimmers, and boaters in the ocean.

19. Rewrite and correct this run-on sentence:
(3, 4)
Although seemingly harmless, dolphins are still wild animals we should not startle them.

For 20–23, tell whether each noun is concrete or abstract.

20. statue   **21.** generosity   **22.** worry   **23.** slippers
(8)   (8)   (8)   (8)

24. Write the two collective nouns from this list:
(8)
South America   school

scientist   journal

25. Unscramble these words to make a declarative sentence:
(1, 3)
interesting   sea   The   dolphin   creature   an   is

26. Unscramble these words to make an exclamatory
(1, 3) sentence: see   it   I

Choose the best word to complete sentences 27–30.

27. The (geology, geography) course included map reading.
(7)

28. Two words that sound alike but have different spellings
(4) and meanings are (homophones, homonyms).

29. The opposite of tardy is (moral, punctual).
(1, 2)

30. The exercise required one to bend at the (waste, waist).
(5)

LESSON
11

Future Tense

Dictation or Journal Entry

Vocabulary:

The prefix *bio-* means "life." *Biology* is the study of life. The students learned about blood types in their *biology* class. A *biography* is the story of one's life written by another. Have you read a *biography* of Albert Einstein? The *biosphere* is all the land, water, and air inhabited by life. Planet Earth has a rich *biosphere*.

The **future tense** refers to action that has not yet occurred. The future tense is usually formed with the helping verbs *shall* or *will*. With the pronouns *I* and *we*, the use of *shall* is preferable in **formal** writing.

He *will* run.	We *shall* run.
They *will* cook.	I *shall* cook.
You *will* ride.	We *shall* ride.
Christie *will* finish.	She and I *shall* finish.
Steph *will* help.	We *shall* help.
Bruce and John *will* enter.	I *shall* enter.

Example 1   Complete the future tense verb form by replacing each blank with *will* or *shall*, as you would do in formal writing.

(a) Bob _____ vote next Tuesday.

(b) Kerry and I _____ win.

(c) It _____ rain tomorrow.

(d) I _____ sing.

Solution   (a) Bob **will** vote next Tuesday.

(b) Kerry and I **shall** win.

(c) It **will** rain tomorrow.

(d) I **shall** sing.

Errors to Avoid   Do not use the present for the future tense.

NO: Tomorrow I <u>walk</u> to school.
YES: Tomorrow I <u>shall walk</u> to school.

NO: We <u>race</u> next Friday.
YES: We <u>shall race</u> next Friday.

                NO: Next week she <u>starts</u> her class.
                YES: Next week she <u>will start</u> her class.

Example 2   Identify the following underlined verbs as present, past or future tense.
             (a) Mexico <u>lies</u> south of California.

             (b) Grandma <u>will fry</u> doughnuts for us.

             (c) Dad <u>walked</u> the dog.

             (d) The coyote <u>chased</u> the rabbit.

Solution   (a) **present**   (b) **future**   (c) **past**   (d) **past**

Example 3   Write the correct form of the verb.
             (a) The basketball team (future of *play*) tonight.

             (b) Some teenagers (present of *drink*) too much soda.

             (c) The captain (past of *watch*) his crew.

             (d) The infant (present of *cry*) when hungry.

Solution   (a) The basketball team **will play** tonight.

             (b) Some teenagers **drink** too much soda.

             (c) The captain **watched** his crew.

             (d) The infant **cries** when hungry.

Practice   For sentences a–d, tell whether the underlined verb is present, past, or future tense.
             a. Small children <u>share</u> their toys at school.

             b. The students <u>will drink</u> orange juice for breakfast.

             c. <u>Shall</u> I <u>walk</u> you home?

             d. Josh <u>picked</u> up all his toys.

             For e–g, write the correct form of the verb.
             e. Deborah (past of *telephone*) Egypt.

f. Tassoula (future of *prove*) her case.

g. The parrot (present of *talk*) loudly.

For h–k, replace each blank with *will* or *shall*, as you would do in formal writing, in order to complete the future tense form of the verb.

h. The value _____ depreciate.

i. I _____ not waste money.

j. They _____ accept you.

k. We _____ devise a plan to improve our health.

For l–o, replace each blank with the correct vocabulary word.

l. The prefix _____ means "life."

m. There is no life on the moon; it has no _____.

n. _____ is the study of living things.

o. You might enjoy reading a _____ of Louis Pasteur or Isaac Newton.

Review Set 11   For 1–3, tell whether the underlined verb is present, past, or future tense.

1. Quilt-making <u>began</u> in the United States during the early
(9, 11)   1700s.

even

2. Today, people <u>make</u> quilts to tell a story or to share
(9, 11)   memories.

3. Quilters <u>will teach</u> others how to make quilts.
(9, 11)

For 4–6, write the correct form of the verb.

4. Soon, the Natural History Museum in Los Angeles,
(9, 11)   California, (future of *open*) a special quilt exhibit.

5. Quilting (past of *begin*) when women sought ways to
(7, 11)   keep their families warm during the winter.

6. Quilters (present of *pass*) their quilts down from
(7, 11)   generation to generation.

For 7 and 8, replace each blank with *will* or *shall* to complete the future tense form of the verb.

7. I _____ learn to make quilts.
(11)

8. _____ Ray sell his house in Chicago, Illinois?
(11)

For 9 and 10, tell whether the noun is singular or plural.

9. women   **10.** pouch
(10)   *(10)*

For 11–14, tell whether the noun is feminine, masculine, indefinite, or neuter.

11. groom   **12.** bride   **13.** elm tree   **14.** clerk
(10)   *(10)*   *(10)*   *(10)*

15. Write the compound noun from this list:
(10)

   harpsichord   brother-in-law   encyclopedia

16. Write the possessive noun from this sentence:
(10)

   She followed the pharmacist's advice.

17. From memory, write the 23 helping verbs from Lesson 9.
(9)

18. Write the simple subject of this sentence:
(2)

   Generally, quilts were heavy and warm and made for homes without adequate heating.

19. Write the verb phrase from this sentence and underline
(5, 7) the helping verbs:

   Many women would make quilts from feed sacks or tobacco pouches.

20. Replace the action verb with one that is more descriptive:
(2, 5)

   Annie Dennis <u>made</u> quilts for those who were ill.

21. Tell whether this expression is a fragment, run-on, or
(3) complete sentence:

   From her mother as a little girl.

22. Rewrite and correct this run-on sentence:
(3, 4)

   Annie Dennis learned to make "fancy quilts" from her mother she made them until she was 97.

For 23 and 24, tell whether the noun is concrete or abstract.

23. quilt
(8)

24. belief
(8)

25. Unscramble these words to make a declarative sentence:
(1, 3)

preserve   history   family   can   quilts

26. Write each proper noun that requires capitalization from
(6) this sentence:

Next friday, peter and paul will visit natalee joe in
phoenix, arizona.

Choose the best word to complete sentences 27–30.

27. The newspaper deliverer (lies, lays) the paper on the
(10) front porch.

28. Do you have the (self-discipline, integrity) to exercise
(6, 9) daily?

29. We have been asked not to (waist, waste) water.
(5)

30. In (geography, geology) one studies land formations and
(7) rocks.

Capitalization: Sentence, Pronoun *I*, Poetry

Dictation or Journal Entry
Vocabulary:
Diligent means "hard-working, persistent." A *diligent* student will succeed.
Conscientious means "careful, painstaking." A *conscientious* student works
steadily and always tries to do his or her best.

There are many reasons why words require capitalization.
Recall that since proper nouns name a specific person, place,
or thing, they need to be capitalized. Remember that a
common noun linked with a proper noun requires a capital
letter. For example, the word "ocean" is capitalized in
"Atlantic Ocean." Also remember that little words such as *a*,
of, *the*, *an*, and *in* are not capitalized when they are part of a
proper noun (as in Republic of China).

We will learn more about capitalization in this lesson.

First Word of Every Sentence

The **first word of every sentence** requires a capital letter.

The judge indicts the criminal for robbery.

Sadly, some people lack morals.

The new skateboard's value depreciates with
constant use.

The Pronoun *I*

The **pronoun *I*** is always capitalized, no matter where it is
placed in the sentence.

I am in such a dilemma!

Do I use a capital letter there?

Rules, I am told, aid students in their writing.

I have three siblings.

First Word in a Line of Poetry

The **first words of each line in most poetry** are usually
capitalized.* For example, Edgar Allan Poe begins "The
Raven" with

Once upon a midnight dreary, while I pondered,
weak and weary,

Over many a quaint and curious volume of forgotten
lore,

* However, for effect, some poets purposely do not capitalize first words of
their lines of poetry.

Amy Lowell's poem "Time" reads:

Looking at myself in my metal mirror,
I saw, faintly outlined,
The figure of a crane
Engraved upon its back.

Example   Add capital letters wherever needed.

(a) Should i start dinner now?

(b) the letter had been mailed three days ago.

(c) Emily Dickenson, capitalizes the first word of each line of
her poem "I Like to See It Lap the Miles:"

i like to see it lap the miles,
and lick the valleys up,
and stop to feed itself at tanks;
and then, prodigious, step...

Solution   (a) The pronoun *I* is capitalized in this sentence.

(b) Since the first word in every sentence must be
capitalized, we write, "**T**he letter had been mailed three
days ago."

(c) We write:

I like to see it lap the miles,
And lick the valleys up
And stop to feed itself at tanks
And then, prodigious, step...

Practice   Write each word that should be capitalized in a–d.

a. have you ever read "i Have a Dream," a famous speech by
martin luther king, junior?

b. T. S. Eliot capitalized the first word of each line in his
poem, "Macavity: The Mystery Cat." Here is the first
stanza:

macavity's a Mystery Cat: he's called the Hidden
Paw—
for he's the master criminal who can defy the Law.
he's the bafflement of Scotland Yard, the Flying
Squad's despair:
for when they reach the scene of crime—Macavity's
not there!

c. in the year 2000, a presidential convention was held in
los angeles, california.

d. rules for capitalization are easy!

Replace each blank with the correct vocabulary word.

✓ **e.** A _____ person works hard on his or her tasks.

✓ **f.** A _____ person works carefully and always tries to do a good job.

Review Set 12

Write each word that should be capitalized in 1–4.

1. William Shakespeare capitalized the first word in each
(12) line of his verses. Here are some famous lines from *Romeo and Juliet*:

> love goes toward love, as schoolboys from their books:
> but love from love, toward school with heavy looks.

2. *topiary* is a new word for me.
(12)

3. *topiary*, originating from the latin word *topiarius*, refers
(12) to the ancient art of using plants for sculptures.

4. in the united states, people have developed a new type of
(6, 12) topiary.

For 5–7, write whether the underlined verb tense is present, past, or future.

5. Today, topiary <u>refers</u> to figures and forms created by
(7, 11) shaping plants while they grow.

6. <u>Will</u> you <u>purchase</u> a small ivy or bush to make an
(7, 11) elephant-shaped topiary?

7. Long ago, only wealthy people <u>owned</u> topiary gardens.
(7, 11)

For 8–11, write the correct form of the verb.

8. People (past of *form*) rosemary or boxwood into
(7) foxhounds, whales, or mythical characters.

9. Someday you (future of *visit*) a topiary display.
(11)

10. I (future of *purchase*) a wire form to cover with ivy.
(11)

(7) **11.** Ivy (present of *cover*) the wire base completely.

For 12 and 13, tell whether the noun is singular or plural.

12. people
(10)

13. garden
(10)

For 14 and 15, tell whether the noun is feminine, masculine, indefinite, or neuter.

14. rhinoceros
(10)

15. vine
(10)

16. Write the compound word from this list: boxwood,
(10) soldiers, topiary.

17. Write the possessive noun from this sentence:
(10)
The gardener's job is to shape the ivy.

18. From memory, write the 23 helping verbs from Lesson 9.
(9)

19. Write the simple subject of this sentence. Then replace
(2, 5) the underlined verb with one that is more descriptive.

In 17th century England, gardeners <u>cut</u> plants into
mazes and labyrinths.

20. Make a complete sentence from this fragment:
(3, 4)
Some topiaries small enough to fit on a table.

For 21 and 22, tell whether the noun is concrete or abstract.

21. Hinduism
(8)

22. book
(8)

23. Unscramble these words to make an imperative sentence:
(1, 3)
trample   topiary   not   do   the

For 24–30, choose the best word to complete each sentence.

24. A (conscientious, coarse) neighbor moved our trash cans
(8, 12) to the backyard.

25. Perhaps the hen will (lie, lay) some brown eggs this
(10) morning.

26. (Geology, Biology) is the study of life.
(7, 11)

27. (Geology, Biology) is the study of the origin and structure
(7, 11) of the earth.

28. The story of one's life written by another is a (biography,
(11) biosphere).

29. The land, water, and air inhabited by life is the
(11) (biography, biosphere).

30. Do you have the (dishonor, willpower) to complete your
(6, 9) homework assignment?

LESSON 13

Irregular Plural Nouns, Part 1

Dictation or Journal Entry

Vocabulary:
Many words begin with the prefixes *uni-*, meaning "one;" *bi-*, meaning "two, both, twice, or double;" and *tri-*, meaning "three." A *uni*cycle has one wheel, a *bi*cycle has two wheels, and a *tri*cycle has three wheels. The word *bilingual* has two parts: *bi-*, meaning "two," and *lingual*, meaning "pertaining to the tongue." A *bilingual* person speaks two languages. Ilbea is *bilingual*; she speaks both Spanish and English.

Plural Nouns

We do not form a plural with an apostrophe. In most cases, we make a singular noun plural by adding an *s*.

SINGULAR	PLURAL
cat	cats
book	books
pencil	pencils
shoe	shoes

Irregular Forms

Some nouns have irregular plural forms. We add *es* to a singular noun ending in the following letters: *s, sh, ch, x, z*.

SINGULAR	PLURAL
Curtis	Curtises
boss	bosses
brush	brushes
church	churches
box	boxes
Ramirez	Ramirezes
buzz	buzzes

We add an *s* when a singular noun ends with *ay, ey, oy,* or *uy*.

SINGULAR	PLURAL
day	days
donkey	donkeys
toy	toys
buy	buys

We change *y* to *i* and add *es* when a singular noun ends in a consonant plus *y*.

SINGULAR	PLURAL
candy	candies
lady	ladies
party	parties
penny	pennies

Example   For a–p, write the plural form of each singular noun.

    (a) towel   (b) porch   (c) fox   (d) bay

    (e) dress   (f) shirt   (g) reply   (h) dish

    (i) valley   (j) boy   (k) waltz   (l) circus

    (m) guy   (n) sky   (o) bus   (p) fizz

Solution   (a) **towels** (regular)   (b) **porches** (ends in *ch*)

    (c) **foxes** (ends in *x*)   (d) **bays** (ends in *ay*)

    (e) **dresses** (ends in *s*)   (f) **shirts** (regular)

    (g) **replies** (ends in consonant plus *y*)

    (h) **dishes** (ends in *sh*)   (i) **valleys** (ends in *ey*)

    (j) **boys** (ends in *oy*)   (k) **waltzes** (ends in *z*)

    (l) **circuses** (ends in *s*)   (m) **guys** (ends in *uy*)

    (n) **skies** (ends in consonant plus *y*)

    (o) **buses** (ends in *s*)   (p) **fizzes** (ends in *z*)

✓ Practice   For a and b, replace each blank with the correct word.

    a. The teacher spoke two languages; she was _____.

    b. A tricycle has _____ wheels.

    For c–p, write the plural form of each singular noun.

    c. moss   **d.** snake   **e.** chimney   **f.** bush

    g. Thomas   **h.** country   **i.** bicycle   **j.** bench

    k. day   **l.** tax   **m.** decoy   **n.** toy

    o. cherry   **p.** baby

    q. Which one of the following words is not in plural form?
       taxes   holidays   student's

**Review Set
13**

For 1–5, write the plural form for each singular noun.

1. turkey   **2.** pantry   **3.** perch   **4.** wax   **5.** weasel
(13)   (13)   (13)   (13)   (13)

For 6–8, replace each blank with the singular present tense form of the italicized verb.

6. I *wax*. Brent _____.
(7)

7. The customers *reply*. Trent _____.
(7)

8. Roosters *crow*. The rooster _____.
(7)

For 9–11, write the past tense of each verb.

9. rip   **10.** brush   **11.** dry
(7)   (7)   (7)

For 12 and 13, write the possessive form of the noun.

12. gentlemen   **13.** lawyers
(10)   (10)

14. Rewrite the following lines from Shakespeare's *King*
(12) *Henry IV, Part I,* and add capital letters where they are
       needed.

       if all the year were playing holidays,
       to sport would be as tedious as to work.

For 15–17, tell whether the underlined verb tense is present, past, or future.

15. I <u>shall learn</u> about calamari.
(7, 11)

16. Some people <u>know</u> calamari is a popular appetizer at
(7, 11) restaurants.

17. Before today, the writer <u>understood</u> little about calamari.
(7, 11)

For 18–20, choose the correct form of the verb.

18. He (present of *like*) squid.
(7)

19. I (future of *taste*) squid at the next opportunity.
(11)

20. Oscar (past of *enjoy*) bringing calamari to school for
(7) lunch.

21. Write the collective noun from this list: pack (of coyotes),
(8) meadow, squid.

22. For a and b, tell whether the noun is feminine,
(10) masculine, indefinite, or neuter.

(a) doe   (b) buck

23. Write the compound word from this list: material,
(10) classroom, marine, octopus.

24. From memory, write the 23 helping verbs from Lesson 9.
(9)

25. Write the simple subject of this sentence. Then write and
(2, 9) underline the simple predicate.

A squid's mouth does look like a parrot's beak.

26. Use a period and capital letter to correct this run-on
(3, 4) sentence:

The squid is not a fish it belongs to a group of
animals called mollusca.

27. Write the abstract noun from this list: eyes, mouth,
(8) democracy, ocean.

Choose the best word to complete sentences 28–30.

28. The prefix (*bio-, geo-*) means "Earth."
(7, 11)

29. A prefix meaning "one" is (*uni-, bi-, tri-*).
(13)

30. A (moral, bilingual) person tries to live a good, clean life.
(2, 13)

Irregular Plural Nouns, Part 2

> **Dictation or Journal Entry**
>
> **Vocabulary:**
> We find the prefix *sub-* in words like *submarine, subsoil,* and *substitute.*
> The prefix *sub-* means "under" or "to put under." We understand that a
> *submarine* is a ship designed to operate beneath the surface of the sea. The
> *submarine* descended to 1000 feet below the surface of the sea. *Subsoil* is
> that layer of earth right beneath the surface soil. The rocky *subsoil* was hard
> to dig. In the word *substitute,* the prefix *sub-* means "to put under." A
> *substitute* is someone or something which is put in the place of another.
> You may *substitute* margarine for butter in the recipe.

We continue our study of plural nouns.

Irregular Forms   Some singular nouns change completely in their plural forms.

SINGULAR	PLURAL
woman	women
man	men
child	children
mouse	mice
goose	geese
cactus	cacti

Other nouns are the same in their singular and plural forms.

SINGULAR	PLURAL
sheep	sheep
deer	deer
trout	trout

Dictionary   When we are uncertain, it is very important that we use a
dictionary to check plural forms. If the plural form of the
noun is regular (only add *s* to the singular noun), then the
dictionary will not list it. Sometimes the dictionary will list
two plural forms for a noun. The first one listed is the
preferred one. (Example: cactus *n., pl.* cacti, cactuses)

Example 1   Write the plural form of each of the following singular nouns.
Use a dictionary if you are in doubt.

(a) goose   (b) woman   (c) child   (d) salmon

Solution   (a) **geese** (irregular form)   (b) **women** (irregular form)

(c) **children** (irregular form)

(d) We check the dictionary and find that the plural of salmon is **salmon.**

Nouns Ending in *f, ff, fe* For most nouns ending in *f, ff,* and *fe,* we add *s* to form the plural.

SINGULAR	PLURAL
cuff	cuffs
gulf	gulfs
safe	safes

However, for some nouns ending in *f* and *fe,* we change the *f* to *v* and add *es.*

SINGULAR	PLURAL
knife	knives
wife	wives
loaf	loaves

Nouns Ending in *o* We usually add *s* to form the plurals of nouns ending in *o,* especially if they are musical terms.

SINGULAR	PLURAL
radio	radios
solo	solos
auto	autos
piano	pianos
alto	altos
soprano	sopranos
banjo	banjos

However, the following are important exceptions:

SINGULAR	PLURAL
echo	echoes
hero	heroes
veto	vetoes
tomato	tomatoes
potato	potatoes
torpedo	torpedoes
mosquito	mosquitoes

(There are more!)

Since there are many more exceptions, we must check the dictionary to be sure of the correct spelling.

Example 2   (a) cliff   (b) solo   (c) echo   (d) thief

Solution   (a) **cliffs** (word ending in *ff*)

(b) **solos** (musical term ending in *o*)

(c) We notice that the word *echo* is in the list of exceptions to words ending in *o*. We check the dictionary and find that the plural of echo is **echoes.**

(d) We check the dictionary and find that the plural of thief is **thieves.**

Compound Nouns   We make the main element plural in a compound noun.

SINGULAR	PLURAL
mother-in-law	mothers-in-law
commander in chief	commanders in chief
officer of the law	officers of the law
justice of the peace	justices of the peace
rule of thumb	rules of thumb
head of state	heads of state
groomsman	groomsmen
bridesmaid	bridesmaids

Nouns Ending in *ful*   We form the plurals of nouns ending in *ful* by adding an *s* at the end of the word.

SINGULAR	PLURAL
tankful	tankfuls
cupful	cupfuls

Example 3   Write the plural form of each of the following singular nouns. Use a dictionary if you are in doubt.
(a) pailful   (b) maid of honor

Solution   (a) **pailfuls** (word ending in *ful*)

(b) **maids of honor** (compound noun)

✓ Practice For a–k, write the plural form of each singular noun. Use the dictionary if you are in doubt.

a. handful   b. mother-in-law   c. chief

d. scarf   e. trout   f. tooth

g. ox   h. cello   i. photo

j. cliff   k. potato

For l–n, replace each blank with the correct vocabulary word.

l. When Mr. Zelaya was sick, his class had a _____ teacher.

m. A vessel built for under the sea is called a _____.

n. Crops grew poorly because the _____ was too sandy.

More Practice Write the plural of each noun.

1. cross   2. bunch   3. boy   4. lunch

5. bush   6. loss   7. berry   8. bay

9. sheep   10. man   11. lady   12. woman

13. child   14. mouse   15. goose   16. cupful

17. wife   18. loaf   19. piano   20. potato

21. father-in-law   22. commander in chief

Review Set 14 For 1–15, write the plural for each noun.

(1–15: 13, 14)

1. handful   2. brother-in-law   3. maid of honor

4. cello   5. solo   6. life

7. whiff   8. octopus   9. monkey

10. sentry   11. march   12. delay

13. fax   14. buoy   15. ferry

16. Replace the blank with the singular present tense form of
(7) the verb.

Cats <u>lurch</u> toward canaries. The cat _____ toward canaries.

17. Replace the blank with the past tense form of the verb.
(7)

The center (tip) _____ the basketball to the opposite team.

18. Write the possessive form of *players*.
(10)

19. Rewrite the following and add capital letters where they
(12) are needed in these lines from Shakespeare's *Julius Caesar*:

friends, romans, countrymen, lend me your ears;
i come to bury caesar, not to praise him.
the evil that men do lives after them:
the good is oft interred with their bones.

For 20–22, write the correct form of the verb.

20. The squid (present of *have*) no backbone.
(7)

21. We (future of *learn*) that the squid is a soft-bodied
(11) invertebrate.

22. Most students have not (past of *touch*) a squid.
(7)

23. Write the collective noun from this list: lamb, donkey,
(8) herd.

24. For a–e, tell whether each noun is feminine, masculine,
(8, 10) indefinite, neuter, or abstract.

(a) bride   (b) groom   (c) caterer

(d) wedding vow   (e) wedding cake

For sentences 25 and 26, write the simple subject. Then write and underline the simple predicate.

25. Squids belong to the cephalopoda class of mollusca.
(2, 5)

(2, 5) **26.** The squid's feet surround the creature's head.

27. Tell whether this group of words is a fragment, run-on, or
(3) complete sentence:

Cephalopod means "head-footed."

For 28–30, choose the best word to complete each sentence.

28. The clown rode a one-wheeled bike, a (tricycle, bicycle,
(13) unicycle).

29. *Rays* and *raise* are (homophones, homonyms).
(4)

30. The (respectful, reliable, generous) baby-sitter always
(3) arrived on time and followed the parents' instructions
exactly.

LESSON 15

Irregular Verbs, Part 1: *To Be, Have, Do*

> **Dictation or Journal Entry**
> **Vocabulary:**
> *Its* and *it's* are often used improperly. *Its* is the possessive form of "it." The kangaroo keeps *its* offspring in *its* pouch. On the other hand, *it's* is the contraction for "it is." *It's* (It is) amazing that the kangaroo keeps its young in its pouch. If in doubt, substitute "it is" for it's to be sure the sentence makes sense.

Three of the most frequently used verbs in the English language are *to be, have,* and *do.* The tenses of these verbs are irregular; they do not fit the pattern of the regular verbs. Therefore, we must memorize them.

Points of View   Verb forms often change according to three points of view: First person (*I* or *we*), second person (*you*), and third person (*he, she, it, they,* and singular or plural nouns). Below are charts showing the verb forms of *to be, have,* and *do.*

To Be

	PRESENT		PAST	
	SINGULAR	PLURAL	SINGULAR	PLURAL
1ST PERSON	I am	we are	I was	we were
2ND PERSON	you are	you are	you were	you were
3RD PERSON	he is	they are	he was	they were

Have

	PRESENT		PAST	
	SINGULAR	PLURAL	SINGULAR	PLURAL
1ST PERSON	I have	we have	I had	we had
2ND PERSON	you have	you have	you had	you had
3RD PERSON	he has	they have	he had	they had

Do

	PRESENT		PAST	
	SINGULAR	PLURAL	SINGULAR	PLURAL
1ST PERSON	I do	we do	I did	we did
2ND PERSON	you do	you do	you did	you did
3RD PERSON	he does	they do	he did	they did

Example   Complete each sentence with the correct form of the verb.

(a) If we (present of *have*) strong, healthy bodies, we can resist disease.

(b) You (present of *to be*) what you eat.

(c) He (past of *to be*) aware that eating proper foods is necessary for good health.

(d) You (past of *do*) know that a balanced diet helps the body function properly.

(e) I (present of *do*) get plenty of sleep.

(f) They (past of *have*) tired, run-down bodies from lack of sleep.

Solution   (a) If we **have** strong, healthy bodies, we can resist disease.

(b) You **are** what you eat.

(c) He **was** aware that eating proper foods is necessary for good health.

(d) You **did** know that a balanced diet helps the body function properly.

(e) I **do** get plenty of sleep.

(f) They **had** tired, run-down bodies from lack of sleep.

Practice   Write the correct verb form to complete sentences a–f.

a. Running, dancing, swimming, and biking (present of *to be*) forms of exercise.

b. In order to relieve muscle tension and maintain healthy muscles and blood vessels, he (present of *have*) to exercise regularly.

c. He (present of *do*) exercises to strengthen his heart.

d. She (past of *have*) studied the food guide pyramid.

e. We (past of *to be*) surprised at the food groups.

f. I (past of *do*) memorize the six basic food groups.

For g–j, replace each blank with *its* or *it's*.

g. _____ important to exercise.

h. The body is at _____ best when it has had enough good food, sleep, and exercise.

i. We learned that _____ essential to get enough sleep to fight off disease.

j. The body gets _____ energy from nutritious food and plenty of sleep.

More Practice   Choose the correct verb form for each sentence.

1. Sam (do, does) like green eggs.

2. He (have, has) brown eyes.

3. Archibald (were, was) my best friend.

4. (Are, Is) you punctual?

5. We (was, were) on time.

6. They (was, were) late.

7. Alba and David (was, were) married last year.

8. Ilbea and Jerry (is, are) planning their wedding.

9. (Was, Were) you considerate of your classmates?

10. (Was, Were) your brother with you?

11. Flora (have, has) a purple unicycle.

12. (Do, Does) Flora speak two languages?

13. Flora (am, are, is) bilingual.

14. Biology (are, is) the study of life.

15. I (are, is, am) studying biology.

16. A tricycle (have, has) three wheels.

17. Kurt (have, has) a tricycle.

18. Freddy (do, does) laundry every day.

19. He (do, did) nine loads of wash today.

√ **Review Set 15** **1.** *(7, 15)* For a–d, choose the correct present tense form of the verb *to be*.

    (a) I (am, are, is)   (b) You (am, are, is)

    (c) He (am, are, is)   (d) They (am, are, is)

2. *(7, 15)* For a–d, choose the correct present tense form of the verb *have*.

    (a) I (have, has)   (b) You (have, has)

    (c) She (have, has)   (d) We (have, has)

3. *(7, 15)* For a–d, choose the correct present tense form of the verb *do*.

    (a) I (do, does)   (b) You (do, does)

    (c) It (do, does)   (d) They (do, does)

4. *(7, 15)* For a–d, choose the correct past tense form of the verb *be*.

    (a) I (was, were)   (b) You (was, were)

    (c) He (was, were)   (d) They (was, were)

Write the correct verb form to complete sentences 5–10.

5. *(7, 15)* An octopus (present of *to be*) a cephalopod like a squid.

6. *(7, 15)* The injured squid (past of *have*) nine arms instead of ten.

7. *(7, 15)* It (present of *do*) amazing things with its suction-capable arms.

8. *(7, 15)* The squid (present of *have*) two longer, retractable arms.

9. *(5, 7)* It caught a fish with its longer tentacles and (past of *pass*) it to its shorter arms.

10. *(5, 11)* We (future of *watch*) the shorter tentacles hand the prey to the squid's mouth.

For 11–19, write the plural for each noun.

11. blueberry   **12.** matron of honor **13.** parade
(11–19: 13, 14)

14. alto   **15.** cupful   **16.** hero

17. cliff   **18.** leaf   **19.** key

20. Replace the blank with the singular present tense form of
(5, 7) the underlined verb.

The finches <u>perch</u> on the branch. The finch
_____ on the branch.

21. Replace the blank with the past tense form of the verb.
(5, 7)

The groomer (clip) _____ the French poodle.

22. Write the possessive noun in this sentence: In the
(10) department store, I was looking for ladies' hats.

23. Rewrite the following and add capital letters where they
(6, 12) are needed.

shakespeare wrote these lines in <u>anthony and
cleopatra</u>:
    i am dying, egypt, dying; only
    i here importune death awhile, until
    of many thousand kisses the poor last
    i lay upon thy lips.

24. Write the collective noun from this list: family, whales,
(8) squid.

25. Write the indefinite noun from this list: tree, lady, man,
(10) squid.

26. Write the simple subject of the following sentence. Then
(2, 5) write and underline the simple predicate.

The squid's siphon brings in water.

27. Tell whether this group of words is a fragment, run-on, or
(3) complete sentence:

The squid with nine arms instead of ten.

Choose the best word to complete sentences 28–30.

28. A (substitute, submarine) must surface cautiously in
(14)   order not to hit another sea vessel.

29. Land, air, and water inhabited by life is called the
(11, 14) (subsoil, biosphere).

30. The prefix meaning "three" is (*uni-, bi-, tri-*).
(13)

LESSON 16

Four Principal Parts of Verbs

Dictation or Journal Entry

Vocabulary:

Persevere is a verb that means "to continue in spite of difficulties." If you *persevere* in your studies, you will succeed. *Perseverance* is a noun meaning "continued effort in spite of difficulties; steadfastness." After years of *perseverance*, Thomas Edison finally invented the light bulb.

Four Principal Parts Every verb has **four** basic forms, or **principal parts.** In order to form all the tenses of each verb, we need to learn these principal parts: the verb, the present participle, the past, and the past participle.

Present Tense The first principal part is the singular verb in its **present tense** form, which is used to express *present time*, something that is *true at all times*, and *future time*.

walk   learn   jump   love

Present Participle The second principal part, the **present participle**, is used to form the *progressive* tenses (continuing action). The present participle is formed by adding *ing* to the singular verb. It is preceded by a form of the *to be* helping verb:

(is) walking   (is) learning   (is) jumping

Past Tense The third principal part of a verb, used to express *past time*, is the **past tense,** which we form by adding *ed* to most verbs.

walked   learned   jumped   loved

Past Participle The fourth principal part of a verb, used to form the *perfect* tenses, is the **past participle.** It is preceded by a form of the *have* helping verb. With regular verbs, the past and the past participle are the same. (Perfect tenses are taught in Lesson 19.)

PAST	PAST PARTICIPLE
walked	(has) walked
jumped	(has) jumped
learned	(has) learned
loved	(has) loved

Example Complete the chart by writing the second, third, and fourth "principal parts" (present participle, past tense, and past participle) of each verb.

VERB	PRESENT PARTICIPLE	PAST TENSE	PAST PARTICIPLE
rest	(is) resting	rested	(has) rested
(a) look	_____	_____	_____
(b) skip	_____	_____	_____
(c) form	_____	_____	_____
(d) hitch	_____	_____	_____
(e) elect	_____	_____	_____

Solution

VERB	PRESENT PARTICIPLE	PAST TENSE	PAST PARTICIPLE
(a) look	**(is) looking**	**looked**	**(has) looked**
(b) skip	**(is) skipping**	**skipped**	**(has) skipped**
(c) form	**(is) forming**	**formed**	**(has) formed**
(d) hitch	**(is) hitching**	**hitched**	**(has) hitched**
(e) elect	**(is) electing**	**elected**	**(has) elected**

Practice For a–e, complete the chart by writing the second, third, and fourth "principal parts" (present participle, past tense, and past participle) of each verb.

VERB	PRESENT PARTICIPLE	PAST TENSE	PAST PARTICIPLE
a. listen	_____	_____	_____
b. help	_____	_____	_____
c. talk	_____	_____	_____
d. prove	_____	_____	_____
e. finish	_____	_____	_____

For f and g, replace each blank with the correct vocabulary word.

√ **f.** To _____ means "to keep trying even when it is difficult."

√ **g.** If you have _____, you will succeed.

Review Set For 1–5, write the present participle, past tense, and past
16 participle of each verb. Example: 1. wait—(is) waiting, waited, (has) waited

1. wait

(7, 16)

2. snore

(7, 16)

(7, 16) **3.** rip   (7, 16) **4.** dry   (7, 16) **5.** pat

6. For a–d, choose the correct present tense form of the
(7, 15) verb *to be*.

  (a) I (am, are, is)   (b) You (am, are, is)

  (c) He (am, are, is)   (d) They (am, are, is)

7. For a–d, choose the correct present tense form of the
(7, 15) verb *have*.

  (a) I (have, has)   (b) You (have, has)

  (c) She (have, has)   (d) We (have, has)

8. For a–d, choose the correct present tense form of the
(7, 15) verb *do*.

  (a) I (do, does)   (b) You (do, does)

  (c) It (do, does)   (d) They (do, does)

9. For a–d, choose the correct past tense form of the verb *to be*.
(7, 15) (a) I (was, were)   (b) You (was, were)

  (c) He (was, were)   (d) They (was, were)

Choose the correct verb form to complete sentences 10–15.

10. Impressionists (past of *do*) paintings with light colors,
(7, 15) few details, and short brush strokes.

11. The museum (past of *have*) some paintings by the
(7, 15) Impressionists on display.

12. The tourists (future of *view*) the works of Mary Cassatt,
(5, 11) Claude Monet, and Pierre Renoir.

(5, 11) **13.** I (future of *purchase*) a Mary Cassatt painting.

14. Mary Cassatt (past of *live*) from 1844–1926.
(7, 16)

15. The Impressionist painter (present of *give*) the observer
(7, 16) the "impression" or "idea" of a painting's subject.

For 16–19, write the plural of each noun.

16. torpedo   **17.** knife   **18.** Smith   **19.** bog
(13, 14)   *(13, 14)*   *(13, 14)*   *(13, 14)*

20. Rewrite the following lines of poetry from Shakespeare's
(12) *Hamlet* and add capital letters where they are needed.

a brother's murder! pray can i not,

though inclination be as sharp as will.

21. Write the possessive form of *salesperson*.
(10)

22. Write the collective noun from this list: television,
(8) collection, book, album.

23. Write the compound noun from this list: skateboard,
(10) wagon, swing, pole.

24. Write the neuter noun from this list: postmaster,
(10) postmistress, mailman, package.

For 25–28, refer to this sentence:

I shall appreciate paintings by the Impressionists.

25. Write the simple subject.
(2, 3)

26. Write the simple predicate or verb phrase.
(2, 11)

27. Write the helping verb.
(9)

28. Tell whether the sentence is interrogative, declarative,
(1) exclamatory, or imperative.

Choose the best word to complete sentences 29–30.

29. (Its, It's) interesting that the squid uses (its, it's) mouth to
(15) move by taking in water.

(10) **30.** Did you (lie, lay) down after the mile run?

Simple Prepositions, Part 1

Dictation or Journal Entry

Vocabulary:

Sometimes people misuse the words *between* and *among*. We use *between* when comparing only two people or things. The wide-eyed toddler couldn't decide *between* an ice-cream cone and a cookie. We use *among* when comparing three or more people or things. The athlete was *among* the best in his sport.

Prepositions   **Prepositions** are words belonging to the part of speech that shows the relationship between a noun or pronoun and another word. Notice how a preposition (italicized) shows the relationship between a bug and the straw:

Bug #1 is *on* the straw. Bug #2 is *under* the straw. Bug #3 is *inside* the straw. Bug #4 is jumping *over* the straw. Bug #5 is walking *around* the straw.

Besides showing spatial relationships, prepositions also show abstract relationships. Below is a list of common prepositions.

aboard	*because of*	*excepting*	*off*	*since*
about	*before*	*for*	*on*	*through*
above	*behind*	*from*	*on account of*	*throughout*
according to	*below*	*from among*	*on behalf of*	*till*
across	*beneath*	*from between*	*on top of*	*to*
across from	*beside*	*from under*	*onto*	*toward*
after	*besides*	*in*	*opposite*	*under*
against	*between*	*in addition to*	*out*	*underneath*
along	*beyond*	*in behalf of*	*out of*	*until*
alongside	*but*	*in front of*	*outside*	*unto*
alongside of	*by*	*in place of*	*outside of*	*up*
along with	*by means of*	*in regard to*	*over*	*up to*
amid	*concerning*	*in spite of*	*over to*	*upon*
among	*considering*	*inside*	*owing to*	*via*
apart from	*despite*	*inside of*	*past*	*with*
around	*down*	*into*	*prior to*	*within*
aside from	*down from*	*like*	*regarding*	*without*
at	*during*	*near*	*round*	
away from	*except*	*near to*	*round about*	
back of	*except for*	*of*	*save*	

Simple   Notice that some prepositions in the list above are single
Prepositions   words while others are groups of words. In this lesson we will learn to recognize single-word prepositions, **simple**

prepositions, which we list alphabetically here. To help you memorize these, we list them in four columns.

1	2	3	4
aboard	beside	inside	since
about	besides	into	through
above	between	like	throughout
across	beyond	near	till
after	but	of	to
against	by	off	toward
along	concerning	on	under
alongside	considering	onto	underneath
amid	despite	opposite	until
among	down	out	unto
around	during	outside	up
at	except	over	upon
before	excepting	past	via
behind	for	regarding	with
below	from	round	within
beneath	in	save	without

Simple prepositions are underlined in the sentences below. Notice how they show the relationship between "ball" and "fence."

The soccer ball went <u>under</u> the fence.

The soccer ball went <u>over</u> the fence.

A person, place, or thing always follows a preposition. We call this word the **object of the preposition.** In the first sentence, we see that *fence* is the object of the preposition *under*. In the second sentence, *fence* is the object of the preposition *over*. We will practice this concept more in a later lesson.

Example   Underline the prepositions in a–d.

(a) A new form of government was finally begun in Mexico after the overthrow of Porfirio Díaz in 1911.

(b) The Spanish colonies in South America also struggled for independence.

(c) Simon Bolivar led the revolution against Spain in South America.

(d) Bolivar came from a wealthy Venezuelan family.

Solution   (a) A new form **of** government was finally begun **in** Mexico **after** the overthrow **of** Porfirio Díaz **in** 1911.

(b) The Spanish colonies **in** South America also struggled **for** independence.

(c) Simon Bolivar led the revolution **against** Spain **in** South America.

(d) Bolivar came **from** a wealthy Venezuelan family.

Practice   **a.** Memorize the first column of prepositions on page 79: Study the column for a moment, then cover it, and say the prepositions to yourself or to a friend. Repeat this until you can say all the preposition in the first column.

b. Now follow the instructions for Practice "a" to memorize the second column of prepositions, and say them to yourself or to a friend.

c. Have a "preposition contest" with yourself or with a friend to see how many prepositions you can write in one minute.

For d–i, list all the prepositions that you find in each sentence.

d. We read *A Wrinkle in Time* by Madeleine L'Engle.

e. Bolivar cried, "I shall march from Panama to Cape Horn, until every Spaniard is expelled!"

f. *Island of the Blue Dolphins* remains a favorite with students.

g. Throughout South America, Simon Bolivar is still called "the Liberator."

h. Boomer wandered out the gate, across the street, around the corner, past the market, and beyond the city limits.

i. After sunrise but before breakfast, we hiked along the river, among the birch trees, and through the valley, during the coolest part of the day.

For j–m, replace each blank with *between* or *among*.

j. Voters will choose from _____ several candidates on election day.

k. We had to decide _____ two people.

l. Teriyaki chicken was _____ the many entrees offered to those attending the banquet.

m. If a diligent student has to choose _____ television and homework, the choice will be homework.

More Practice Write each preposition that you find in these sentences.

1. Jake dug under the fence and crawled through the tunnel to the neighbor's yard.

2. He searched throughout the garden, beneath each tree, and among the cabbage plants for his bone.

3. Beyond the pond, under a lilac bush, beside the road, he discovered a burrow in loose soil.

4. Inside this hole, he found his bone.

5. Without a doubt, it had been stolen by a prairie dog.

Review Set 17 For 1 and 2, replace each blank with the missing preposition from your alphabetical list on page 79.

1. aboard, about, _____, across, _____,
   (17) against, along, alongside, amid, among, _____, at,
   _____ behind, _____, beneath.

2. beside, besides, _____, beyond, _____, by,
   (17) concerning, considering, despite, _____, during,
   except, _____, for, _____, in.

Write each preposition from sentences 3–5.

3. The golden lion tamarin, a kind of monkey, is
   (17) endangered in its native Brazil.

4. At the Los Angeles Zoo, in December, 2001, a golden lion
   (17) tamarin, Terra, gave birth to twins.

5. One of the twins fell from a tree and was rescued by his
   (17) protective parents.

6. Tell whether this group of words is a sentence fragment,
   (3) run-on sentence, or complete sentence:

   The monkey fell, his dad picked him up.

7. Make a complete sentence from this fragment:
(3, 4)

Climbing high in the tree from branch to branch.

8. Write the present participle, past tense, and past
(7, 16) participle of the verb *wrap*.

9. For a–d, choose the correct present tense form of the verb.
(7, 15) (a) I (am, are, is)   (b) You (am, are, is)
(c) He (do, does)   (d) We (have, has)

10. For a–d, choose the correct past tense form of the verb.
(7, 15) (a) He (was, were)   (b) It (had, have)
(c) She (do, did)   (d) They (was, were)

Write the correct verb form to complete sentences 11–14.

11. The zookeepers (future of *protect*) the tamarins by
(5, 11) constant surveillance.

12. We (future of *share*) the responsibility of saving the
(5, 11) world's endangered animals.

13. The Golden Lion Tamarin Conservation Project (present
(7, 16) of *exist*) to help the Brazilian government return these
monkeys to the rain forests.

14. Visitors (past of *examine*) the living arrangements of the
(7, 16) tamarins.

For 15–18, write the plural of each noun.

15. soprano   **16.** half   **17.** cuff   **18.** six
(14)   *(14)*   *(14)*   *(14)*

19. Rewrite the following, adding capital letters where they
(6, 12) are needed.

langston hughes capitalizes the first word of each line in
his poem "the negro speaks of rivers":
i bathed in the euphrates when dawns were young.
i built my hut near the congo and it lulled me to sleep.

20. Replace the underlined verb with an alternative that
(5, 7) might be more precise: Cleo <u>went</u> to the river.

21. Write the concrete noun from this list: love, trust, chair,
(8) Latin, loyalty.

22. Write the singular noun from this list: monkeys, trees,
(10) groomsmen, cage.

23. Write the compound feminine noun from this list: nail
(10) polish, volleyball, mother-in-law, commander in chief.

For 24–28, refer to this sentence:

The tamarins are living in trees at the zoo.

24. Write the simple subject.
(2)

25. Write the simple predicate.
(2, 5)

26. Write the present participle.
(15, 16)

27. Write the helping verb.
(9)

28. Write each preposition.
(17)

For 29–30, choose the best word to complete each sentence.

29. Playwright John Stothers demonstrated (consideration,
(1, 16) perseverance), for he never gave up hope of producing
his show, *Pilgrim*.

30. The hair on a tamarin is not (course, coarse) but rather
(8) fine.

LESSON 18

Simple Prepositions, Part 2

> **Dictation or Journal Entry**
>
> **Vocabulary:**
> The little words *to*, *two*, and *too* cause some people confusion. *To* is a preposition that means "in the direction of." The class will go *to* the zoo. *Two* is the number that follows the number one. Some families own *two* cars. *Too* is an adverb meaning "also," "in addition," "besides," "more than enough," or "very." I have *too* many freckles on my face to count.

In this lesson, we continue to practice memorizing prepositions and identifying them in a sentence.

We will focus on memorizing the third and fourth columns of simple prepositions:

3	4
inside	*since*
into	*through*
like	*throughout*
near	*till*
of	*to*
off	*toward*
on	*under*
onto	*underneath*
opposite	*until*
out	*unto*
outside	*up*
over	*upon*
past	*via*
regarding	*with*
round	*within*
save	*without*

Practice **a.** Memorize the third column of prepositions. Study the column for a moment, then cover it, and say the prepositions to yourself or to a friend. Repeat this until you can say all the prepositions in the third column.

b. Now, follow the Practice "a" instructions to memorize the fourth column of prepositions so that you can say them to yourself or to a friend.

c. Have a "preposition contest" with yourself or with a friend to see how many prepositions you can write in one minute.

Write each preposition that you find in sentences d–i.

d. With compassion, they handed blankets to those living under the bridge.

e. Barbara stuck a geranium in her hat.

f. She came to the well for water, but she left with something more.

g. Until dark, Celly trotted along the mountain trail.

h. From morning till night, he was searching for Lady.

i. With diligence, they practiced their prepositions for several days.

For j–m, replace each blank with *to, two,* or *too.*

j. It is _____ cold to surf in Alaska.

k. Surfing and skiing are _____ sports requiring balance and coordination.

l. I said I was _____ tired to do my homework!

m. My mom said, "Go _____ your room and do your homework now!"

More Practice Number your paper 1–32. Tell whether each word is a noun, verb, or preposition. Write "N" for noun, "V" for verb, or "P" for preposition.

1. went	**2.** hamburger	**3.** upon	**4.** looked
5. with	**6.** joy	**7.** swam	**8.** under
9. tree	**10.** into	**11.** ran	**12.** airplane
13. from	**14.** flew	**15.** like	**16.** until
17. sweater	**18.** during	**19.** sky	**20.** jumped
21. write	**22.** beyond	**23.** synonym	**24.** oven
25. integrity	**26.** except	**27.** after	**28.** polygon
29. below	**30.** lay	**31.** biosphere	**32.** out

Review Set
18

Write each preposition that you find in sentences 1–5.

1. Besides me, only Charles came to the party.
   (17, 18)

2. A python slithered by me.
   (17)

3. Aunt Dorothy whizzed around the rink.
   (17)

4. How many stars can you see in the night sky?
   (18)

5. After lunch, I'll sit beneath the tree and eat cherries with
   (17, 18) you.

6. Write the abstract nouns from this list:
   (8)
   raspberry   adoration   sibling   moral

7. Write each helping verb from this sentence:
   (9, 15)
   You should have seen the golden lion tamarin, the
   squirrel-sized monkey with brightly-colored hair!

8. Write the present participle, past tense, and past
   (7, 16) participle of the verb *fizz*.

9. Write the three helping verbs that begin with the letter *m*.
   (9)

10. For a–d, choose the correct present tense form of the verb.
    (7, 15) (a) I (have, has)   (b) You (am, are, is)
    (c) He (am, are, is)   (d) They (do, does)

11. For a–d, choose the correct past tense form of the verb.
    (7, 15) (a) She (do, did)   (b) It (was, were)
    (c) They (was, were)   (d) We (does, did)

Write the correct verb form to complete sentences 12 and 13.

12. The golden lion tamarin (present of *eat*) yogurt, sunflower
    (7) seeds, giant mealworms, carrots, and grapes.

13. At the new preservation facilities, birds caught in oil spills
    (9, 11) (future of *receive*) a cleaning and treatment.

14. Tell whether this group of words is a sentence fragment,
    (3) run-on sentence, or complete sentence:

    To volunteer at a shelter to help the aquatic birds.

15. Correct this run-on sentence:

(3, 4) Oil spilled into the ocean birds wallowed helplessly in the black muck.

For 16 and 17, write the plural of each noun.

16. tooth   **17.** deer
(14)   (14)

18. Rewrite the following and add capital letters where they
(6, 12) are needed.

robert frost capitalized the first word of each line in his poem, "stopping by woods on a snowy evening":

whose woods these are i think i know.
his house is in the village though;
he will not see me stopping here
to watch his woods fill up with snow.

19. Write the possessive form of *somebody*.
(10)

20. Write the concrete noun from this list: raspberry,
(8) polytheism, moral, love.

21. Unscramble these words to make an imperative sentence:
(1, 3)
me   meet   the   at   library

22. Write the indefinite noun from this list: father-in-law,
(10) grandmother, sister-in-law, grandparent.

For 23–27, refer to this sentence:

Injured birds will be examined for pollution poisoning.

23. Write the simple subject.
(2)

24. Write the simple predicate
(2, 11)

25. Write the helping verbs.
(2, 9)

26. Write the action verb.
(2, 5)

27. Write the preposition.
(17)

For 28–30, choose the best word to complete the sentence.

(18) **28.** The bird was (to, too, two) sick to fly.

29. Please select one video from (among, between) this
(17) collection of videos.

30. (Its, It's) difficult to decide.
(15)

The Perfect Tenses

Dictation or Journal Entry
Vocabulary:
The words *who's* and *whose* are frequently misused. *Whose* is a possessive pronoun. It shows ownership. *Whose* boots are these? *Who's* is the contraction for "who is." *Who's* the young boy standing next to your mother?

We have already learned the simple forms of the present, past, and future tenses. In this lesson, we will examine the three **perfect tenses**—present perfect, past perfect, and future perfect. The perfect tenses show that an action has been completed or "perfected." To form these tenses, we add a form of the helping verb *have* to the past participle.

Present Perfect

has + -ed
have + -ed

The present perfect tense describes an action that occurred in the past and is complete or continuing in the present. We add the present forms of the verb *have* to the past participle.

PRESENT PERFECT TENSE = HAVE OR HAS + PAST PARTICIPLE

Jamie <u>has walked</u> to the store many times.

Joe and Frank <u>have discovered</u> the buried treasure.

Past Perfect

had + -ed

The past perfect tense describes past action completed before another past action. We use the helping verb *had* before the past participle.

PAST PERFECT TENSE = HAD + PAST PARTICIPLE

Jamie <u>had walked</u> to the store before she went to school.

Joe and Frank <u>had discovered</u> the buried treasure before the pirates arrived.

Future Perfect

will have + -ed
shall have + -ed

The future perfect tense describes future action to be completed before another future action. We add the future form of the helping verb *have* to the past participle.

FUTURE PERFECT TENSE = WILL HAVE OR SHALL HAVE + PAST PARTICIPLE

Jamie <u>will have walked</u> to the store and back twice by noon.

We <u>shall have discovered</u> the buried treasure prior to Joe and Frank's arrival.

I <u>shall have washed</u> three loads of clothes by this evening.

Example   In sentences a–d, tell whether each perfect tense verb phrase is present, past, or future.

(a) Father <u>had walked</u> five miles to get help for the stranded motorist.

(b) The class <u>will have gathered</u> two barrels of trash for their community service project.

(c) <u>Have</u> you <u>curled</u> your hair yet?

(d) Priscilla <u>has joined</u> the Daughters of the American Revolution organization.

Solution   (a) We notice the past tense (had) form of the helping verb *have*, so we know that the perfect tense is **past perfect.**

(b) We see the future tense form of *have* (will have), so we know that the perfect tense is **future perfect.**

(c) The present tense form of *have* is used, so we know that the perfect tense is **present perfect.**

(d) The helping verb *have* is in present tense, so we know that the perfect tense is **present perfect.**

Practice   For a–f, replace each blank with *who's* or *whose*.

a. The contraction for "who is" is _____.

b. _____ is a possessive pronoun showing ownership.

c. _____ copy of *The Adventures of Tom Sawyer* is this?

d. _____ taking the minutes of this meeting?

e. I want to know _____ responsible for this mischief!

f. Do you know _____ sweater this is?

For g–j, tell whether the verb is present perfect, past perfect, or future perfect.

g. By noon, I <u>had killed</u> hundreds of mosquitoes.

h. The polio vaccine <u>has saved</u> many people from death or paralysis.

i. We <u>will have vaccinated</u> one hundred school children by five o'clock today.

j. The volcanoes <u>have erupted</u> regularly on the Hawaiian Islands.

Choose the correct word to complete k and l.

k. The "perfect" verb tense shows action that has been "perfected" or (continuing, completed).

l. To form the perfect tense, we add a form of the helping verb (have, must) to the past participle.

Review Set 19 ^(17, 18) **1.** From memory, write as many prepositions as you can in two minutes.

2. Tell whether each word is a helping verb or a ^(9, 17) preposition. Write "HV" for helping verb or "P" for preposition.

(a) is   (b) in   (c) was

(d) to   (e) are   (f) by

3. Write each preposition from this sentence:
⁽¹⁸⁾ Since yesterday, I have memorized thirty prepositions without difficulty.

For 4–6, tell whether the verb is present perfect, past perfect, or future perfect.

4. By the end of this year, volunteers <u>will have washed</u> ^(9, 19) many oil-soaked birds.

5. Donors <u>had wished</u> for even more facilities for injured ^(9, 19) animals.

6. Workers <u>have soaked</u> birds in tubs filled with dish ^(9, 19) detergent and hot, soft water.

For 7–10, write the verb phrase, including helping verbs.

7. Volunteers will wash birds with soft water.
^(9, 11)

8. Soft water does not wash away the water-repelling oils ^(7, 9) from the bird's feathers.

9. Helpers will rinse the birds with water under high
(9, 11) pressure.

10. Workers have washed many birds.
(9, 19)

11. For a–d, choose the correct present tense form of the verb.
(7, 15)

(a) He (am, are, is)   (b) We (have, has)

(c) I (do, does)   (d) You (am, are, is)

12. Tell whether the following word group is a sentence
(3) fragment, a run-on sentence, or a complete sentence:

Jane Goodall's passion for African animals in the wild.

13. Correct this run-on sentence:
(3, 4)

Jane loved animals she was a dreamer.

14. Write the present participle, past tense, and past
(7, 16) participle of the verb *persevere.*

Write the correct verb form to complete sentences 15–17.

15. Jane (past of *do*) all she could to go to Africa.
(7, 15)

16. She (present of *work*) for a big company in Kenya to
(7, 16) support her stay there.

17. Later, Jane (future of *meet*) Dr. Louis Leakey, a famous
(9, 11) scientist.

For 18–21, write the plural for each noun.

18. bucketful   **19.** mosquito   **20.** branch   **21.** key
(13, 14)   (13, 14)   (13, 14)   (13, 14)

22. Langston Hughes capitalized the first word of each line in
(6, 12) his poem below. Write each word that needs a capital
letter in the following:

     langston hughes wrote this poetry in "helen keller":

         she,
         in the dark,
         found light
         brighter than many ever see.

For 23–27, refer to this sentence:

We shall learn about Jane Goodall and her study of chimpanzees.

23. Write the simple subject.
(2)

24. Write the simple predicate, and tell whether the verb is
(2, 16) present, past, or future tense.

25. Write each preposition that you find in the sentence.
(17, 18)

26. Write the indefinite noun and tell whether it is singular
(10) or plural.

27. Write the abstract noun.
(8)

For 28–30, choose the best word to complete each sentence.

28. To form the perfect tense, we add a form of the helping
(19) verb *have* to the (present, past) participle.

29. There are (to, too, two) many facts to remember about
(18) Jane Goodall.

30. Jane Goodall's goal was (to, too, two) travel (to, too, two)
(18) Africa (to, too, two) study animals.

Capitalization: Titles, Outlines, Quotations

Dictation or Journal Entry

Vocabulary:
In the poem "I like to see it lap the miles," Emily Dickinson described her train as *prodigious*. Do you know what that word means? *Prodigious* (pronounced pr-DIJ-s) is an adjective and means "enormous or extraordinary in size, quantity, or degree; vast." The weightlifter lifted 300 pounds in a *prodigious* feat of strength.

We have learned to capitalize the following: Proper nouns, common nouns when they are a part of proper nouns, the pronoun *I*, the first word of every sentence, and the first word in every line of most poetry. We have also learned that little words like *of*, *and*, and *an* are not capitalized when part of a proper noun.

Titles **Titles** require special capitalization. In titles, we capitalize the following:

1. The first and last words of a title

2. All verbs (action or being words)

3. All other words in the title except certain short words

4. A preposition with five or more letters (such as outside, underneath, between, etc.)

Notice the examples below.

Animal Farm

The Secret Garden

When We Were Very Young

Unless located first or last in the title, words like *a*, *an*, *and*, *the*, *but*, *or*, *for*, *nor*, and prepositions with four letters or less do not need a capital letter.

The Call of the Wild

"I Have a Dream"

Romeo and Juliet

The Wind in the Willows

Outlines We learn to organize written material by outlining. **Outlines** require capital letters for the Roman numerals and for the letters of the first major topics. We also capitalize the first letter of the first word in each line of an outline.

> I. Capitalization
>   A. First word of a sentence
>   B. The pronoun *I*
> II. Punctuation
>   A. Commas
>   B. Periods

Quotations We capitalize the first word of a dialogue **quotation,** as shown below.

> Stephen asked, "Have you finished your math?"
>
> The student encouraged his friend, "You can do it!"
>
> Debby said, "Yes, I could be wrong, but I think I'm right."

Example Provide capital letters as needed.

(a) *oliver twist*

(b) *little house on the prairie*

(c) i. school
        a. math
        b. science
     ii. sports
        a. basketball
        b. softball

(d) The coach instructs, "we keep our heads up when dribbling the basketball."

Solution (a) ***O**liver **T**wist.* We capitalize the first and last words in a book title.

(b) ***L**ittle **H**ouse on the **P**rairie* is also a book. The little words *on* and *the* are not capitalized. The first and last words as well as the important words require a capital letter.

(c) We remember that outlines require capital letters for their Roman numerals, major topics, and first words.

> I. **S**chool
>   A. **M**ath
>   B. **S**cience
> II. **S**ports
>   A. **B**asketball
>   B. **S**oftball

(d) We use a capital *w* in "**W**e need to keep our heads up" because it is the beginning of a direct quotation.

√ **Practice** Rewrite a–d, and use correct capitalization.
  a. i. grammar lessons
       a. sentence types
       b. capitalization

  b. *the call of the wild*

  c. The guide said, "the mountain range is prodigious and beautiful."

  d. The judge stated, "a person must be indicted before he can be placed on trial."

  Replace each blank with the correct vocabulary word.

  e. We might say that the clown's large, red nose was _____.

  f. The enormous mountain rose to a _____ height.

More Practice See "More Practice Lesson 20" in Student Workbook.

Review Set 20 **1.** For one minute, study your list of prepositions from *(17, 18)* Lessons 17 and 18. Then write as many as you can from memory.

13+ = good
23+ = excellent
33+ = superb
43+ = genius
53 = photographic memory!

  2. Write each preposition from this list:
  (17, 18)

at	it	on	he
of	me	up	for
four	to	too	till

  3. Write each preposition from this sentence:
  (17, 18) A fish beneath the surface of the sea swam past a treasure chest inside a sunken ship.

4. Rewrite these book titles and use correct capitalization:
(6, 20)

    (a) a wind in the door

    (b) the adventures of tom sawyer

    (c) the lion, the witch, and the wardrobe

Rewrite 5 and 6 and use correct capitalization.

5. i. washing oil-soaked fowl
(20) a. use tubs of soapy, soft water

    b. rinse with strong stream of water

6. after jane goodall arrived in kenya, someone told her, "if
(6, 20) you are interested in animals, you must meet dr. louis leakey."

For 7 and 8, tell whether the verb is past perfect, present perfect, or future perfect.

7. Jane Goodall <u>has discovered</u> the chimps in Tanzania.
(16, 19)

8. Dr. Leakey <u>had offered</u> Jane the opportunity of studying
(16, 19) the chimpanzees.

Write the correct verb form for sentences 9–11.

9. As soon as her tent is pitched, Jane (present of *waste*) no
(7, 16) time before beginning her search for chimps.

10. The soccer player (past of *slip*) on the muddy grass.
(7, 16)

11. The assistant (past of *reply*) politely.
(7, 16)

12. Write the plural of nouns a–d.
(13, 14) (a) leaf   (b) wolf   (c) banjo   (d) ring

13. Choose the concrete noun from this list: plate, joy, idea,
(8) patience.

14. Unscramble these words to make an imperative sentence.
(1, 3)
    me   please   understand

15. Write the present participle, past tense, and past
(7, 16) participle of the verb *waste.*

For 16–18, refer to this sentence:

The prodigious jet sliced through the clouds.

16. Write the simple subject.
(2)

17. Write the simple predicate.
(2, 5)

18. Write the preposition.
(17, 18)

19. Correct this run-on sentence:
(3, 4)

She flew to Oregon on Monday she returned on Tuesday.

Choose the best word to complete sentences 20–30.

20. The "perfect" verb tense shows action that has been
(19) "perfected" or (continuing, completed).

21. (Who's, whose) the villain in the melodrama?
(19)

22. The director must choose from (between, among) many
(17) talented actors for the leading part.

23. That type of decision is (to, two, too) difficult for most
(18) people.

24. Abraham Lincoln demonstrated (dishonor, perseverance)
(6, 16) when trying to free the slaves.

25. The chimpanzee cared for (it's, its) young.
(15)

26. Please (lay, lie) down if you are tired.
(10)

27. The cross country (course, coarse) challenged even the
(8) most elite runner.

28. Because of inadequate rainfall, consumers must not
(5) (waste, waist) water.

29. The prefix meaning "two" is (*bio-, geo-, tri-, uni-, bi-*).
(13)

30. *Whose* and *who's* are (homophones, homonyms).
(4, 19)

The Progressive Verb Forms

Dictation or Journal Entry
Vocabulary:
Sometimes we misuse the words *fewer* and *less*. We use *fewer* with nouns that can be counted. February has *fewer* days than December. We use *less* when referring to nouns that cannot be counted. We spent *less* time in England than in Israel.

We have learned the six main verb tenses:

1. present   walk(s)
2. past   walked
3. future   will/shall walk
4. present perfect   has/have walked
5. past perfect   had walked
6. future perfect   will/shall have walked

All six of these main verb tenses also have a **progressive form.** A progressive verb phrase shows action in "progress" or continuing action.

Present progressive	=	action still in progress at the time of speaking
Past progressive	=	action in progress throughout a specific time in the past
Future progressive	=	action that will be in progress in the future
Present perfect progressive	=	action begun in the past and still continuing in the present
Past perfect progressive	=	past action begun, continued, and terminated in the past
Future perfect progressive	=	continuous future action completed at some time in the future

Progressive verb forms are expressed with some form of the verb *to be* and the present participle ("ing" added to the main verb).

Present Progressive

The present progressive form consists of the appropriate present tense of *to be* (am/is/are) plus the present participle (verb + *ing*).

PRESENT PROGRESSIVE = IS OR AM OR ARE + PRESENT PARTICIPLE

Henry <u>is coming</u> to the party.

We <u>are discussing</u> the details for the party.

I <u>am baking</u> banana bread for a treat.

am
is
are
+ -ing

Past Progressive The past progressive form consists of a past form of *to be* (was/were) plus the present participle.

Was
were
+ -ing

> PAST PROGRESSIVE = <u>WAS</u> OR <u>WERE</u> + <u>PRESENT PARTICIPLE</u>
>
> The cat <u>was nibbling</u> at the dry food.
>
> The crows <u>were dropping</u> pecans to the ground.

Future Progressive We form the future progressive by adding the present participle to the future of the *to be* verb (shall be/will be).

shall be
will be
+ -ing

> FUTURE PROGRESSIVE = <u>SHALL BE</u> OR <u>WILL BE</u> + <u>PRESENT PARTICIPLE</u>
>
> Our family <u>will be going</u> to the beach on Saturday.
>
> I <u>shall be celebrating</u> my twenty-first birthday this year.

Present Perfect Progressive We form the present perfect progressive by using *has* or *have*, *been*, and the present participle.

have been
has been
+ -ing

> PRESENT PERFECT PROGRESSIVE = <u>HAVE BEEN</u> OR <u>HAS BEEN</u> + <u>PRESENT PARTICIPLE</u>
>
> Jenny and Trisha <u>have been studying</u> their math tonight.
>
> Jim <u>has been attending</u> this organ class for the last two years.

Past Perfect Progressive The past perfect progressive consists of *had*, *been*, and the present participle.

had been
+ -ing

> PAST PERFECT PROGRESSIVE = <u>HAD BEEN</u> + <u>PRESENT PARTICIPLE</u>
>
> The plants <u>had been growing</u> rapidly from the moment the experiment began.
>
> Last month we <u>had been looking</u> for a new car.

Future Perfect Progressive We form the future perfect progressive with *will* or *shall* have, *been*, and the present participle.

will have been
shall have been
+ -ing

> FUTURE PERFECT PROGRESSIVE =
> <u>WILL HAVE BEEN</u> OR <u>SHALL HAVE BEEN</u> + <u>PRESENT PARTICIPLE</u>
>
> The minister <u>will have been marrying</u> couples for twenty years when he retires.
>
> On our next anniversary, I <u>shall have been cooking</u> for him for thirty years.

Example For sentences a–f, tell whether the progressive verb form is present, past, future, present perfect, past perfect, or future perfect.

(a) The girls <u>were chatting</u> on the Internet.

(b) You <u>will be playing</u> the piano well soon.

(c) The neighbor <u>had been talking</u> about his garden for hours.

(d) The air-traffic controller <u>is guiding</u> the plane safely.

(e) This June, I <u>shall have been teaching</u> aerobics for twenty years.

(f) Grandpa <u>has been helping</u> me with my science project.

Solution (a) We notice that "were" is the past tense form of *to be*, so we know that "were chatting" is the **past progressive.**

(b) "Will be" is the future form of *to be*, so the verb phrase is **future progressive.**

(c) "Had been" is the past perfect form, so the verb phrase is **past perfect progressive.**

(d) "Is" is a present form of *to be*, so the verb phrase is **present progressive.**

(e) The verb phrase "shall have been" is a future perfect form, so the entire phrase is **future perfect progressive.**

(f) The verb phrase "has been" indicates the present perfect tense, so the entire verb phrase is **present perfect progressive.**

Practice For sentences a–c, tell whether the verb is present progressive, past progressive, or future progressive.

a. A doll <u>is missing</u> from Emily's wish list.

b. The tiger <u>was carrying</u> her cub with her teeth.

c. Eric <u>will be representing</u> his high school at the league cross-country meet.

For sentences d–f, tell whether the verb is present perfect progressive, past perfect progressive, or future perfect progressive.

d. At noon, the policemen <u>will have been searching</u> for four hours for the missing person.

e. The waitress <u>had been opening</u> the restaurant at the request of her employer.

f. The dentist <u>has been treating</u> the homeless for many years.

For g–k, replace each blank with *fewer* or *less.*

g. There was _____ oil in the can than the boy thought.

h. If the noun can be counted, we use _____.

i. If the noun cannot be counted, we use _____.

j. Did you bring _____ candy bars than you had planned?

k. The ill patient had _____ energy than normal.

Choose the correct word to complete sentences l and m.

l. The progressive tense shows action that is (continuing, completed).

m. To make the progressive tense, we use some form of the verb *to be* plus the (present, past) participle which ends in *ing.*

Review Set 21

1. Write each preposition in this sentence:
(17, 18) In the fight against evil, the hero stood opposite a villain with deceitful powers.

Choose the best word to complete sentences 2–5.

2. The White Rabbit in *Alice in Wonderland* checks his
(1, 2) watch continually because he tries to be (moral, punctual).

3. A (diligent, considerate) hostess tries to make her guests
(1, 12) feel comfortable and welcome.

4. (Respectful, Reliable) men rise when a lady enters the
(3) room.

5. Jurors must demonstrate (willpower, integrity) when
(6, 9) delivering a verdict.

For 6–8, refer to this sentence:

Jane Goodall has been watching chimpanzees.

6. Write the simple subject.
(2)

7. Write the simple predicate.
(2, 21)

8. Write each helping verb.
(9, 21)

9. For a–c, tell whether each group of words is a fragment,
(3) run-on, or complete sentence.

(a) About four feet tall with brown skin and black, coarse
hair.

(b) They are the smallest of the great apes they weigh
between 100 and 150 pounds.

(c) Chimpanzees have small noses, large ears, big lips,
and brown eyes.

Rewrite sentences 10–12, and add capital letters where they
are needed.

10. in africa, jane goodall learned more about chimpanzees.
(6, 12)

11. she said, "let us persevere in our studies."
(12, 20)

12. the book was called <u>the sign of the beaver</u>.
(12, 20)

13. Write the word from this list that is *not* a helping verb.
(9, 17)

is, am, are, was, were, be, being, been
about, has, have, had, may, might, must
can, could, do, does, did, shall, will

✓**14.** Write the feminine noun from this list: host, baker,
(10) hostess, teacher.

✓**15.** Write the collective noun from this list: hamburger,
(8) bunch, faith, Latin, soda.

16. Write the present participle, past tense, and past
(5, 16) participle of the verb *talk*.

17. Replace each blank with the missing prepositions from your memorized list.

(17)

aboard, about, _____, across, after, against, _____, alongside, amid, among, around, _____, before, behind, below

For 18–21, choose the correct verb form.

18. We (will, shall) remember that chimpanzees depend more on sight than smell to detect danger.

(9, 11)

19. Jane (will, shall) report her findings to other animal enthusiasts.

(9, 11)

20. I (am, is, are)   **21.** We (has, have)

(7, 15)   (7, 15)

For 22 and 23, write the plural of each noun.

22. box   **23.** sheep

(13)   (13)

24. Tell whether the underlined verb phrase is past perfect, present perfect, or future perfect.

(19)

The Amur leopard <u>will have joined</u> the list of endangered animals.

For 25–27, tell whether the verb tense is present progressive, past progressive, or future progressive.

25. The lumberjacks <u>were chopping</u> down trees.

(9, 19)

26. I <u>shall be celebrating</u> Monty and Tom's birthdays.

(9, 19)

27. Scientists <u>are discussing</u> how to protect the Amur leopard.

(9, 19)

For 28 and 29, tell whether the verb tense is present perfect progressive, past perfect progressive, or future perfect progressive.

28. In May, I <u>shall have been studying</u> Greek for three years.

(9, 19)

29. Fewer than two hundred Amur leopards <u>had been living</u> in zoos.

(9, 19)

30. Choose the correct word to complete sentences a and b.

(9, 19)

(a) The (perfect, progressive) tense shows continuing action.

(b) The (past, present) participle ends in *ing*.

Linking Verbs

Dictation or Journal Entry
Vocabulary:
Compassion, a noun, is "sympathy for the suffering or sorrow of another person, with a desire to help." Juan had *compassion* for the homeless man and offered him a hamburger.

Sympathy, a synonym for compassion, means "sharing another person's feelings." Bo had *sympathy* for Jan after Jan's dog died.

Linking Verbs   A **linking verb** "links" the subject of a sentence to the rest of the predicate. It does not show action, and it is not "helping" an action verb. Its purpose is to connect a name or description to the subject.

Ray <u>is</u> a policeman.

In the sentence above, *is* links "Ray" with "policeman." The word *policeman* names Ray's occupation.

Ray <u>is</u> trustworthy.

In the sentence above, *is* links "Ray" with "trustworthy." The word *trustworthy* describes Ray.

Watch Out!   We must carefully examine our sentences. Some verbs can be used as either linking or action verbs, as shown in the two sentences below.

Jill <u>looks</u> ill today. (*Looks* is a linking verb. It links "Jill" with "ill.")

Jill <u>looks</u> at the helicopter in the sky. (*Looks* is an action verb, not a linking verb. Jill is doing something.)

Common Linking Verbs   Common linking verbs include all of the "to be" verbs:

> *is, am, are, was, were, be, being, been*

The following are also common linking verbs. Memorize these:

> *look, feel, taste, smell, sound*
>
> *seem, appear, grow, become*
>
> *remain, stay*

Identifying Linking Verbs To tell whether a verb is a linking verb, we replace it with a form of the verb "to be"—*is, am, are, was, were, be, being, been*, as in the example below.

> The firefighter *feels* anxious about the burn victim.

We replace *feels* with *is*:

> The firefighter *is* anxious about the burn victim.

Since the sentence still makes sense, we know that *feels* is a linking verb in this sentence. Now let us examine the word *feels* in the sentence below.

> The firefighter *feels* the heat of the fire.

We replace *feels* with *is*:

> The firefighter *is* the heat of the fire.

The sentence no longer makes sense, so we know that *feels* is not a linking verb in this sentence.

Example Identify and write the linking verb, if any, in each sentence.
   (a) Porfirio Díaz was the successor of Benito Juárez.

   (b) Díaz seemed successful as a leader.

   (c) Mexico became more prosperous under his dictatorship.

   (d) Unfortunately, Díaz remained unconcerned about the landless farmworkers.

   (e) Díaz looked at the people.

Solution (a) The linking verb **was** links "Díaz" to "successor."

   (b) The verb **seemed** links "Díaz" to "successful."

   (c) The verb **became** links "Mexico" to "prosperous."

   (d) The verb **remained** links "Díaz" to "unconcerned."

   (e) We replace the verb *looked* with *was*: Díaz *was* at the people. The sentence no longer makes sense, so we know that the word *looked* is not a linking verb in this sentence. There are **no linking verbs** in this sentence.

Practice   a. Study the linking verbs (including the "to be" verbs) listed in this lesson. Memorize them line by line. Then say them to your teacher or to a friend.

b. Have a "linking verb contest" with yourself or with a partner: Write as many as you can from memory in one minute.

Write the linking verbs, if any, from sentences c–j.

c. The farmworkers became poorer under Díaz's leadership.

d. Díaz's treatment of the Yaquis Indians was cruel and vicious.

e. Pancho Villa and Emiliano Zapata became the leaders of Mexico after Díaz.

f. Zapata remains famous for his battle cry, "Land and liberty!"

g. Mexican history seems turbulent during this time.

h. Zapata appeared more idealistic than Villa.

i. Zapata smelled the meat.

j. The meat smelled rotten.

For k–m, replace each blank with the correct vocabulary word.

k. The word *compassion* means "_____ for the suffering or sorrow of others."

l. A synonym for sympathy is _____.

m. When we are sad or hurting, we appreciate people who show _____ or _____ toward us.

More Practice   Write each linking verb from sentences 1–15.

1. The substitute teacher seemed conscientious.

2. Mr. Vásquez remains the best electrician in the area.

3. He appears self-disciplined.

4. Frank felt healthy after hiking in the fresh air.

5. Reliable workers remain diligent on the job.

6. The two friends stayed loyal to one another through many years.

7. After dinner, he grew tired.

8. Rotten eggs smell sulfurous.

9. Young people with integrity usually become honorable adults.

10. Christie's voice sounded hoarse after she officiated at the game.

11. Jaime looks intelligent.

12. His brother is a genius.

13. His parents were scholars.

14. The milk tasted sour.

15. Tom was the groom.

For 16–20, tell whether each verb is action or linking.

16. She <u>tasted</u> the pie.   **17.** The pie <u>tasted</u> sweet.

18. Joe <u>sounded</u> the horn.   **19.** It <u>sounded</u> urgent.

20. Peter <u>smelled</u> the rose.

Review Set 22 **1.** Write all the linking verbs, including the "to be" verbs, *(15, 22)* listed in this lesson.

2. From your memory, write all the common helping verbs *(9, 15)* from Lesson 9. If necessary, refer to Lesson 9 to check your list.

For 3–8, write the linking verbs, if any.

3. Juárez is respected for his honesty and sincerity. *(15, 22)*

(5, 22) **4.** Steve tasted the soup.

5. The soup tasted bitter.
(22)

6. The quartet sounds harmonious.
(22)

7. A bear appeared out of the darkness.
(5, 22)

8. It appeared ferocious.
(22)

9. Write each preposition from these sentences:
(17, 18)
    (a) Fewer tourists travel during winter.

    (b) All except Ned hiked up Mount Whitney.

10. Rewrite the following and add capital letters where they
(6, 12) are needed.

william shakespeare wrote these lines of poetry in *as you like it*:

the fool doth think he is wise, but
the wise man knows himself to be a fool.

11. For a–c, tell whether the group of words is a fragment,
(3) run-on, or complete sentence.

    (a) In many countries, manatees and dugongs are hunted for their hides, bones, and meat.

    (b) Some manatees die in speedboat accidents many are crushed in locks and dams.

    (c) The manatee on the beach near the bay.

For 12–15, refer to this sentence:

Man's influence has endangered the manatee's existence.

12. Write the simple subject.
(2)

13. Write the simple predicate.
(2, 19)

14. Write each possessive noun.
(10)

15. Write the helping verb.
(9, 19)

Choose the best word to complete sentences 16–19.

16. *Rock*, a stone, and *rock*, to move back and forth, are
(4) (homophones, homonyms).

17. Chefs prefer (course, coarse) salt because less is required
(8)   for taste.

18. If one speaks two languages fluently, one is (bilingual,
(12, 13) conscientious, lucky).

19. The customer could not choose (among, between) the
(17)   two pies.

20. Unscramble these words to make an imperative sentence.
(1, 3)

   trash   the   to   remember   take   out

21. For a and b, write the plural of each noun.
(13)   (a) tablet   (b) tabby

22. Write the present participle, past tense, and past
(16)   participle of the verb *pitch*.

23. Replace each blank with the missing preposition from
(17)   column 2 in Lesson 17.

   beside, _____, between, beyond,
   _____, by, concerning, considering, despite,
   _____, during, except, _____, for, from, in

24. Write each preposition from this sentence:
(17, 18)

   Henry Sugimoto's paintings showed the bravery of
   Japanese-American soldiers during World War II.

25. Write the correct verb form for a–c.
(7, 15) (a) I (was, were) (b) They (has, have) (c) He (do, does)

For 26–28, tell whether the underlined verb phrase is present
perfect, past perfect, or future perfect.

26. The Japanese women <u>had provided</u> a *senninbari* for the
(9, 19) brave soldier to wrap around his waist.

27. The observers <u>have learned</u> that a *senninbari* is a simple
(9, 19) white cloth containing a thousand stitches.

28. The soldiers <u>will have recognized</u> the *senninbari* as a
(9, 19) symbol of the prayers of each person who stitched a knot
   for the soldier's safe return.

For 29 and 30, write the progressive tense verb phrase from each sentence.

29. The Japanese women had been encouraging their soldiers
(9, 21) for years through the *senninbari.*

30. Visitors are discussing the paintings of Henry Sugimoto.
(9, 21)

LESSON 23

Diagramming Simple Subjects and Simple Predicates

> **Dictation or Journal Entry**
>
> **Vocabulary:**
> *Morale* (pronounced mo-RAL) is a noun and means "a mental state or attitude, particularly one of well-being." Scoring a point boosted the players' *morale*.

We learned to analyze a sentence for its simple subject and simple predicate. Now we will learn how to **diagram** our sentence according to this pattern:

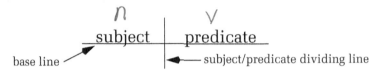

The subject and predicate sit on a horizontal "base line" and are separated by a vertical line that passes through the base line. Below is a **simple subject and simple predicate diagram** of this sentence: (At our school) the teachers possess high morale.

As you can see above, we place the simple subject on the left and the simple predicate on the right. We separate the two with a vertical line.

Example 1 Diagram the simple subject and predicate of the following sentence:

At our school, the students respect each other.

Solution The "who or what" (subject) of the sentence is "students." The action word connected with students (predicate) is "respect."

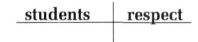

Example 2 Diagram the simple subject and predicate of the following sentence:

The moral (of the story) is "to do unto others as you would have them do unto you."

Solution We refer to the list of helping verbs and linking verbs in the previous lessons. "Is" is a linking verb in this sentence. We ask ourselves, "What *is*?" The answer is the subject, the moral.

moral	is

Example 3 Diagram the simple subject and predicate of this sentence:

Mr. Do-it-later Procrastinator <u>might have neglected</u> something important.

Solution We recall our list of helping verbs and see that the verb phrase <u>might have neglected</u> is the simple predicate telling what *Mr. Do-it-later Procrastinator* (subject) did.

Mr. Do-it-later Procrastinator	**might have neglected**

Practice Diagram the simple subject and the simple predicate of sentences a–d.

  a. The siblings have demonstrated high morals and high morale.

  b. The boy's dilemma caused great confusion.

  c. *Anne Frank: The Diary of a Young Girl* portrays the struggles of a young girl during the time of the Nazis.

  d. Anne hid from the Nazis for two years.

For e and f, replace each blank with the correct vocabulary word.

  e. We say your *morale* is good if you have an _____ of well-being.

  f. Happy, successful people generally have high _____.

Review Set 23 Choose the best word to complete sentences 1–4.

  1. People (waist, waste) a great deal of time in front of the
  (5) television.

  2. What a(n) (honor, dishonor) to eat lunch with President
  (6) Barack Obama!

3. The prefix meaning "same" is (*geo-*, *homo-*, *bio-*).
(7, 11)

4. A (perfect, progressive) tense verb shows continuing
(19, 21) action.

5. Tell whether this sentence is declarative, interrogative,
(1, 3) imperative, or exclamatory: What day of the week is it?

6. Tell whether the following group of words is a fragment,
(3) run-on, or complete sentence: Severo Ochoa, an
intelligent man from Spain.

7. Write the abstract noun from this list: piano, ship,
(8) football, jacket, Christianity, book.

For 8–11, write the plural of each noun.

8. branch   **9.** airplane   **10.** turkey   **11.** cactus
(13, 14)   *(13, 14)*   *(13, 14)*   *(13, 14)*

Rewrite sentences 12–14, adding capital letters where they
are needed.

12. severo ochoa emigrated to the united states in 1941 and
(6, 12) did research at the new york university's College of
Medicine.

13. i was not aware that dr. ochoa made synthetic dna.
(6, 12)

14. here is an outline: i. severo ochoa
(12, 20)   a. physician
                                                  b. researcher

15. Replace each blank with the missing prepositions from
(17) the third column in Lesson 17.

inside, into, _____, near, _____ off, on,
onto, opposite, _____, outside, _____
past, regarding, round, save

16. Write the 23 helping verbs.
(9)

17. Write the linking verbs, including the "to be" verbs,
(22) listed in Lesson 22.

18. Replace the blank with the singular present tense form of
(7) the verb.

Gorillas <u>belch</u>.   A gorilla _____.

19. Choose the correct future tense helping verb.

(11)   We (will, shall) begin our state project next week.

20. For a–c, choose the correct form of the irregular verb *to be*.

(15)   (a) I (am, are, is) (b) He (was, were) (c) You (am, are, is)

21. Write the present participle, past tense, and past

(16)   participle of the verb *walk.*

22. Write the present perfect verb phrase from this sentence:

(16, 19)   Archie has misbehaved in class today.

23. Write the present progressive verb phrase from this

(9, 21)   sentence:

Nathan is cooking dinner tonight.

24. Write the past perfect progressive verb phrase from this

(9, 21)   sentence:

Emily had been growing several inches a year.

For 25–28, tell whether the verb is an action verb or linking verb.

25. Robert <u>grew</u> a foot last year.

(5, 22)

26. Sherry <u>grew</u> thirsty during the marathon.

(5, 22)

27. The nurse <u>felt</u> his forehead.

(5, 22)

28. With a proper diet, she <u>felt</u> healthy.

(5, 22)

Diagram the simple subject and simple predicate of sentences 29 and 30.

29. Gloriana enjoys cheerleading.

(2, 23)

30. Eric plays the harp.

(2, 23)

Phrases and Clauses

Dictation or Journal Entry
Vocabulary:
The homophones *whole* and *hole* cause some people difficulty. *Whole* means "all, complete, or entire." Robert ate the *whole* pizza. A *hole* is a hollow place or a cavity. I dug a *hole* to plant the tree.

Phrases   A **phrase** is a group of words used as a single word in a sentence. A phrase may contain nouns and verbs, but it does not have both a subject and a predicate. Below are some phrases.

One

across the field

instead of the blue dress

should have eaten

during the Industrial Revolution

will have finished

Clauses   A **clause** is a group of words with a subject and a predicate. In the clauses below, we have italicized the simple subjects and underlined the simple predicates.

Both

after the steam *engine* <u>was invented</u>

as *you* <u>may know</u>

but one *invention* <u>led</u> to another

Eli Whitney's *cotton gin* <u>speeded</u> fabric production.

(*you*) <u>Imagine</u> that!

Example 1   Tell whether each group of words is a phrase or a clause.

(a) when electrical energy came

(b) into widespread use

(c) beside the deep and wide Mississippi River

(d) before I went

(e) Look up!

Solution   (a) This group of words is a **clause.** It has both a subject (energy) and a predicate (came).

(b) This group of words is a **phrase.** It does not have a subject or predicate.

(c) This is a **phrase.** It has no subject or predicate.

(d) This is a **clause.** Its subject is *I*; its predicate is went.

(e) This is a **clause.** We remember that the subject, *you*, of an imperative sentence is understood. (*You*) Look up!

Every complete sentence has at least one clause. Some sentences have more than one clause. We have italicized the simple subjects and underlined the simple predicates in each clause of the sentence below. Notice that it contains three clauses (three subject and predicate combinations).

After *I* ate my breakfast, but before *I* went to school, *I* brushed my teeth.

Below, we have diagrammed the simple subjects and simple predicates of each clause from the sentence above.

After I ate my breakfast,   I | ate

but before I went to school,   I | went

I brushed my teeth.   I | brushed

Example 2   Diagram the simple subjects and simple predicates of the clauses in this sentence:

Steam remained the most important energy source until electrical energy came into widespread use.

Solution   We examine the sentence and find that there are two clauses:

1. *Steam* remained the most important energy source

2. until electrical *energy* came into widespread use

We diagram the first clause: steam | remained

We diagram the second clause: energy | came

✓ **Practice**   For a–d, tell whether the group of words is a phrase or a clause.

a. because steam can be made anywhere

b. into another century

c. then you can weave your cloth

d. after Independence Day, July 4, 1776

Diagram each simple subject and simple predicate in clauses e–g.

e. although their home is over there

f. and loud trains drive cows crazy

g. after James Watt invented the steam engine

Replace each blank with *hole* or *whole.*

h. The dentist informed his patient that there was a cavity, or _____, in his tooth.

i. I read the entire, or _____, novel in one sitting.

Review Set 24

Choose the best word or prefix to complete sentences 1–4.

1. Please (lie, lay) my beach towel on the sand.
(10)

2. A (biography, biosphere) is the story of one's life written
(11) by another.

3. The study of life is called (geography, biology, geology).
(7, 11)

4. A fictional horse having one horn in its forehead is called
(13) a (uni-, bi-, tri-)corn.

5. Tell whether this sentence is declarative, interrogative,
(1) imperative, or exclamatory:

Barbara McClintock studied the variations in corn kernels under a microscope.

6. Tell whether this group of words is a fragment, run-on, or
(3) complete sentence:

Severo Ochoa received a medical degree at the age of twenty-four.

7. Write the concrete noun from this list: French, Islam,
(8) friendship, Mr. Rogers, loyalty.

For 8–11, write the plural of each noun.

8. cliff   **9.** tomato   **10.** lady   **11.** deer
(13, 14)   *(13, 14)*   *(13, 14)*   *(13, 14)*

Rewrite sentences 12–14, and add capital letters where they are needed.

12. there was a big race to discover the structure of dna.
(12)

13. james watson, an american scientist, and francis crick, an
(6, 12) english scientist, won the race.

14. their research paper began, "we wish to suggest a
(6, 12) structure...[that has] novel features which are of considerable biological interest."

15. Replace each blank with the missing prepositions from
(17) the fourth column in Lesson 17.

      _____,   through,   _____,   till,
      _____, toward, under, underneath, until, unto,
      _____, upon, via, _____, within, without

16. Write the word from this list that is *not* a helping verb.
(9, 17)

is, am, are, was, were, be, being, been, by, has, had, have, do, does, did, can, could, shall, will, should, would, may, might, must

17. Write the word from this list that is *not* a linking verb.
(5, 22)

is, am, are, was, were, be, being, been, hop, look, feel, taste, smell, sound, seem, appear, grow, become, remain, stay

18. Replace the blank with the past tense form of the verb.
(7, 16)

Ken and Barbie <u>dance</u>. Yesterday they_____.

19. Complete the future tense verb form by choosing *will*
(9, 11) or *shall.*

In *Beauty and the Beast,* the Beast (shall, will) transform into a prince.

20. For a–c, choose the correct form of the irregular verb *have.*
(7, 15) (a) I (has, have)   (b) He (has, have)   (c) You (has, have)

21. Write the present participle, past tense, and past
(7, 16) participle of the verb *finish*.

22. Write the past perfect verb phrase from this sentence:
(9, 19)
LeRoy had skated for five miles.

23. Write the past progressive verb phrase from this sentence:
(9, 21)
Boomer was barking at the door.

24. Write the future perfect progressive verb phrase from this
(9, 21) sentence.

Soon, Veronica will have been practicing the piano
for one hour.

For 25 and 26, tell whether the verb is action or linking.

25. Andrea <u>tasted</u> the guacamole.
(5, 22)

26. The guacamole <u>tasted</u> creamy and delicious.
(5, 22)

For 27 and 28, tell whether the group of words is a phrase or
a clause.

27. because James Watson and Francis Crick shared the same
(2, 24) belief

28. the simple pattern of DNA's molecular structure
(2, 24)

Diagram the simple subject and simple predicate of sentences
29 and 30.

✓ **29.** The scientists deduced the truth.
(2, 23)

✓ **30.** DNA has a double helix structure.
(2, 23)

Diagramming a Direct Object

Dictation or Journal Entry
Vocabulary:
The prefix *mono-* means "one" or "single." A *monorail* is a railway using a single track. We rode the *monorail* to our hotel. A *monologue* is a dramatic sketch performed by one person. Jason needed a drink of water after delivering his *monologue.* A *monopoly* is the control of a product or service by one company. One bus company has a *monopoly* of the city's transportation.

Finding the Direct Object

A **direct object** follows an *action verb* and tells who or what receives the action.

Nancy's cat Easton caught a mouse.

action verb   direct object

We can answer these three questions to find the direct object of a sentence:

1. What is the verb in the sentence?

2. Is it an *action verb*?

3. Who or what receives the action? (direct object)

We will follow the steps above to find the direct object of this sentence:

Johnny repaired the computer.

QUESTION 1:   What is the verb?
   ANSWER: The verb is "repaired."

QUESTION 2:   Is it an *action verb*?
   ANSWER: Yes.

QUESTION 3:   Who or what receives the action?
   ANSWER: The *computer* was "repaired."

Therefore, "computer" is the direct object.

Example 1   Follow the procedure above to find the direct object of this sentence:

Loud music damages the ears.

Solution   We answer the questions as follows:

QUESTION 1:   What is the verb?
   ANSWER: The verb is "damages."

QUESTION 2:   Is it an *action verb*?

ANSWER: Yes.

QUESTION 3:   Who or what receives the action?
ANSWER: *Ears* receive the "damage."

Therefore, **ears** is the direct object.

Example 2   Answer the three previous questions to find the direct object of this sentence:

Dr. Livingstone was an explorer in Africa.

Solution   We answer the questions as follows:

QUESTION 1:   What is the verb?
ANSWER: The verb is "was."

QUESTION 2:   Is it an *action verb*?
ANSWER: No. "Was" is a linking verb.

Therefore, this sentence has **no direct object.**

Diagramming the Direct Object   Below is a diagram of the simple subject, simple predicate, and direct object of this sentence:

Johnny repaired the computer.

Johnny	repaired	computer
(subject)	(verb)	(direct object)

Notice that a vertical line after the action verb indicates a direct object.

Example 3   Diagram the simple subject, simple predicate, and direct object of this sentence:

Loud music damages the ears.

music	damages	ears
(subject)	(verb)	(direct object)

√ **Practice**   For a–d, write the direct object, if there is one, in each sentence.

a. The Industrial Revolution spread economic ideas.

b. Capitalism and socialism were two economic ideas.

c. In capitalism, individuals control their money.

d. The United States practices capitalism today.

e. Diagram the simple subject, simple predicate, and direct object of sentence *a* on page 122.

f. Diagram the simple subject, simple predicate, and direct object of sentence *d* above.

For g–j, replace each blank with the correct vocabulary word.

g. The prefix _____ means "one" or "single."

h. We call a train a _____ if it rides on a single track.

i. Jaqueline practiced her character's _____ in the mirror last night.

j. Does that company have a _____ of the potato market in this country?

Review Set 25

Choose the best word to complete sentences 1–4.

1. The amusement park (substitute, submarine) circles around a lagoon and dazzles spectators with underwater sights.
(14)

2. The (coarse, subsoil) contains too much clay to absorb water properly.
(8, 14)

3. The gopher snake will shed (its, it's) skin soon.
(15)

4. That little boy is (to, too, two) intelligent for his own good!
(18)

For 5 and 6, tell whether the sentence is declarative, interrogative, imperative, or exclamatory.

5. Sound the alarm.
(1, 3)

6. That story sounds scary!
(1, 3)

7. Tell whether this group of words is a fragment, run-on, or
(2, 3) complete sentence:

Severo Ochoa did research in Europe then he studied
proteins that cause chemical reactions.

8. Write the collective noun from this list: patriotism, cat,
(8) flock, truck, ocean.

For 9–12, write the plural for each noun.

9. fox   **10.** boy   **11.** louse   **12.** bluff
(13, 14)   (13, 14)   (13, 14)   (13, 14)

Rewrite sentences 13–15, adding capital letters where they
are needed.

13. percy julian was born in montgomery, alabama, in 1899.
(6, 12)

14. soybeans, i suspect, have many uses.
(6, 12)

15. she said, "percy julian synthesized cortisone from
(12, 20) soybeans."

16. List each preposition from this sentence:
(17)

Cortisone, one of a group of hormones called
steroids, is used by people with arthritis.

17. Replace each blank with the missing helping verb.
(9)

is, am, _____, was, were, be, being,
_____, has, _____, had, do, does, did,
shall, _____, can, could, may, might,
_____, should, would

18. Write the past tense form of the verb *ship*.
(7)

19. Choose the correct helping verb form: Neil (shall, will)
(9, 11) enter his Porsche in an auto show.

20. For a–c, choose the correct form of the irregular verb *do*.
(7, 15)
(a) She (do, does) (b) You (do, does) (c) They (does, do)

21. Write the present participle, past tense, and past
(9, 16) participle of the verb *help*.

22. Write the future perfect verb phrase from this sentence:

(9, 19)

Skooter will have finished high school in June.

23. Write the future progressive verb phrase from this

(9, 21) sentence:

Our family will be going to camp in August.

24. Write the present perfect progressive verb phrase from

(9, 21) this sentence:

Mark has been planning a visit to France this summer.

25. For a–d, tell whether the verb is action or linking.

(5, 22) (a) The mother <u>sounded</u> angry.

(b) The soldier <u>sounded</u> the bugle.

(c) The captain <u>felt</u> seasick.

(d) She <u>felt</u> the heat from the sun.

26. For a and b, tell whether each group of words is a phrase

(2, 24) or a clause.

(a) because people suffer from arthritis

(b) a painful and crippling disease

27. Write the direct object from this sentence:

(2, 25)

Some people take cortisone for pain.

For 28–30, diagram the simple subject, simple predicate, and direct object for each sentence.

28. A <u>scientist</u> <u>synthesized</u> cortisone (from soybeans.)

(23, 25)

29. <u>Percy Julian</u>, an African American, <u>received</u> his

(23, 25) education (at DePauw University.)

30. <u>Harvard University</u> <u>awarded</u> a fellowship (to Julian.)

(23, 25)

Capitalization: People Titles, Family Words, School Subjects

Dictation or Journal Entry
Vocabulary:
Conscience, a noun, is the "sense of the rightness or wrongness of one's own acts." Quan trusts his *conscience* to guide his behavior.

We continue to learn about capitalization. We have learned that proper nouns require capital letters and that common nouns are capitalized when they are a part of a proper noun. We also capitalize parts of an outline, the first word of a sentence, the first word of every line of poetry, the pronoun *I*, the first word in a direct quotation, and the important words in titles. Now we will add more capitalization rules.

Titles Used with Names of People

Titles used with names of people require a capital letter. Often, these are abbreviations. We capitalize initials because they stand for names of people.

> Mr. and Mrs. Hugh Young
>
> Dr. Richard Curtis
>
> General E. K. Gee
>
> Aunt Mary
>
> Sir Lawrence
>
> Grandma Angles

Family Words

When **family words** such as *father, mother, grandmother,* or *grandfather* are used instead of a person's name, these words are capitalized. However, they are not capitalized when words such as *my, your, his, our,* or *their* are used before them.

> *Dad*, did you finish painting?
>
> I asked *my dad* if he had finished painting.
>
> She wanted *Grandma* to help her.
>
> She wanted *her grandma* to help her.

School Subjects

When the name of a school subject comes from a proper noun, it is capitalized. Otherwise it is not.

> English   math
>
> French   biology
>
> Spanish   language arts

Example Correct the following sentences by adding capital letters.

(a) I asked professor r. u. flubber if i could attend his class.

(b) please ask mother for directions to the party.

(c) my morning classes are english, history, and spanish.

Solution (a) We capitalize **Proffesor** because it is a title used with the name of a person. We capitalize **R. U. Flubber** because it is a proper noun, and the letters *R* and *U* are initials. Also, the pronoun *I* is always capitalized.

(b) We capitalize **Please** because it is the first word of the sentence. **Mother** requires a capital because it is used instead of a person's name.

(c) **My** is the first word of the sentence. **English** and **Spanish** come from proper nouns, so we capitalize them.

✓ Practice Add capital letters where they are needed.

a. do you need latin to graduate?

b. grandma, please come to my party.

c. have you visited your dentist, dr. hanfu lee?

d. i am important to my grandfather.

Replace each blank with the correct vocabulary word.

e. Your _____ tells you what is right or wrong.

f. We are wise to listen to our _____ to know right from wrong.

More Practice See "More Practice Lesson 26" in Student Workbook.

Review Set 26 Choose the best word to compete sentences 1–4.

1. Minerva got a headache when she ate her ice cream (to, *(18)* two, too) fast.

2. The doctor prescribed (to, two, too) aspirin.
(18)

3. Busy people should remember (to, two, too) relax and eat *(18)* slowly.

4. The words *to*, *two*, and *too* are (homonyms,
(4, 18) homophones).

5. Tell whether this sentence is declarative, interrogative,
(1, 3) imperative, or exclamatory:

There are many unique types of sharks.

6. Tell whether this word group is a sentence fragment,
(2, 3) run-on sentence, or complete sentence:

Adapting to its environment differently.

7. Write the concrete noun from this list: generosity,
(8) friendship, greeting card, love, joy.

8. Write the plural form of a–c.
(13, 14) (a) boat   (b) banjo   (c) coach

9. Write the noun from this list whose gender is
(10) neuter: assistant, sow, buck, flower, bull.

Rewrite sentences 10–14, adding capital letters as needed.

10. the flores family lives in paris, france.
(6, 12)

11. you have a ten o'clock appointment with doctor riggs.
(12, 26)

12. kay suggested that her mother come for a visit.
(12, 26)

13. i think mother should see the doctor soon.
(12, 26)

14. is your favorite class greek or math?
(12, 26)

15. Replace each blank with the missing preposition from the
(17) your memorized list.

aboard, about, _____, across, _____,
against, along, alongside, amid, among, _____,
at, _____, behind, _____, beneath

16. Write the word from this list that is *not* a helping verb.
(9)

is, am, are, was, were, what, be, being, been, has,
have, had, do, does, did, shall, will, should, would,
can, could, may, might, must

17. Replace the blank with the singular present tense form of
(5, 7) the verb.

Alina and Britni <u>brush</u> their hair. Celina
_____ her hair.

18. Write the present progressive verb phrase from this
(9, 21) sentence:

Sharks are swimming in the bay!

19. Write the past progressive verb phrase from this sentence:
(9, 21)
The sharks were nibbling on a surfboard.

For 20 and 21, tell whether the verb is an action or linking verb.
20. The watchman <u>sounds</u> the alarm.
(5, 22)

21. The music <u>sounds</u> scary.
(5, 22)

22. For a and b, tell whether the word group is a phrase or a
(2, 24) clause.

  (a) although most sharks have fusiform

  (b) for the animal's mobility and speed

For 23–26, write the direct object, if there is one.
23. In socialism, government controls the money.
(2, 25)

24. Karl Marx was an influencial socialist thinker.
(2, 25)

25. The dorsal fin provides stability.
(2, 25)

26. The pectoral fins steer the shark.
(2, 25)

Diagram the simple subject, simple predicate, and direct
object of sentences 27–30.
27. Jenny mailed the letter.
(23, 25)

28. Hector usually rides his scooter.
(23, 25)

29. Fins help the shark in different ways.
(23, 25)

30. The caudal fin provides forward movement.
(23, 25)

Descriptive Adjectives

Dictation or Journal Entry
Vocabulary:
The words *affect* and *effect* are different parts of speech. *Affect* is always a verb and means "to influence." Using drugs *affects* our health. *Effect* is usually a noun that means "the result." The *effect* of drugs on the nervous system is obvious.

An adjective is a word that describes a person, place, or thing. There are many different kinds of adjectives. There are **limiting** adjectives such as *a*, *an*, and *the*; **demonstrative** adjectives such as *this, that, those,* and *these*; and **possessive** adjectives such as *his, her, their, our, its, your,* and *my.*

Descriptive Adjectives In this lesson we will concentrate on **descriptive adjectives**, which describe a person, place, or thing. Sometimes they answer the question, "What kind?" Descriptive adjectives are italicized below.

rusty nail

multiplication problem

heavy, leather briefcase

Often descriptive adjectives come before the person, place, or thing, as in the sentences below.

Shy puppies hide in corners.

African artwork gave Picasso *new* ideas.

Sometimes descriptive adjectives come after the noun or pronoun, as in the example below.

Boomer, *gentle* and *beautiful,* is a retriever.

Some descriptive adjectives end in suffixes like these:

-*able*	*lovable, suitable, breakable, believable*
-*al*	*gradual, natural, eventual, casual*
-*ful*	*thankful, helpful, graceful, tuneful*
-*ible*	*incredible, sensible, visible, possible*
-*ive*	*decorative, secretive, decisive, extensive*
-*less*	*fearless, hopeless, useless, careless*
-*ous*	*enormous, dangerous, famous, horrendous*
-*y*	*sunny, salty, shiny, hasty*

Example 1 Write each descriptive adjective in sentences a–c.

(a) Disciplined people can accomplish incredible feats.

(b) Tireless scientists studied different theories about atoms.

(c) Are you familiar with prime numbers?

Solution (a) **disciplined** (describes "people"), **incredible** (describes "feats")

(b) **tireless** (describes "scientists"), **different** (describes "theories")

(c) **prime** (describes "numbers")

Improving Our Writing Descriptive adjectives help us to draw pictures using words. They make our writing more precise and more interesting. For example, a nose can be *bulbous, straight, pug, thin, broken, ski-shaped, swollen, glossy, purple*, or *runny*. Eyes can be *bloodshot, clear, sparkling, healthy, sunken, round*, or *almond*. When we write, we can use descriptive adjectives to create more detailed pictures.

Example 2 Replace each blank with a descriptive adjective to add more detail to the word "smile" in this sentence:

The news reporter had a _____, _____ smile.

Solution Our answers will vary. Here are some possibilities: ***happy, playful, phony, deceitful, friendly, broad, wicked, sarcastic, bright, joyful, sanctimonious, proud, arrogant, slight, tentative***, and ***confident***.

✓ **Practice** Identify each descriptive adjective in sentences a–d.

a. Remember that positive integers are usually written without positive signs.

b. Thankful people make pleasant companions.

c. Do you like abstract art?

d. Lithographs sometimes look like black-and-white drawings.

For e–g, write two descriptive adjectives to describe each noun.

e. dog   **f.** noise   **g.** hiker

Replace each blank with *affect* or *effect*.

h. Lack of sleep can _____ our concentration.

i. The _____ of more sleep might be better concentration.

✓ **More Practice**   See "Silly Story #2" in Student Workbook.

Review Set 27   Choose the best word to complete sentences 1–4.

1. One needs (perseverance, compassion) to master the game of golf.
(16, 22)

2. The (prodigious, considerate) dorsal fin of a shark alarms many swimmers.
(1, 20)

3. (Whose, Who's) lunch is this?
(19)

4. I wonder (whose, who's) going to help do the dishes.
(19)

5. Tell whether this sentence is declarative, interrogative, imperative, or exclamatory:
(1, 3)

Did you know that Severo Ochoa was the first scientist to chain together molecules outside of a living organism?

6. Tell whether this word group is a sentence fragment, run-on sentence, or complete sentence:
(1, 3)

Severo Ochoa won widespread recognition he also won the 1959 Nobel Prize in medicine.

7. Write the abstract noun from this list: monkey, television, swimming pool, religion, slide.
(8)

8. For a–c, write the plural of each noun.
(13, 14)

(a) crunch   (b) Sunday   (c) commander in chief

Rewrite sentences 9 and 10, adding capital letters as needed.

9. mr. van genderen, our neighbor, represents us in the
(6, 12) house of representatives.

10. here is an outline:
(20)
  i. friends
     a. holly
     b. laura

11. Replace each blank with the missing preposition from
(17, 18) your memorized list.

_____, besides, between, _____, but, _____, concerning, considering, despite, _____, during, except, _____, for, from, in

12. Write two helping verbs that rhyme with *could*.
(9)

13. Write the linking verbs, including the "to be" verbs,
(22) listed in Lesson 22.

14. Write the past tense of the verb *mop*.
(7, 16)

15. Write the present perfect verb phrase from this sentence:
(9, 19)

Severo Ochoa has demonstrated perseverance in his research on RNA.

16. Write the future progressive verb phrase from this
(9, 21) sentence:

Alejandra will be leaving the sixth grade in June.

For 17 and 18, tell whether the underlined verb is action or linking.

17. The seamstress <u>feels</u> the texture of the cloth.
(5, 22)

18. Monica <u>feels</u> anxious about the upcoming test.
(5, 22)

For 19 and 20, tell whether the word group is a phrase or a clause.

19. the artist Monet with the tiny paintbrush
(2, 24)

20. even though Monet wanted to show the marvels of the
(2, 24) real world

Choose the correct word to complete sentences 21 and 22.

21. To make the (perfect, progressive) tense, we use some
(19, 21) form of the verb *to be* plus the present participle, which
ends in *ing*.

22. The (perfect, progressive) tense shows action that has
(19, 21) been "perfected," or completed.

Diagram the simple subject, simple predicate, and direct
object of sentences 23 and 24.

23. The Wright Brothers opened a bicycle shop.
(23, 25)

24. The brothers built a glider.
(23, 25)

Write each descriptive adjective that you find in sentences
25–30.

25. The inexperienced hiker froze on the dangerous cliff.
(27)

26. Everyone enjoys a cheerful person.
(27)

27. Lovable puppies please us.
(27)

28. Andy likes salty tortillas.
(27)

29. Fuji has a filthy face.
(27)

30. The fearless Wright Brothers flew the new airplane.
(27)

The Limiting Adjective • Diagramming Adjectives

Limiting adjectives help to define, or "limit," a noun or pronoun. They tell "which one," "what kind," "how many," or "whose." There are six categories of limiting adjectives. They include articles, demonstrative adjectives, numbers, possessive adjectives (both pronouns and nouns), and indefinites.

Articles   Articles are the most commonly used adjectives, and they are also the shortest—*a, an,* and ***the.***

a flower	*the* flower
a pencil	*the* pencil
an octopus	*the* octopus
an example	*the* example

We use *a* before words beginning with a consonant sound, and *an* before words beginning with a vowel sound. It is the sound and not the spelling that determines whether we use *a* or *an*:

an hour	*a* human being
an umbrella	*a* university
an R-rating	*a* rat
an X-ray	*a* xylophone

Demonstrative Adjectives   WHICH ONE?

this lesson	*that* haircut
these shoes	*those* socks

Numbers   HOW MANY?

three potatoes	*four* carrots	*one* onion
seventy-six trombones	*fifteen* years	*thirty* miles

Possessive Adjectives   Both pronouns and nouns commonly function as adjectives. They answer the question, WHOSE?

Pronouns   WHOSE?

his hat   *her* gloves

their sweaters   *our* class

its place   *your* reward

my idea

Nouns   WHOSE?

Amanda's horse   *Julio's* cat

Dad's chair   *Monty's* wife

Allison's husband   *Sergio's* mom

Indefinites   HOW MANY?

some people   *few* voters   *many* ballots

several mice   *no* errors   *any* pests

Example 1   Write each limiting adjective that you find in these sentences.

(a) I admire Dr. Livingstone because he loved the African people.

(b) That man set out to find the source of the Nile River.

(c) Henry Stanley stayed with the doctor three or four months.

(d) Our desire is to learn about these men.

(e) Dr. Livingstone's dream of finding the source of the Nile never materialized.

(f) Few people pursue their dream for as many years as Dr. Livingstone did.

Solution   (a) **the**   (b) **That, the, the**

(c) **the, three, four**   (d) **Our, these**

(e) **Dr. Livingstone's, the, the**   (e) **Few, their, many**

Diagramming Adjectives   We diagram adjectives by placing them on a slanted line beneath the noun or pronoun they describe, or "limit."

Jasmine's (possessive adjective) *best* (descriptive adjective) friend is Mallory.

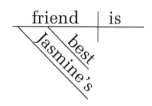

In this sentence, *Jasmine's* and *best* tell "whose" and "what kind" of friend, so we attach them to the word "friend."

Example 2   Diagram this sentence:

Many intelligent students remember Dr. Livingstone.

Solution   We see that the adjectives *many* and *intelligent* describe "students," so we diagram the sentence like this:

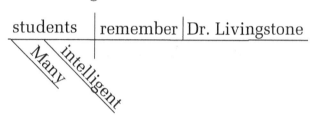

√Practice   For a–d, replace each blank with *faint, feign,* or *feint.*

a. The actor's _____ of tears and howls convinced the audience of his injury.

b. General Robert E. Lee and General Ulysses S. Grant _____ed friendship at the end of the Civil War.

c. The pink paint appeared too _____ to add much color to the bedroom.

d. Lack of food can cause one to _____.

Write each limiting adjective that you find in sentences e–h.

e. Kristen's teacher taught several lessons about sharps and flats.

f. Some music reflects people's origins.

g. This key has two sharps, and that key has three flats.

h. Music is Jeremy's major.

i. Diagram this sentence: Jeremy enjoys his music class.

class

More Practice   See "More Practice Lesson 28" in Student Workbook.

Review Set 28   Choose the best word to complete sentences 1–4.

1. Shelly was able to memorize her (conscience,
(25, 26) monologue) before opening night.

2. Did Pierre tell the (hole, whole) truth?
(24)

3. Residents hope there will be (less, fewer) smog in the future.
(21)

4. Jasmine filled (less, fewer) Easter baskets this year.
(21)

5. Tell whether this sentence is declarative, interrogative,
(1, 3) imperative, or exclamatory:

Please research James Watson and Francis Crick for
tomorrow's quiz.

6. Tell whether this word group is a sentence fragment,
(3) run-on sentence, or complete sentence:

James Watson and Francis Crick discovered that DNA
is twisted into a double spiral, or helix.

7. Write the collective noun from this list: notebook, paper,
(8) pen, crayon, congregation.

8. Write the plural form of a–c.
(13, 14) (a) cuff   (b) candy   (c) pailful

Rewrite sentences 9 and 10, adding capital letters as needed.

9. the answer, i know, can be found in the back of the book.
(12)

10. grandma hoppy was my favorite grandma.
(12, 20)

11. Replace each blank with the missing preposition from your memorized list.
(17, 18)

inside, _____, like, near, _____, off, _____, onto, opposite, _____, outside, over, past, regarding, _____, save

12. List 8 prepositions that begin with the letter *o.*
(17, 18)

13. Replace the blanks with the missing helping verbs.
(9)

is, am, _____, was, were, be, _____, been, shall, will, should, would, _____, might, must, can, _____, has, _____, had, do, does, did

14. Write the word from this list that is *not* a linking verb: is, am, are, was, were, be, being, been, what, look, feel, taste, smell, sound, seem, appear, grow, become, remain, stay.
(22)

15. Choose the correct word to complete this sentence: The progressive verb tense shows (completed, continuing) action.
(21)

16. For a–c, choose the correct form of the irregular verb *have.*
(15)

(a) You (has, have) (b) They (has, have) (c) It (have, has)

17. Write the present perfect verb phrase from this sentence:
(9, 19)

Crick and Watson have demonstrated the double helix of DNA.

18. Write the present perfect progressive verb phrase from this sentence:
(9, 21)

Crick and Watson have been studying the structure of viruses.

For 19 and 20, tell whether the underlined verb is an action or linking verb.

19. Jeremy <u>looks</u> petrified at the prospect of climbing the ladder.
(5, 22)

20. Betty <u>looks</u> at Jeremy as he slowly struggles up the ladder.
(5, 22)

For 21 and 22, tell whether the word group is a phrase or a clause.

21. even though much of their knowledge came from reading
(2, 24)

22. born with a knack for invention
(2, 24)

Write the direct object of sentences 23 and 24, if there is one.

23. Kitty Hawk was the location of the first powered flight.
(2, 25)

24. The Wright Brothers' first flight received little attention.
(2, 25)

Diagram the simple subject, simple predicate, and direct object of sentences 25 and 26.

25. Cleo read the newspaper.
(23, 25)

26. Chico swam a mile.
(23, 25)

27. Write the present participle, past tense, and past
(9, 16) participle of the verb *feign*.

28. Write the articles from this sentence: Does an apple a day
(28) keep the doctor away?

29. Write the indefinite adjective in this sentence: Some
(28) people hoard their possessions.

30. Diagram this sentence: This sweet red strawberry stained
(27, 28) her hand.

LESSON 29

Capitalization: Areas, Religions, Greetings

Dictation or Journal Entry

Vocabulary:
We know that the prefix *in-* often means *"not."* The word *incredible* means "not credible or believable." Many people use the word to mean "wonderful" or "great," but if something is *incredible*, it is unbelievable. The burglary suspect told the police an *incredible* story. *Incapacitate* (in-k-PAS-i-tat) ends with the word *capacitate*, which means "to make capable." Therefore, *incapacitate* means "to disable" or "to make incapable." Sickness *incapacitated* the workers.

Proper capitalization becomes easier with practice. We remember to capitalize titles, family words when used as names, and the names of school subjects that come from proper nouns. Refer to an earlier capitalization lesson if you are in doubt. Now let's look at a few more capitalization rules.

Areas of the Country

We capitalize North, South, East, West, Midwest, Northeast, etc., when they refer to **certain areas of the country.**

The Midwest is famous for its corn.

The large Southern farms were called plantations.

In 1849, many people from the North, South, and East left their jobs and homes to go to California in search of gold.

Recorded history began in the Middle East.

However, we do not capitalize these words when they indicate a direction. See the examples below.

Christie lives south of the foothills and north of the center of town.

New Jersey is east of Pennsylvania.

The Nile River flows from south to north.

Religious References

We capitalize **religions and their members, works regarded as sacred,** and **references to a supreme being.**

My best friend is Jewish.

Muslims worship Allah.

The Presbyterians organized a weekend retreat.

Those passages are from the King James Bible.

Greeting and Closing of a Letter

We capitalize the first words in the **greeting and closing of a letter.** For example:

> Dear Beth,
>
> My generous uncle,
>
> To whom it may concern:
>
> Yours truly,
>
> Love,
>
> Sincerely,

Example Provide capital letters as needed.

(a) The tourists live in the south.

(b) According to the compass, the ship was headed northeast.

(c) There is a lutheran church on the corner.

(d) The girl wrote, "my dear sis," and ended her letter with, "love, mary."

Solution

(a) We capitalize **S**outh, because it refers to a specific section of the United States.

(b) No correction is needed.

(c) We capitalize **L**utheran because it is the name of a religion.

(d) We capitalize **M**y because it is the first word of a letter's greeting. However, because "sis" is not the name of a specific person, and because it is preceded by the word "my," we do not capitalize it. **L**ove needs a capital because it is the first word of the closing. We capitalize **M**ary because it is a proper noun, or a specific person.

✓ Practice Rewrite a–d with correct capitalization.

a. in his book *the lion, the witch, and the wardrobe*, c. s. lewis created aslan, the lion, to represent jesus christ.

b. when i visited the south, i ate catfish and grits.

c. please look at the northwest corner of the map.

d. dear mom,
> i miss you so much.
> > your daughter,
> > maria

For e–h, replace each blank with the correct vocabulary word.

e. If something is unbelievable, it is _____.

f. The idea of an unidentified flying object (UFO) is so incredible that most people do not _____ it.

g. Disable is another word for _____.

h. Lack of fuel will _____ an engine.

Review Set 29

Choose the best word to complete sentences 1–5.

1. My nephew will (faint, feint, feign) at the sight of blood.
(28)

2. Rumaldo's (morale, conscience) prevented him from keeping the stolen item.
(23, 26)

3. A prefix meaning "one" or "single" is (*in-*, *bi-*, *mono-*).
(25)

4. A railway using only one track is called a (monorail, monopoly).
(25)

5. A progressive tense verb shows (completed, continuing) action.
(21)

6. Tell whether this sentence is declarative, interrogative, imperative, or exclamatory:
(1, 3)

Did you know that Percy Lavon Julian created a treatment for the eye disease glaucoma?

7. Tell whether this word group is a sentence fragment, run-on sentence, or complete sentence:
(3)

Julian earned the reputation of being one of the most gifted chemists of all time.

8. Write the concrete noun from this list: courage, loyalty, Latin, Pacific Ocean, French.
(8)

9. For a and b, write the plural of each noun.
(13, 14) (a) hobo   (b) syllabus

Rewrite sentences 10–16, adding capital letters as needed.

10. my sister becky thinks she's a southern belle.
(12, 26)

11. irene's school schedule includes algebra, english, french,
(12, 26) and history.

12. the son asked his dad if he could play little league
(6, 26) baseball.

13. hey, dad, may i play baseball?
(6, 26)

14. was the union army from the north or the south?
(12, 29)

15. go two blocks west of the library to the methodist church.
(6, 29)

16. the principal began the letter with "dear ms. johnson,"
(12, 29) and ended with "gratefully, mrs. strobel."

17. Replace each blank with the missing preposition from
(17, 18) your memorized list.

since, _____, throughout, _____, to,
_____, under, underneath, _____,
unto, up, _____, with, within, without

18. Write the word from this list that is *not* a helping
(5, 9) verb: is, am, are, was, were, be, being, been, shall, will,
should, would, can, could, work, may, might, must, have,
had, has, do, does, did.

19. Replace the blanks with the missing linking verbs.
(22)

is, am, _____, was, were, _____, being,
been, look, feel, _____, smell, sound, seem,
_____, grow, _____, remain, stay

20. For a–c, choose the correct form of the irregular verb *to be*.
(7, 15) (a) I (am, are, is) (b) we (am, are, is) (c) you (was, were)

21. Write the past perfect verb phrase from this sentence:
(9, 19)

Julian had worked as chief chemist for The Glidden
Manufacturing Company.

22. Write the past perfect progressive verb phrase from this
(9, 21) sentence:

Julian had been experimenting with soybeans for firefighting foam.

23. For a and b, tell whether the underlined verb is an action
(5, 22) or linking verb.

(a) The serviceman <u>smells</u> gas.

(b) The air <u>smells</u> fresh.

24. For a and b, tell whether the word group is a phrase or a
(2, 24) clause.

(a) widely and cheaply available to physicians

(b) with the freedom Glidden gave him

25. Write the present participle, past tense, and past
(9, 16) participle of the verb *affect*.

Write each adjective (descriptive, demonstrative, possessive, indefinite, article, or number) from sentences 26 and 27.

26. No persons entered the building through the two doors.
(27, 28)

27. This lesson contains my description of Felix's guinea pig.
(27, 28)

Diagram each word of sentences 28–30.

✓ **28.** Some classic books interest Scott's dad.
(25, 28)

✓ **29.** Her ten red fingernails attracted attention.
(25, 28)

✓ **30.** Those wet socks chilled my feet.
(25, 28)

Proper Adjectives

Dictation or Journal Entry

Vocabulary:

The words *capitol* and *capital* differ by one letter. A *capitol* is a building in which a state legislature convenes. When *capitol* is capitalized, it refers to the official building of the U.S. Congress in Washington D.C. The tourists visited the *Capitol* Building while in Washington D.C. The word *capital* refers to the city or town that houses the state or national government. The *capital* of Nevada is Carson City. The word *capital* has several other meanings as well. When used as an adjective, *capital* means "first in importance," (the *capital* points in a discussion) or "not lowercase" (*capital* letter). The *capital* topics in an outline should begin with a *capital* letter.

Common Adjectives An adjective can be common or proper. Common adjectives are formed from common nouns and are not capitalized.

COMMON NOUN	COMMON ADJECTIVE
truth	truthful
talent	talented
cloud	cloudy
grace	graceful

Proper Adjectives Proper adjectives are formed from proper nouns and are always capitalized. Sometimes the word doesn't change at all, as in the examples below.

PROPER NOUN	PROPER ADJECTIVE
Franklin	Franklin (stove)
Easter	Easter (basket)
Harvard	Harvard (graduate)
Texas	Texas (toast)

Often the form of the proper adjective does change, as in the examples below.

PROPER NOUN	PROPER ADJECTIVE
Britain	British (history)
Japan	Japanese (art)
Rome	Roman (architecture)
Greece	Greek (myths)

Example 1 For sentences a–d, write each proper adjective followed by the noun it describes.

(a) The American flag arouses patriotism in our country.

(b) Chinese food usually includes rice and chow mein.

(c) My grandparents enjoy listening to the Scottish bagpipes.

(d) Johnny ordered French toast and bacon.

Solution (a) **American flag**   (b) **Chinese food**

(c) **Scottish bagpipes**   (d) **French toast**

Example 2 Diagram this sentence:

Mr. Kawakami helped a Japanese student.

Solution We place the proper adjective "Japanese" underneath the word it describes—"student."

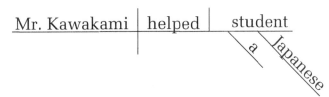

✓Practice For sentences a–d, write each proper adjective followed by the noun it describes.

a. Do you like Swiss or American cheese on your sandwich?

b. *Pride and Prejudice*, a popular novel by Jane Austen, was written during the Victorian era.

c. My brother was hit in the face with a Boston cream pie.

d. Are New York drivers notorious for their wild driving?

e. Diagram this sentence: Stella tasted the Danish pastry.

For f–j, replace each blank with *capitol* or *capital*.

f. In fifth grade, most students memorize the _____ city of each state.

g. Sacramento is the _____ city of California.

h. The Congress of the United States meets in the _____ Building.

i. A proper adjective begins with a _____ letter.

j. The most important reason is the _____ reason.

Review Set 30 Choose the best word to complete sentences 1–5.

1. Hector's (hole, incredible) pole vault exceeded all his
(24, 29) expectations.

2. A flu epidemic can (incapacitate, waist) an entire work
(5, 29) force.

3. The (affect, effect) of kind words is a friendly
(27) relationship.

4. One can (affect, effect) another person's confidence with
(27) words of encouragement.

5. A perfect tense verb shows (completed, continuing)
(19, 21) action.

6. Tell whether this sentence is declarative, interrogative,
(1, 3) imperative, or exclamatory:

    I'll never be as smart as Albert Einstein!

7. Tell whether this word group is a sentence fragment,
(3) run-on sentence, or complete sentence:

    After WWI, the general public learned that Albert
    Einstein's predictions about space, time, and gravity
    were true they were astonished.

8. Write the abstract noun from this list: scooter, plant, bag,
(8) shirt, truth.

9. Write the compound noun from this list: rabbit, basket,
(10) grass, chalkboard, ears, chicks.

10. Write the plural of a–c.
(13, 14) (a) salmon   (b) ditch   (c) mess

11. Rewrite this sentence, adding capital letters as needed.
(6, 26)

    tigger, winnie the pooh, and eeyore are characters in
    a. a. milne's *winnie the pooh*.

12. Write the prepositions from this sentence:
(17, 18)

    Albert Einstein looked like a person with a lot on his
    mind.

13. Write three helping verbs that begin with the letter *d*.
(9)

14. Write the word from this list that is *not* a linking verb: is,
(5, 22) am, are, was, were, be, being, been, slide, look, feel, taste,
smell, sound, seem, appear, grow, become, remain, stay.

15. For a–c, choose the correct form of the irregular verb *do*.
(7, 15)
(a) you (do, does) (b) she (do, does) (c) we (did, done)

16. Write the future perfect verb phrase from this sentence:
(9, 19)

We shall have discussed several brilliant scientists by
the end of this book.

17. Write the future perfect progressive verb phrase from this
(9, 21) sentence:

In June, he will have been playing the violin for four
years.

For 18 and 19, tell whether the underlined verb is an action
or linking verb.

18. The secret service person <u>appeared</u> at the front door.
(5, 22)

19. The person at the door <u>appeared</u> frightened.
(5, 22)

For 20 and 21, tell whether the word group is a phrase or a
clause.

20. but he became enchanted by the logic of geometry at the
(2, 24) age of twelve

21. writing some of the most revolutionary scientific papers
(2, 24)

22. Write the present participle, past tense, and past
(9, 16) participle of the verb *incapacitate*.

Write each adjective from sentences 23–25.

23. The flamboyant woman had red, curly hair.
(27, 28)

24. No mail was delivered today.
(28)

(28) **25.** I like that haircut!

For 26–28, write each proper adjective followed by the noun it describes.

26. The Easter basket contained jelly beans and chocolate
(30) eggs.

27. The American flag arouses pride in the citizens.
(30)

28. The British people remember their kings and queens.
(30)

Diagram each word of sentences 29 and 30.

29. The hungry man ate French toast.
(25, 28)

30. Mexican food includes Spanish rice.
(25, 28)

No Capital Letter

Vocabulary:
Independence (in-di-PEN-dəns) means "possessing the quality or condition of being independent," or "not depending on another." We notice that the prefix "in-,"meaning *not*, gives us a clue to the word's definition. As children grow up, they gain *independence*. An *injustice* is something that is *not* fair. It is a wrong. You do people an *injustice* by gossiping about them.

Most grammar books teach us when to capitalize words, but this lesson reminds us when **not** to capitalize words.

Common Nouns

Common nouns such as animals, plants, foods, objects, medical conditions, and pastimes are not capitalized. If a proper adjective (descriptive word) appears with the noun, we capitalize only the proper adjective, not the common noun. Below are some examples:

COMMON NOUN	COMMON NOUN WITH PROPER ADJECTIVE
beagle	Doberman pinscher
tulip	Boston fern
saxophone	French horn
influenza	Lyme disease
rollercoaster	Ferris wheel
soccer	Chinese checkers

Example 1 Add capital letters where needed.

(a) Our neighbors planted a chinese elm and an oak tree in their yard.

(b) Do you prefer italian sandwiches or hamburgers?

(c) The library loans out games such as checkers and chess.

(d) John plays the guitar, the french horn, the piano, and the drums.

(e) Mumps, chicken pox, and measles require vaccination for immunity.

Solution (a) We capitalize *Chinese,* a proper adjective. However, *elm* and *oak* are not capitalized because trees are common nouns.

(b) We capitalize *Italian,* a proper adjective. However, *sandwiches* and *hamburgers* are not capitalized because foods are common nouns.

(c) We do not add capital letters. Games and pastimes such as *checkers* and *chess* are common nouns.

(d) We capitalize *French,* a proper adjective. However, we do not capitalize *guitar, horn, piano, or drums* because objects such as musical instruments are common nouns.

(e) We do not add capital letters. Most medical conditions are common nouns.

Seasons of the Year We do not capitalize **seasons of the year**: fall, winter, spring, and summer.

> In the winter, families play indoors more often than they do in the summer.

Hyphenated Words We treat a **hyphenated word** as if it were a single word. If it is a proper noun or the first word of a sentence, we capitalize only the first word, not all the parts of the hyphenated word. See the examples below.

> Twenty-one years is considered the age of adulthood in most states.

> After dinner, Mother-in-law Isabel bathed her grandchildren.

Example 2 Add capital letters where needed in this sentence:

> Last spring I found my fifty-year-old victorian dollhouse in grandma's attic.

We capitalize *Victorian* because it is a proper adjective. We capitalize *Grandma* because it is a family word used as a name. We do not capitalize *spring* because it is a season of the year.

✓ Practice For a–c, replace each blank with the correct vocabulary word.

a. If you are independent, you do not _____ on someone or something else.

b. The Declaration of _____ (1776) remains a vital part of American history.

c. Something that is wrong or unfair is called an _____.

Rewrite the following sentences, using proper capitalization.

d. Brian's favorite sport is basketball.

e. Brass instruments include the trumpet, trombone, baritone, and tuba.

f. Have you ever tasted english muffins?

g. wise squirrels store their seeds and nuts in summer and fall.

h. thirty-four children played the game of tug-of-war.

More Practice See "More Practice Lesson 31" in Student Workbook.

Review Set 31

Choose the best word to complete sentences 1–4.

1. The moths chewed a tiny (whole, hole) in the wool
(24) sweater.

2. Considered a (morale, monopoly) by the federal
(23, 25) government, AT&T was forced to break up into smaller companies.

3. The opossum will (feign, faint) death in order to fool its
(28) pursuers.

4. Company layoffs destroyed the workers' (compassion,
(22, 23) morale).

5. Tell whether this sentence is declarative, interrogative,
(1, 3) imperative, or exclamatory:

Why, water expands when it changes from a liquid to a solid!

6. Tell whether this group of words is a sentence fragment,
(3) run-on sentence, or complete sentence:

Most chemical reactions depend on substances dissolving in water, without water life would not exist.

7. Write the common concrete noun from this list: hunger,
(6, 8) Uncle Wyatt, marriage, wallpaper, idea.

8. Write the singular noun from this list: glasses, forks,
(10, 13) plate, spoons, knives.

For 9 and 10, write the plural of each noun.

9. gulf
(13, 14)

10. loaf
(13, 14)

Rewrite sentences 11 and 12, adding capital letters where they are needed.

11. is your favorite season of the year fall, winter, spring, or
(12, 31) summer?

12. surfing is better in the pacific ocean than in the atlantic
(6, 12) ocean.

13. Tell whether this word group is a phrase or a clause:
(2, 24)

an acid with a base

14. Write five simple prepositions that begin with the letter *t.*
(17, 18) (Refer to Lesson 17 if necessary.)

15. Replace the blanks with the missing helping verbs.
(9)

is, _____, are, was, _____, be,
_____, been, may, might, _____, can,
could, should, would, shall, _____, do, does,
did, has, have, had

✓**16.** Write the linking verb from this sentence: You seem
(22) intelligent.

17. Replace each blank with the missing linking verb.
(22)

is, am, are, was, _____, be, being, been,
_____, feel, taste, smell, sound, seem,
_____, grow, remain, become, stay

18. Replace the blank with the singular present tense form of
(7, 16) the verb: The wasp _____ (buzz) around the
flower.

19. For a–c, choose the correct form of the irregular verb *have.*
(7, 15)

(a) I (has, have) (b) she (have, had) (c) they (has, have)

20. Write the four principal parts (present tense, present
(9, 16) participle, past tense, and past participle) of the verb *talk.*

For 21–23, choose the correct word to complete each sentence.

21. The progressive tense shows action that is (continuing, completed).
(21)

22. To make the progressive tense, we use some form of the verb *to be* plus the (present, past) participle.
(16, 21)

23. The (present, past) participle ends in *ing.*
(16)

For sentences 24 and 25, tell whether the underlined verb is an action verb or a linking verb.

24. An acid <u>is</u> a compound with a hydrogen atom.
(5, 22)

25. An acid <u>reacts</u> with other atoms or molecules when dissolved in water.
(5, 22)

26. Write the descriptive adjective from this sentence: Sometimes iron has red-colored rust.
(27)

✓ **27.** Write each article from this sentence: Oxidation occurs when an element or a compound joins with oxygen.
(28)

28. Write the proper adjective followed by the noun it describes in this sentence:
(30)

Niels Bohr, a Danish scientist, proposed that the electrons in each kind of atom gave the element its characteristics.

Diagram each word of sentences 29 and 30.

✓ **29.** The winter pageant included beautiful music.
(25, 28)

✓ **30.** The German university attracted American students.
(25, 28)

LESSON 32

Transitive and Intransitive Verbs

Dictation or Journal Entry

Vocabulary:

The prefix *post-* means "after." The word *postwar* refers to what happens "after" a war. The *postwar* economy resulted in mass unemployment. *Postmortem* refers to those things happening "after" death. The *postmortem* success of her book made the author's family wealthy. A *postscript* is a sentence or paragraph added to a piece of correspondence "after" the writer's signature. A *postscript* on the invitation contained directions to the party. A *postgraduate* is one who pursues additional studies "after" taking an advanced degree. The *postgraduate* applied at several institutions to further his education.

Transitive Verbs A **transitive verb** is an action verb that has a direct object. The sentences below have transitive verbs.

Jan <u>polished</u> the nails of her client.

Paul <u>presented</u> an orchid to his mom on Mother's Day.

Intransitive Verbs An **intransitive verb** is an action or linking verb that has no direct object. The sentences below have intransitive verbs.

Pilgrim <u>is</u> a music drama.

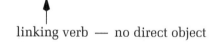

Bob <u>was sleeping</u> peacefully.

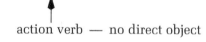

The same verb can be transitive in one sentence and intransitive in another.

Tony <u>ate</u> five tacos for lunch. (transitive)

Tony <u>ate</u> quickly. (intransitive)

↑

action verb — no direct object

Some action verbs are *always* intransitive. See the examples below.

A traffic jam <u>occurred</u> on the freeway.

The owl's eyes <u>glowed</u>.

Example Rewrite the following sentences. Underline the verb and star the direct object if there is one. Tell whether the verb is transitive or intransitive.

(a) The math test was very difficult.

(b) Ted computed the problems correctly.

Solution (a) **The math test <u>was</u> very difficult.** The verb "was" is **intransitive.** It has no direct object.

(b) **Ted <u>computed</u> the *problems correctly.** The verb "computed" is **transitive.** It has a direct object.

Practice Rewrite sentences a–d. Underline the verb and star the direct object if there is one. Tell whether the verb is transitive or intransitive.

a. Julie grated cheese for the enchiladas.

b. The seagull flew gracefully over the beach.

c. Did Dad answer the phone?

d. Marx's socialism was named "communism."

For e–i, replace each blank with the correct vocabulary word.

e. The prefix *post-* means "_____."

f. When writers want to say more after signing a letter, they might add a _____.

g. One must be a _____ to attend orthodontics school.

h. The _____ years following the Vietnam War have included both prosperous and depressed economic times.

i. After the patient's death, the doctor did a _____ examination to determine the cause of death.

Review Set 32
Choose the best word to complete sentences 1–10.

1. The (prodigious, conscientious) physician examined the
(12, 20) patient thoroughly.

2. (It's, Its) always challenging to begin a new job.
(15)

3. The prefix *sub-* means "(three, not, under)."
(14)

4. Organizations like the Salvation Army demonstrate
(16, 22) (perseverance, compassion) for others by providing shelter, food, and clothing.

5. The sentence below is (declarative, interrogative,
(1, 3) imperative, exclamatory).

The Vasquez Rocks provided shelter for the Tataviam Indians.

6. This word group is a (fragment, run-on, complete)
(1, 3) sentence: The Tataviam Indians used the Vasquez Rocks for their grindstones.

7. The perfect verb tense shows action that has been
(19) "perfected," or (continuing, completed).

8. To form the perfect tense, we add a form of the helping
(19) verb (have, must) to the past participle.

9. A(n) (transitive, intransitive) verb has no direct object.
(25, 32)

10. A(n) (transitive, intransitive) verb is an action verb with a
(25, 32) direct object.

11. Write the abstract common noun from this list: Latin,
(6, 8) pity, flower, confetti, Spain.

12. Write the plural noun from this list: smile, eye, hand,
(13, 14) cookies, ship.

For 13 and 14, write the plural of each noun.

13. sheep
(13, 14)

14. alto
(13, 14)

Write each word that should be capitalized in sentences 15 and 16.

15. the cheetah raced after the cottontail rabbit but was
(12, 31) unable to catch it.

16. *charlotte's web* is a story about a spider named charlotte
(6, 26) and a pig named wilbur.

17. Tell whether this word group is a phrase or a
(2, 24) clause: because the Vasquez Rocks are used as settings for movies and television shows

18. Write ten simple prepositions that begin with the letter *b*.
(17, 18) (Refer to Lesson 17 if necessary.)

19. Write three helping verbs that begin with the letter *m*.
(9)

20. Write the five linking verbs that are related to our five
(22) senses.

21. Replace the blank with the past tense form of the
(7, 16) verb: The farmer _____ (pry) open the barn door.

22. Write the four principal parts (present tense, present
(9, 16) participle, past tense, and past participle) of the verb *polish*.

For sentences 23 and 24, tell whether the underlined verb is an action or linking verb.

✓ **23.** In the mid-1800s, Tiburcio Vásquez and his band of
(5, 22) cattle-rustling desperados <u>hid</u> in the caves and rocks.

✓ **24.** Vasquez Rocks <u>is</u> the only national park named after a
(5, 22) notorious bandit.

For 25 and 26, write the direct object if there is one, and tell whether the underlined verb is transitive or intransitive.

25. "The Flintstones," "The Lone Ranger," and "Star Trek"
(25, 32) <u>were filmed</u> at Vasquez Rocks.

26. Vasquez Rocks <u>provides</u> sites for picnicking and
(25, 32) camping.

27. Write the three descriptive adjectives from this
(27) sentence: Horseback riders may only use the sandy trails
in dry weather.

28. Write the demonstrative adjective from this sentence:
(28) This information interests historians.

29. Write the proper adjective from this sentence followed by
(30) the noun it describes: The Tataviam people lived among
the rocks until the late 1700s.

30. Diagram each word of this sentence:
(25, 28)
This Los Angeles County park fascinates visitors.

Object of the Preposition •
The Prepositional Phrase

Dictation or Journal Entry

Vocabulary:

We will examine the homophones *oar, or,* and *ore.* An *oar* is a paddle used to row or steer a boat. Put the *oar* in the water. *Or* is a conjunction introducing an alternative. Would you like milk *or* water to drink? *Ore* is a natural material, like a mineral or a rock, that contains a valuable metal. The *ore* contained iron.

Object of the Preposition

We have learned to recognize common prepositions—connecting words that link a noun or pronoun to the rest of the sentence. In this lesson, we will identify the **object of the preposition,** which is the noun or pronoun that follows the preposition. Every preposition must have an object. Otherwise, it is not a preposition. We italicize prepositions and star their objects in the phrases below.

at the *store	*down* the *stairs
on the *desk	*through* the *door
around the *park	*like* a *rocket
within a *month	*for* your *convenience
across *town	*behind* *her
except *him	*with* *love
in the *book	*considering* the *rain

Prepositions may have compound objects:

Brent skis *on* (*snow and *ice.)

Celebration galloped *over* *mountains and *streams.

Example 1 Star the object (or objects) of each preposition in these sentences.

(a) *Before* lunch, I chased *after* my runaway dog and cat.

(b) I noticed them hiding *near* the big tree *past* the neighbor's garage and driveway.

Solution (a) *Before* ***lunch,** I chased *after* my runaway ***dog** and ***cat.**

(b) I noticed them hiding *near* the big ***tree** *past* the neighbor's ***garage** and ***driveway.**

Prepositional Phrase A prepositional phrase begins with a preposition and contains a noun and its modifiers. We italicize prepositional phrases below.

> Al's fickle friends led him *into dangerous activities.*
>
> We talked *on the phone* yesterday.
>
> The teacher is *in the wrong classroom.*
>
> Brent skied *beyond Bill and me.*

There can be more than one prepositional phrase in a sentence:

> Brent skis *in the remotest parts* (1) *of the large ski resort* (2).
>
> Celebration galloped *out the gate* (1) and *through the pasture* (2).
>
> *After breakfast* (1), let's walk *along the bike path* (2) *to the zoo* (3).

Example 2 For each sentence, write each prepositional phrase and star the objects of the prepositions.

(a) Communicable diseases are spread in a variety of ways.

(b) Some microbes are spread from one person to another person through direct contact.

(c) Colds and flu can spread via sneezing and coughing.

Solution (a) **in a *variety / of *ways**

(b) **from one *person / to another *person / through direct *contact**

(c) **via *sneezing and *coughing**

✓Practice For sentences a–d, write each prepositional phrase and star the object of the preposition.

a. People worry needlessly about noncommunicable diseases.

b. Noncommunicable diseases are not spread by human contact or airborne microbes.

c. Some noncommunicable diseases are spread from parent to child through their genes.

d. Hemophilia, a blood disease, can be passed to the next generation.

For e–g, replace each blank with *oar, or,* or *ore.*

e. While rowing my boat upstream, I lost an _____ in the water.

f. Would I sink, _____ would I swim?

g. The miners searched for _____.

More Practice Write each prepositional phrase and star the object of each preposition in these sentences.

1. For exercise, Mrs. Rivas ran for miles along the levee, through historic battlefields, and beyond the suburbs of Princeton.

2. She ran fast past some golfers at a country club, and she sprinted by a ferocious dog without a leash.

3. After an hour, and with a sigh of relief, she turned toward home.

4. At the end of her run, she spied two deer in the woods at the edge of the water.

5. With inquisitive eyes, they watched her cross over the bridge near her apartment.

6. Despite weariness, Mrs. Rivas smiled to herself at the thought of the wildlife around her.

Review Set 33 Choose the best word to complete sentences 1–6.

1. Murder is a (capital, capitol) offense.
(30)

2. Please begin each sentence with a (capital, capitol) letter.
(30)

3. The House of Representatives resides in the (Capital, *(30)* Capitol) Building.

4. There is a (capitol, capital) city in each state of the United
(30) States.

5. This sentence is (declarative, interrogative, imperative,
(1, 3) exclamatory): How amazing that woodwinds appeared
around 20,000 years ago!

6. This word group is a (fragment, run-on, complete)
(2, 3) sentence: a long, hollow tube

7. Write the collective noun from this list: plastic hoop, rock,
(8) congregation, soloist, pulpit.

8. Write the possessive noun from this list: tree's, benches,
(10) women, children.

For 9 and 10, write the plural form of each noun.

9. gentleman   **10.** hero
(13, 14)   (13, 14)

Write each word that should be capitalized in sentences 11
and 12.

11. twenty-one years is geraldine's age.
(6, 12)

12. tourists enjoy the gulf of mexico because it is warmer
(6, 12) than the pacific ocean.

13. Tell whether this word group is a phrase or a
(2, 24) clause: made from bear, bird, and deer bones

14. Write the twelve simple prepositions that begin with the
(17) letter *a*. (Refer to Lesson 17 if necessary.)

For sentences 15–17, write each prepositional phrase and star
each object of the preposition.

15. Gabriel's present came in a big box tied with string.
(18, 33)

16. Until sundown, Hiawatha paddled his canoe around the
(17, 33) lake, over the beaver dam, with the current, against the
current, and through enemy territory.

17. Early woodwinds were made of bones with holes pierced
(18, 33) in them.

18. Write the word from this list that is *not* a helping
(5, 9) verb: is, am, are, was, were, be, being, been, shall, will,
should, would, may, might, must, write, can, could, do,
does, did, has, have, had.

19. Write the linking verb from this sentence: Early
(22) woodwinds looked different than today's.

20. Choose the correct future tense form of the verb: We
(9, 11) (shall, did) produce sounds on a woodwind.

21. Write the present perfect verb phrase from this
(9, 19) sentence: Musicians and historians have discovered
wooden woodwinds from the 1700s.

22. Write the past progressive verb phrase from this
(9, 21) sentence: The musician was playing a woodwind.

For sentences 23 and 24, tell whether the underlined verb is
an action or linking verb.

23. The musician <u>sounded</u> the first note of the song.
(5, 22)

24. The woodwind <u>sounded</u> soothing to the ears.
(5, 22)

For 25 and 26, write the direct object if there is one, and tell
whether the underlined verb is transitive or intransitive.

25. Today, woodwinds <u>are made</u> from wood and metal.
(25, 32)

26. To make different notes, musicians <u>cover</u> different holes
(25, 32) along the side of the tube.

27. Write each descriptive adjective from this sentence: The
(27) popular clarinet is a single-reed woodwind.

28. Write the number used as an adjective in this
(28) sentence: The bassoon is a woodwind with two reeds.

29. Write the proper adjective from this sentence, followed
(30) by the noun it describes: That New York City orchestra
charms listeners each year.

30. Diagram each word of this sentence: Mozart's music
(25, 28) features the versatile woodwinds.

The Prepositional Phrase as an Adjective • Diagramming

Dictation or Journal Entry

Vocabulary:

Let's compare the homophones *pore*, *pour*, and *poor*. *Pore* has two meanings. As a noun, a *pore* is an opening in the skin or a leaf. A leaf absorbs moisture through the pores on its surface. *Pore*, the verb, means "to gaze steadily or intently." The avid reader *pored* over the riveting book. *Pour* means "to flow in a continuous stream." Please *pour* water into the glasses. *Poor* means "needy." The *poor* children needed warm winter clothes. *Poor* can also mean "less than adequate." He got *poor* grades in chemistry.

Adjective Phrases

We remember that a phrase is a group of words that functions as a single word. Prepositional phrases function as a single word, and some modify a noun or pronoun, so we call them **adjective phrases.** This type of prepositional phrase answers an adjective question— "Which one?" "What kind?" or "How many?" The adjective phrases are italicized in the following examples:

The delicious food was *from Mexico.* (The adjective phrase *from Mexico* modifies the noun "food," and tells "what kind.")

The man *on the phone* is Joel. (The adjective phrase *on the phone* modifies the noun "man," and tells "which one.")

The mysteries *of human growth and development* are fascinating. (The adjective phrase *of human growth and development* modifies the noun "mysteries," and tells "what kind.")

My car has room *for six.* (The adjective phrase *for six* modifies the noun "room," and tells "how many.")

Example 1

Write the adjective phrase and tell which noun or pronoun it modifies.

(a) The picture on the wall is an antique.

(b) Have you read a book about biology?

(c) Mom made reservations for twelve.

Solution

(a) The phrase **on the wall** modifies **picture.** It tells "which one."

(b) The phrase **about biology** modifies **book.** It tells "what kind."

(c) The phrase **for twelve** modifies **reservations.** It tells "how many."

Diagramming Prepositional Phrases

To diagram a prepositional phrase, we place the preposition on a slanted line attached to the word that the phrase modifies. We place the object of the preposition on a horizontal line at the bottom of the slanted preposition line:

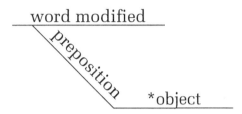

Let's diagram this sentence:

The table had seats (with cushions.)

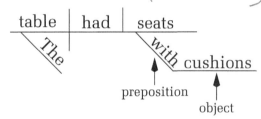

Example 2 Diagram this sentence:

The inside of our bones contains marrow.

Solution The phrase **of our bones** modifies the subject of the sentence, **inside.** We place the preposition **of** on a slanted line connected to **inside.** Then we place the object, **bones**, on the horizontal line. The word **our** describes **bones**, so we place it on a slanted line connected to the word it modifies.

The inside of our bones contains marrow.

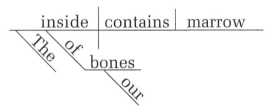

Sometimes a prepositional phrase immediately follows another one, as in the sentence below.

Some (of the food)(from Mexico) causes heartburn.

In the sentence above, the first prepositional phrase, **of the food**, modifies the subject **some.** The second prepositional phrase, **from Mexico**, modifies the noun **food.** We show this by diagramming the sentence:

Some of the food from Mexico causes heartburn.

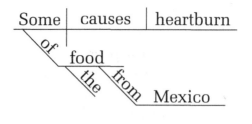

Example 3   Diagram this sentence:

I saw a boat \with a flag/on its smokestack.)

Solution   We place each preposition on a slanted line underneath the word it modifies. Then we place each object on a horizontal line attached to its preposition.

I saw a boat with a flag on its smokestack.

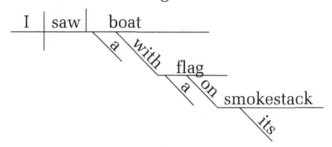

√ Practice   For a–c, tell which noun or pronoun is described by each italicized prepositional phrase.

a. A picture *of a young skeleton* shows bones *of cartilage.*

b. Cartilage is a strong, flexible tissue that pads the ends *of bones.*

c. The material *inside our ears and noses* is also cartilage.

Write the prepositional phrase in sentences d–f, and tell which noun or pronoun it describes.

d. Do you know the names of all your bones?

e. The bone in the upper leg is called the femur.

f. Without ligaments, your skeleton would come apart.

Diagram sentences g and h.

   g. Some ligaments support the organs in your body.

   h. Chris read an article regarding the skeleton.

For i–l, replace each blank with *pore, pour,* or *poor.*

   i. The _____ people had no food on their table.

   j. Please _____ over this contract, and make sure all of the details are correct.

   k. Julie will _____ punch at the wedding.

   l. The clogged _____ on Jethro's face resulted in a pimple.

Review Set 34

Choose the best word to complete sentences 1–6.

1. To become a licensed orthodontist, one must do
(32) (postmortem, postgraduate, postscript) work.

2. In the (postmorten, postgraduate, postwar) years, the
(32) economy sank into a recession.

3. The letter included a (postmortem, postscript,
(32) postgraduate) asking for a response.

4. Racial prejudice is an example of social (independence,
(31) injustice).

5. This sentence is (declarative, interrogative, imperative,
(1, 3) exclamatory): Did you know Albert Einstein?

6. This word group is a (fragment, run-on, complete)
(2, 3) sentence: Einstein's first paper proved the existence of atoms.

7. Write the proper collective noun from this list: batch,
(6, 8) United Nations, tribe, class, multitude.

8. Write the compound noun from this list: squash,
(10) cantaloupe, volleyball, corn, tee.

For 9 and 10, write the plural form of the noun.

(13, 14) **9.** arch   **10.** maid of honor

Write each word that should be capitalized in sentences 11 and 12.

11. in the summer, the family visits the beach for fun in the
(12, 31) sand and water.

12. do i turn right or left at the next corner?
(12)

13. Tell whether this word group is a phrase or a clause: if
(2, 24) light is made up of bundles called quanta or photons

14. Write eight simple prepositions that begin with the letter *o*.
(17, 18) (Refer to Lesson 17 if necessary.)

15. Write each prepositional phrase and star each object of
(17, 33) the preposition in this sentence:

Amid the confusion, Rawlin sang in the key of
C with no one besides Caleb until midnight.

16. Refer to the sentence below and write the prepositional
(33, 34) phrase that is used as an adjective. Then write the word
that the phrase modifies.

Albert Einstein proposed the most famous formula in
modern science.

17. Write the three helping verbs that begin with the letter *h*.
(9)

18. Write the linking verb from this sentence: The deep end
(22) of the pool appeared bottomless.

19. For a–c, choose the correct form of the irregular verb *to be*.
(7, 15) (a) we (am, is, are) (b) they (am, is, are) (c) you (was, were)

For sentences 20 and 21, write the entire verb phrase.

20. This September, Mr. Newkirk will have been teaching
(9, 21) biology for twenty years.

21. The ranger will have guided three lost hikers home before
(9, 19) ending his work day.

For 22 and 23, tell whether the underlined verb is an action
or linking verb.

22. Albert Einstein <u>became</u> world famous after winning the
(5, 22) Nobel Prize.

23. Albert Einstein <u>took</u> American citizenship in 1940.
(5, 22)

For sentences 24 and 25, write the direct object if there is one, and tell whether the underlined verb is transitive or intransitive.

24. Albert Einstein <u>was</u> a Jew.
(25, 32)

25. Einstein <u>discovered</u> incredible truths about our universe.
(25, 32)

26. Write each descriptive adjective from this sentence: The
(27) great scientist became an unelected statesman.

27. Write the possessive adjective from this sentence: His
(28) worry was the atomic bomb.

28. Write the proper adjective from this sentence, followed
(30) by the noun it describes: The American scientists worked hard on a counter-weapon.

Diagram each word of sentences 29 and 30.

29. Did you see a man with a beard?
(25, 34)

30. Each of the dogs ate dinner.
(25, 34)

LESSON 35

Indirect Objects

Indirect Objects

We have learned that a transitive verb is an action verb with a direct object. A transitive verb may have two kinds of objects. A direct object receives the action directly. An **indirect object** receives the action indirectly. It tells *to whom* or *for whom* the action was done. In the sentences below, we have starred the direct objects and placed parentheses around the indirect objects.

Bob <u>bought</u> (Christie) *flowers.

Ron <u>gave</u> (Spot) a *bath.

<u>Did</u> *you* <u>leave</u> (me) any *pizza?

Please <u>pass</u> (me) the *menu.

In order to have an indirect object, a sentence must have a direct object. The indirect object usually follows the verb and precedes the direct object. One test of an indirect object is that it can be expressed alternately by a prepositional phrase introduced by *to* or *for:*

Bob bought flowers *for Christie.*

Ron gave a bath *to Spot.*

Did you leave any pizza *for me?*

Please pass the menu *to me.*

Indirect objects can be compound:

The band *director* <u>gave</u> (Erin) and (Megan) *music to practice.

Example 1 Identify the indirect objects, if any, in each sentence.

(a) *Nancy* <u>ordered</u> her husband a new car on their anniversary.

(b) Each year the *boss* <u>gives</u> her hard-working staff a cash bonus.

(c) *Rodney* <u>tossed</u> the punchball (into the cart.)

(d) The caring young *girl* <u>found</u> the lost dog a new home.

Solution (a) Nancy ordered a new car *for* her husband. Therefore, **husband** is the indirect object.

(b) The boss gives a bonus *to* her staff. Therefore, **staff** is the indirect object.

(c) This sentence has **no indirect object.**

(d) The girl found a home *for* the dog. Therefore, **dog** is the indirect object.

Below is a diagram showing the simple subject, simple predicate, direct object, and indirect object of this sentence:

Monty <u>sent</u> (Allison) an *invitation to the party.

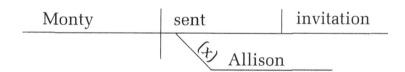

Notice that the indirect object (Allison) is attached beneath the verb by a slanted line, as though it were a prepositional phrase with the preposition (x) understood, not stated.

Example 2 Diagram the simple subject, simple predicate, direct object, and indirect object of the sentences from Example 1.

Solution (a) Nancy ordered her husband a new car on their anniversary.

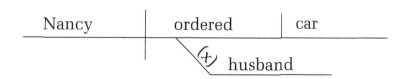

(b) Each year the boss gives her hard-working staff a cash bonus.

boss	gives	bonus

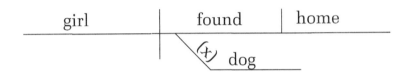

(c) Rodney tossed the punchball into the cart.

Rodney	tossed	punchball

(d) The caring young girl found the lost dog a new home.

girl	found	home

✓**Practice** For a–d, replace each blank with the correct vocabulary word.

a. Another word for conversation between two or more people is _____.

b. The prefix meaning "through, across, between" or "apart" is _____.

c. A line segment across a circle through the center is called a _____.

d. The quarterback scored a touchdown by running at a _____, or from corner to corner.

Write the indirect object, if any, in sentences e–h.

e. The *policeman* <u>issued</u> the speeding driver a ticket.

f. The *dog* <u>brought</u> his owner the newspaper.

g. The birthday *girl* <u>gave</u> her guests party favors.

h. The *student* <u>returned</u> to the library.

i, j. Diagram the simple subject, simple predicate, direct object, and indirect object of sentences e and f.

Review Set 35

Choose the best word to complete sentences 1–7.

1. He couldn't multiply without a calculator because his
(34) math skills were (pore, poor, pour).

2. A clogged (pore, poor, pour) in the skin can result in a
(34) blemish.

3. An (ore, or, oar) can help steer a rowboat.
(33)

4. The mine produced iron (ore, or, oar).
(33)

5. This sentence is (declarative, interrogative, imperative,
(1, 3) exclamatory): A banana tree is really a big herb.

6. This word group is a (fragment, run-on, complete)
(2, 3) sentence: Everyone eats bananas, bugs eat them too.

7. The (direct, indirect) object receives the action of a verb
(25, 35) indirectly.

8. Write the abstract proper noun from this list: Rembrandt,
(6, 8) love, Seattle, President's Day, car.

9. Write the masculine noun from this list: thorn, doe,
(10) muscle, stallion, doctor.

For 10 and 11, write the plural of each noun.

10. handful   **11.** toy
(13, 14)   (13, 14)

Write each word that should be capitalized in sentences 12 and 13.

12. the bengal tiger, the giraffe, and the hippopotamus lived
(12, 31) at the zoo.

13. king lear uttered these lines of poetry in william
(12, 20) shakespeare's *king lear*:

i am a man
more sinned against than sinning.

14. Tell whether this word group is a phrase or a clause: one
(2, 24) of five hundred names

15. Write the six simple prepositions that begin with the letter *u*. (Refer to Lesson 17 if necessary.)
_(17, 18)

16. Write the prepositional phrase and star the object of the preposition in this sentence:
_(17, 33)

A plantain is a large banana used for cooking.

17. Write the adjective phrase from the sentence below. Then write the word it modifies.
_(33, 34)

I eat bananas from Ecuador.

18. Write the two helping verbs that begin with the letter *c*.
₍₉₎

19. Write the linking verb from this sentence: A ripe, yellow banana tastes sweet.
₍₂₂₎

20. For a–c, choose the correct form of the irregular verb *do*.
_(7, 15) (a) you (does, do) (b) he (does, do) (c) they (does, do)

21. Write the past perfect progressive verb phrase from this sentence: Sunny had been growing bananas for decades.
_(9, 21)

22. For a and b, tell whether the underlined verb is an action or linking verb.
_(5, 22)

(a) This banana muffin <u>tastes</u> fresh.

(b) The baker <u>tastes</u> his muffins for freshness.

For sentences 23 and 24, write the direct object if there is one, and tell whether the underlined verb is transitive or intransitive.

23. Bananas <u>are</u> very healthful.
_(25, 32)

24. People <u>eat</u> bananas with cold or hot cereal.
_(25, 32)

Write the indirect object of sentences 25 and 26.

25. The ape gave the zookeeper a banana.
_(25, 35)

26. The zookeeper gave the elephant a banana.
_(25, 35)

27. Write the indefinite adjective from this sentence: Some monkeys devour bananas greedily.
₍₂₈₎

Diagram sentences 28–30.

28. The monkey threw the banana.
(25)

29. Have you seen a banana on a tree?
(25, 34)

30. The frisky gorilla picked me an orange.
(25, 35)

The Period, Part 1

Dictation or Journal Entry

Vocabulary:

Discretion and *prudence* are synonyms. Both words mean "good judgment" or "good sense." A person with *discretion* or *prudence* makes wise, careful choices. James exercised *discretion* in his choice of a movie. With *prudence*, he chose a non-violent cartoon for his little brother.

Punctuation marks help the reader to understand the meaning of what is written. **Periods** help the reader to know where a sentence begins and ends, but there are other uses for the period as well.

Declarative Sentence

A **declarative sentence** (statement) needs a period at the end.

A muscle cramp can incapacitate a runner.

I wonder why she had to leave so soon.

Imperative Sentence

An **imperative sentence** (command) needs a period at the end.

Look in both directions before crossing the street.

Clean up that mess before Mom gets home.

Initials

We place periods after the **initials** in a person's name.

Michael W. Smith

D. J. Williams

F. Scott Fitzgerald

Outline

In an **outline**, letters and numbers require a period after them.

I. Breeds of horses
   A. Thoroughbred
   B. Appaloosa

Example

Add periods where they are needed in each expression.

(a) I The British Empire
   A Queen Victoria
   B British imperialism

(b) Learn about Queen Victoria

(c) Queen Victoria is described as a stern and serious woman

(d) Composer J S Bach wrote beautiful music in Germany

Solution (a) We place periods after the numbers and letters in an **outline.**

  I. The British Empire
    A. Queen Victoria
    B. British imperialism

(b) We place a period at the end of an **imperative sentence.**
Learn about Queen Victoria.

(c) We place a period at the end of a **declarative sentence.**
Queen Victoria is described as a stern and serious woman.

(d) We place periods after **initials** in a person's name. This is also a **declarative sentence.**

J. S. Bach wrote beautiful music in Germany.

✓Practice Add periods as needed in a–d.

a. I Children's literature
    A Picture books
    B Modern fantasy and humor

b. She read *The Swiss Family Robinson* by J D Wyss

c. Don't be insensitive

d. Reading different types of books is fun

For e–g, replace each blank with the correct vocabulary word.

e. A synonym for discretion is _____.

f. One who has good judgment, or prudence, has _____.

g. John exercises prudence, or _____, in carefully choosing good friends.

Review Set 36 Choose the best word to complete sentences 1–8.

1. The prefix (*bi-, mono-, dia-*) means "through, across, between,"
(25, 35) or "apart."

2. A (diameter, diagonal, dialogue) is a line segment passing
(35) through the center of a circle.

3. You may choose either cake (ore, or, oar) ice cream for
(33) dessert.

4. The prefix meaning "after" is (*in-*, *post-*, *tri-*).
(29, 32)

5. The object of the (preposition, noun, adjective) is the
(33) noun or pronoun that follows the preposition.

6. A prepositional phrase that answers an adjective
(33, 34) question such as "Which one?" "What kind?" or "How
many?" is an (noun, verb, adjective) phrase.

7. The (direct, indirect) object receives the action indirectly.
(25, 35)

8. The (direct, indirect) object receives the action directly.
(25, 35)

9. Tell whether this word group is a fragment, run-on, or
(3) complete sentence: Snakes have no external ears.

10. Write the possessive noun from this list: monkeys,
(10) alligators, dolphins, giraffes, elephant's.

For 11–13, write the plural of each noun.

11. mouse   **12.** veto   **13.** monkey
(13, 14)   (13, 14)   (13, 14)

Rewrite 14–16, adding capital letters as needed.

14. lake erie is one of the great lakes.
(6, 12)

15. the teacher wrote this outline:
(6, 20) i. book report
        a. plot
        b. characters

16. some farms in the south raise tobacco and cotton.
(6, 20)

17. Tell whether this word group is a phrase or a clause:
(2, 24) when the snake sheds its skin

18. Write the prepositional phrase and star the object of the
(17, 33) preposition from this sentence:

Humans have only thirty-two vertebrae, but some
snakes have more than four hundred of them!

(9) **19.** Write the 23 helping verbs.

20. Write the four principal parts (present tense, present participle, past tense, and past participle) of the verb *love*.
(7, 16)

Write the entire verb phrase from sentences 21 and 22.

21. Gloria had loved that kitten dearly.
(9, 19)

22. Laura and Maggie have been making quilts.
(9, 21)

23. Write the demonstrative article from this sentence:
(28)

That coast redwood is taller than the Statue of Liberty!

Replace each blank with the correct word to complete sentences 24–29.

24. The _____ helps the reader to know where a sentence ends, but there are other uses for it as well.
(36)

25. A declarative sentence ends with a _____ .
(1, 36)

26. An exclamatory sentence ends with an _____ point.
(1, 36)

27. We place a _____ after an initial in a person's name.
(36)

28. In an outline, letters and numbers require a _____ after them.
(20, 36)

29. The _____ participle of a verb ends with *ing*.
(16, 21)

√**30.** Diagram each word of this sentence:
(25, 34)

She hung a painting of a Victorian house.

Coordinating Conjunctions

Dictation or Journal Entry

Vocabulary:

The words *so*, *sew*, and *sow* sound the same but have different spellings and meanings. *So* is a conjunction meaning "in order that." Dad washed the car in the morning, *so* he could drive it to work. *Sew*, a verb, means "to take a stitch." Uncle Bob will *sew* this button back on my shirt. *Sow*, a verb, means "to plant." The farmer *sowed* his crops in orderly rows.

Conjunctions are connecting words. They connect words, phrases, and clauses. There are three kinds of conjunctions: coordinating, correlative, and subordinating. In this lesson, we will learn to recognize coordinating conjunctions.

Coordinating Conjunctions

We use a **coordinating conjunction** to join parts of a sentence that are equal in form, or **parallel**. (Notice that grammarians use the term *parallel* in a different way than do mathematicians.) Parts of sentences, such as words, phrases, and clauses, are called **elements**. A coordinating conjunction connects a word to a word, a phrase to a phrase, or a clause to a clause. When joined by a conjunction, they are called **compound elements**.

Here are the common coordinating conjunctions:

✳ *and   but   or   nor   for   yet   so*

They may join a **word** to another **word**:

Mom *and* Dad	John *or* James	slowly *but* surely
firm *yet* kind	hop *and* skip	sooner *or* later

They may join a **phrase** to another **phrase**:

playing inside *or* playing outside

out of the frying pan *and* into the fire

They may connect a **clause** to another **clause**:

Bruce sprinted out the door, *for* he was late.

Lisa searched for her iguana, *but* she couldn't find it.

Example   Underline each coordinating conjunction that you find in these sentences.

(a) Tracy washed and ironed her pants, but she still did not like them.

(b) The traveler appeared lost, for he was wandering in circles.

(c) The teacher wanted to go home and plant daisies, yet she had too many papers to grade.

(d) Mom bought carrots and celery, but she forgot the cake and ice cream.

(e) You may wear a dress or skirt today.

Solution (a) Tracy washed **and** ironed her pants, **but** she still did not like them.

(b) The traveler appeared lost, **for** he was wandering in circles.

(c) The teacher wanted to go home **and** plant daisies, **yet** she had too many papers to grade.

(d) Mom bought carrots **and** celery, **but** she forgot the cake **and** ice cream.

(e) You may wear a dress **or** skirt today.

Practice **a.** Replace each blank to complete the list of coordinating conjunctions:

_____, but, _____, nor, _____, yet, _____

b. Replace each blank to complete the list of coordinating conjunctions.
and, _____, or, _____, for, _____, so

c. Memorize the seven coordinating conjunctions, and say them to a friend or teacher.

Write each coordinating conjunction, if any, that you find in sentences d–g.

d. Many important developments in medicine have helped to treat certain diseases, yet scientists need to do further research.

e. The growth of bacteria is slowed or killed by antibiotics without killing the healthy cells in the body.

f. Penicillin, an antibiotic, fights bacteria, but it is ineffective against viruses.

g. Penicillin has saved lives, for it is effective against pneumonia, strep throat, and other bacterial diseases.

For h–j, replace each blank with *so, sew,* or *sow.*

h. The farmer taught the workers how to _____ seed.

i. If you want to make your own clothes, you have to learn to _____ .

j. The group was tired, _____ they went to bed.

Review Set 37   Choose the best word to complete sentences 1–7.

1. Wise people use (perseverance, discretion, dishonor)
(16, 36) when spending their money.

2. When a person no longer needs help from another
(31, 36) person, he or she has achieved (prudence, conscience, independence).

3. The doctor performed a (postmortem, postwar, diagonal)
(32, 35) examination on the accident victim.

4. One must (persevere, waste, honor) in training to
(5, 16) improve one's performance.

5. A (transitive, intransitive) verb is an action verb that has
(25, 32) a direct object.

6. An intransitive verb has no direct (object, noun,
(25, 32) adjective).

7. The progressive tense shows action that is (continuing,
(9, 21) completed).

8. Tell whether this word group is a fragment, run-on, or
(1, 3) complete sentence: Helping snakes locate prey.

9. Write the collective noun from this list: chair, cart,
(8) chorus, clock, cars.

10. Write the indefinite noun from this list: bull, mother,
(10) steak, professor, rose.

For 11 and 12, write the plural of each noun.

11. deer
(13, 14)

12. father-in-law
(13, 14)

Write each word that should be capitalized in sentences 13–15.

13. the house of commons assists the queen in ruling great
(6, 12) britain.

14. huck finn explains, "miss watson she kept pecking at me,
(6, 20) and it got tiresome and lonesome."

15. first names in ms. smith's homeroom include daniel,
(6, 12) david, derrick, and doug.

16. Write the two simple prepositions that begin with *c*.
(17, 18)

17. Write the prepositional phrase and star the object of the
(17, 33) preposition in this sentence:

Some snakes are thirty feet in length.

18. Write the adjective phrase from this sentence and tell
(33, 34) which noun or pronoun it modifies.

Perhaps the winner of the national tree contest will be the giant sequoia.

Write the entire verb phrase and underline each helping verb in sentences 19–21.

19. Do you know California's two state trees?
(7, 9)

20. Diane and Ted shall have washed all the windows by
(9, 19) evening.

21. The pine tree had been growing for ten years.
(9, 21)

22. Replace the blank with the correct verb form:
(9, 11)

Manuel and I _____ (future of *go*).

23. Write each adjective from this sentence:
(27, 28)

Some people have never seen a giant sequoia.

Rewrite 24–26, adding periods as needed.

24. Redwoods date back 100 million years
(3, 36)

25. Let us protect the redwoods
(3, 36)

26. Here is an outline:
(20, 36)
      I California's state trees
        A Coast redwood
        B Giant sequoia

27. Replace each blank with the correct word in this
(37) sentence:

We use a _____ _____ to join parts of a sentence that are equal.

28. List the seven common coordinating conjunctions.
(37)

29. Write the coordinating conjunction from this sentence:
(37)
Have you ever seen a coast redwood or a giant sequoia?

30. Diagram each word of this sentence:
(25, 34)
The thoughtful groom gave his bride a piece of cake.

Diagramming Compound Subjects and Predicates

Compound Subjects   The predicate or verb of a sentence may have more than one subject, as in the sentence below.

Quan and Sheung <u>raced</u>.

In this sentence, the verb "raced" has two subjects: "Quan" and "Sheung." We call this a **compound subject**.

Compound Predicates   Likewise, a subject may have more than one predicate, as in the sentence below.

Robbie <u>ran</u> and <u>jumped</u>.

In this sentence, the subject "Robbie" has two predicates: "ran" and "jumped." We call this a **compound predicate**.

Diagramming   To diagram a compound subject or a compound predicate, we place each part of the compound on a separate, horizontal line. We write the conjunction on a vertical dotted line that joins the horizontal lines.

COMPOUND SUBJECT DIAGRAM:

Mr. Fish and Mrs. Gold <u>bought</u> a goldfish.

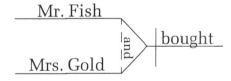

COMPOUND PREDICATE DIAGRAM:

Mr. Flea <u>purchased</u> and <u>bathed</u> a puppy.

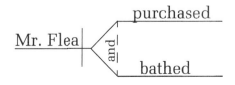

COMPOUND SUBJECT AND COMPOUND PREDICATE DIAGRAM:

Mr. Flea and *Mrs. Suds* <u>shampooed</u> and <u>brushed</u> a litter of Dalmatian puppies.

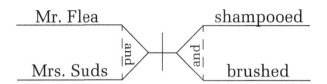

Example   Diagram the subjects and predicates of each sentence.
  (a) The dog and cat fought.

  (b) The canary chirped and sang beautifully.

  (c) A monkey, a chimpanzee, and a gorilla yelled and screamed at the spectators.

Solution   (a) This sentence contains a compound subject.

The *dog* and *cat* <u>fought</u>.

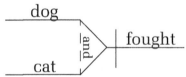

  (b) This sentence has a compound predicate. The subject *canary* did two things. It <u>chirped</u> and it <u>sang</u>.

The canary <u>chirped</u> and <u>sang</u> beautifully.

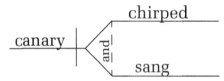

  (c) This sentence has a compound subject (*monkey, chimpanzee, gorilla*) and a compound predicate (<u>yelled</u>, <u>screamed</u>).

A *monkey*, a *chimpanzee*, and a *gorilla* <u>yelled</u> and <u>screamed</u> at the spectators.

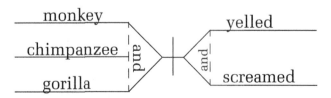

Practice For a–d, replace each blank with *their, they're,* or *there.*

    a. They received _____ report cards in the mail.

    b. _____ very thoughtful people.

    c. Please place your belongings over _____.

    d. What do you think _____ going to do?

Diagram the simple subjects and simple predicates of sentences e–g.

    e. *Sense and Sensibility* and *Pride and Prejudice* were written by Jane Austen.

    f. Her *Mansfield Park* excites and entertains readers.

    g. White blood cells and antibodies attack intruders and protect our bodies.

More Practice See "More Practice Lesson 38" in Student Workbook.

Review Set 38 Choose the best word to complete sentences 1–5.

    1. Put that book down (so, sew, sow) we can leave.
    (37)

    2. (Homophones, Homonyms) are spelled and pronounced
    (4) alike but differ in meaning.

    3. *Sow,* "a pig," and *sow,* "to plant," (are, aren't) homonyms
    (4) because they are not pronounced alike.

    4. A person with (integrity, dishonor, morale) tells the truth.
    (6, 23)

    5. To make the progressive tense, we use some form of the
    (15, 21) verb *to be* plus the (present, past) participle.

    6. Tell whether this sentence is declarative, exclamatory,
    (1, 3) imperative, or interrogative:

    Remember the facts on reptiles.

    7. Write the abstract proper noun from this list: Labor Day,
    (6, 8) friendship, Princess Beatrice, hammer.

For 8–10, write the plural of each noun.

8. pig
(13)

9. fox
(13)

10. tankful
(13)

Write each word that should be capitalized in sentences 11–15.

11. snakes have eyes but no eyelids.
(12)

12. aunt nova served an excellent meal.
(6, 12)

13. the patient wrote, "dear dr. camiling," and ended with,
(12, 29) "gratefully, mrs. hernandez."

14. Write five simple prepositions that begin with the letter *a*.
(17, 18)

15. Write each prepositional phrase and star each object of
(17, 33) the preposition in this sentence:

Four hundred vertebrae are a lot of bones for one snake!

For 16 and 17, choose the correct form of the verb.

16. We (is, are) friends.
(7, 15)

17. They (was, were) here.

18. Write the common linking verbs from Lesson 22.
(22)

19. For sentences a and b, tell whether the underlined verb is
(5, 22) an action or linking verb.

(a) Fernando <u>smelled</u> garlic in the spaghetti.

(b) Pietro <u>smelled</u> smoky after the barbecue.

For 20 and 21, tell whether the underlined verb is transitive or intransitive.

20. The bird <u>swallowed</u> quickly.
(25, 32)

21. The bird <u>swallowed</u> a sunflower seed.
(25, 32)

22. Write each adjective in this sentence:
(27, 28) The salty, stale potato chip satisfied the hungry pigeon.

Rewrite sentences 23 and 24, adding periods as needed.

23. We find coast redwoods only between southern Oregon
(1, 36) and central California

24. We see giant sequoia trees only on the western slopes of
(1, 36) the Sierra Nevada Mountains

25. List the seven coordinating conjunctions.
(37)

Write each coordinating conjunction in sentences 26 and 27.

26. The cinnamon-red bark of both trees is thick and fibrous.
(37)

27. I can't decide if I should walk or drive.
(37)

Diagram each word of sentences 28–30.

✓ **28.** Mr. French and Mrs. Fries fried French fries.
(25, 38)

✓ **29.** The hungry infant cried and cried.
(25, 38)

30. The biggest tree in my yard shades the house.
(25, 34)

Correlative Conjunctions

Dictation or Journal Entry

Vocabulary:

Indict (pronounced in-DYT) is a verb that means "to formally accuse or charge with a fault or offense." The grand jury *indicted* the official for fraud.

Correlative Conjunctions

Correlative conjunctions are similar to coordinating conjunctions. They connect elements of a sentence that are equal in form, or parallel. Correlative conjunctions are always used in pairs. Here we list the most common ones:

both—and   either—or

neither—nor   not only—but also

The parts they join must be equal in form, or parallel. In the sentences below, the parallel elements are italicized.

Both *the girls* **and** *the boys* will participate in the soccer tournament.

Either *Patti* **or** *Liz* will finish the task.

Neither *the chicken* **nor** *the beef* was eaten.

The traffic frustrated **not only** *the drivers* **but also** *the pedestrians*.

Example Underline the correlative conjunctions in each sentence.

(a) Both ice cream and whipped cream taste good on top of pumpkin pie.

(b) Jack took not only a chemistry final but also a physics final today.

(c) The tourists wanted to visit either the arboretum or the observatory.

(d) Neither rain nor snow will keep me from traveling today.

Solution (a) **Both** ice cream **and** whipped cream taste good on top of pumpkin pie.

(b) Jack took **not only** a chemistry final **but also** a physics final today.

(c) The tourists wanted to visit **either** the arboretum **or** the observatory.

(d) **Neither** rain **nor** snow will keep me from traveling today.

Diagramming   We diagram correlative conjunctions this way:

Nigel enjoys *both* jogging *and* swimming.

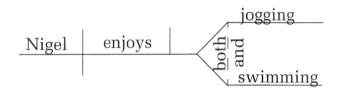

Example 2   Diagram this sentence:

Either Brian or Gia will blow the whistle.

Solution   We diagram the sentence as follows:

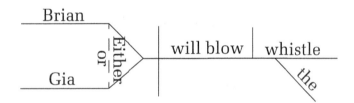

√**Practice**   Replace each blank with the correct vocabulary word.

a. If the authorities charge a person with an offense, they _____ them.

b. The court will _____ the criminal accused of robbery.

Write the correlative conjunctions from sentences c–f.

c. You may either sit in the shade or swim in the pool this afternoon.

d. Neither her complaints nor her arguments will change my mind.

e. Both dogs and cats can be good pets.

f. Not only his strength but also his bravery made him a hero.

g. Diagram this sentence:

I will cook either beans or rice.

Choose the best word to complete sentences 1–5.

1. *To, two,* and *too* are (homonyms, homophones).
(4, 18)

2. After a day at the zoo, the grandfather was (to, two, too)
(18) tired to carry his granddaughter.

3. That address was not listed (between, among) the many
(17) others.

4. The (coarse, subsoil, biosphere) includes all the air,
(11, 14) water, and land inhabited by life.

5. The (present, past) participle of a verb ends in *ing*.
(16, 21)

6. A linking verb "links" the (subject, verb) of a sentence to
(22) the rest of the predicate.

7. Tell whether this sentence is declarative, interrogative,
(1, 3) exclamatory, or imperative:

I saw stars!

8. Write the concrete common noun from this
(6, 8) list: Yamaha, Toyota, car, Honda, Ford, Pontiac.

For 9 and 10, write the plural form of each noun.

9. lady   **10.** chimney
(13)   *(13)*

Write each word that should be capitalized in sentences 11–14.

11. snakes, i am told, have eyes that are protected by a clear
(12) scale.

12. hey, mom, have you seen my jacket?
(12, 26)

13. the poinsettia plant gave the room a holiday feeling.
(12, 31)

14. jennifer ware, the maid-of-honor, wore a beautiful gown.
(6, 12)

15. Write the simple preposition that begins with the letter *l*.
(17, 18)

16. Write the prepositional phrase in this sentence, and star
(18, 33) the object of the preposition.

"The Star Spangled Banner" is the national anthem
of the United States.

17. Write the action verb from this sentence:
(5, 22)

Chief Sequoyah invented the eighty-six character Cherokee alphabet.

For 18 and 19, choose the correct form of the verb.

18. You (has, have) a cold.   **19.** It (do, does) matter.
(15)   *(15)*

20. Write the entire verb phrase from this sentence:
(9, 21)

The injured soccer player was hopping on one foot.

21. Write each adjective from this sentence:
(27, 28)

One coast redwood is ten feet in diameter.

Rewrite 22 and 23, adding periods as needed.

22. I Television sets   **23.** I miss James R. Roe
(20, 36)

    A Screens

    B Channels

24. Replace each blank with the missing coordinating
(37) conjunction: _____, but, _____, nor, for, _____, so

25. Write the coordinating conjunction from this sentence:
(37)

Will the weather be warm or cool today?

26. List the four most common pairs of correlative
(39) conjunctions.

Write the correlative conjunctions from sentences 27–29.

27. Neither Heather nor Ashley knew the location of
(39) Zachary's game.

28. David was not only high scorer but also MVP of the game.
(39)

29. The clown sold both peanuts and popcorn.
(39)

30. Diagram each word of this sentence:
(2, 38)

Both Mary and Martha served the guests their desserts.

The Period, Part 2:
Abbreviations, Decimals

Dictation or Journal Entry
Vocabulary:
The words *accept* and *except* have slightly different initial sounds. *Accept* (pronounced ak-SEPT) means to "receive with favor" or "to take." Will you *accept* my invitation to have lunch? *Except* (pronounced ek-SEPT) means "but" or "excluding." I exercise every day *except* Mondays.

Abbreviations

Sometimes we shorten words by abbreviating them. **Abbreviations** often require periods. Because there are so many abbreviations, and because some abbreviations are used for more than one word, we check our dictionaries. Below are some common abbreviations that require periods. While it is important to become familiar with these abbreviations, we do not normally use abbreviations in formal writing. **When in doubt, spell it out.**

Time of Day

a.m. (Latin *ante meridiem*, "before noon")

p.m. (Latin *post meridiem*, "after noon")

Days of the Week

Sun. (Sunday)	Thurs. (Thursday)
Mon. (Monday)	Fri. (Friday)
Tues. (Tuesday)	Sat. (Saturday)
Wed. (Wednesday)	

Months of the Year

Jan. (January)	July (no abbreviation)
Feb. (February)	Aug. (August)
Mar. (March)	Sept. (September)
Apr. (April)	Oct. (October)
May (no abbreviation)	Nov. (November)
June (no abbreviation)	Dec. (December)

Personal Titles

Mr. (Mister)	Miss (no abbreviation)
Mrs. (Mistress; a married woman)	
Ms. (any woman, especially one whose marital status is unknown)	
Jr. (Junior)	Sr. (Senior)
Dr. (Doctor)	Rev. (Reverend)
Prof. (Professor)	Pres. (President)

| Gen. (General) | Capt. (Captain) |
| Sen. (Senator) | Rep. (Representative) |

Proper Place Names We may abbreviate the following words when they appear in addresses as part of a proper place name (as in *Main Street*). They are not abbreviated when they are used as common nouns (as in *down the street*).

St. (Street)	Rd. (Road)
Dr. (Drive)	Blvd. (Boulevard)
Pl. (Place)	Ave. (Avenue)
Mt. (Mount, Mountain)	Bldg. (Building)

Compass Directions Compass directions may be abbreviated when they appear in addresses as part of a proper place name.

N. (North)	N.E. (Northeast)
S. (South)	N.W. (Northwest)
E. (East)	S.E. (Southeast)
W. (West)	S.W. (Southwest)

Others Here are a few other commonly-used abbreviations.

Inc. (Incorporated)	etc. (Latin *et cetera,* "and so forth")
Co. (Company)	est. (estimated)
Ltd. (Limited)	cont. (continued)
govt. (government)	anon. (anonymous)
dept. (department)	misc. (miscellaneous)

Decimal Point We use a period as a **decimal point** to show dollars and cents and to show the place value of numbers. (Note: When we read a number, the "and" shows where the decimal point belongs.)

$2.50 (two dollars and fifty cents)

4.5 (four and five tenths)

Example Add periods as needed in a–d.

(a) Mrs Sánchez lives at 443 W Live Oak Ave

(b) Ground beef costs $199 (one dollar and 99 cents) per pound at the market.

(c) The sign read "Homework due Tues, Jan 7."

(d) My appointment with Dr Riggs is at 10 am today.

Solution (a) **Mrs.** (Mistress), **W.** (West), and **Ave.** (Avenue), are abbreviations that require periods.

(b) **$1.99** requires a period as a decimal point to show one dollar *and* ninety-nine cents.

(c) **Tues.** (Tuesday) and **Jan.** (January) are abbreviations that require periods.

(d) **Dr.** (doctor) and **a.m.** (*ante meridiem*, "before noon") are abbreviations that require periods.

Practice Add periods as needed in a–h. (Hint: When a sentence ends with an abbreviation that requires a period, that same period serves as the final punctuation!)

a. Mr and Mrs Pauly drove west on Sunset Blvd

b. School begins at 8 a m each weekday

c. Everybody admired Ms Webster's Easter bonnet

d. Our marriage ceremony was performed by Rev John Harrison

e. David R Jones, Jr, plans to visit South America

f. "Acme Toy Co" was the name printed on the box

g. Most of us will never climb Mt Everest

h. Meg is sure that 725 (seven and twenty-five hundredths) is the answer to Prof Wang's math problem

For i–m, replace each blank with *accept* or *except*.

i. The candidate will _____ the nomination graciously.

j. The high school student hoped the college would _____ her.

k. Quan did not like vegetables, so he ate everything on his plate _____ the spinach.

l. To happily receive a gift means to _____ it.

m. All the teachers _____ Mr. O'Rourke went home.

More Practice See "More Practice Lesson 40" in Student Workbook.

Review Set 40 Choose the best word to complete sentences 1–8.

1. You may use honey as a (morale, substitute, biography)
(14, 23) for sugar.

2. A race containing three activities is called a (biathlon,
(13) triathlon).

3. The (moral, morale) of *The Adventures of Huckleberry*
(2, 23) *Finn* is to be true to yourself.

4. If you cheat on a test, you (dishonor, poor, feint) your
(6, 28) school.

5. The perfect verb tense shows action that has been
(16, 19) "perfected," or (continuing, completed).

6. To form the perfect tense, we add a form of the helping
(9, 19) verb (have, must) to the past participle.

7. We (shorten, lengthen) words by abbreviating them.
(40)

8. Abbreviations often require (commas, periods).
(40)

9. Tell whether this sentence is declarative, interrogative,
(1, 3) imperative, or exclamatory:

Snakes have thin, forked tongues that collect scents
from the air and the ground.

10. Write the proper noun from this list: state, mountain,
(6) Sunday, hymn, pew.

For 11 and 12, write the plural form of each noun.

11. half   **12.** hoof
(13, 14)   (13, 14)

Rewrite sentences 13–15, adding capital letters where they
are needed.

13. last year, the senior class at kentridge high school
(12, 20) performed william shakespeare's *romeo and juliet.*

(12, 26) **14.** my first two subjects of the day are french and geometry.

15. school generally begins in the fall.
(12, 31)

16. Write two simple prepositions that begin with the letter s.
(17, 18)

Write each prepositional phrase in sentences 17 and 18, and star the object of each preposition.

17. The national flower of the United States is the rose.
(18, 33)

18. The tallest of the coast redwoods grows in Montgomery
(18, 33) State Reserve.

19. Replace the underlined verb in this sentence with one
(5, 7) that is more descriptive: Aimee <u>hit</u> a home run to win the softball game.

For 20–22, replace each blank with the correct form of the verb.

20. A dog _____ (present of *scratch*) when it has fleas.
(7, 16)

21. Snakes _____ (present of *hiss*) at threats.
(7, 16)

22. The nervous man _____ (past of *tap*) his shoe.
(7, 16)

23. Write each adjective from this sentence and underline
(27, 28) each article: The cinnamon-red bark of a giant sequoia is a natural fire extinguisher.

24. Rewrite a and b, adding periods as needed.
(40) (a) Tues   (b) $175 ($1 and 75¢)

Write each correlative conjunction from sentences 25–27.

25. Neither Henri nor Alberto knew the rules.
(39)

26. José is not only a pianist but also a singer.
(39)

27. I ordered both carrots and peas with the meal.
(39)

Diagram each word of sentences 28–30.

28. The groom tossed the best man the garter.
(25, 35)

29. Dot and Doc not only bake but also sell fresh bread.
(38, 39)

(25, 34) **30.** The lizard on her kitchen floor frightened my mom.

LESSON
41

The Predicate Nominative

Dictation or Journal Entry

Vocabulary:

The prefix *mal-* means "bad; ill; wrong." *Malnutrition* refers to bad or faulty nutrition. *Malnutrition* is a serious problem in many third-world countries. To be *maladjusted* means "to be badly adjusted to a situation." The *maladjusted* child could not function normally in a school classroom. The verb *maltreat* means "to treat badly or abuse." The veterinarian taught his clients not to *maltreat* their pets.

More than one name can identify people, animals, or things.

Scamp is a Siamese cat.

In the sentence above, "cat" is another name for "Scamp."

Renames the Subject A **predicate nominative** is a noun that follows the verb and renames the subject person, animal, or thing. It explains or defines the subject and is identical with it. The subject and the predicate nominative are joined by a <u>linking verb</u> such as *am, is, are, was, were, be, being, been, become,* or *seem.* We remember that a linking verb does not show action, nor does it "help" the action verb. Its purpose is to connect the person, animal, or thing (the subject) to its new name (the predicate nominative).

Predicate nominatives are circled in the sentences below.

Lincoln <u>was</u> our sixteenth (president).

"president" renames "Lincoln"

Joyce <u>is</u> my (mother).

"mother" renames "Joyce"

If we reverse the subject and the predicate nominative, as in the sentences below, the meaning of the sentence is not affected.

Our sixteenth *president* <u>was</u> (Lincoln).

My *mother* <u>is</u> (Joyce).

Identifying the Predicate Nominative Reversing the subject and predicate nominative in this manner helps us identify predicate nominatives. If the linking verb is not a "to be" verb, we replace it with a "to be" verb to determine whether there is a predicate nominative that renames the subject.

John Adams <u>became</u> president after George Washington.

John Adams <u>was</u> president after George Washington.

"to be" linking verb

Now we reverse the subject and predicate nominative, and we see that the predicate does indeed rename the subject. The meaning is the same, so we have identified a predicate nominative.

The *president* after George Washington <u>was</u> John Adams.

Predicate nominatives are more difficult to identify in interrogative sentences. Turning the question into a statement will help.

Question: Is Professor Plum the man with purple hair?

Statement: Professor Plum is the man with the purple hair.

In the statement above, we see that "man" renames "Professor Plum." Therefore, "man" is a predicate nominative.

Compound Predicate Nominatives

Predicate nominatives may be compound, as in the sentences below.

My favorite *sports* <u>are</u> soccer, baseball, and rugby.

The best *players* that day <u>were</u> Randy and Martin.

Diagramming

In a diagram, the predicate nominative is indicated by a line that slants toward the left. Here we diagram the simple subject, linking verb, and predicate nominatives of some of the sentences the sentences on the previous page.

Lincoln was our sixteenth president.

Lincoln | was \ president

My mother is Joyce.

mother | is \ Joyce

My favorite sports are soccer, baseball, and rugby.

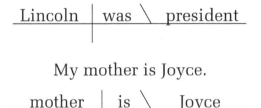

Example Diagram the simple subject, linking verb, and predicate nominatives of the following sentences. The simple subject is italicized and the linking verb is underlined to help you.

(a) The *countries* of the United Kingdom <u>are</u> Scotland, Wales, Northern Ireland, and England.

(b) *Great Britain* <u>became</u> the most powerful and prosperous country in Europe in the 1800s.

(c) *Queen Victoria* <u>was</u> the queen of Britain during this time.

(d) The current *ruler* of Great Britain <u>is</u> Queen Elizabeth II.

Solution (a)

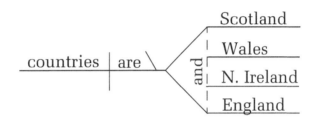

(b)

Great Britain | became \ country

(c)

Victoria | was \ queen

(d)

ruler | is \ Queen Elizabeth II

 Practice For a–d, replace each blank with the correct vocabulary word.

a. Children must learn not to abuse or _____ animals.

b. When people suffer from vitamin and mineral deficiencies, we say that they suffer from _____.

c. One who is not well-adjusted is _____.

d. A prefix meaning "bad," "ill," or "wrong" is _____.

For e–h, diagram the simple subject, linking verb, and predicate nominatives in each sentence.

e. In the 1800s, *England* <u>became</u> a more democratic nation.

f. *Queen Victoria* <u>was</u> the monarch.

g. The *queen* <u>was</u> a stern and serious woman.

h. The *queen* <u>became</u> a widow at a young age.

Review Set 41 Choose the best word to complete sentences 1–7.

1. That speckled hen (lays, lies) three eggs each day.
(10)

2. Snakes (lay, lie) in the sun to keep warm.
(10)

3. Do you know (who's, whose) keys these are?
(19)

4. The judges haven't yet revealed (who's, whose) going to the finals.
(19)

5. A proper noun names a (specific, common) person, place, or thing.
(6)

6. A (singular, plural) noun names only one person, place, or thing.
(10)

7. A (compound, possessive) noun tells "who" or "what" owns something.
(10)

8. Tell whether this sentence is declarative, interrogative, exclamatory, or imperative: Be considerate of the feelings of others.
(1, 3)

9. Tell whether this word group is a fragment, run-on, or complete sentence: *Homo-, geo-, bio-, uni-, tri-,* and *sub-* are common prefixes, do you know any others?
(3)

For 10 and 11, write the plural of each noun.

10. biography
(13, 14)

11. attorney at law
(13, 14)

12. Write each word that should be capitalized in this sentence: the prince of wales enjoyed reading mark twain's *a connecticut yankee in king arthur's court.*
(12, 26)

13. Write the five words from this list that are *not*
(17, 18) prepositions: aboard, about, and, above, across, the, after, against, me, along, alongside, think, amid, among, around, at, very, before, behind, below.

14. Write the adjective phrase from this sentence and tell
(33, 34) which noun or pronoun it modifies: A TV with a very small screen required a magnifying glass.

Choose the correct verb form to complete sentences 15 and 16.

✓ **15.** Yesterday we (chat, chatted) about the early versions of
(7, 16) television.

✓ **16.** The RCA 630, built in 1946, (were, was) the first TV to be
(7, 15) mass-produced.

Write the entire verb phrase from sentences 17 and 18.

17. Oscar has discovered much about the first portable TV set
(9, 19) from 1948. (present perfect)

18. We have been learning about the beginnings of television.
(9, 21) (present perfect progressive)

19. For parts a and b, tell whether the underlined verb is
(25, 32) transitive or intransitive.

    (a) The lost child <u>was</u> whimpering softly.

    (b) The relieved child <u>found</u> the babysitter.

20. Write each adjective from this sentence: In 1956, Zenith
(27, 28) introduced the Space Command System, the first wireless remote control.

21. Rewrite this address, adding periods as needed:
(26, 40) Mrs Henrietta B Highbrow
1265 S Higginbottom Blvd
Uppity City, Ohio 44873

22. Write the seven common coordinating conjunctions.
(37)

For 23 and 24, replace each blank with the correct word to complete each sentence.

23. A _____ nominative follows the verb and renames
(41) the subject.

24. The _____ and the predicate nominative are
(22, 41) joined by linking verbs such as *am, is, are, was, were, be, being, been, become,* or *seem.*

Write the predicate nominative in sentences 25 and 26.

25. The Mercury 7 is an unusual TV.
(22, 41)

26. The TV with a Sumsung tube atop an upside-down
(22, 41) Chinese wok was the Mercury 7.

Diagram each word of sentences 27–30.

Choose 2

27. Grapes may become juice, raisins, or wine.
(22, 41)

28. Either Marco or Maria will bring you.
(25, 39)

29. Dr. Yu washed and scoured pots and pans.
(25, 38)

30. The cat with the pink nose brought me her favorite toy.
(34, 35)

Noun Case, Part 1: Nominative, Possessive

> **Dictation or Journal Entry**
> **Vocabulary:**
> People often misuse the words *sit* and *set*. *Sit* means "to put the body into a seated position." When I'm tired of standing, I *sit* on a chair. *Set* means "to place something." The florist *set* the vase of red roses on the counter.

We can group nouns into three **cases:** *nominative, possessive,* and *objective.* The case of the noun explains how the noun is used in the sentence. In this lesson, we will learn to identify nouns that are in the nominative and possessive cases.

Nominative Case

SUBJECT OF A SENTENCE

A noun is in the **nominative case** when it is the subject of a sentence. In the sentence below, the noun *mice* is in the nominative case because it is the subject of the sentence.

> The *mice* ate the cheese greedily.

PREDICATE NOMINATIVE

A noun is also in the **nominative case** when it is used as a predicate nominative. A predicate nominative follows a linking verb and renames the subject. In the sentence below, *rodents* renames the subject, mice. *Rodents* is in the nominative case because it is a predicate nominative.

> Mice are *rodents.*

Possessive Case

We are familiar with nouns that show possession or ownership. These nouns are in the **possessive case**. In the sentence below, the possessive noun *Grandma's* is in the possessive case.

> *Grandma's* apple pie tasted yummy.

Example

Tell whether the italicized noun in each sentence is in the nominative case or the possessive case. If it is in the nominative case, tell whether it is the subject of the sentence or a predicate nominative.

(a) The *glass* fell and shattered.

(b) Grandpa Angles was a *plumber.*

(c) *Monty's* wife is a nurse.

Solution (a) The word *glass* is in the **nominative case**. It is the **subject of the sentence.**

(b) The word *plumber* is in the **nominative case**. It is a **predicate nominative**; it follows the linking verb *was,* and it renames the subject.

(c) *Monty's* is in the **possessive case**. It shows possession; it tells "whose wife."

√Practice For sentences a–e, tell whether the italicized noun is in the nominative case or the possessive case. If it is in the nominative case, tell whether it is the subject of the sentence or a predicate nominative.

   a. The growing *boy* ate three doughnuts.

   b. That clown is *Henry.*

   c. The *plumber's* toolbox weighs at least twenty pounds.

   d. Did an *artist* draw this sketch of your home?

   e. Robert Frost is my favorite *poet.*

For f–i, replace each blank with *sit* or *set.*

   f. We _____ in chairs.

   g. We _____ our backpacks on the ground.

   h. I told my lively dog to _____.

   i. The kitchen crew helped to _____ dishes on the table.

Review Set Choose the best word to complete sentences 1–6.
42
   1. No large company wants to be labeled a(n) (independent,
(8, 25) monopoly, honorable).

   2. In order to be (punctual, bilingual, coarse), the employee
(1, 13) arrived at 7 a.m. every morning.

   3. Refusing to eat sweets takes (respect, willpower, reliance)
(3, 9) for most people.

(15) **4.** (It's, Its) hair was matted with mud.

5. The word *veterinarian* is (masculine, feminine, indefinite, neuter) in gender.
(10)

6. We use a coordinating (conjunction, verb, pronoun) to join parts of a sentence that are equal, or parallel.
(37)

7. Tell whether this sentence is interrogative, exclamatory, imperative, or declarative: What is the moral of the story?
(1, 3)

8. Tell whether this word group is a phrase or a clause: if you waste your time
(2, 24)

9. Write the common noun from this list: month, July, Tuesday, President Ronald Reagan.
(6)

10. Write the singular noun from this list: brushes, potatoes, dramas, mice, holiday.
(10)

For 11 and 12, write the plural of each noun.

11. course
(13, 14)

12. capful
(13, 14)

13. Write each word that should be capitalized in this sentence: a dog named fido lives on danbury street in portland, oregon.
(12, 26)

14. Write the five words from this list that are *not* prepositions: beside, besides, persevere, between, beyond, but, by, unicycle, concerning, considering, submarine, despite, down, during, prodigious, except, excepting, fewer, for, from.
(17, 18)

15. Write the twenty-three helping verbs.
(9)

16. Choose the correct verb form for this sentence: Yes, scientists (does, do) understand why deserts are so dry.
(7, 15)

Write the entire verb phrase from sentences 17 and 18.

17. Deserts had existed far away from large bodies of water. (past perfect)
(9, 19)

18. Deserts had been expanding due to lack of moisture. (past perfect progressive)
(9, 21)

Write the direct object of sentences 19 and 20.

19. The earth's general weather patterns form deserts.
(2, 25)

20. Have you visited a desert?
(2, 25)

21. Rewrite this sentence, adding periods as needed: The
(36, 40) bus left at 11:00 am and returned at 3:30 pm

Write the predicate nominative in sentences 22 and 23.

22. For lack of moisture, the Gobi became a desert.
(22, 41)

23. Dr. Monty will be an orthodontist.
(22, 41)

For sentences 24–27, replace each blank with the correct word.

24. We group nouns into three cases: _____,
(42) possessive, and objective.

25. The _____ of a noun explains how the noun is
(42) used in the sentence.

26. When a noun is a subject or a predicate nominative, it is
(42) in the _____ case.

27. Nouns that show possession are in the _____ case.
(10, 42)

Diagram each word of sentences 28–30.

28. Dr. Bryce has become an orthodontist.
(2, 41)

29. The carpenter taught Steph tricks of the trade.
(25, 35)

30. Julio is a teacher and friend.
(2, 41)

Noun Case, Part 2: Objective

Dictation or Journal Entry
Vocabulary:
The homophones *principle* and *principal* differ in the spelling of their final syllable. A *principle* is a fundamental truth, law, or belief. Our government is based on the *principle* that all people are equal. A *principal* is the administrative head of an elementary or secondary school. The *principal* of Gidley Elementary School is my pal. *Principal* also means "first in importance." Safety is the fire department's *principal* concern.

We have learned to identify nouns that are in the nominative and possessive cases. In this lesson, we will see examples of nouns that are in the objective case.

Objective Case   A noun is in the **objective case** when it is used as a *direct object*, an *indirect object*, or the *object of a preposition*. Let's review these "objects."

Direct Object   A noun or pronoun is called a **direct object** when it is the direct receiver of the action of the verb. Direct objects are starred in the sentences below.

Sarah prepared *breakfast.
(Sarah prepared *what*?)

I cleaned the *barn.

Who built the *Sphinx?

Indirect Object   An **indirect object** is the noun or pronoun that tells "to whom" or "for whom" the action was done. In the following examples, the indirect objects are starred.

Did you bring *me a cookie?
(Did you bring a cookie for *me*?)

The player passed *Ron the football.
(The player passed the football to *Ron*.)

Please write *Tedmond a letter.
(Please write a letter to *Tedmond*.)

Object of a Preposition   A noun or pronoun that follows a preposition is called the **object of a preposition.** Objects of the prepositions are starred in the examples below.

at *school	over the *fence
through the *gate	except *you
beside *him	within two *months

Example 1 For sentences a–c, tell whether each italicized noun is a direct object, an indirect object, or the object of a preposition.

(a) The chef baked *Irene* a birthday cake.

(b) We take the *garbage* out on Wednesdays.

(c) The squirrel climbed up the *tree.*

Solution (a) *Irene* is an **indirect object.** It tells "for whom" the cake was baked.

(b) *Garbage* is a **direct object.** It is the receiver of the action verb *take.*

(c) *Tree* is the **object of the preposition** *up.*

Example 2 Tell whether the italicized noun is in the nominative, ~ownership~ possessive, or objective case. DO, IO, OP S PN

(a) Karina and Kristina planted *geraniums.*

(b) *Jumana's* mother sang beautifully.

(c) Fong is a good *student.*

(d) Spot crawled under the *gate.*

Solution (a) *Geraniums* is a direct object. Therefore, it is in the **objective case.**

(b) *Jumana's* is a possessive noun. Therefore, it is in the **possessive case.**

(c) *Student* is a predicate nominative. Therefore, it is in the **nominative case.**

(d) *Gate* is the object of a preposition. Therefore, it is in the **objective case.**

✓ **Practice** For sentences a–f, tell whether the italicized noun is a direct object (D.O.), an indirect object (I.O.), or the object of a preposition (O.P.).

a. Freddy drove across *town.*

b. Sal threw *Sergio* the basketball.

c. Tony missed the basketball *game.*

d. The detective came upon a *clue.*

e. The school principal called the *parents.*

f. He gave his *teacher* his homework.

For g–j, replace each blank with *principle* or *principal.*
g. The law of gravity is a scientific _____.

h. The _____ of the school awarded students who were improving their reading skills.

i. Faithfulness is an important _____ in friendship.

j. Higher pay was the union's _____ demand.

For k–n, tell whether the italicized noun or pronoun is in the nominative, possessive, or objective case.
k. Do *you* like surfing?

l. The horses devoured the *grain.*

m. Quan remains *John's* faithful friend.

n. Juan loaned *Quan* a dollar.

Review Set 43

Choose the best word to complete sentences 1–7.

1. Sometimes small children have a difficult time (setting, (42) sitting) still.

2. (Sit, Set) the egg carefully on the kitchen counter.
(42)

3. The clogged (pour, pore, poor) on Ned's face hurt.
(34)

4. Malia has an (incredible, capitol, diligent) story to tell.
(29, 30)

5. A (proper, common) noun requires a capital letter.
(6)

6. A (concrete, abstract) noun names something that can be (8) seen or touched or smelled.

7. The present participle of the word *heat* is (*heating,* (16, 21) *heated*).

8. Tell whether this sentence is declarative, interrogative, (1, 3) exclamatory, or imperative: It's hot!

9. Tell whether this word group is a phrase or a (2, 24) clause: integrity in all parts of your life

For 10 and 11, write the plural for each noun.

10. stingray
(13, 14)

11. bluff
(13, 14)

Rewrite 12 and 13, adding capital letters as needed.

12. these lines, i recall, come from william shakespeare's *as* (12, 20) *you like it*:

all the world's a stage,
and all the men and women merely players.

13. i. the prefix *bio-*
(20)   a. biology
        b. biography
        c. biosphere

14. Write the five words from this list that are not (17, 18) prepositions: inside, into, bicycle, like, subsoil, near, substitute, of, off, on, onto, opposite, out, outside, over, past, morale, regarding, become, round.

15. Write the action verb from this sentence: The gas station (5) attendant pours oil into the engines.

16. Replace the underlined verb with one that is more (5) descriptive: The prodigious man <u>is</u> on the sofa.

Write the entire verb phrase and underline each helping verb in sentences 17–19.

17. People have made several deserts. (present perfect)
(9, 19)

18. By the end of this lesson, we shall have discovered some (9, 19) reasons for deserts. (future perfect)

19. At the end of this decade, the oak tree in the town square (9, 21) will have been growing for at least a century. (future perfect progressive)

20. Write the indirect object from this sentence: Ricardo (25, 35) ordered his girlfriend flowers for the prom.

21. Write each article from this sentence: The Thar, a desert
(28) in western India, was created by people in an area that
was once a forest.

Replace each blank with the correct word to complete
sentences 22 and 23.

22. We use a coordinating _____ to join parts of a
(37) sentence that are equal, or parallel.

23. A noun is in the _____ case when it is used as a
(43) direct object, an indirect object, or the object of a
preposition.

24. Write the coordinating conjunction in this sentence: To
(37) collect firewood and to make fields, the Romans cut
hillside forests.

25. Write the predicate nominative in this sentence: The
(41) spread of deserts is a problem.

For sentences 26–28, tell whether the italicized noun is a
direct object, an indirect object, or the object of a preposition.

26. The golden retriever caught the *ball* high in the air.
(43)

27. The jet flew high above the *clouds*.
(43)

28. Joyce showed *Nadine* her beautiful doll collection.
(43)

Diagram sentences 29 and 30.

29. The journalist with the great sense of humor told me a
(25, 35) funny joke.

Hint:

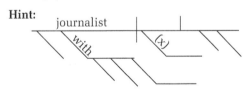

✓ **30.** Rose either trots or gallops.
(38, 39)

LESSON 44

The Predicate Adjective

Dictation or Journal Entry
Vocabulary:
The prefix *ultra-* suggests "going beyond the bounds of moderation; extreme." The word *ultraconservative* describes something that is extremely conservative. The *ultraliberal* politician describes his opponent as an *ultraconservative*. *Ultraviolet* refers to the high-frequency wavelengths lying beyond the violet end of the visible spectrum. *Ultraviolet* light appears purple in the dark. The adjective *ultramodern* refers to something that is extremely modern. *Ultramodern* homes feature built-in computers.

Describes the Subject We have learned that a predicate nominative follows a linking verb and *renames* the subject. A **predicate adjective** follows a linking verb and *describes* or gives more detail about the subject.

Chocolate <u>is</u> delicious.

In the sentence above, the word "delicious" is a predicate adjective. It describes "chocolate"— delicious chocolate.

Laural <u>was</u> busy.

In the sentence above, the word "busy" is a predicate adjective. It describes "Laural"— busy Laural.

The linking verb that connects the subject to the predicate adjective may be a form of the verb "to be" (*is, am, are, was, were, be, been*), but other linking verbs such as *become, seem, feel, appear, look, taste,* and *smell* also can link the predicate adjective to the subject.

My *teacher* <u>looks</u> prepared.

Freshly baked *bread* <u>smells</u> good.

Identifying Predicate Adjectives To help us identify the predicate adjective, we can replace a possible linking verb with a "to be" verb.

My *teacher* <u>is</u> prepared.

↑
"to be" verb

In the sentence above, we see that "prepared" describes the subject "teacher"— prepared teacher. Therefore, "prepared" is a predicate adjective.

Freshly baked *bread* <u>is</u> good.

↑
"to be" verb

In the sentence above, we see that "good" describes the subject "bread"— good bread. "Good" is a predicate adjective.

Compound Predicate Adjectives A predicate adjective may be compound, as in the sentence below. Predicate adjectives are circled.

The *cake* <u>is</u> (scrumptious) and (attractive).

Diagramming We diagram a predicate adjective in the same way we diagram a predicate nominative. Here is a diagram of the simple subject, linking verb, and predicate adjectives of the sentence above:

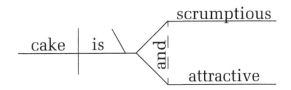

Example Diagram the simple subject, linking verb, and predicate adjectives in sentences a–d.

(a) *Imperialism* <u>was</u> popular with the British people in the 1800s.

(b) *Imperialism* <u>seemed</u> very unfair to the native people.

(c) The *British* <u>felt</u> superior to the Asian and African people during this time.

(d) *Asia* and *Africa* <u>appeared</u> backward and primitive to them.

Solution (a)

Imperialism | was \ popular

(b)

Imperialism | seemed \ unfair

(c)

British | felt \ superior

(d)

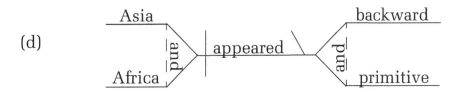

√ **Practice** For sentences a–d, diagram the simple subjects, linking verbs, and predicate adjectives.

  a. *India* <u>was</u> special to the British.

  b. The *temples* and religious *art* in India <u>were</u> magnificent.

  c. The *West India Company* <u>became</u> greedy, dishonest, and cruel to the Indian subjects.

  d. The British and Indian *soldiers* <u>were</u> brutal in the Sepoy Rebellion in 1857.

For e–h, replace each blank with the correct vocabulary word.

  e. A prefix meaning "extreme" is _____.

  f. Sunbathers ignore the warnings about the _____ rays of the sun.

  g. _____ technology is usually expensive.

  h. A person who is extremely conservative is said to be _____.

Review Set 44 Choose the best word to complete sentences 1–11.

  1. There is never an excuse to (maltreat, feign, willpower) an animal.
  (28, 41)

  2. Violent people are considered (incredible, principal, maladjusted).
  (28, 41)

  3. The criminal was (affected, indicted, incapacitated) for murder.
  (29, 39)

  4. Let us show (prudence, monopoly, dialogue) when planning how we will spend our money.
  (35, 36)

  5. The main word in a sentence that tells who or what is doing or being something is called the simple (subject, predicate).
  (2)

  6. A (concrete, abstract) noun names something that cannot be seen or touched.
  (8)

7. A (singular, plural) noun names more than one person,
(10) place, or thing.

8. The past tense of the verb *cry* is (*cried, crying*).
(7)

9. We (shall, will) attend the baseball game this evening.
(9, 11)

10. The predicate adjective describes the (subject, verb,
(44) object).

11. The predicate adjective follows a (linking, action) verb
(44) and gives more detail about the subject.

12. Tell whether this sentence is declarative, exclamatory,
(1, 3) imperative, or interrogative: Homonyms are spelled and
pronounced alike.

For 13 and 14, write the plural of each noun.

13. moose   **14.** radio
(13, 14)   (13, 14)

Write each word that should be capitalized in sentences 15
and 16.

15. informing the employee of a pay raise, the manager
(12, 20) complimented, "you are diligent and conscientious about
every aspect of your job."

16. hey, mr. wilson, did you know that my mom is an english
(12, 26) teacher?

17. Write the five words from this list that are not
(17, 18) prepositions: since, tricycle, through, throughout,
bilingual, till, to, toward, under, underneath, its, until,
unto, up, upon, too, with, within, whose, without.

18. Replace the blank with the singular present tense form of
(7, 16) the italicized verb: Bees *buzz*. A bee _____.

19. Write the present progressive verb phrase in this
(9, 21) sentence: In my history class, we are discussing the
struggle for independence in the Americas.

20. Write the five verbs from this list that are *not* linking
(22) verbs: is, am, are, was, were, teach, be, being, been, skate,
look, feel, taste, skip, smell, sound, seem, swing, appear,
grow, become, cook, remain, stay.

21. Write the demonstrative adjective in this sentence: This
(28) nation, the United States, was once a colony under the control of a faraway government.

22. Write the indefinite adjective in this sentence: Within
(28) fifty years, many people in Mexico, Central America, and South America would gain their independence from Spain and Portugal.

23. Write the predicate adjective in this sentence: The
(27, 44) triathlete appeared exhausted after the race.

Replace each blank with the correct word to complete sentences 24 and 25.

24. We diagram a predicate adjective the same way that we
(41, 44) diagram a _____ nominative.

25. _____ conjunctions always come in pairs.
(39)

For sentences 26 and 27, tell whether the italicized noun is in the nominative, possessive, or objective case.

26. Haiti was the next *colony* to win its independence.
(42)

27. The store on the corner lowered its *prices*.
(43)

Diagram sentences 28–30.

28. The lonely dog grew bored.
(23, 44)

29. Fresh flowers smell delightful.
(23, 44)

30. Sam served us fettucine with broccoli and chicken.
(34, 35)

Hint: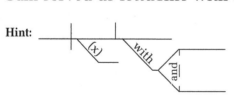

Comparison Adjectives

Adjectives are often used to compare nouns or pronouns. These **comparative adjectives** have three forms that show greater or lesser degrees of quality, quantity, or manner: **positive**, **comparative**, and **superlative**. Below are examples of the positive, comparative, and superlative forms of some adjectives.

POSITIVE	COMPARATIVE	SUPERLATIVE
tall	taller	tallest
fast	faster	fastest
soft	softer	softest
funny	funnier	funniest
busy	busier	busiest

Positive Form The positive form describes a noun or pronoun without comparing it to any other. (Do not confuse *positive* with *good.* In this context, positive simply means "possessing the quality." The quality itself may be good, bad, or neutral.)

Zeus is *strong.*

Athena is *smart.*

Bacchus is *lazy.*

Comparative Form The comparative form compares **two** persons, places, or things.

Zeus is *stronger* than Athena.

Is Athena *smarter* than Zeus?

Bacchus is *lazier* than Pan.

Superlative Form The superlative form compares **three or more** persons, places, or things.

Of Zeus, Athena, and Bacchus, Zeus is the *strongest.*

Athena is the *smartest* of the three.

Bacchus is the *laziest* of all the Greek gods.

Example 1 Choose the correct adjective for each sentence.

    (a) My car is (new, newer, newest) than yours.

    (b) Of the three, Cole is the (wise, wiser, wisest).

    (c) Samantha is the (tall, taller, tallest) of the two players.

    (d) Of all the boys in the room, Tim was the (silly, sillier, silliest).

Solution (a) My car is **newer** than yours. We use the comparative form because we are comparing two cars.

    (b) Of the three, Cole is the **wisest**. We use the superlative form because we are comparing three or more people.

    (c) Samantha is the **taller** of the two players. We use the comparative form because we are comparing two players.

    (d) Of all the boys in the room, Tim was the **silliest**. We use the superlative form because we are comparing three or more boys.

Forming Comparison Adjectives How we create the comparative and superlative forms of an adjective depends on how the adjective appears in its positive form. There are three main categories to remember.

One-Syllable Adjectives We create the comparative form of most one-syllable adjectives by adding *er* to the end of the word. The superlative form is created by adding *est*.

POSITIVE	COMPARATIVE	SUPERLATIVE
green	greener	greenest
brave	braver	bravest
big	bigger	biggest

Two-Syllable Adjectives Most adjectives with two or more syllables do not have comparative or superlative forms. Instead, we use the word "more" (or "less") before the adjective to form the comparative, and the word "most" (or "least") to form the superlative.

POSITIVE	COMPARATIVE	SUPERLATIVE
loyal	more loyal	most loyal
timid	less timid	least timid
valuable	more valuable	most valuable

Two-Syllable Adjectives That End in *y* — When a two-syllable adjective ends in *y,* we create the comparative and superlative forms by changing the *y* to *i* and adding *er* or *est.*

POSITIVE	COMPARATIVE	SUPERLATIVE
lovely	lovelier	loveliest
scratchy	scratchier	scratchiest
happy	happier	happiest

Exceptions — There are exceptions to these guidelines. Below are a few examples of two-syllable adjectives whose comparative and superlative forms are created by adding *er* or *est.*

POSITIVE	COMPARATIVE	SUPERLATIVE
little (size, not amount)	littler	littlest
quiet	quieter	quietest
able	abler	ablest
narrow	narrower	narrowest
clever	cleverer	cleverest
simple	simpler	simplest

We check the dictionary if we are unsure how to create the comparative or superlative form of a two-syllable adjective.

Spelling Reminders — Remember that when adding *er* or *est* to the positive form of an adjective, we often must alter the word's original spelling. We apply the same rules we use when adding *ed* to form a past-tense verb.

When an adjective ends with **two or more consonants**, *er* or *est* is simply added to the positive form of the adjective.

dark	darker	darkest
young	younger	youngest
light	lighter	lightest

When an adjective ends with a **single consonant following one vowel**, we double the final consonant before adding *er* or *est.*

red	redder	reddest
fit	fitter	fittest

When an adjective ends with a **single consonant following two vowels**, we do not double the final consonant.

loud	louder	loudest
cool	cooler	coolest

When a one-syllable adjective ends in **w, x, or y preceded by a vowel**, we do not double the final consonant.

new	newer	newest
gray	grayer	grayest

When a two-syllable adjective ends in **y**, we change the *y* to *i* before adding *er* or *est*.

wavy	wavier	waviest
sloppy	sloppier	sloppiest

When an adjective ends with a **silent e**, we drop the *e* and add *er* or *est*.

safe	safer	safest
blue	bluer	bluest

Example 2 Complete the comparison chart by adding the comparative and superlative forms of each adjective.

POSITIVE	COMPARATIVE	SUPERLATIVE
(a) sweet	_____	_____
(b) harsh	_____	_____
(c) risky	_____	_____
(d) obvious	_____	_____
(e) wet	_____	_____
(f) fine	_____	_____

Solution

POSITIVE	COMPARATIVE	SUPERLATIVE
(a) sweet	sweeter	sweetest
(b) harsh	harsher	harshest
(c) risky	riskier	riskiest
(d) obvious	more obvious (or less obvious)	most obvious (or least obvious)
(e) wet	wetter	wettest
(f) fine	finer	finest

√ **Practice** Choose the correct adjective for each sentence, and tell whether it is comparative or superlative.

    a. Your pancake is (flatter, flattest) than mine.

    b. Allison is the (younger, youngest) of the four children.

    c. Patricia is the (more, most) graceful dancer in her class.

    d. Are you (hungrier, hungriest) in the morning or in the evening?

    e. Isn't this puppy the (cute, cuter, cutest) of the litter?

    f. Debby raced Scot to the phone, but Scot was (faster, fastest).

For g and h, give the comparative and superlative of each adjective.

    g. high   **h.** talkative

For i–l, replace each blank with *advice* or *advise*.

    i. The word _____ is a verb meaning "to give counsel."

    j. The word _____ is a noun meaning "counsel given to persuade or encourage."

    k. Good _____ is sometimes hard to follow.

    l. Please _____ me on my choice of a college.

Review Set 45 Choose the best word to complete sentences 1–8.

    1. Please (except, accept) this gift as a token of our gratitude.
    (40)

    2. Class, you will have play rehearsals every day this week
    (40) (accept, except) Friday.

    3. There are many charitable organizations that help
    (26, 41) children who suffer from (conscience, malnutrition, independence).

    4. (There, They're, Their) are just too many things to
    (38) accomplish in the next hour.

    (2) **5.** The simple (subject, predicate) is the verb.

6. A (collective, common) noun names a collection of persons, places, animals, or things.
_(6, 8)

7. A (compound, possessive) noun is made up of two or more words.
_(8, 10)

8. Julita and Julio (is, are) conscientious and diligent.
_(7, 15)

9. Write the past participle of the verb *smoke*.
_(9, 16)

10. Tell whether this word group is a fragment, run-on, or complete sentence: Homophones sound alike but have different meanings and spellings.
₍₃₎

For 11 and 12, write the plural of each noun.

11. cactus
_(13, 14)

12. mosquito
_(13, 14)

Write each word that should be capitalized in sentences 13 and 14.

13. grandma and grandpa curtis want dad to pick them up at the airport.
_(12, 26)

14. the donkeys migrated south in the winter.
_(12, 31)

15. Write the prepositional phrase and star each object of the preposition in this sentence: Hamlet sat between Gertrude and Ophelia.
_(17, 33)

16. Replace the blank with the singular present tense form of the verb.
_(7, 16)

Baseball players <u>hit</u> home runs. A baseball player _____ home runs.

17. Write the past progressive verb phrase in this sentence: Fernando was studying colonial Mexico.
_(9, 21)

18. Write the linking verb in this sentence: Another name for today's Mexico was "New Spain."
₍₂₂₎

19. Write the number adjective from this sentence: Of all the colonies, "New Spain" was the first concern of Spain.
₍₂₈₎

For 20 and 21, replace each blank with the correct word.

20. A predicate adjective follows a _____ verb and gives more detail about the subject.
_(22, 44)

21. The three forms of adjectives showing greater or lesser
(45) degrees are the positive, the _____, and the superlative.

Choose the correct adjective for sentences 22 and 23.

22. New Spain was the (large, larger, largest) and most
(45) important of all the Spanish colonies.

23. The number of Spaniards in New Spain was (great,
(45) greater, greatest) than the number of Creoles, who were people of Spanish background born in Mexico.

24. Rewrite this sentence, adding periods as needed: Be here
(36, 40) at 8 a m sharp

25. List the four most common pairs of correlative
(39) conjunctions.

26. Write the predicate nominative in this sentence: The
(41) second most powerful group in New Spain were the Creoles.

For 27 and 28, tell whether the italicized noun is in the nominative, possessive, or objective case. If it is in the nominative case, tell whether it is the subject of the sentence or a predicate nominative. If it is in the objective case, tell whether it is a direct object, indirect object, or object of a preposition.

27. Many Creoles became prosperous *landowners* and
(42) *merchants.*

28. Even the wealthiest Creoles had very little say in the
(43) *government.*

Diagram sentences 29 and 30.

29. The poorest people in New Spain were the
(28, 44) oppressed indigenous people.

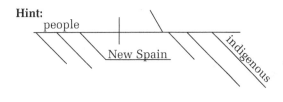
Hint:

(2, 44) **30.** These people felt mistreated and abused.

LESSON 46

Irregular Comparison Adjectives

Some adjectives have irregular comparative and superlative forms. We must learn these if we haven't already.

POSITIVE	COMPARATIVE	SUPERLATIVE
little (amount, not size)	less	least
good, well	better	best
bad, ill	worse	worst
far	farther	farthest
many, much	more	most

Little or Few? We use *little, less,* and *least* with things that cannot be counted. We use *few, fewer,* and *fewest* with things that can be counted.

CANNOT BE COUNTED:
The pet store owner has *less* affection for his finches than for his puppies.

CAN BE COUNTED:
Does he sell *fewer* finches than puppies?

Much or Many? We use *much* with things that cannot be counted, and we use *many* for things that can be counted.

CANNOT BE COUNTED:
There is not *much* confidence in the stock market today.

CAN BE COUNTED:
Many investors still purchase stock.

Example 1 Choose the correct adjective for each sentence.

(a) (Little, less, least) rain falls on the desert than in the mountains.

(b) This cold is the (baddest, worst) one I've ever experienced.

(c) There are (less, fewer) hot days in January than in August.

(d) Last year, (less, fewer) snow fell on the local mountains.

(e) (Many, Much) of the students are working hard.

Solution   (a) **Less** rain falls on the desert than in the mountains. (The sentence is comparing two places, so we use the comparative form of "little.")

(b) This cold is the **worst** one I've ever experienced. ("Baddest" is not a word.)

(c) There are **fewer** hot days in January than in August. ("Days" can be counted.)

(d) Last year, **less** snow fell on the local mountains. ("Snow" cannot be counted.)

(e) **Many** of the students are working hard. ("Students" can be counted.)

Avoid Double Comparisons   We do not use double comparisons. In other words, we do not use *more* with *er,* or *most* with *est.*

NO: Marilyn Monroe was *more prettier* than Tony Curtis.
YES: Marilyn Monroe was *prettier* than Tony Curtis.

NO: She was not the *most happiest* person in the world.
YES: She was not the *happiest* person in the world.

Absolute Adjectives   Some adjectives do not normally permit comparison. Adjectives that represent an ultimate condition (*square, round, maximum, equal, fatal, unique, dead,* etc.) cannot be increased by degree. (For example, a square can't be "squarer" than another square; it's either square or it's not!) When necessary, careful writers can modify these adjectives by using words like *almost, near,* and *nearly* instead of more/less and most/least.

NO: Arsenic is *more fatal* than strychnine.
YES: He swallowed an *almost fatal* dose.

Example 2   Choose the correct adjective for each sentence.

(a) She is (friendlier, more friendlier) than her sister.

(b) That was the (bravest, most bravest) thing he ever did.

Solution   (a) She is **friendlier** than her sister. ("More friendlier" is a double comparison. We do not use *more* with *er*.)

            (b) That was the **bravest** thing he ever did. ("Most bravest" is a double comparison. We do not use *most* with *est*.)

✓ Practice   For a–f, choose the correct adjective for each sentence.

    a. (Much, Many) countries claimed unsettled areas for their own.

    b. The natives expressed (many, much) dislike of this practice.

    c. One of the (worse, worst) effects of nationalism was the "scramble for Africa."

    d. (More, Most) rubber could be found in Africa than in Europe.

    e. (Few, Little) palm oil was available in England.

    f. The pony was (more timider, more timid) last time.

For g–i, replace each blank with *raise*, *rays*, or *raze*.

    g. Students _____ their hands before speaking out in class.

    h. The city council voted to _____ the old theater in order to build the new library.

    i. Skin specialists warn sunbathers to avoid the direct _____ of the sun.

More Practice   Choose the correct adjective for each sentence.

    1. (Little, Less) snow falls in the desert than in the mountains.

    2. Sheung plays tennis (gooder, better) than Hung.

    3. This storm is the (worse, worst) since 1982.

    4. I feel (better, weller) today than yesterday.

    5. Our old car is (reliabler, more reliable) than our new one.

6. He has (more, most) courage than I have.

7. Who is the (more clever, most clever) of the three?

8. Are you the (braver, bravest) of the two?

Review Set 46 Choose the best word to complete sentences 1–10.

1. The (maladjustment, maltreatment, malnutrition) of
(41) Ethiopian children leads to skinny bodies but extended bellies.

2. Please (sit, set) the tax documents on the table.
(42)

3. The (dialogue, diagonal, diameter) of the two foreign
(35) spies revealed their plans to the CIA agent.

4. What (affect, effect) will this secret information have on
(27) this country?

5. An (imperative, interrogative, exclamatory) sentence asks
(1, 3) a question and ends with a question mark.

6. The past tense of the verb *pat* is (*pated, patted*).
(7, 16)

7. Elephants (is, are) the largest living land mammals.
(7, 15)

8. A (positive, comparative, superlative) adjective compares
(45) three or more persons, places, or things.

9. A (positive, comparative, superlative) adjective describes
(45) a noun or pronoun without comparing it to any other.

10. A (positive, comparative, superlative) adjective compares
(45) two persons, places, or things.

11. Tell whether this word group is a fragment, run-on, or
(3) complete sentence: An ostrich can run up to forty miles per hour.

12. Tell whether this word group is a phrase or a
(2, 24) clause: with the very long legs of an ostrich

13. Write the concrete noun from this list: squid, fright,
(8) appreciation, honor

Grammar and Writing 6   **231**   **Student Edition**
Lesson 46

For 14–16, write the plural of each noun.

14. ostrich
(13, 14)

15. elephant
(13, 14)

16. studio
(13, 14)

17. Write each word that should be capitalized in this
(12, 20) sentence: the zookeeper said, "the ostrich is the fastest
animal on two legs."

For 18 and 19, write each prepositional phrase and star the
object of each preposition.

18. The ostrich has strides of fifteen feet.
(17, 33)

19. The wings of an ostrich serve many functions.
(17, 33)

Write the entire verb phrase in sentences 20 and 21.

20. Scientists have counted 150,000 muscles in an elephant's
(9, 19) trunk. (present perfect)

21. The baby elephant will be using his trunk for touching,
(9, 21) smelling, eating, and drinking. (future progressive)

22. Write the 19 linking verbs from this list: is, about, above,
(22) am, are, was, were, be, before, but, being, been, look, like,
because, after, while, feel, taste, smell, should, so, sound,
seem, what, appear, while, grow, become, remain, stay.

For 23–25, write the comparative and superlative forms of
each adjective.

23. new
(45)

24. intelligent

25. little (size)

26. Write the seven common coordinating conjunctions.
(37)

27. Add periods as needed in this sentence: John C Fremont
(36, 40) explored many parts of the U S

28. Tell whether the italicized noun in this sentence is in the
(42, 43) nominative, objective, or possessive case: The giraffe,
hippopotamus, and orangutan are other interesting
animals.

Diagram sentences 29 and 30.

✓ **29.** The indulgent grandmother purchased her grandson a
(28, 35) souvenir.

30. The wings of an ostrich control its body temperature and
(25, 33) its balance.

The Comma, Part 1: Dates, Addresses, Series

Dictation or Journal Entry

Vocabulary:
The words *brake* and *break* (pronounced brāk) are homophones. *Brake* means "to slow and stop." When you see a stop sign, begin to *brake*. *Break* means "to shatter or render useless." Falling rock might *break* your windshield.

Commas are the most frequently-used form of punctuation. We use commas to separate elements within sentences. Using commas correctly helps us clarify the meaning of a phrase or a sentence.

Parts of a Date
We use commas to separate the **parts of a date.** When we write a complete date, we always place a comma between the day and the year.

> July 20, 1969

If a complete date appears in the middle of a sentence, we place a comma after the year.

> On July 20, 1969, humans first walked on the moon.

If the day of the week appears as part of the date, we place a comma after the day.

> I'll never forget Sunday, July 20, 1969.

Note: When just the month and the year appear in a sentence, no comma is required.

> Many people remember July 1969 as an exciting time.

Example 1
Insert commas wherever they are needed in the parts of the date in this sentence:

> Monty's birth occurred on Thursday March 9 1976 at eleven o'clock in the morning.

Solution
We place a comma after day of the week (Thursday). We also place a comma after the day (March 9). Lastly, because the date appears in the middle of a sentence, we place a comma after the year.

> Monty's birth occurred on Thursday, March 9, 1976, at eleven o'clock in the morning.

Parts of an Address We use commas to separate the **parts of an address** and the names of geographical places or political divisions.

The parts of a street address are separated by commas according to the following pattern:

house number and street, city, state and zip code

10662 Lora Street, Monrovia, California 91016

305 Faraway Drive, Princeton, NJ 08540

Note: We use the state abbreviation when addressing a letter or package.

We also use commas to separate the names of geographical places or political divisions.

King County, Washington   San José, Costa Rica

Inverness, Scotland, UK   Banff, Alberta, Canada

If the city and state or country appear in the middle of the sentence, a comma is required after the state or country.

I live in Paris, France, during the summer.

Example 2 Insert commas wherever they are needed in these sentences.

(a) The lost puppy's tag indicated that his home was at 123 Dogwood Street Wagsburg Alabama.

(b) The jet landed in Tokyo Japan at precisely nine o'clock.

Solution (a) We separate the parts of the address with commas. One comma goes after the house number and street, and another goes between the city and the state.

The lost puppy's tag indicated that his home was at 123 Dogwood Street, Wagsburg, Alabama.

(b) We place a comma between the city and the country. We place another comma after the country because it is in the middle of a sentence.

The jet landed in Tokyo, Japan, at precisely nine o'clock.

Words in a Series We use commas to separate **three or more words or phrases in a series**.

Fido, Spot, and Rover used to be popular names for dogs.

The dessert cart featured cream puffs, blueberry cobbler, cheesecake with cherry topping, and three kinds of cookies.

Example 3 Insert commas as needed in this sentence:

> Commas periods quotation marks and semicolons help make the meaning of a sentence clearer.

Solution We separate the items in the series with commas.

> Commas, periods, quotation marks, and semicolons help make the meaning of a sentence clearer.

√Practice For a–d, replace each blank with *break* or *brake*.

a. When approaching a stop sign, new drivers often _____ too quickly.

b. Glass will usually _____ when dropped.

c. If you _____ something while shopping, you should tell the salesclerk.

d. Always be ready to _____ for rambunctious squirrels.

Rewrite sentences e–g, inserting commas where necessary to separate parts of a date.

e. Flying 670 miles per hour, American test pilot Charles Yeager broke the sound barrier on October 14 1947.

f. The news spread in January 1849 that gold had been discovered in California.

g. Christmas fell on Monday December 25 in the year 2000.

Rewrite sentences h–j, inserting commas to separate parts of an address.

h. The doctor moved his office to 1712 W. Duarte Road Arcadia California 91007.

i. Rome Italy attracts many tourists each year.

j. Are your friends going to Salem Massachusetts or Salem Oregon?

Rewrite sentences k–m, inserting commas to separate words in a series.

k. The eight parts of speech include nouns pronouns verbs adverbs adjectives prepositions conjunctions and interjections.

l. I have a sweet gum tree two spruce trees two lilac bushes and several junipers in my front yard.

m. Siti wants to visit Tibet Mongolia and Indonesia.

More Practice See "More Practice Lesson 47" in Student Workbook.

Review Set 47 Choose the best word to complete sentences 1–5.

1. A moth chewed a (whole, hole) in Martha's red cashmere
(24) sweater.

2. The two friends trusted each other because both believed
(43) in the (principle, principal) of honesty.

3. Remember to protect your skin from the (ultramodern,
(44) ultraconservative, ultraviolet) rays of the sun.

4. The monkey ate (less, fewer) bananas today.
(21, 46)

5. A (declarative, interrogative) sentence makes a statement
(1, 3) and ends with a period.

6. Tell whether this word group is a phrase or a clause: on a
(2, 24) boat in the waters near Anacapa Island

A transitive verb has a direct object. For 7 and 8, tell whether the underlined verb is transitive or intransitive.

7. A biologist <u>can hold</u> a murrelet, a bird, in the palm of his
(25, 32) hand.

8. Black rats <u>appear</u> harmful to the murrelets.
(25, 32)

9. Write the common abstract noun from this list: iguana,
(6, 8) Jurassic Period, extinction, dinosaur.

For 10–12, write the plural of each noun.

10. torpedo   **11.** baby   **12.** commander in chief
(13, 14)   (13, 14)   (13, 14)

13. Rewrite this outline, adding capital letters as needed:
(20)
　　i. saving the birds by destroying the rats

　　　a. black rats eat murrelet eggs

　　　b. the tiny murrelet nears extinction

Write each prepositional phrase from sentences 14 and 15, and star the object of each preposition.

14. The murrelets are vulnerable to black rats in the cliffs and
(17, 33) grottoes of Anacapa Island.

15. For the murrelets' survival on the island, the rats must be
(17, 33) removed.

16. Write the 23 helping verbs.
(9)

17. For a–c, choose the correct form of the irregular verb *have*.
(7, 15)

    (a) That mother murrelet (have, has) eggs.

    (b) The many murrelets (have, has) eggs.

    (c) (Have, Has) you ever seen a murrelet?

Write the entire verb phrase in sentences 18 and 19.

18. Other sea birds had joined the murrelets on Anacapa
(9, 19) Island. (past perfect)

19. Scientists have been observing the murrelets for some
(9, 21) time. (present perfect progressive)

20. Tell whether the underlined verb is an action or linking
(5, 22) verb: The murrelets <u>nudge</u> their young offspring down
the cliffs and into the sea.

Write each adjective in sentences 21 and 22.

21. The endangered murrelets live in the water.
(27, 28)

22. One hundred pairs of murrelets live on this island.
(27, 28)

23. Write the four common pairs of correlative conjunctions.
(39)

24. Rewrite this outline, adding periods as needed:
(20, 36)   I Polar bears

      A Weight

      B Length

Add periods and commas as needed in sentences 25 and 26.

25. On Wednesday July 4 2001 the United States celebrated
(20, 47) Independence Day with barbecues fireworks and parades

26. Please return this lost dog to 321 Beagle Ave Roverton
(40, 47) Connecticut

Tell whether the italicized nouns in sentences 27 and 28 are in the nominative case, objective case, or possessive case.

✓ **27.** Polar *bears* frighten people because of their prodigious
(42, 43) size.

✓ **28.** Most female polar bears give *birth* once every three years.
(42, 43)

Diagram sentences 29 and 30.

✓ **29.** Newborn cubs are small and blind.
(23, 41)

✓ **30.** Polar bears risk extinction.
(25, 28)

LESSON 48

Appositives

Dictation or Journal Entry

Vocabulary:
People often misuse the words *may* and *can. Can* means "able to." *Can* I reach the roof on this ladder? *May* means "permitted to." *May* I go outside to play?

Appositives A word or group of words that immediately follows a noun to identify or give more information about the noun is called an **appositive.** In the sentences below, the appositives are italicized.

> President Abraham Lincoln, *our sixteenth president,* freed the slaves.

> Janna's friends *Bob and Kate* are coming to visit this weekend.

> Richard Curtis, *my father,* can fix anything.

> The sport *tennis* requires a racquet and a ball.

Example 1 Identify the appositives from each sentence.

(a) My favorite treat, eggnog, is available only during the holidays.

(b) Julia looks like her sister Amanda but acts like her sister Laura.

Solution (a) The appositive *eggnog* gives more information about the noun "treat."

(b) The appositive *Amanda* identifies the noun "sister." The appositive *Laura* identifies the second noun "sister."

Improving Our Writing Using appositives skillfully can improve our writing. With an appositive, we can combine two choppy sentences to make one good one.

> TWO CHOPPY SENTENCES:
> Fred Smith is a pitcher for the Mitford Giants. Fred mows the neighborhood lawns.

> ONE GOOD SENTENCE:
> Fred Smith, *a pitcher for the Mitford Giants,* mows the neighborhood lawns.

Example 2 Combine each pair of choppy sentences to make one longer sentence by using an appositive.

> (a) Some say that Secretariat was the fastest racehorse ever born. Secretariat was the winner of the 1973 Kentucky Derby.

> (b) You can see da Vinci's *Mona Lisa* at the Louvre. The Louvre is the world's largest art museum.

Solution (a) **Some say that Secretariat, the winner of the 1973 Kentucky Derby, was the fastest racehorse ever born.**

> (b) **You can see da Vinci's *Mona Lisa* at the Louvre, the world's largest art museum.**

Diagramming an Appositive We diagram an appositive by placing it in parentheses beside the noun it identifies or describes.

My mother, *Isabel Curtis*, is a teacher.

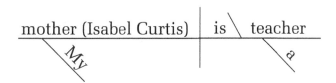

If the appositive contains adjectives, we place them on slanted lines directly beneath the appositive.

The man in the yellow shirt is Ricardo, *our team's goalie.*

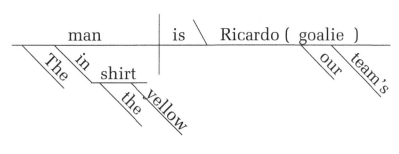

✓ Practice For a–f, replace each blank with *can* or *may.*

> **a.** We use the word _____ when we are asking permission to do something.

> **b.** If we are able to do something, we use the word _____.

> **c.** _____ the track meet be finished before dark?

d. _____ the runners use shoes with cleats on them?

e. Mother, _____ I walk to Kendie's house?

f. _____ I walk the distance, or should I ride my bike?

For g and h, write the appositive from each sentence.

g. Pumpkin pie, a popular Thanksgiving dessert, uses many spices for flavoring.

h. The spice cinnamon is used in pumpkin pie.

i. Diagram this sentence: Joe Lu, class president, writes mystery novels.

For j and k, combine each pair of sentences into one sentence by using an appositive.

j. Mrs. Smith is my teacher. Mrs. Smith wants me to succeed.

k. Mr. Dunn encourages students to try hard. Mr. Dunn is principal of Gidley School.

More Practice See "Silly Story #3" in Student Workbook.

Review Set 48 Choose the best word to complete sentences 1–7.

1. The (feint, pore, prodigious) pile of laundry discouraged
(20, 28) the homemaker.

2. Do you heed the (advice, advise) of your teacher?
(45)

3. The operator asked if I would (accept, except) the collect
(40) phone call.

4. The (independence, injustice) of punishing one and not
(31) the other angered the crowd.

5. An (interrogative, exclamatory) sentence shows
(1, 3) excitement or strong feeling and ends with an exclamation point.

(25, 32) **6.** A(n) (transitive, intransitive) verb has no direct object.

7. A(n) (appositive, pronoun, conjunction) is a word or
(48) group of words that immediately follows a noun to
identify or give more information about the noun.

8. Rewrite this run-on sentence to make one or two
(3, 4) complete sentences: Shirley Temple was a very famous
child actress she was also called "The Little Princess."

9. Choose the concrete proper noun from this list: dancer,
(6, 8) famous, singer, Shirley Temple, actress.

For 10 and 11, write the plural of each noun.

10. bluff   **11.** Wednesday
(13, 14)

Write each word that should be capitalized in sentences
12–14.

12. at a very young age, shirley temple loved to sing and
(6, 12) dance.

13. *stand up and cheer*, i recall, featured the song "baby, take
(12, 20) a bow."

14. *the little colonel*, which takes place during the civil war,
(12, 20) features shirley temple and bill "bojangles" robinson in a
classic tap dance on a flight of stairs.

Write each prepositional phrase and star the object of each
preposition in sentences 15 and 16.

15. After her film contract was signed, Shirley Temple
(17, 33) starred in short films that made fun of adult movies.

16. During 1934, Shirley Temple played in seven short films.
(17, 33)

17. For a–c, choose the correct form of the irregular verb *to be*.
(7, 15) (a) I (is, am, are) punctual.

(b) That show-off (is, am, are) maladjusted.

(c) These two books (is, am, are) for you.

Write the entire verb phrase in sentences 18–20.

18. By age six, Shirley Temple had become the most famous
(9, 19) actress in the United States. (past perfect)

19. By noon tomorrow, I shall have watched Shirley
(9, 19) Temple's *Bright Eyes* four times. (future perfect)

20. Movie scouts had been looking for a talented young child
(9, 21) like Shirley Temple. (past perfect progressive)

21. Write the present participle, past tense, and past
(9, 16) participle of the verb *dance*.

22. Write the proper adjective in this sentence: During the
(30, 22) Depression, young girls everywhere desired a Shirley
Temple doll.

23. Write the predicate adjectives in this sentence: Shirley
(27, 44) Temple was bright and cheery.

24. Write the correlative conjunctions in this sentence:
(39) Shirley Temple danced in both *The Little Colonel* and
Captain January.

25. Rewrite this sentence, adding the needed periods and
(40, 47) commas: On Sunday June 1 2002 we were asked to send
a copy of the *St Louis Post-Dispatch* to 32 Marshall Blvd
Green City Alaska

26. Write the predicate nominatives in this sentence: During
(22, 41) the Depression, two bright spots of hope and happiness
were Shirley Temple and the dog Rin Tin Tin.

27. Tell whether the italicized noun in this sentence is in the
(42, 43) nominative, objective, or possessive case: Her talent,
cheerful personality, and hopeful attitude captured the
admiration of many *people.*

Write each appositive in sentences 28 and 29.

✓ **28.** My grandmother, a Shirley Temple fan, often sings
(48) "Animal Crackers in My Soup."

✓ **29.** Shirley Temple's mother, Gertrude Temple, helped
(48) Shirley learn her lines every evening.

✓ **30.** Diagram this sentence: My friend Patricia Cheung
(33, 48) traveled to China.

LESSON 49

The Comma, Part 2: Direct Address, Appositives, Academic Degrees

---

Dictation or Journal Entry

Vocabulary:

Let us look at the homophones *peace* and *piece*. *Peace* means "calmness," "tranquility," or "lack of hostility." After the war, there was *peace* in the land. *Piece* refers to a part of a whole. Would you like a *piece* of this cake?

In this lesson, we will discuss more uses for commas.

Nouns of Direct Address

A **noun of direct address** names the person who is being spoken to (the person who is receiving the information in the sentence). The noun can be the person's name or a "name" you are using for him or her. Nouns of direct address can appear anywhere in a sentence. We offset them with commas.

> Albert, please give us the definition of a homonym.

> Where, Mom, did you put the mail?

> Don't step in that paint again, silly.

There may be more than one noun of direct address in a sentence. Also, like any noun, a noun of direct address can be modified by adjectives. We offset the entire noun phrase with commas, as in the sentences below.

> Stop running around the pool, Darrin and Ed!

> Be careful, my dear Betsy, or you'll bother the bees.

Example 1 Insert commas to offset the noun of direct address in the sentence below.

> Jason where did you see van Gogh's painting?

Solution We insert a comma after "Jason" because Jason is being spoken to. It is a noun of direct address.

> **Jason, where did you see van Gogh's painting?**

Example 2 Insert commas to offset the noun of direct address in the sentence below.

> Go into the kitchen wet dog until you are dry.

Solution We offset the entire noun phrase "wet dog" because the dog is being spoken to and "wet" modifies "dog."

> **Go into the kitchen, wet dog, until you are dry.**

Appositives We have learned that an **appositive** is a word or group of words that immediately follows a noun to identify or give more information about the noun. In the sentence below, "Mr. Goodheart" is an appositive. Notice how commas offset it from the rest of the sentence.

> Our principal, Mr. Goodheart, appreciates the high morals of his students.

In the sentence below, "Gerardus Mercator" is also an appositive. But it is not offset by a comma. Why?

> The first person to project the earth's surface onto a flat map was the cartographer Gerardus Mercator.

Essential and Nonessential Appositives Whether or not an appositive is offset with commas depends on how essential it is to the meaning of the sentence.

Let's look at the first sentence, above. If we remove the appositive, the sentence still makes sense:

> Our principal appreciates the high morals of his students.

The phrase "our principal" has already identified the person the sentence is about. The appositive "Mr. Goodheart" is informative but **nonessential** to the meaning of the sentence. **Nonessential appositives are offset with commas.**

Now let's remove the appositive from the second sentence:

> The first person to project the earth's surface onto a flat map was the cartographer.

The cartographer? Which cartographer? This sentence no longer makes sense. The appositive "Gerardus Mercator" is **essential** to the meaning of the sentence. **Essential appositives are not offset by commas**.

Example 3 Insert commas where necessary in the sentence below.

> Roald Dahl author of *Charlie and the Chocolate Factory* is admired by most students.

Solution If we remove the appositive, "author of *Charlie and the Chocolate Factory*," the meaning of the sentence is still clear. (Roald Dahl is admired by most students.) Therefore, it is a nonessential appositive, and we offset it with commas.

> **Roald Dahl, author of *Charlie and the Chocolate Factory*, is admired by most students.**

Example 4 Insert commas where necessary in the sentence below.

Vincent van Gogh's painting *The Starry Night* is more famous than any of my paintings.

Solution If we remove the appositive, "*The Starry Night,*" the reader is left to wonder *which* painting by van Gogh, and the meaning of the sentence is lost. Therefore, it is an essential appositive, and we do not offset it with commas.

Vincent van Gogh's painting *The Starry Night* is more famous than any of my paintings.

Academic Degrees When an **academic degree** or similar title follows a person's name, it is usually abbreviated. Here are some abbreviations you're likely to see:

M.D. (Doctor of Medicine)

D.D.S. (Doctor of Dental Surgery)

D.V.M. (Doctor of Veterinary Medicine)

Ph.D. (Doctor of Philosophy)

Ed.D. (Doctor of Education)

LL.D (Doctor of Laws)

D.D. (Doctor of Divinity)

R.N. (Registered Nurse)

L.P.N. (Licensed Practical Nurse)

M.B.A. (Master of Business Administration)

We use commas to offset academic degrees or other titles that follow a person's name.

Allison Ramos, R.N., works at Huntington Memorial Hospital.

The children called the dentist Doctor Monty, but his licensed name was Richard Montgomery, D.D.S.

Example 5 Insert commas to offset the academic degree in this sentence.

Phyllis Jensen Ph.D. teaches art appreciation at Citrus Elementary School.

Solution Since "Ph.D." is an academic degree, it is offset with commas.

Phyllis Jensen, Ph.D., teaches art appreciation at Citrus Elementary School.

Practice Rewrite sentences a and b, using commas to offset nouns of direct address.

    a. Peter we learned about negative integers yesterday.

    b. How long good friends must we wait before lunch?

Rewrite sentences c and d, using commas where necessary to to offset nonessential appositives.

    c. Charles Dickens author of *Oliver Twist* wrote several notable literary works.

    d. The artist Claude Monet painted a peaceful water scene by using a special method of brushing.

Rewrite sentences e and f, using commas to offset academic degrees or other titles.

    e. Patti Anderson R.N. applied to be a school nurse instead of a hospital nurse.

    f. My dog's health is very important to Don Russell D.V.M.

For g–j, replace each blank with *peace* or *piece*.

    g. The nun had a sense of tranquility or _____ about her.

    h. Mom, may I have a _____ of pie?

    i. Claude Monet's *Bridge Over a Pool of Water Lilies* often brings a sense of calmness or _____ to the viewer.

    j. We searched everywhere for the last _____ of the jigsaw puzzle.

More Practice See "More Practice Lesson 49" in Student Workbook.

Review Set 49 Choose the best word to complete sentences 1–10.

    1. The (reliable, respectful, compassionate) American
    _(3, 22) citizen placed his hand over his heart when the national anthem was sung.

    ₍₈₎ **2.** Of (course, coarse), parents will chaperone the party.

3. Cleaning one's room sometimes seems like (two, to, too)
(18) difficult a task.

4. Getting up early each morning requires (integrity,
(6, 9) discipline).

5. An (exclamatory, imperative, interrogative) sentence
(1, 3) expresses a command or a request and ends with a
period.

6. Scamp, our Siamese cat, (empty, empties) his dish
(5, 8) quickly.

7. We (shall, will) carefully wash our cantaloupe before
(9, 11) cutting into it.

8. The present participle of the verb *dance* is (*dance,
(5, 16) danced, dancing*).

9. An action verb that has a direct object is called a
(25, 32) (transitive, intransitive) verb.

10. *A, an,* and *the* are called (descriptive adjectives, articles).
(27, 28)

11. Write the proper noun from this list: country, fruit,
(6) cantaloupe, Mexico, melon, salmonella.

12. Write the abstract proper noun from this
(6, 8) list: conservatism, liberalism, journalism, Marxism,
prism.

13. Write the word from this list that is *not* a compound
(10) noun: watermelon, maid of honor, cantaloupe, nail
polish, basketball.

14. Write the plural of *child*.
(13, 14)

Write each word that should be capitalized in sentences
15–17.

15. grandma lillian warned her grandchildren to wash
(12, 26) cantaloupe to avoid salmonella.

16. hey, grandpa, did you know that bacteria can grow on the
(12, 26) skins of cantaloupe?

17. i learned in my biology class, not my spanish class, that
(12, 26) fever and abdominal cramps are symptoms of salmonella.

Write each prepositional phrase in sentences 18 and 19, and star the object of each preposition.

18. Although not generally dangerous, salmonella can cause
(17, 33) serious problems for young children and the elderly.

19. When a knife cuts through the cantaloupe's rind, the
(17, 33) knife may spread bacteria to the fruit.

Write the entire verb phrase in sentences 20 and 21.

20. In some cases, salmonella will have tainted such fruits as
(9, 19) cantaloupe and strawberries. (future perfect)

21. By the day of the festival, the townsfolk will have been
(9, 21) preparing food for weeks. (future perfect progressive)

Replace each blank with the correct word to complete sentences 22 and 23.

22. Comparison adjectives have these three forms: the
(45) positive, the comparative, and the _____.

23. The comparative and superlative forms of the adjective
(45) *stormy* are _____ and _____.

For sentences 24–26, add periods and commas as needed.

24. On Thursday February 14 2002 my brother and his
(40, 47) fiancée became Mr and Mrs Rodríguez

25. "Thank you Joyce for the delicious meal" commented
(36, 47) Van the polite boyfriend of Jan

26. Kenneth Hopkins PhD authored several books on
(40, 47) psychology while teaching at the University of Boulder

27. Tell whether the italicized noun in this sentence is
(42, 43) nominative, objective, or possessive case: The *cat's* fur stood straight up when she saw the gigantic dog.

28. Write the appositive in this sentence: Holly, Jenny's best
(48) friend, visited Death Valley with the geology class.

29. Use an appositive to combine these sentences into one
(48) sentence: Dr. Flealess is a veterinarian. Dr. Flealess
prescribes treatment for fleas and ticks.

30. Diagram this sentence: Dr. Itchfree, the veterinarian, gave
(35, 48) Rover some ointment for his fleabites.

Hint:

LESSON 50

Overused Adjectives • Unnecessary Articles

Dictation or Journal Entry
Vocabulary:
The words *right, write, wright,* and *rite* are homophones. *Right* means "correct or proper." It is also a direction opposite of left. It is *right* to wait until everyone is served before eating. Go to the corner and turn *right*. *Write* means "to record in print." Did you *write* your essay yet? *Wright* is one who constructs, creates, or contrives. It is usually used in compounds. The play*wright* presented his play to the cast. *Rite* means a "ritual or ceremonial act." The baby received the *rite* of baptism at church.

Overused Adjectives

Many people make the mistake of using the same adjectives over and over again. In this lesson we will learn to choose more vivid adjectives. Some of the adjectives that people use too often are as follows:

great	bad	wonderful
nice	terrible	fine
good	awful	okay

While there is nothing wrong with the adjectives above, we should try to use more specific or interesting ones if we can. We can always consult the dictionary or thesaurus for more choices.

WEAK: It was a *great* movie.
BETTER: It was a *thrilling* (or *moving, stimulating, breathtaking, exciting, hilarious, hair-raising*) movie.

WEAK: My grandpa is *nice*.
BETTER: My grandpa is *kind* (or *gracious, generous, warmhearted, loving, jovial, friendly*).

WEAK: I felt *bad* today.
BETTER: I felt *ill* (or *depressed, guilty, disappointed, miserable, sad, unhappy, wretched*) today.

Example 1

Rewrite each sentence, replacing each overused adjective with a more vivid one.

(a) It was a *good* party.

(b) The weather was *bad*.

(c) That book is *terrible*.

(d) My vacation was *wonderful*.

Solution   Our answers will vary. Here are some possibilities:

(a) It was a (*fabulous, extraordinary, marvelous*) party.

(b) The weather was (*stormy, depressing, foul, inclement*).

(c) That book is (*atrocious, boring, worthless, dreadful*).

(d) My vacation was (*relaxing, refreshing, invigorating, stimulating*).

Unnecessary Articles   We have learned that the articles *a, an,* and *the* are adjectives. Sometimes they are used unnecessarily. Avoid these errors:

We do not use *the* before "both."

NO: I invited *the both* of them.
YES: I invited *both* of them.

NO: Please help *the both* of them with their spelling.
YES: Please help *both* of them with their spelling.

We do not use *a* or *an* after the phrases "kind of," "sort of," or "type of."

NO: I like that *kind of a* sandwich.
YES: I like that *kind of* sandwich.

NO: She is not that *type of a* person.
YES: She is not that *type of* person.

Example 2   Rewrite each sentence correctly.

(a) Rondo fixed the both of those trucks.

(b) What kind of a car does Letha drive?

Solution   (a) **Rondo fixed both of those trucks.** (We remove the word *the*. It is not used before "both.")

(b) **What kind of car does Letha drive?** (We remove the word *a*. We do not use it after "kind of.")

√**Practice**   Rewrite sentences a–d, replacing each overused adjective with a more interesting or specific one.

a. Last night I had an *awful* dream.

b. You wrote a *good* essay.

c. Tom had a *nice* day.

d. My dessert tastes *bad.*

Rewrite sentences e and f correctly.

    e. That sort of a test makes me nervous.

    f. The toddlers were tired, so we put the both of them to bed.

For g–j, replace each blank with *right, write, wright,* or *rite.*

    g. Some people think they are always _____.

    h. Please _____ legibly.

    i. Many cultures have similar customs surrounding the _____ of marriage.

    j. The play_____ won several awards for his dramas.

Review Set 50   Choose the best word to complete sentences 1–10.

    1. (There, They're, Their) socks stank after the hike.
    (38)

    2. The lawyers showed discretion and (capital, monopoly, prudence) when selecting the jury for the case.
    (25, 36)

    3. The company's absence of compassion and sympathy lowered the (morals, morale, perseverance) of its employees.
    (16, 23)

    4. Your punctuality shows your (diligence, dishonor, consideration) for others.
    (1, 12)

    5. Intertidal creatures (brush, brushes) against death almost every day.
    (5, 7)

    6. He (do, does) his homework conscientiously each day.
    (7, 15)

    7. The past tense of the verb *dance* is (*dance, danced, dancing*).
    (7, 16)

    8. *This, that, those,* and *these* are called (descriptive, demonstrative) adjectives.
    (28)

    9. *His, our, my, her, its, their,* and *your* are called (descriptive, demonstrative, possessive) adjectives.
    (28)

    10. *Some, few, many, several, no,* and *any* are called (descriptive, demonstrative, possessive, indefinite) adjectives.
    (28)

11. Tell whether this word group is a sentence fragment,
(1, 3) run-on sentence, or complete sentence: To protect the
creatures in the tide pools.

12. Choose the correctly written proper noun from this
(6) list: Pacific ocean, atlantic Ocean, Indian Ocean.

13. Choose the common collective noun from this
(6, 8) list: United States, Europe, multitude, Latin America.

14. Write the possessive noun in this sentence: The
(10, 28) intertidal zones (shorelines) are among the Earth's most
threatened ecosystems.

15. Write the plural of *life*.
(13, 14)

Write each word that should be capitalized in sentences
16–18.

16. along the west coast, the rocky seashore has changed
(6, 12) dramatically from twenty years ago.

17. one of the main christian holidays is easter.
(6, 12)

18. dear sierra club,
(6, 29)

      sadly, the animal life in the tidepools is decreasing.
can we save our tidepools?

                sincerely,

                an animal lover

For sentences 19 and 20, write each prepositional phrase, and
star the object of each preposition.

19. People, pollution, and disease have destroyed the
(17, 33) octopus, black abalone, and clumps of mussels in the
tidepools.

20. Oceanographers have charted temperature increases
(17, 33) throughout the Pacific Ocean since the late 1970s.

21. Write the present progressive verb phrase in this
(9, 21) sentence: Oceanographers are warning of serious
consequences if people do not respect the tidepools.

22. Tell whether the underlined verb is transitive or
(25, 32) intransitive: The polar bear <u>was sleeping</u> peacefully on
the iceberg.

23. Write the comparative and superlative of the positive
(45, 46) adjective *lovely*.

24. Write the adjective from this list that is *not* overused:
(50) great, bad, nice, flamboyant, good, terrible.

✓ **25.** Rewrite this sentence correctly: Please give the both of
(50) them directions to the sports arena.

26. Add periods and commas as needed to this
(36, 49) sentence: Chandler please show me that you are reliable

27. Tell whether the italicized noun in this sentence is in the
(42, 43) nominative, objective, or possessive case: Haley gave
Spencer a hug.

28. Write each appositive in this sentence: One of my
(48) favorite movies, *Mary Poppins*, features Julie Andrews, a
talented vocalist.

29. Use an appositive to combine these two sentences into
(48) one sentence: Rin Tin Tin was a famous dog. Rin Tin Tin
captured the hearts of the American people during the
Depression.

✓ **30.** Diagram this sentence: The little dog across the street, a
(25, 34) poodle, loves peanut butter.

LESSON 51

Pronouns and Antecedents

> **Dictation or Journal Entry**
>
> **Vocabulary:**
> The words *fracture*, *fraction*, and *fractious* all come from the Latin word *frangere*, meaning "to break." As a verb, *fracture* means just that: "to break." Used as a noun, *fracture* refers to the result of a break. An X-ray of the runner's ankle revealed that he had *fractured (verb)* a bone. He had a stress *fracture (noun)*. A *fraction* is a portion or part of something; it is a piece "broken off" of the whole. Because she had insurance, the motorist paid only a *fraction* of the auto repair bill. The word *fractious* means "unruly" or "quarrelsome." An adjective, *fractious* implies a "breaking" of order. The *fractious* mob hurled insults at the speaker.

Pronouns   A **pronoun** is a word that takes the place of a noun or a noun phrase. Rather than using the same noun over and over again, we use pronouns.

Without pronouns, our language would be quite tiresome:

> Mrs. Peabody drove into Mrs. Peabody's driveway and honked at Mrs. Peabody's dog. Mrs. Peabody's dog barked happily to see that Mrs. Peabody was finally home. Then Mrs. Peabody called Mrs. Peabody's husband and asked Mrs. Peabody's husband to help Mrs. Peabody unload Mrs. Peabody's groceries…

Pronouns (italicized) simplify the passage:

> Mrs. Peabody drove into *her* driveway and honked at *her* dog, *who* barked happily to see that *she* was finally home. Then *she* called *her* husband and asked *him* to help *her* unload *her* groceries…

Pronouns are the words (such as *he, she, it, we, they*) we use to refer to people, places, and things that have already been mentioned. Pronouns are italicized in the examples below.

> The girl served the volleyball, and *she* watched *it* land out of bounds.

In the sentence above, the pronoun *she* replaces "girl," and the pronoun *it* replaces "volleyball."

Antecedents   The noun or noun phrase to which the pronoun refers is called the **antecedent.** The prefix *ante-* means "before," and the root *ced* means "go." The antecedent usually "goes before" the pronoun. In the example above, "girl" and "volleyball" are antecedents for the pronouns *she* and *it.*

Notice the antecedents for the pronouns *her* and *it* in this sentence:

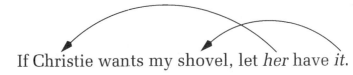

If Christie wants my shovel, let *her* have *it*.

The antecedent of the pronoun *her* is "Christie," and the antecedent of the pronoun *it* is "shovel."

Often we find an antecedent in an earlier sentence:

> Last night Joe (antecedent) made a burrito (antecedent).
> *He* ate *it* before school this morning.

Sometimes the antecedent comes after the pronoun:

> Although *he* disliked going to the shopping mall,
> Brian (antecedent) reluctantly agreed to accompany Kim.

An antecedent might be another pronoun:

> *I* (antecedent) finished all *my* homework.

A pronoun can also have more than one antecedent:

> After Joyce (antecedent) and John (antecedent) purchased fabric, *they* sewed shorts for the children.

Likewise, a noun can serve as the antecedent for more than one pronoun.

> Grandpa (antecedent) was eighteen years old when *he* served *his* country in the army.

Example 1 List the italicized pronouns in a–d. Beside each pronoun, write its antecedent. (Example: his/Tony)

(a) Heather injured *her* toe when *she* kicked the soccer ball.

(b) Although *he* disliked flying, Uncle Carl agreed to fly to Hawaii.

(c) Nettie baked the cake. *She* also decorated *it*.

(d) It takes them a whole day to mow *their* enormous lawn.

Solution (a) *her*/Heather, *she*/Heather

(b) *he*/Uncle Carl

(c) *she*/Nettie, *it*/cake

(d) *their*/them

Each pronoun needs a clear antecedent. The meaning of the sentence below is unclear because the antecedent is unclear:

The nutritionist said *she* eats too much fat.
Who eats too much fat?
What is the antecedent of *she*?

The following sentences are unclear because they each contain a pronoun that has more than one possible antecedent:

Sandra and Mom drove to *her* house.
Whose house?
Mom's? Sandra's?

Gordy left Joe alone with *his* brother.
Which is the antecedent of *his*?
Is it Gordy, or is it Joe?

Emily picked up Jane when *she* was finished.
Does *she* refer to Emily or to Jane?

To make our meaning clear, we can use nouns instead of pronouns, we can rearrange a few words, or we can rewrite the whole sentence:

Sandra and Mom drove to Mom's house.

Gordy left his brother alone with Joe.

When Emily was finished, she picked up Jane.

Example 2 Write the clearer sentence of each pair.
(a) She left for the market.

Mother left for the market.

(b) Ted played baseball with Ned and broke his bat.

Ted broke his bat while playing baseball with Ned.

Solution (a) We choose the second sentence because it clearly tells *who* went to the market.

Mother left for the market.

(b) We choose the second sentence because it clearly tells *whose* bat broke.

Ted broke his bat while playing baseball with Ned.

Practice For a–d, give the antecedent for each italicized pronoun.
a. James left at two o'clock, but *he* returned at dinnertime.

b. Jenny wants to learn all *she* can.

c. Natalie and Nicholas rode their bikes to the store, and *they* parked *them* outside the entrance.

d. Although the jacket is old, *it* still keeps Jerry warm.

For e and f, write the clearer sentence of each pair.

e. While Ellen and Tracy were waiting, she completed her math assignment.

While Ellen and Tracy were waiting, Ellen completed her math assignment.

f. It dated back to colonial times.

The primer dated back to colonial times.

For g–i, replace each blank with the correct vocabulary word.

g. The _____ criminal spent extra time in isolation.

h. The talkative child ate only a _____ of the food on his plate.

i. Our bones may become more susceptible to _____ as we age.

Review Set 51

Choose the best word to complete sentences 1–10.

1. The employee received a big (raise, rays, raze) for a job
(46) well-done.

2. The driver applied his foot to the (break, brake) pedal in
(47) order to stop the vehicle.

3. Randa and I (can, may) not stay past visiting hours.
(48)

4. A (peace, piece) of good chocolate pleases most people.
(49)

5. The (positive, comparative, superlative) form of an
(45) adjective compares two persons, places, or things.

6. Nouns in the (nominative, objective, possessive) case are
(42, 43) used as direct objects, indirect objects, or objects of a preposition.

7. A noun or pronoun is called a (direct, indirect) object
(25) when it is the direct receiver of the action of the verb.

8. An (appositive, adjective, pronoun) is a word or group of
(48) words that immediately follows a noun to identify or give
more information about the noun.

9. We usually separate an appositive from the rest of the
(48, 49) sentence with (periods, commas, adverbs).

10. They (was, were) wise to postpone the beach excursion.
(7, 15)

11. Tell whether this sentence is declarative, interrogative,
(1, 3) exclamatory, or imperative: Did the X-ray reveal a fracture
of the femur?

12. Write each word that should be capitalized in this
(6, 12) sentence: the lewis and clark expedition crossed the
mississippi river when exploring the united states of
america.

13. Rewrite this outline, adding capital letters and periods as
(20, 36) needed:

i book list

a *the indian in the cupboard*

b *the house at pooh corner*

14. Write each prepositional phrase in this sentence, and star
(17, 33) the object of each preposition: Despite the rain, we had
fun at the beach.

15. Write the present participle, past tense, and past
(9, 16) participle of the verb *snip*.

16. Write each proper adjective in this sentence: You can tell
(27, 30) Asian elephants from an African elephant by their ears.

17. Replace the overused (underlined) adjective in this
(27, 50) sentence with one that is more descriptive: The bus
driver was <u>nice</u>.

18. Rewrite this sentence, adding periods and commas as
(40, 47) needed: The three planets closest to our sun are Mercury
Venus and Earth

19. Write the missing pair of common correlative
(39) conjunctions: both/and; either/or; not only/but also;
_____/_____.

20. Write the appositive in this sentence: The fourth planet
(48) from the sun, Mars, is 4,200 miles in diameter.

21. Use an appositive to combine these two choppy
(48) sentences into one longer sentence: Mercury is the
nearest planet to the sun. Mercury orbits the sun in about
eighty-eight Earth days.

Replace each blank with the correct word to complete
sentences 22–26.

22. A _____ is a word that takes the place of a noun.
(51)

23. The word to which the pronoun refers is called the
(51) _____.

24. The prefix *ante-* means "_____."
(51)

25. The root *ced* means "_____."
(51)

26. The antecedent usually goes _____ the pronoun.
(51)

27. Write the pronoun in this sentence: The moon is the
(51) closest natural body to the Earth, but it is not a planet.

Diagram sentences 28–30.

28. Lions and tigers sniffed and devoured the raw meat.
(23, 25)

29. His favorite sport is swimming.
(28, 41)

30. Tide pools provide homes for mussels, starfish, and
(25, 33) abalone.

LESSON 52

The Comma, Part 3: Greetings and Closings, Last Name First

> **Dictation or Journal Entry**
> **Vocabulary:**
> Note the difference in spelling between the homophones *hanger* and *hangar*. A *hanger* is a frame for hanging clothes. Put your shirt on a *hanger,* or it will wrinkle. A *hangar* is a shed for an airplane. The ground crew moved the smaller airplanes into *hangars* before the windstorm.

In this lesson, we will learn more uses for commas.

Greeting   We use a comma after the **greeting** of a friendly letter.

Dear George,

My generous uncle,

Closing   We use a comma after the **closing** of a letter.

Sincerely yours,

Gratefully,

Example 1   Place commas where they are needed in the letter below.

Dear Paula
    Thank you for the lovely gift.
        Love
        Kerry

Solution   We place commas after the greeting and closing of the letter.

Dear Paula,
    Thank you for the lovely gift.
        Love,
        Kerry

Last Name First   When we alphabetize a list of names, we usually alphabetize by the person's last name. We place the last name first and the first name (followed by middle names, if any) last. They are separated by a comma, as shown:

Bashford, John

Duong, Mai

Johnson, Renee Marie

Martínez, Bruce J.

Stuart, M'kalah

Zertuche, Nicole

Grammar and Writing 6   **263**   **Student Edition** Lesson 52

Other than in lists, we don't often write names this way. When we do, we are usually referring to or "quoting from" a list. Quotation marks are a good way of indicating this:

The last name on the class list was "Zertuche, Nicole."

"Twain, Mark" completed the list of famous American authors.

I'm known as "Williams, George E." in the phone book.

Example 2 Insert a comma where it is needed in the sentence below.
"Bashford John" was the first name on the class list.

Solution We use a comma in inverted names.

"Bashford, John" was the first name on the class list.

Practice Rewrite a and b, inserting commas as needed.

a. Dear Rosie

Thank you for arranging my student list in alphabetical order. I can see that the first name on the list is "Adams Laurie."

Gratefully
Suzanne

b. The index lists "Poe Edgar A." as the author of "The Raven."

For c–f, replace each blank with *hangar(s)* or *hanger(s)*.

c. El Monte Airport rents _____ to store small airplanes.

d. Dry cleaners place clean garments on wire frames called _____.

e. Howard Hughes owned a gigantic _____ to house his famous airplane, the *Spruce Goose*.

f. My sisters always raid my closet when they need more _____ for their clothes.

More Practice See "More Practice Lesson 52" in Student Workbook.

Review Set 52 Choose the best word to complete sentences 1–9.

1. The copy____ (right, write, wright, rite) date of a book
(50) indicates the year it was written or revised.

2. With rain in the forecast, the weatherperson (advised,
(45) adviced) people to carry umbrellas.

3. A word similar in meaning to *compassion* is (respectful,
(3, 22) sympathy, conscientious).

4. When an author writes about the life of another person,
(8, 11) we call it a (biosphere, course, biography).

5. We form the perfect verb tense by adding a form of the
(9, 19) helping verb (*be, have, do*) to the past participle.

6. The (positive, comparative, superlative) form compares
(45) three or more persons, places, or things.

7. We use a (comma, period, question mark) when we invert
(52) names and write the last name first.

8. A (verb, conjunction, predicate nominative) follows a
(41) linking verb and renames the subject.

9. A(n) (direct, indirect) object is the noun or pronoun that
(25, 35) tells "to whom" or "for whom" the action was done.

10. A transitive verb has a direct object. Tell whether the
(25, 32) underlined verb in this sentence is transitive or
intransitive: The famous playwright William Shakespeare
wrote both comedies and tragedies.

11. Write the collective noun from this list: audience, Utah,
(8) father, table, Paris.

12. Write each word that should be capitalized in this
(12, 26) sentence: dr. and mrs. robert turner suggested, "mom,
why don't you ride in our car to the english tea party?"

13. Write the adjective phrase in this sentence, and tell
(33, 34) which noun it modifies: The squid has eight arms with
suckers.

14. Write the predicate adjective in this sentence: Emerson
(22, 44) and Wendy became husband and wife last weekend.

15. Write each adjective in this sentence: Wendy's bridal
(27, 28) bouquet contained tiny pink roses, some mint sprigs, and
three enormous white lilies tied with a long silk ribbon.

16. Rewrite this sentence correctly: I had never seen that
(50) kind of a bouquet before.

Replace each blank with the correct word to complete
sentences 17–21.

17. We use a comma after the greeting and _____ of a
(52) friendly letter.

18. We use a _____ after the closing of a letter.
(52)

19. A noun or pronoun that follows a preposition is called
(33) the _____ of the preposition.

20. A pronoun takes the place of a _____.
(51)

21. An _____ is the word to which a pronoun refers.
(51)

22. Place commas and periods where they are needed in this
(40, 52) letter:

Dear Sunny

  Your appointment is at 9 am

    Sincerely

    Bala

Write the appositive in sentences 23 and 24.

✓ **23.** The book my father gave me is full of short stories by his
(48, 49) favorite author, Ray Bradbury.

✓ **24.** Bradbury's classic novel *Fahrenheit 451* takes place in
(48, 49) the future.

✓ **25.** Use an appositive to combine these two sentences into
(48, 49) one longer sentence: One of my favorite books is *To Kill
a Mockingbird*. *To Kill a Mockingbird* isn't about killing
birds.

26. Write the pronoun and its antecedent in this
(51) sentence: Annabel choked when she tried to talk and eat at the same time.

Write the entire verb phrase in sentences 27 and 28.

27. By nightfall, the army will have marched sixteen miles.
(9, 19)

28. The troops have given their best effort all day.
(9, 19)

Diagram sentences 29 and 30.

√ **29.** The soldiers were tired and hungry.
(23, 41)

√ **30.** The security guard gave me keys to the locked gate.
(25, 34)

LESSON
53

Personal Pronouns

Dictation or Journal Entry
Vocabulary:
The word *depreciate* (di-PRE-she-ate) is a verb that means "to lower in estimation or esteem" or "to fall in value." When Kevin told a lie, Sally's opinion of him *depreciated*. A car *depreciates* as its mileage increases.

There are five main categories of pronouns: personal, relative, indefinite, interrogative, and demonstrative. We will begin with personal pronouns.

Just like nouns, **personal pronouns** refer to people and things (and also places, if you think of a place as an "it"). In the following sentences, the personal pronouns are italicized.

I want to see *them.*

Do *you* have *my* hammer?

They say *you* can't take *it* with *you.*

It is the largest county in the state.

There are three forms of personal pronouns: person, number, and case.

Person *First person* is the speaker: *I, me, mine, we, us, ours*

I shall vote today.

We live in a democracy.

That ballot is *mine.*

Second person is the person being spoken to: *you, yours*

Will *you* vote also?

All of *you* are important.

That ballot is *yours.*

Third person is the person being spoken about: *he, she, it, him, her, his, hers*

He and *she* will vote.

They shall vote also.

That ballot is *hers.*

Give *it* to *them.*

Example 1 For each sentence below, write the pronoun and tell whether it is first person, second person, or third person.

(a) We ate spaghetti.

(b) Dale gave her a rose.

(c) Did you finish the assignment?

Solution (a) *We* is **first person.** It indicates the speaker.

(b) *Her* is **third person,** the person being spoken about.

(c) *You* is **second person,** the person being spoken to.

Number Some personal pronouns are <u>singular:</u>

> *I, me, mine, you, yours, he, him, his, she, her, hers, it*

Others are <u>plural:</u>

> *we, us, ours, you, yours, they, them, theirs*

Notice that *you* and *yours* appear in both lists. These words can be either singular or plural. In fact, we won't always be able to tell which is meant.

Example 2 For a–d, write each personal pronoun and tell whether it is singular or plural.

(a) *They* saw the car.   (b) That's *mine.*

(c) Tom lost *his.*   (d) *You* can go now.

Solution (a) *They* is **plural.**   (b) *Mine* is **singular.**

(c) *His* is **singular.**   (d) *You* might be **singular** or **plural.** We can't tell.

Case Just like nouns, pronouns appear in **cases**. We remember that case shows how a noun or pronoun is used in a sentence.

Some pronouns are used as <u>subjects:</u>

> *He* ate snails. *They* ordered some too. *I* refused the offer. Did *she* save the shells?

Others are used as <u>objects:</u>

> Isabel ate **them* also. (direct object)

Robert fed *her the last bite. (indirect object)

Bill paid for all of *us. (object of a preposition)

Some pronouns show *possession*:

Where is *yours?*

Dad ate *his.*

I hid *mine.*

Theirs are green.

Example 3 Tell whether each italicized pronoun shows possession or whether it is used as a subject or an object. If it is an object, tell what kind (direct object, indirect object, object of a preposition).

(a) Christie sent *her* an email.

(b) Yesterday *she* replied to Christie by phone.

(c) Dale asked *him* for a ride.

(d) Sorry, I lost *yours.*

Solution (a) The pronoun *her* is an **indirect object.**

(b) The pronoun *she* is the **subject** of the sentence.

(c) The pronoun *him* is a **direct object.**

(d) The pronoun *yours* shows **possession.**

✓ **Practice** Choose the best word to complete sentences a and b.

a. The word *depreciate* is a (noun, verb, adjective).

b. When something depreciates, it becomes (more, less) valuable.

For sentences c–e, write the personal pronoun and tell whether it is first, second, or third person.

c. Homer agrees with me.

d. She agrees with Homer.

e. Do you agree with Homer?

For f and g, write the personal pronoun and tell whether it is singular or plural.

f. Let us go.   **g.** Take me too.

For h–k, tell whether the italicized personal pronoun is used as a subject, direct object, indirect object, object of a preposition, or whether it shows possession.

h. *I* wonder what will happen today.

i. John greeted *her* at the door.

j. Mom handed *us* the fresh peach pie.

k. That bike is *ours*.

More Practice   Write each personal pronoun from sentences 1–10, and tell whether it is first, second, or third person. Also tell whether it is singular or plural. (Example: 1. we, first person plural; you, second person singular)

1. May we help you?

2. Did they feign ignorance?

3. Please pour him some juice.

4. They're folding their laundry and placing it over there.

5. Will you accept my apology?

6. All the students except her were punctual.

7. We took our frogs to the pond and let them go.

8. I advised them to study diligently.

9. They took my advice and studied hard.

10. She broke the news to us this morning.

11–20. Tell how each pronoun is used in sentences 1–10 above. Write "subject," "object," or "possessive."

Review Set 53 Choose the best word to complete sentences 1–10.

1. (There, They're, Their) running a few minutes late.
(38)

2. The baker put all the spices in the apple pie (accept,
(40) except) for the cinnamon.

3. Some people consider chrome furniture (prodigious,
(44, 20) ultramodern, poor).

4. Several current television shows focus on (incredible,
(29, 32) substitute, postgraduate) feats of strength.

5. The progressive verb tense indicates (completed,
(21) continuing) action.

6. The (positive, comparative, superlative) degree, or basic
(45) form, describes a noun or pronoun without comparing it
to any other.

7. Personal pronouns refer mainly to (people, animals,
(53) things).

8. The personal pronouns *I, me, mine, we, us,* and *ours* refer
(53) to the speaker, or the (first, second, third) person.

9. The personal pronouns *you* and *yours* refer to the person
(53) being spoken to, or the (first, second, third) person.

10. The personal pronouns *he, she, it, him, her, his,* and *hers*
(53) refer to the person being spoken about, or (first, second,
third) person.

11. Tell whether this word group is a fragment, run-on, or
(1, 3) complete sentence: Squids can swim very fast they are
shaped like torpedoes.

12. Write the masculine noun from this list: nurse, buck,
(10) lamb, bush, technician.

13. Write each word that should be capitalized in this
(12, 29) sentence: the amish people, most of whom live in the
east, resist modern conveniences.

14. Replace the underlined action verb in this sentence with
(5) one that is more descriptive: Thousands of prospectors
<u>went</u> to South Africa to find diamonds.

15. Write the article from this sentence: Today, South Africa
(28) is the largest producer of diamonds.

16. Write the comparative and superlative forms of the
(45) positive adjective *large*.

Rewrite 17–21, adding periods, commas, and capital letters as
needed.

17. read henry w longfellow's "the psalm of life" by
(20, 40) tomorrow

18. "zorilla britnii" was the last name on the list
(6, 52)

19. the last entry in the encyclopedia was "zweig arnold"
(12, 52)

20. dear isabel
(29, 52) please use these boxes racks
and hangers for your clothes
        love
        mom

21. thomas gillespie the president of princeton seminary
(6, 49) preached about god's justice and mercy

22. Write and circle the indirect object, then write and star
(25, 35) the direct object of this sentence: In the late 1860s, a Boer
boy gave his mother a diamond from the riverbank.

23. Write the predicate nominative in this sentence: Cecil
(22, 41) Rhodes became the owner of the world's largest diamond
company.

24. Tell whether the underlined verb in this sentence is
(25, 32) transitive or intransitive: Cecil Rhodes <u>made</u> his fortune
in the diamond fields of South Africa.

25. Tell whether the italicized objective case noun in this
(43) sentence is a direct object, an indirect object, or the object
of a preposition: The Boer boy played jacks with the
diamond before taking it to his mother.

Write the appositive in sentences 26 and 27.

26. Cecil Rhodes, a young Englishman, also got involved in
(48, 49) gold mining.

27. The country South Africa proved rich in both gold and
(48, 49) silver.

28. Use an appositive to combine these two choppy
(48, 49) sentences to make one longer one: Cecil Rhodes was a
man with great ambition. Cecil Rhodes went into politics.

29. Write the pronoun and its antecedent from this
(51, 53) sentence: Cecil Rhodes admitted that his greatest
ambition was to increase the power and size of the British
empire.

30. Diagram this sentence: Cecil Rhodes, a fanatical
(25, 48) imperialist, desired more countries for England.

LESSON 54

Irregular Verbs, Part 2

Dictation or Journal Entry
Vocabulary:
Let us examine the words *continuous* and *continual Continuous* refers to something that doesn't stop happening. The *continuous* rain caused mudslides and flooding. *Continual* refers to something that happens again and again. The troubled student exhibited *continual* misbehavior.

Regular verbs form the past tense by adding *d* or *ed* to the present tense of the verb. Irregular verbs form the past tense in different ways. There are no rules for forming the past tense and past participles of these verbs. Fortunately, we recognize the principal parts of most irregular verbs just by hearing them. We must memorize the irregular verb parts that we do not know already.

Irregular verbs cause people trouble because it is easy to confuse the past and past participle.

I had gone (NOT went) to school.

She began (NOT begun) her work on time.

We can group many irregular verbs because they follow similar patterns. Here we list four groups of irregular verbs:

VERB	PAST	PAST PARTICIPLE
1. blow	blew	(has) blown
know	knew	(has) known
throw	threw	(has) thrown
grow	grew	(has) grown
2. bear	bore	(has) borne
tear	tore	(has) torn
wear	wore	(has) worn
swear	swore	(has) sworn
3. begin	began	(has) begun
ring	rang	(has) rung
shrink	shrank	(has) shrunk

Grammar and Writing 6 **275** **Student Edition** Lesson 54

sing	sang	(has) sung
drink	drank	(has) drunk
4. choose	chose	(has) chosen
freeze	froze	(has) frozen
speak	spoke	(has) spoken
break	broke	(has) broken
steal	stole	(has) stolen

Remember, there are many more irregular verbs. Some of them follow the patterns above, but others don't. Always consult the dictionary if you are unsure.

Example Write the correct verb form for sentences a–d.

(a) Jeff has (chose, chosen) his classes for the spring semester.

(b) The howling wind (blew, blown) all night.

(c) The church bells (rang, rung) on the hour.

(d) Victoria has (drank, drunk) all her milk.

Solution (a) Jeff has **chosen** his classes for the spring semester.

(b) The howling wind **blew** all night.

(c) The church bells **rang** on the hour.

(d) Victoria has **drunk** all her milk.

√ **Practice** For a–d, replace each blank with *continual* or *continuous*.

a. The fax machine has _____ breakdowns.

b. Anne in *Anne of Green Gables* chatters _____ly.

c. A _____ noise in a car's engine signals a need to see a mechanic.

d. Finding a substitute for a regular classroom teacher is a _____ frustration for the principal.

For e–l, write the correct verb form for each sentence.

e. The fifth grader (knew, known) the capital of every state in the United States.

f. The juror was (swore, sworn) in for the trial.

g. The rock has (sank, sunk) to the bottom of the pool.

h. Just as Grandpa predicted, the farm pond had (froze, frozen) by mid-January.

i. I have (wore, worn) out my shoes.

j. Austin (swore, sworn) to tell the truth.

k. Lucius had (grew, grown) weary of her chatter.

l. My sweater (shrank, shrunk) when I washed it.

For m–z, write the past and past participle of each verb.

m. blow   **n.** know   **o.** throw   **p.** grow

q. bear   **r.** tear   **s.** wear   **t.** swear

u. begin   **v.** ring   **w.** sing   **x.** drink

y. choose   **z.** speak

Review Set 54 Choose the best word to complete sentences 1–9.

1. The (poors, pours, pores) in our skin provide openings
(34) for drops of perspiration to cool our bodies.

2. My (principle, principal) reason for coming was to see
(43) you.

3. Valuable (oars, ors, ores) include such metals as iron,
(33) copper, and silver.

4. Popeye ate a (hole, whole) can of spinach for strength to
(24) rescue the victims.

5. (Nouns, Verbs, Conjunctions) are connecting words.
(37, 39)

6. *I, me, mine, you, yours, he, him, his, she, her, hers,* and *it*
(53) are (singular, plural) personal pronouns.

7. *We, us, ours, you, yours, they, them,* and *theirs* are
(53) (singular, plural) personal pronouns.

8. Pronoun (number, case) shows how the pronoun is being
(53) used in the sentence.

9. Some pronouns are used as subjects; some pronouns
(53) show possession; and some are used as (objects, nouns,
verbs) such as direct objects, indirect objects, and objects
of prepositions.

10. Make a complete sentence from this fragment: The coat
(4) on the hanger.

11. Write the plural of the noun *peony*.
(13, 14)

For sentences 12 and 13, tell whether the underlined verb is
action or linking.

12. The talkative child <u>grew</u> quiet when an unknown person
(5, 22) entered the room.

13. The boy's foot <u>grew</u> two sizes in six months.
(5, 22)

14. Write each word that should be capitalized in this letter:
(12, 29)
dear father-in-law jeremy,

thirty-five years ago, you planted an oak tree in the
spring. it is still thriving.

gratefully,
son-in-law francis

15. Write the past and past participle of each verb.
(54)
(a) freeze   (b) break   (c) steal

Write the correct verb form for sentences 16–19.

16. The friends have (knew, known) each other for thirty
(54) years.

17. Robert (grew, grown) several inches last year.
(54)

18. Molly's dog had (tore, torn) her homework paper.
(54)

19. Has the vivacious lady (sang, sung) yet?
(54)

20. Write the comparative and superlative forms of adjectives
(45, 46) a and b.

(a) loyal   (b) happy

21. Add periods and commas as needed in this
(40, 47) sentence: The abbreviations for the days of the week
are Sun Mon Tue Wed Thurs Fri and Sat

Replace each blank with the correct word to complete
sentences 22 and 23.

22. We can group nouns into three cases: _____,
(42) objective, and possessive.

23. A noun is in the nominative case when it is the subject of
(42) a sentence or when it is used as a _____
nominative.

24. Tell whether the italicized objective case noun in this
(43) sentence is a direct object, an indirect object, or the object
of the preposition: Peter Lassen guided *settlers* through
the Cascade Mountains in the 1800s.

Write each appositive in sentences 25 and 26.

25. Lassen Peak, a 10,457-foot volcano, is named after Peter
(48, 49) Lassen.

26. The Atsugewi, an American Indian group, met in the
(48, 49) Lassen area.

27. Use an appositive to combine these two choppy
(48) sentences into one longer sentence: Lassen Peak is a
volcano in Northern California. Lassen Peak erupted from
1914 to 1921.

28. Tell whether the italicized pronoun in this sentence is
(53) used as a subject or an object: Aunt Dottie sent *her* a
telegram.

Diagram sentences 29 and 30.

29. The four types of volcanoes are cinder cones, composite
(23, 41) volcanoes, shield volcanoes, and plug domes.

30. Lassen Peak, a plug dome, is one of the world's largest
(41, 48) volcanoes.

LESSON 55

Nominative Pronoun Case

Dictation or Journal Entry

Vocabulary:
Invalid means two things. When pronounced IN-ve-lid, it refers to one who suffers from a disease or disability. The *invalid* remained in bed for a week. *Invalid* (pronounced in-VAL-id) means "not valid," or "without foundation in fact, truth, or law." Because the contract had never been signed, it was declared *invalid*.

Nominative Case

We remember that nouns can be grouped into three cases: nominative, objective, and possessive. We also remember that the same is true of pronouns. In this lesson we will concentrate on the **nominative case.** A pronoun used as a subject or predicate nominative is in the nominative case.

She lives next door. (subject)

The girl next door is *she.* (predicate nominative)

I baked the cake. (subject)

It was *I* who baked the cake. (predicate nominative)

He will be late. (subject)

It is *he* who will be late. (predicate nominative)

We are the grammar experts. (subject)

The grammar experts are *we.* (predicate nominative)

Example 1 Complete this chart by replacing each blank with the correct nominative case pronoun.

Number	Person		Nominative Case (subject or predicate nominative)
Singular	First		_____
	Second		_____
	Third	(masc.)	_____
		(fem.)	_____
		(neuter)	_____
Plural	First		_____
	Second		_____
	Third		_____

Solution   We complete the chart as follows:

NUMBER	PERSON		NOMINATIVE CASE (subject or predicate nominative)
Singular	First		I
	Second		you
	Third	(masc.)	he
		(fem.)	she
		(neuter)	it
Plural	First		we
	Second		you
	Third		they

Subjects   These sentences use nominative case personal pronouns as subjects:

I wrote Mary a letter.

He joined the team.

When we use the pronoun *I* as part of a compound subject, it is polite to refer to ourselves last:

Deanne and *I* share many of the same beliefs.

Sherry and *I* are sisters.

Example 2   Which sentence is more polite?

Both we and they hope it rains.

Both they and we hope it rains.

Solution   It is more polite to refer to ourselves (we) last.

Both they and we hope it rains.

Example 3   Write a sentence using a nominative case personal pronoun as a subject.

Solution   Your answer will be unique. Here are some correct examples:

We can memorize these pronouns.

They won the basketball game.

Barbara and *she* returned safely.

Predicate Nominatives These sentences use nominative case personal pronouns as predicate nominatives.

The owner is *he* in the black suit.

The guest who brought the soda is *she*.

Predicate nominatives can also be compound:

The painters are Marilyn and *he*.

The violinists will be *she* and *I*.

Example 4 Write a sentence using a nominative case pronoun as a predicate nominative.

Solution Your answer will be unique. Here are some correct examples:

It was *I* who ate all the chocolate.

The best candidate is *he*.

Your chefs tonight will be *they* and *I*.

Practice **a.** Study the nominative case pronoun chart from Example 1. Then try to reproduce it from memory. You may abbreviate (1st, 2nd, 3rd, sing., pl., etc.).

b. Unscramble these words to make a sentence with a personal pronoun as a subject:

friends   faithful   they   are

c. Unscramble these words to make a sentence with a personal pronoun as a predicate nominative:

writer   best   she   was   the

For d and e, replace each blank with the correct word.

d. If a person is an _____, he or she suffers from a disease or disability.

e. When something is without foundation in fact, truth, or law, we say it is _____.

f. Write the sentence that is more polite:

I and she will come.

She and I will come.

g. Write each nominative case pronoun from this list: me, him, I, she, them, they, he, her, we, us.

Choose the nominative case pronoun for sentences h–k.

h. The person in the photo is (he, him).

i. The fastest runners were Christie and (her, she).

j. The man in the green sweatshirt was (him, he).

k. It is (I, me).

Review Set 55

Choose the best word to complete sentences 1–6.

1. The (affect, effect) of yeast on dough is to make it "rise,"
(27) or double in size.

2. The (diagonal, diameter, dialogue) of a circle cuts the
(35) circle into two equal half-circles.

3. The captain wisely used (discretion, injustice, reliance)
(31, 36) when choosing his team.

4. At the sight of blood, the rector (razed, fainted, set).
(28, 46)

5. A (clause, phrase) is a group of words with a subject and
(2, 24) a predicate.

6. Nouns that show possession or ownership are in the
(10, 42) (nominative, objective, possessive) case.

7. Write the plural form of *goose.*
(13, 14)

8. Write each prepositional phrase and star the object of
(17, 33) each preposition in this sentence: Squids suck water into
their bodies, squeeze it through a funnel, and propel
themselves like missiles through the ocean.

9. Write the entire verb phrase in this sentence and
(5, 9) underline each helping verb: With their water jets,
squids can escape sea lions and birds.

10. Write the past tense and past participle of the irregular
(54) verb *wear.*

For 11 and 12, write the comparative and superlative forms of
each irregular comparison adjective.

11. bad   **12.** many or much
(45, 46)

13. Rewrite this sentence, adding commas as
(47) needed: Father's Day fell on Sunday June 17 in the year 2001.

14. Write the missing coordinating conjunctions in this
(37) list: and, _____, or, _____, for, yet, _____.

For sentences 15 and 16, tell whether the italicized noun is in the nominative or possessive case.

15. The *squid's* two extra tentacles are used to capture
(10, 42) fast-moving food like shrimp and fish.

16. The market squid is the most common *species*.
(4, 42)

17. Tell whether the italicized objective case noun in this
(35, 43) sentence is a direct object, an indirect object, or the object of the preposition: The squid's arms bring its *beak* the captured food.

For sentences 18 and 19, write each appositive.

18. The colors brown and red mean the squid is either
(48, 49) frightened or excited.

19. Market squids, an easy catch, are captured in nets.
(48, 49)

20. Use an appositive to combine these two choppy
(48, 49) sentences to make one longer sentence: My birthday is in July. July is the hottest month of the year.

21. Write the pronoun and its antecedent in this
(51) sentence: Winnie gave her cookie to a friend.

For sentences 22–24, write each personal pronoun and tell whether it is first, second, or third person. Also tell whether it is singular or plural.

22. That watch is mine.
(51, 53)

23. They agree to the selling price of the house.
(51, 53)

24. Gayle offered you a piece of boysenberry pie.
(51, 53)

25. Reproduce the nominative case pronoun chart from
(55) Example 1. You may abbreviate (1st, 2nd, 3rd, sing., pl., etc.).

√ **26.** Unscramble these words to make a sentence with a

$^{(53,\ 55)}$ personal pronoun as a subject.

belongs to it Henrietta

√ **27.** Unscramble these words to make a sentence with a

$^{(53,\ 55)}$ personal pronoun as a predicate nominative.

race you winner the the was of

28. Write the sentence that is more polite (a or b).

$^{(48,\ 49)}$ (a) I and you are invited to the grand opening.

(b) You and I are invited to the grand opening.

29. Write the second person, singular or plural, personal

$^{(53,\ 55)}$ pronoun.

√ **30.** Diagram this sentence: Our guides are she and he.

$^{(41,\ 55)}$

LESSON 56

The Comma, Part 4: Introductory and Interrupting Elements, Afterthoughts, Clarity

> **Dictation or Journal Entry**
>
> **Vocabulary:**
> The homophones *your* and *you're* (pronounced yôr) cause some people difficulty. *Your* means "belonging to you." Please put *your* name on *your* paper. *You're* is a contraction of "you are." *You're* intelligent.

Comma = Pause   When we speak, we often pause between words. If we wrote down exactly what we were saying, most of those pauses would be indicated by commas. Pauses usually occur when we insert words or phrases that interrupt the natural flow of the sentence. Notice how commas are used to offset the italicized words, phrases, and clauses in the sentences below.

> *No,* I would not like to live in the desert.

> There are, *I assume,* people who feel differently.

> The mountains are more hospitable, *after all.*

These sentences demonstrate the natural pauses that occur with introductory elements, interrupting elements, and afterthoughts. Let's look at each of these elements.

Introductory Elements   An **introductory element** begins a sentence. It sometimes expresses the writer's attitude about what is being said. An introductory element can also be a request or command.

> *Yes,* I stayed up too late studying last night.

> *On the other hand,* I managed to read the whole book.

> *Obviously,* you didn't get enough sleep.

> *Please remember,* I thought I was doing the right thing.

Example 1   Rewrite these sentences, using commas to offset introductory phrases.

(a) Amazingly that cat slept in the same spot all day.

(b) In my opinion she is the laziest cat in the neighborhood.

Solution   (a) "Amazingly" is an introductory element. We offset it with a comma.

Amazingly, that cat slept in the same spot all day.

(b) The phrase "In my opinion" is an introductory element. We offset it with a comma.

In my opinion, she is the laziest cat in the neighborhood.

Interrupting Elements An **interrupting element** appears in the middle of a sentence, interrupting the flow from subject to verb to object. An interrupting element can be removed without changing the meaning of the sentence.

Deserts, *it would seem*, are home to many species.

Catch the camels, *if you can*, before they find the gate.

Beverly, *not Jane*, was going to search for water.

Example 2 Rewrite these sentences, using commas to offset interrupting phrases.

(a) How in the world you ask did we finish on time?

(b) I wanted pizza not spaghetti for dinner.

Solution (a) We look for a word or phrase that interrupts the flow of the sentence and can be removed without changing its meaning. (It's not unusual to find that you must read the sentence two or three times in order to decide.) In this sentence, the phrase "you ask" is an interrupting element, so we offset it with commas.

How in the world, **you ask,** did we finish on time?

(b) The phrase "not spaghetti" is an interrupting element. We offset it with commas.

I wanted pizza, **not spaghetti,** for dinner.

Afterthoughts **Afterthoughts** are similar to introductory and interrupting elements except that they are added to the ends of sentences.

The box is still on the porch, *by the way.*

Second place was just fine, *thank you.*

Her father will chaperone, *if I remember correctly.*

Some afterthoughts turn the sentence into a question:

It's not too late to order tickets, *is it?*

Pass me that screwdriver, *would you?*

We all have to do our part, *don't we?*

Example 3 Rewrite these sentences, using commas to offset afterthoughts.

    (a) Green means "go" of course.

    (b) You don't wear shoes to bed do you?

Solution (a) The phrase "of course" is an afterthought, so we offset it with a comma.

    Green means "go," **of course.**

    (b) The questioning phrase "do you" is an afterthought. We offset it with a comma.

    You don't wear shoes to bed, **do you?**

Clarity To *clarify* is to "make clear." When something is clear, it has *clarity*. We use commas to separate words, phrases, or clauses in order to **clarify meaning**, or to "make clear" the meaning of our sentences. Without commas, the meaning of the sentences below is unclear.

    UNCLEAR: To Jesse James was always a problem.
    CLEAR: To Jesse, James was always a problem.

    UNCLEAR: Shortly after the old barn collapsed.
    CLEAR: Shortly after, the old barn collapsed.

Example 4 Rewrite each sentence, using commas to clarify meaning.
    (a) During the week it snowed.

    (b) To Bob the plumber was a lifesaver.

Solution (a) Without a comma, this sentence seems incomplete. During the week it snowed... *what?* They missed school? We built a snowman? To avoid confusion, we insert a comma to clarify our intended meaning:

    During the week, it snowed.

    (b) Is Bob a plumber? If we read the sentence carefully, we see that he is not. A comma makes this much clearer.

    To Bob, the plumber was a lifesaver.

✓ **Practice** Rewrite sentences a and b, inserting commas to offset introductory elements.

    a. Yes I've heard that the Arabian camel can go without water for over two weeks.

    b. Of course a horse cannot do that.

Rewrite sentences c and d, inserting commas to offset interrupting elements.

c. The jackrabbit I believe cools itself on the hot deserts through his tall, thin ears.

d. The camel it is said is a difficult animal to ride.

Rewrite sentences e and f, using commas to clarify meaning.

e. Of all the ideas rafting the river was our favorite.

f. When we were through the glass door sparkled.

For g–k, replace each blank with *your* or *you're*.

g. The contraction for "you are" is _____.

h. The word that means "belonging to you" is _____.

i. _____ likely to succeed if you keep trying.

j. Here is _____ coat.

k. When I finally arrived, my friend said to me, "_____ late!"

More Practice See "More Practice Lesson 56" in Student Workbook.

Review Set 56 Choose the best word to complete sentences 1–8.

1. Admiring the beauty and grandeur of the giant redwoods
(49) gives one a sense of (peace, piece).

2. William Shakespeare is a famous play(right, write,
(50) wright, rite).

3. The band of (fracture, fraction, fractious) coyotes caused
(51) anxiety in the camp.

4. (May, Can) I become computer-literate in one day?
(48)

5. In the 1800s, Japan was (little, less, least) developed than
(45, 46) Europe.

6. People (do, does) not know what will happen tomorrow.
(7, 15)

7. Nouns or pronouns that show possession or ownership
(42, 43) are in the (nominative, objective, possessive) case.

8. We diagram pronouns in the same way we diagram
(51) (verbs, nouns, conjunctions).

9. Write the plural form of *jack-o'-lantern*.
(13, 14)

10. Tell whether this sentence is declarative, interrogative,
(1, 3) imperative, or exclamatory: For two centuries, the
Japanese had been sealed off from the rest of the world.

Rewrite 11 and 12, adding capital letters as needed.

11. the cabreras and i visited hoover dam and lake mead on
(6, 12) our visit to nevada.

12. william shakespeare wrote these lines in *king lear*:
(6, 12) men must endure
their going hence, even as their coming hither.
ripeness is all.

13. Write five missing prepositions from this list. Refer to
(17, 18) Lesson 17, if necessary. aboard, _____, above,
across, _____, against, along, _____, amid,
among, around, _____, before, _____, below

14. Write each adjective from this sentence: No new goods or
(27, 28) ideas could enter Japan because oppressive leaders
forbade it.

Tell whether the underlined verb in sentences 15 and 16 is
transitive or intransitive.

15. Steam <u>poured</u> from the ship's chimneys.
(25, 32)

16. The ship's chimneys <u>poured</u> steam into the air.
(25, 32)

17. Write the seven common coordinating conjunctions.
(37)

18. Write the correlative conjunctions in this sentence:
(39) Neither the Japanese leaders nor the people expected the
U.S. warships.

For 19–21, tell whether the italicized noun is in the
nominative or possessive case. If it is in the nominative case,
tell whether it is the subject of the sentence or a predicate
nominative.

19. The *United States* sent Commodore Matthew Perry to
(42, 43) meet with the Japanese leaders.

20. *Perry's* steamships convinced the Japanese to begin
(42, 43) trading with the United States.

21. Commodore Perry was the American *representative*.
(42, 43)

22. Rewrite this sentence, adding periods and commas as
(40, 47) needed: Ayeesha's address is 327 W Longden Ave
Eureka Kansas

23. Write the appositive in this sentence: For several
(48, 49) hundred years, Japan had been ruled by the shogun, a
military dictator.

Replace each blank with the correct word to complete
sentences 24 and 25.

24. A _____ is a word that takes the place of a noun so
(51) that we do not have to use the same noun over and over
again.

25. We can group pronouns into three cases: _____,
(53, 55) _____, and possessive.

26. Write each nominative case pronoun from this list: me,
(53, 55) him, I, she, them, they, he, her, we, us.

27. Unscramble these words to make a sentence that uses a
(53, 55) personal pronoun as an object of a preposition:

    me   for   waited   driver   bus   the

For 28 and 29, tell whether the italicized pronoun is
nominative, objective, or possessive case.

28. *She* sprinkled Roxanne with water.
(53, 55)

29. Cerissa gave *him* another chance.
(53, 55)

30. Diagram this sentence: He and I gave her the clothes and
(38, 41) food.

Objective Pronoun Case

Dictation or Journal Entry
Vocabulary:
Let us learn to use the words *lend* and *borrow* correctly. When we *borrow* something, we take it. May I *borrow* one cup of sugar? When we *lend* something, we give it. I will *lend* you my garden hose.

We have learned that pronouns used as subjects and predicate nominatives are in the **nominative case**, and that pronouns that show possession are in the **possessive case**. In this lesson, we will focus on the **objective case**.

Pronouns are in the **objective case** when they are used as direct objects, indirect objects, or objects of a preposition.

Kurt was watching *me*. (direct object)

Pass *me* the potatoes. (indirect object)

You can ride with *me*. (object of a preposition)

Please take *them* to the airport. (direct object)

Did you give *them* directions? (indirect object)

I'll sit by *them*. (object of a preposition)

I think Mrs. Seifert likes *us*. (direct object)

Will somebody please cook *us* dinner? (indirect object)

These supplies belong to *us*. (object of a preposition)

Example 1 Complete this chart by replacing each blank with the correct objective case pronoun.

NUMBER	PERSON		OBJECTIVE CASE (direct object, indirect object, or object of a preposition)
Singular	First		_____
	Second		_____
	Third	(masc.)	_____
		(fem.)	_____
		(neuter)	_____
Plural	First		_____
	Second		_____
	Third		_____

Solution   We complete the chart as follows:

NUMBER	PERSON		OBJECTIVE CASE (direct object, indirect object, or object of a preposition)
Singular	First		me
	Second		you
	Third	(masc.)	him
		(fem.)	her
		(neuter)	it
Plural	First		us
	Second		you
	Third		them

Direct Objects   The following sentences use personal pronouns as direct objects. We remember to use objective case pronouns.

My dog chased *her.* (not *she*)

Jim's sister hugged Jim and *me.* (not *I*)

Benito warned *them.* (not *they*)

Example 2   Write a sentence using a personal pronoun as a direct object.

Solution   Your answer will be unique. Here are some correct examples:

Hector didn't recognize *him.*

Gloria will call Randy and *her.*

The cat wouldn't eat *it.*

Indirect Objects   These sentences use personal pronouns as indirect objects. Note that the pronouns are in the objective case.

Mrs. Peacock gave *her* a book. (not *she*)

Lucy loaned Robert and *me* a dollar. (not *I*)

Christie baked *us* a pumpkin pie. (not *we*)

Example 3   Write a sentence using an objective case personal pronoun as an indirect object.

Solution Your answer will be unique. Here are some correct examples:

Jan will tell *her* the story.

Colonel Mustard sent *them* a clue.

Arnold read Agnes and *him* the article.

Objects of a Preposition The sentences below use personal pronouns as objects of a preposition. The pronouns are in the objective case.

The author read his book to *them*. (not *they*)

Professor Plum waited for *me*. (not *I*)

The goose flew over *us*. (not *we*)

Example 4 Write a sentence using a personal pronoun as an object of a preposition.

Solution Your answer will be unique. Here are some correct examples:

The goose landed near *them*.

Gabi collected money from *us*.

My uncle sat behind *me*.

Compound Objects Objective case pronouns can be compound. We politely mention ourselves last.

Mom hugged *him* and *me*. (compound direct object)

Jim gave *her* and *him* a present. (compound indirect object)

The bicyclist veered around *them* and *us*.
(compound object of a preposition)

Example 5 Choose the sentence that is both correct and polite.

She sliced a bagel for me and him.

She sliced a bagel for he and I.

She sliced a bagel for him and me.

She sliced a bagel for him and I.

Solution The objective case pronouns are *him* and *me*. Also, we politely mention ourselves last.

She sliced a bagel for him and me.

√ **Practice**   **a.** Study the objective case pronoun chart from Example 1. Then try to reproduce it from memory.

b. Unscramble these words to make a sentence with a personal pronoun as a direct object:

wind   the   blew   down   her

c. Unscramble these words to make a sentence with a personal pronoun as an indirect object:

sang   John   lullaby   a   me

d. Unscramble these words to make a sentence with a personal pronoun as an object of a preposition:

sung   has   he   us   to

For e–h, replace each blank with *lend* or *borrow*.

e. Please _____ me five dollars.

f. You may _____ our lawn mower to mow your lawn.

g. Students are permitted to _____ books from the school library.

h. Ruth's parents will _____ her their car for the field trip.

i. Write the sentence that is more polite.

Don't overlook me or him.
Don't overlook him or me.

j. Write each objective case pronoun from this list:

me	him	I	she	them
they	he	her	we	us

Choose the objective case pronoun for sentences k–m.

k. The goose bit James and (he, him).

l. I'll give Jayne and (him, he) the soup recipe.

m. The boa wrapped itself around Hung and (me, I).

1. Study the nominative case pronoun chart from Lesson 55. (55) From memory, reproduce the nominative case pronoun chart.

2. From memory, reproduce the objective case pronoun (57) chart.

Choose the best word to complete sentences 3–8.

3. Because the certification had expired, it was (prodigious, (20, 55) invalid, continual).

4. The selling price of machinery (fractures, breaks, (51, 53) depreciates) with age and use.

5. A (direct, indirect) object follows an action verb and tells (25, 35) who or what receives the action.

6. A (preposition, coordinating conjunction, pronoun) (37) connects a word to a word, a phrase to a phrase, or a clause to a clause.

7. I'll bet (your, you're) smarter than you think you are. (56)

8. (Your, You're) keys unlock every door in the house. (56)

9. Write the simple predicate in this sentence: Orpheus, a (2, 5) son of one of the Muses, played the lyre, a stringed instrument.

10. Write the abstract noun from this list: son, goddess, (8) forest, animals, charisma.

11. Rewrite this outline, adding capital letters and periods as (20, 36) needed:
    i william shakespeare
       a *king lear*
       b *the merchant of venice*

12. Replace each blank with the missing prepositions from (17, 18) Lesson 18: inside, _____, like, near, _____, off, _____, onto, opposite, _____, outside, over, past, regarding, _____, save

13. Write the demonstrative adjective from this sentence: (28) This instrument soothed wild beasts.

14. Write the overused adjective in the sentence below. Then write one that is more descriptive.

(27, 50)

People thought Orpheus's music was good.

15. Write the four principal parts (present tense, present participle, past tense, and past participle) of the verb *charm*.

(7, 16)

16. Write the direct object in this sentence: Orpheus loved Eurydice, a lovely maiden.

(2, 25)

Replace each blank with the correct word to complete sentences 17–20.

17. We can group nouns into three cases: nominative, _____, and _____.

(42, 43)

18. When a noun is used as a direct object, an indirect object, or the object of a preposition, it is in the _____ case.

(42, 43)

19. The word to which a pronoun refers is called the _____.

(51)

20. A pronoun used as a subject or predicate nominative is in the _____ case.

(53, 55)

For sentences 21–23, tell whether the italicized noun is a direct object, an indirect object, or an object of a preposition.

21. Eurydice was bitten by a venomous *snake* on her and Orpheus's wedding day.

(33, 43)

22. Orpheus played *Pluto* his charming music.

(35, 43)

23. Pluto gave *Eurydice* back to Orpheus.

(25, 43)

24. Choose the nominative case pronoun for this sentence: This is (she, her).

(53, 55)

25. Unscramble these words to make a sentence with a personal pronoun as an indirect object:

(53, 57)

sent   caterer   menu   the   them   a

26. Tell whether the italicized pronoun in this sentence is
(55, 57) nominative, objective, or possessive case: *She* howled
with laughter.

27. Write the appositive in this sentence: Cerberus, the
(48, 49) three-headed watchdog of the underworld, guarded the
world of the dead.

Diagram sentences 28–30.

28. Eurydice, a lovely maiden, both rejoiced and suffered.
(23, 48)

29. She sent him and me the letter.
(25, 33)

30. The nurse gave me an ointment for poison ivy.
(33, 35)

Personal Pronoun Case Forms

Case Forms   The following chart helps us to sort out the three personal pronoun **case forms**: (1) If a pronoun is a subject or predicate nominative, it is *nominative case*. (2) A pronoun used as a direct object, indirect object, or object of a preposition is *objective case*. (3) If a pronoun shows possession, it is *possessive case*.

NUMBER	PERSON	CASE		
		NOMINATIVE	OBJECTIVE	POSSESSIVE
Singular	First	I	me	mine
	Second	you	you	yours
	Third (masc.)	he	him	his
	(fem.)	she	her	hers
	(neuter)	it	it	its
Plural	First	we	us	ours
	Second	you	you	yours
	Third	they	them	theirs

Example 1   Tell whether each italicized pronoun is nominative, objective, or possessive case.

(a) Gerry, Kay, and *she* laughed.

(b) Mariya tickled *her.*

(c) *Yours* is on the counter.

Solution   (a) **nominative case**

(b) **objective case**

(c) **possessive case**

The pronoun case form depends on how the pronoun is used in the sentence. We refer to the chart to decide which pronoun is correct for this sentence:

(We, Us) trumpet players will lead the parade.

The pronoun *we* identifies "trumpet players," which is the subject of the sentence. We use the nominative case pronoun *we* (NOT *us*) as a subject. Therefore, we write:

We trumpet players will lead the parade.

Example 2 Tell how the pronoun is used in each sentence (subject, direct object, indirect object, object of a preposition, or possession).
(a) Irina thanked *him* for the spinach.

(b) That plate is *hers.*

(c) *We* served Kristina another helping.

(d) Karina gave *her* a fork.

(e) Tucker and Tim laughed at *them.*

Solution (a) *Him* is a **direct object.**

(b) *Hers* shows **possession.**

(c) *We* is the **subject.**

(d) *Her* is an **indirect object.**

(e) *Them* is an **object of a preposition.**

Example 3 Determine how the pronoun is used in each sentence. Then refer to the chart on page 300 to help you choose the correct pronoun. Rewrite each sentence correctly.
(a) The class elected Edward and (*he, him*).

(b) Both Bob and (*she, her*) have read the book.

(c) The card was addressed to Delilah and (*she, her*).

Solution   (a) The pronoun is a **direct object,** so we choose the objective case pronoun **him.**

The class elected Edward and *him.*

(b) The pronoun is the **subject** of the sentence, so we choose the nominative case pronoun **she.**

Both Bob and *she* have read the book.

(c) The pronoun is an **object of the preposition** *to,* so we choose the objective case pronoun **her.**

The card was addressed to Delilah and *her.*

√ Practice   For a–c, tell whether the pronoun is nominative, objective, or possessive case.

   a. Luke noticed *her.*

   b. *He* imitated a parrot.

   c. The window he broke was *hers.*

For d–h, tell how the pronoun is used in each sentence (subject, direct object, indirect object, object of a preposition, or possession).

   d. The manatee rolled over *me.*

   e. *I* gasped.

   f. A bee stung *him.*

   g. Tom tossed *her* the football.

   h. That touchdown was *hers.*

For i and j, choose the correct pronoun.

   i. The Stothers and (*they, them*) like flowers.

   j. Charlie giggled at Maggie and (*I, me*).

For k–n, replace each blank with *rise* or *raise.*

   k. Tomorrow, the sun will _____ at 5:55 a.m.

   l. The hotel is going to _____ its rates.

m. Who wants to _____ the flag?

n. You may _____ from your seat when the speaker is finished.

Review Set 58

Choose the best word to complete sentences 1–7.

1. A new car is often more (respectful, considerate, reliable) than an old one.
(1, 3)

2. The prefix *homo-* means "(same, one, before)."
(4, 13)

3. Someone needs to empty the (waste, waist)basket.
(5)

4. The contractor purchased both fine and (course, coarse) sandpaper.
(8)

5. The (direct, indirect) object tells to whom or for whom the action was done.
(25, 35)

6. Our gate is (more tall, taller) than theirs.
(45, 46)

7. Can you believe I have (wore, worn) these socks three days in a row?
(54)

8. Tell whether this word group is a fragment, run-on, or complete sentence: Narcissus, vain and conceited.
(3)

9. Write the possessive noun in this sentence: The conceited man's beauty melted the heart of a lovely nymph named Echo.
(10, 28)

10. Write each word that should be capitalized in this sentence: annette shouted, "grandpa, I'm going to play first base this season!"
(12, 20)

Replace each blank with the correct word to complete sentences 11–13.

11. The noun or pronoun that follows the preposition is called the _____ of the preposition.
(25, 57)

12. The _____ of the noun explains how the noun is used in a sentence.
(42)

13. Pronouns are in the _____ case when they are
(57) used as direct objects, indirect objects, or objects of a
preposition.

14. Write the proper adjective in this sentence: In one Greek
(30) myth, Echo follows Narcissus everywhere.

15. Write the action verb in this sentence: The nymph Echo
(5, 7) repeated words.

16. Write the future perfect progressive verb phrase in this
(9, 21) sentence: Juno will have been punishing Echo for
protecting Jupiter.

17. Write the coordinating conjunction from this
(37) sentence: Narcissus looked into a silvery pool and fell in
love with his own reflection.

For sentences 18–20, tell whether the italicized noun is
nominative, objective, or possessive case.

18. *Echo's* love for Narcissus destroyed everything except
(42, 43) Echo's voice.

19. *Narcissus* could not tear himself away from his
(42, 43) reflection.

20. Where Narcissus died, there grew a flower with a yellow
(42, 43) *center* and white petals.

Rewrite 21 and 22 and add commas and periods as needed.

✓ **21.** Apollo Daphne Orpheus Eurydice Echo and Narcissus
(36, 47) are all characters from Greek myths

22. Dear Adrienne
(36, 52)   School will begin on September 9 2001
                         Your friend
                         Michelle

Write the antecedent of the italicized pronoun in sentences
23 and 24.

✓ **23.** The supervisor watched *his* employees complete the job.
(51, 58)

✓ **24.** When Marta has a test, *she* studies diligently.
(51, 55)

25. Reproduce the nominative case pronoun chart from
(55) Lesson 55.

26. Unscramble these words to make a sentence with a
√ (53, 57) personal pronoun as a direct object:

me   my   rescued   brother

For sentences 27 and 28, tell whether the italicized pronoun is nominative, objective, or possessive case.

27. *We* volunteered to give blood to the Red Cross.
(56, 58)

28. The farmers depended on *them.*
(56, 58)

Diagram sentences 29 and 30.

√ **29.** My computer is faster.
(23, 44)

30. Narcissus broke Echo's heart.
√ (25, 28)

Diagramming Pronouns

Dictation or Journal Entry

Vocabulary:
Devise (pronounced di-VYZ or dee-VYZ) is a verb that means "to work out" or "to think up." Please *devise* a plan to finish your homework on time. *Sibling* (pronounced SIB-ling) is a noun that means "a brother or a sister." Your brothers and sisters are your *siblings*.

As you may have already noticed, we diagram pronouns in the same way we diagram nouns.

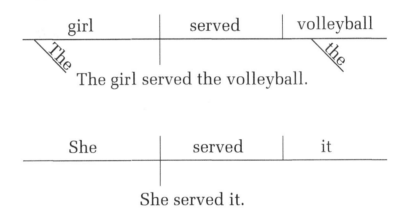

The girl served the volleyball.

She	served	it

She served it.

Diagramming a sentence helps us determine which pronoun to use because it clearly shows *how* the pronoun is used in the sentence. We diagram the sentence below to help us choose the correct pronoun:

Samuel waited for my brother and (*I, me*).

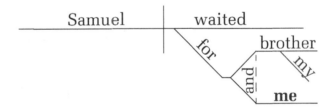

We see from the diagram that the pronoun is an object of the preposition *for*, so we choose the objective case pronoun *me*.

Samuel waited for my brother and *me*.

Note: For some reason, we are more likely to use the wrong pronoun when it is part of a compound subject or object, as in the sentence above. If we remove the other half of the subject or object, the correct pronoun is usually obvious:

Samuel waited for ~~my brother and~~ (I, me).

Our ears tell us that "waited for me" is correct. "Waited for I" does not sound right; it is incorrect.

Example Diagram the following sentence in order to choose the correct pronoun. Then rewrite the sentence correctly.

Julius and (*he, him*) might play football.

Solution We diagram the sentence this way:

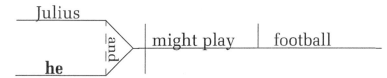

We see from our diagram that the pronoun is part of the subject of the sentence, so we choose the nominative case pronoun *he*.

Julius and *he* might play football.

Practice Diagram sentences a–c, choosing the correct pronoun.

a. Michael and (*him, he*) play water polo.

b. Dana wrote Dan and (*me, I*) a letter.

c. The president called Lucy and (*she, her*).

Replace each blank with the correct vocabulary word.

d. A _____ is a brother or a sister.

e. To _____ something means "to work it out or think it up."

f. The politician wants to _____ a better system for health care.

g. Young Olaf, an only child, felt lonely because he had no _____.

Review Set 59 Choose the best word to complete sentences 1–7.

1. People will value your (substitute, integrity, dishonor).
(6, 14)

2. If you (persevere, waste, discipline), you will complete your work.
(5, 16)

3. (Who's, Whose) idea was that?
(19)

4. Let's keep the surprise (among, between) you and me!
(17)

5. Grace is fast, but Libby is (more fast, faster, fastest).
(45, 46)

6. Thursday was undoubtedly the (most hot, hottest) day
(45, 46) this week.

7. To his friends, Pygmalion (reply, replies), "Never again
(7, 16) shall I fashion marble into shapes of beauty."

8. Rewrite and correct this run-on sentence: Once there
(3) lived a sculptor named Pygmalion he made statues of the
finest design.

9. Write the plural of *stingray*.
(13, 14)

10. Write each word that should be capitalized in this
(26, 29) sentence: i did not find as many spanish-speaking
people in the north as i did in the west.

11. Write the prepositional phrase in this sentence, and star
(17, 33) the object of the preposition: Pygmalion worked all day
at his art.

12. Write the predicate adjectives in this sentence:
(27, 44) Pygmalion was content and happy staring at his marble
statue.

13. Write the past perfect tense verb phrase from this
(9, 19) sentence: Pygmalion had loved his statue so intensely
that Venus brought Galatea, the statue, to life.

14. Write the indirect object in this sentence: Galatea gave
(25, 35) Pygmalion a gentle embrace.

Replace each blank with the correct word to complete
sentences 15–17.

15. Correlative _____ connect parts of a sentence and
(39) always come in pairs.

16. When used as the subject of a sentence, a noun is in the
(42) _____ case.

17. _____ pronouns refer mainly to persons and things.
(53)

Rewrite sentences 18–22, adding commas and periods as needed.

18. Look under "London Jack" in the catalog to find *The Call*
(36, 52) *of the Wild*

19. Hey Pop have you ever read about Pygmalion a famous
(36, 49) sculptor?

20. Dr U R Fine I think practices in Omaha
(40, 56)

21. Yes Pygmalion died a happy man
(36, 56)

22. After studying the students practice basketball soccer
(56) and volleyball

23. Write the sentence that is more polite (a or b).
(55) (a) We and they picked up trash after the picnic.
(b) They and we picked up trash after the picnic.

24. Reproduce the objective case pronoun chart.
(57)

25. Choose the objective case pronoun for this sentence: The
(57) teacher is depending on you and (I, me).

Tell how the italicized pronoun is used in sentences 26–28 (subject, direct object, predicate nominative, indirect object, possessive, object of a preposition).

26. The veterinarian offered *her* a treat.
(25, 35)

27. The winners were *they*.
(41, 55)

28. Would *you* rather see a play or go to a movie?
(2, 55)

Diagram sentences 29 and 30.

29. Those shoes on the floor are mine.
(41, 55)

30. Galatea, a statue, became a living woman.
(28, 48)

Possessive Pronouns and Possessive Adjectives

Dictation or Journal Entry
Vocabulary:
The verbs *leave* and *let* sometimes confuse us. *Leave* means "to go away or depart from." Will you *leave* from the local airport? *Leave* also means "to allow to remain behind." My parents will *leave* us at home while they go out. *Let* means "to allow or permit." My aunt *let* my cousin go to the park.

Possessive Pronouns

We have learned that a pronoun takes the place of a noun. The possessive pronouns *mine*, *yours*, *his*, *hers*, *ours*, and *theirs* replace nouns to tell "whose."

That's *mine,* not *yours.*

His is in the car, and *hers* is on the porch.

Theirs are done, so why aren't *ours?*

Notice that in each of the sentences above, the possessive pronoun **replaces a noun** and stands alone.

Possessive Adjectives

There is another group of words that is very similar to possessive pronouns except that they **come before a noun** rather than replace it. These words are the possessive adjectives *my, your, his, her, its, our,* and *their.*

It may be *your* saddle, but it's *my* horse.

Her mother doesn't like *his* father.

Tim and I moved *our* trailer closer to *their* cabin.

In each of the sentences above, the possessive adjective comes before a noun to tell "whose."

Many people consider these words pronouns. Others see them as adjectives because they always come before nouns to modify them. What is important is using them correctly.

POSSESSIVE ADJECTIVE (IN FRONT OF A NOUN)	POSSESSIVE PRONOUN (STANDING ALONE)
my	mine
your	yours
his	his
her	hers
its	its *(very seldom used)*
our	ours
their	theirs

Errors to Avoid Possessive pronouns do not have apostrophes. The words *yours*, *hers*, *its*, and *ours* are already possessive.

> INCORRECT: I can drive Mom's car but not **your's**.
> CORRECT: I can drive Mom's car but not **yours**.

> INCORRECT: The details are **her's** to handle.
> CORRECT: The details are **hers** to handle.

Also, we must not confuse contractions and possessive adjectives.

POSSESSIVE ADJECTIVE	CONTRACTION	
your	you're	(you are)
their	they're	(they are)
its	it's	(it is)

Example Choose the correct word to complete each sentence.

(a) (*Your, you're*) dog is a golden retriever.

(b) (*Its, It's*) name is Boomer.

(c) The collie is (*your's, yours*) also.

(d) That Great Dane is bigger than (*theirs, their's*).

Solution (a) **Your** dog is a golden retriever.

(b) **Its** name is Boomer.

(c) The collie is **yours** also.

(d) That Great Dane is bigger than **theirs.**

√ **Practice** Choose the correct word to complete sentences a–e.
   a. The chair was wobbly; (*its, it's*) legs were broken.

   b. In the late 1700s, the British sent (*their, they're*) convicted criminals to Australia.

   c. Once the convicts had served (*their, they're*) sentences, they couldn't afford to return to England.

   d. Give me (*your, you're*) opinion.

   e. The blue tent is (*ours, our's*).

For f–i, replace each blank with *leave* or *let*.

f. Please do not _____ me alone in this dark alley.

g. The surgeon _____ me stand by her.

h. You must _____ the room just as you found it.

i. Will you _____ me walk to school with you?

More Practice Choose the correct word(s) to complete each sentence.

1. Thanks to (there, their) keen sense of smell, Labrador retrievers can find and rescue people.

2. (They're, There, Their) able to safely explore areas that would be risky for humans.

3. That springer spaniel will protect (its, it's) master.

4. Dogs' hearing is usually more sensitive than (ours, our's).

5. Are all these cats (her's, hers)?

6. Is the German shepherd (your's, yours)?

7. A well-trained dog could save (your, you're) life.

8. When the dog hears an alarm, (its, it's) ears twitch.

9. (It's, Its) willing to risk danger to protect (it's, its) owner.

10. (Your, You're) dog is long-haired, but (our's, ours) is short-haired.

11. (Their, They're, There) dog's name is Checkers.

12. (They're, Their, There) training Checkers to chase decoys.

Review Set 60 Choose the best word to complete sentences 1–14.

1. The toddler was (to, too, two) on his last birthday.
(18)

2. The workers appear to have (less, fewer) stress than
(21) usual.

3. Buses, trains, and (monotheism, monorails, bicycles)
(11, 25) carry many passengers at a time.

4. The *P.S.* at the end of a letter is the abbreviated form of
(32) (postmortem, postgraduate, postscript).

5. We place (commas, periods) after the initials in a
(40) person's name and after letters and numbers in an
outline.

6. (First, Second, Third) person indicates the speaker.
(53)

7. (First, Second, Third) person is the person being spoken to.
(53)

8. (First, Second, Third) person is the person being spoken
(53) about.

9. *You* and *yours* are examples of (first, second, third)
(53) person.

10. *I, me, mine, we, us,* and *ours* are examples of (first,
(53) second, third) person.

11. *He, she, it, him, her, his,* and *hers* are examples of (first,
(53) second, third) person.

12. Both Rimaldo and (him, he) attended the stock car races.
(55)

13. Are all these gasoline receipts (her's, hers)?
(60)

14. (Your's, Yours) are over there.
(60)

15. Write the plural of *sheep.*
(13, 14)

16. Write each word that should be capitalized in this letter:
(12, 29) dear mieko,

an article in the school paper said, "one of our
japanese students is studying the history of christianity
in japan." are you that student?

sincerely,
professor knowings, ph.d.

17. Write the prepositional phrase used as an adjective
(33, 34) in this sentence: Cupid, the son of Venus, was a
Roman god.

18. Write the 23 helping verbs.
(9)

19. Write the linking verb in this sentence: Cupid became
(22) enamored of Psyche.

20. Write the two sentence types from this list that end with a
(1, 36) period: interrogative, exclamatory, imperative, declarative.

21. Write the four pairs of common correlative conjunctions.
(39)

22. Replace the blank with the correct word to complete this
(42, 55) sentence: When used as a predicate nominative, a noun
or pronoun is in the _____ case.

23. Write the pronoun in this sentence, and tell whether it is
(51, 53) first, second, or third person: Psyche loved her unseen
husband, Cupid.

24. Write the pronoun in this sentence, and tell whether it is
(51, 53) singular or plural: We are excited!

25. Unscramble these words to make a sentence with a
(53, 55) personal pronoun as a subject:

wore she dress same the Caitlin as

26. Write the sentence that is more polite (a or b).
(53, 57) (a) Elena husked corn for me and him.
(b) Elena husked corn for him and me.

27. Replace each blank with the missing objective case
(57) pronoun from this list: me, you, _____, her, it,
_____, you, them.

28. Write each possessive pronoun from this list: my, your,
(60) they're, his, her, it's, its, their, you're, mine.

Diagram sentences 29 and 30.

29. Venus was jealous of Psyche.
(23, 41)

30. They had mailed him an invitation.
(25, 35)

LESSON 61

Dependent and Independent Clauses • Subordinating Conjunctions

Dictation or Journal Entry

Vocabulary:
The prefix *poly-* means "many." A *polygon* is a many-sided, closed, geometric figure with straight sides. Rectangles, squares, triangles, and octagons are all *polygons*. A word that contains many syllables is *polysyllabic*. *Watermelon* is a *polysyllabic* word. *Chroma* is a Greek word that means "color." Therefore, *polychromatic* means "having many colors." Guang's design was *polychromatic*.

Independent Clauses There are two types of clauses. One type is the **independent clause**, also called the main clause. An independent clause expresses a complete thought.

> Polygons have more than two sides.

> James Watt invented the steam engine.

Dependent Clauses The other type of clause is the **dependent clause**. It cannot stand by itself and is sometimes called the subordinate clause. It depends upon additional information to complete a thought.

> If instructions are followed

> When you write on stationery

Even though the dependent clauses above each contain a subject and a predicate, they do not complete a thought. However, if we remove the introductory words "if" and "when," they become independent clauses and can stand alone:

> Instructions are followed.

> You write on stationery.

Example 1 For a–d, tell whether the clauses are dependent or independent.

(a) as soon as you go

(b) many countries were ruled by dictators

(c) although Jose de San Martin dreamed of a free South America

(d) the military leaders betrayed his dream

Solution (a) This is a **dependent** clause. It depends on another clause in order to complete a thought.

(b) This is an **independent** clause. It can stand alone and does not require another clause in order to complete a thought.

(c) This is a **dependent** clause.

(d) This is an **independent** clause and can stand by itself.

Subordinating Conjunctions

A **subordinating conjunction** introduces a dependent clause. We can turn an independent clause into a dependent clause by adding a subordinating conjunction. In the dependent clauses below, *though* and *because* are subordinating conjunctions.

INDEPENDENT CLAUSE	DEPENDENT CLAUSE
I like tacos.	*Though* I like tacos,...
He was smart.	*Because* he was smart,...

Below are some common subordinating conjunctions. There are many more.

after	*because*	*so that*	*when*
although	*before*	*than*	*whenever*
as	*even though*	*that*	*where*
as if	*if*	*though*	*wherever*
as soon as	*in order that*	*unless*	*while*
as though	*since*	*until*	

Many of these words also function as prepositions. Sometimes phrases begin with prepositions such as *after*, *before*, *since* or *until*. In this case, these words are not subordinating conjunctions but prepositions. Remember that a clause has both a subject and a verb. Notice how the word *after* is used in the two sentences below.

SUBORDINATING CONJUNCTION:
Miners hurried to California *after* gold was found at Sutter's Mill. (introducing the **clause** "after gold was found at Sutter's Mill.")

PREPOSITION:
Miners hurried to California *after* gold. (part of the **phrase** "after gold.")

Example 2   Identify the subordinating conjunctions in the following sentences.

(a) Brazil was never colonized by Spain because Portugal had already claimed it.

(b) If I go, I'll need a ride.

Solution   (a) **Because** is the subordinating conjunction. It introduces the dependent clause "because Portugal had already claimed it."

(b) **If** is the subordinating conjunction. It introduces the dependent clause "If I go."

√ **Practice**   For a–d, tell whether the clauses are dependent or independent.

a. although I put antifreeze in the drain

b. the pipes froze

c. she did not waste time

d. because she was in a hurry

For e–g, write each subordinating conjunction.

e. Unless you have already finished your homework, you are not ready to play.

f. I was able to lift the statue even though it was prodigious in size.

g. When the engine died, the car was incapacitated.

For h–l, replace each blank with the correct vocabulary word.

h. _____ means "having more than one color."

i. *Chroma* is a Greek word meaning "_____."

j. The prefix *poly-* means "_____."

k. A polygon is a geometric figure with _____ sides.

l. A polysyllabic word has many _____.

More Practice   See ""More Practice Lesson 61" in Student Workbook.

Review Set 61   Choose the best word to complete sentences 1–9.

1. (You're, Your) eyes blink when lights flash.
(56)

2. Don't (lend, borrow) money to a fool.
(57)

3. The ocean waves will (rise, raise) tall before they "break."
(58)

4. Can you (right, brake, devise) a plan to build a birdhouse?
(47, 59)

5. They wish. She (wish, wishes).
(7, 16)

6. The emperor (swore, sworn), "The bad customs of the past shall be abolished, and our government shall tread in the paths of civilization and enlightenment."
(54)

7. Rather than using the same noun over and over again, we may use (adjectives, pronouns).
(51)

8. A (transitive, intransitive) verb has a direct object.
(25, 32)

9. A personal pronoun that comes before a noun and tells "whose" is a (possessive, objective) adjective.
(60)

10. Tell whether this sentence is declarative, imperative, interrogative, or exclamatory: Get off your bicycle when you cross the street.
(1, 3)

11. Tell whether this group of words is a phrase or a clause: but the Japanese had reopened trade with a number of countries
(24, 61)

12. List six common subordinating conjunctions that begin with *a*.
(61)

13. Write the subordinating conjunction from this sentence: Matt has permission to go to the concert if his homework is completed.
(61)

14. Write the proper noun in this sentence: The entrance of foreigners to Japan led to the overthrow of her government.
(6)

15. Write each word that should be capitalized in this sentence: wiltshire, yorkshire, oxfordshire, and cornwall are all counties in england.

(6, 12)

16. Write the future perfect verb phrase in this sentence: At this rate, we will have covered all of Japanese history by the end of next year.

(9, 21)

17. Write the prepositional phrases and star the objects of the prepositions in this sentence: The shogun was overthrown by the emperor in 1868.

(17, 33)

18. Write the "number" adjective in this sentence: With intelligence and dignity, Emperor Meiji ruled Japan for the next forty-five years.

(28)

19. Rewrite this sentence correctly: The Japanese liked that kind of an emperor.

(50)

20. Rewrite the following, adding periods and capital letters as needed: meiji ruled wisely his first concern was to unite the country

(4, 12)

21. Write the four common pairs of correlative conjunctions.

(39)

22. Tell whether the italicized noun in this sentence is nominative or possessive case: Japan steadily became an industrialized *nation*.

(42)

23. Rewrite this sentence, adding commas as needed: On July 28 2001 a big event occurred at 323 March Street Bridle City Iowa.

(47)

24. Reproduce the nominative case pronoun chart.

(55)

25. Tell whether the italicized pronoun in this sentence is used as a direct object, indirect object, or object of a preposition: The lost child rushed toward *them*.

(33, 57)

For 26 and 27, tell whether the italicized pronoun is nominative, objective, or possessive case.

26. Kirsten brought *her* to the hair salon.

(57, 60)

27. Kyle and *he* waited outside.

(55, 58)

Diagram sentences 28–30.

28. Jack gave Jill and me a bucket of water.
(34, 35)

29. Japan became a modern, industrialized nation.
(23, 41)

30. The Japanese overtook Korea, a nation between China and Japan.
(25, 48)

Reflexive and Intensive Pronouns

Dictation or Journal Entry
Vocabulary:
Do not confuse the words *teach* and *learn*. *Teach* means "to give instruction." The coach will *teach* us how to pass a basketball. *Learn* means "to gain knowledge." I will *learn* how to pass a basketball.

Reflexive Pronouns

Reflexive pronouns end in "-self" or "-selves." A reflexive pronoun throws the action back upon the subject of the sentence. **The antecedent of a reflexive pronoun is always the subject of the sentence.** It is a necessary part of the sentence and cannot be omitted. The singular reflexive pronouns are *myself, yourself, himself, herself,* and *itself.*

The arrogant contestant patted *herself* on the back.

I injured *myself* in the contest.

The plural reflexive pronouns are *ourselves, yourselves,* and *themselves.*

Sam and Wes prepared *themselves.*

We protected *ourselves* from the sun.

Like all pronouns, reflexive pronouns match their antecedents in person, number, and gender. Reflexive pronouns are used as direct objects, indirect objects, and objects of a preposition. They are diagrammed like this:

INDIRECT OBJECT:

I gave *myself* a party.

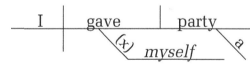

DIRECT OBJECT:

He bruised *himself.*

OBJECT OF A PREPOSITION:

They were whispering among *themselves.*

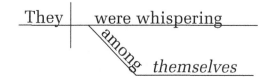

Errors to Avoid   We do not use *hisself* and *theirselves*. They are not words.

> NO: He cut *hisself*.
> YES: He cut *himself*.
>
> NO: They tested *theirselves* on the spelling words.
> YES: They tested *themselves* on the spelling words.

We do not use a reflexive pronoun in place of the simple personal pronoun.

> NO: Judy and *myself* attended the opera.
> YES: Judy and *I* attended the opera.

Example 1   Choose the correct pronoun for each sentence.

(a) The girls muttered to (*themselves, theirselves*) as they fixed the flat tire.

(b) Letha, are Julie and (*you, yourself*) going to type all day?

Solution   (a) We do not use *theirselves*. It is not a word.

The girls muttered to *themselves* as they fixed the flat tire.

(b) We do not use a reflexive pronoun in place of a personal pronoun.

Letha, are Julie and you going to type all day?

Intensive Pronouns   **Intensive pronouns** have the same form as reflexive personal pronouns. However, they are used to emphasize or intensify another noun or pronoun. We can leave an intensive pronoun out of a sentence without changing the meaning of the sentence. The antecedent is whatever word the intensive pronoun emphasizes; it need not be the subject of the sentence. Notice that the sentences below make sense without the intensive pronoun.

> Sally *herself* chose the material for her suit.
>
> Anela and Jordan *themselves* waxed the family car.
>
> I suppose I will have to do it *myself*.
>
> This book was given to me by the author *himself*.

Again, we do not use *hisself* and *theirselves*. They are not words. Also, we do not replace simple personal pronouns with intensive pronouns.

We diagram intensive personal pronouns like this:

We will behave *ourselves*.

$$\underline{\text{We } (\textit{ourselves})\ \big|\ \text{will behave}}$$

They mowed the lawn *themselves*.

$$\underline{\text{They } (\textit{themselves})\big|\ \text{mowed}\ \big|\ \text{lawn}}$$
$$\diagdown \textit{the}$$

Example 2 Choose the correct pronoun for each sentence.

(a) Either George or (*yourself, you*) will play the saxophone.

(b) Henry (*hisself, himself*) told me the story.

(c) They gave up and fixed dinner (*theirselves, themselves*).

Solution (a) We do not replace a simple personal pronoun with an intensive pronoun.

Either George or *you* will play the saxophone.

(b) *Hisself* is not a word.

Henry *himself* told me the story.

(c) *Theirselves* is not a word.

They gave up and fixed dinner themselves.

√ **Practice** Choose the correct personal pronoun for sentences a–d.

a. Both James and (*myself, I*) plan to go.

b. We made the curtains (*ourself, ourselves*).

c. (*Yourself, You*) will complete all your homework.

d. They bought (*theirselves, themselves*) a new table.

For e–h, replace each blank with *teach* or *learn*.

e. When will you _____ me to play the guitar?

f. I _____ aerobics classes every morning.

g. Where did Tom _____ to waltz?

h. You must _____ to multiply before you can _____ someone else.

More Practice Choose the correct personal pronoun for each sentence.

1. He painted it (himself, hisself).

2. They wanted to fix the car (theirselves, themselves).

3. They helped (theirself, themselves) to dessert.

4. Cecilia and (I, myself) raised the flag.

5. He taught Steve and (me, myself) to use the computer program.

6. Bryon and John wrote the song (theirselves, themselves).

7. John created the music (hisself, himself).

8. They don't bake the bread (theirselves, themselves).

9. He learned to make bread (hisself, himself).

10. Tom and (he, himself) attended the meeting.

Review Set 62 Choose the best word to complete sentences 1–8.

1. (Leave, Let) the mail on the table.
(60)

2. Some religions permit multiple spouses, or (polytheism, polygamy, polygon).
(61)

3. Which is easier to (brake, break), glass or diamond?
(47)

4. (May, Can) you swim well?
(48)

5. Some lucky people are (bear, bore, born) with a wide voice range.
(54)

6. Many sopranos have (sing, sang, sung) Mozart's songs, which can contain very high notes.
(54)

7. A personal pronoun that stands alone and replaces a noun to tell "whose" is a (possessive, concrete) noun.
(53, 58)

8. (Reflexive, Possessive) pronouns end in "-self" or "-selves."
(62)

Write the subordinating conjunctions from sentences 9 and 10.

9. Since fall is here, the leaves on the liquid amber tree are
(24, 61) red, yellow, and orange.

10. I cannot complete this task unless you help me.
(24, 61)

11. List the five common subordinating conjunctions from
(61) this list: and, because, but, before, or, even though, if, in
order that.

12. Write the concrete noun from this list: gentleness,
(8) meekness, self-control, cupcake, honesty.

13. Rewrite this outline, adding capital letters and periods as
(20, 36) needed:
i voices
   a soprano
   b alto
   c tenor
   d bass

14. Write the entire verb phrase and underline the helping
(9, 7) verb in this sentence: We can categorize people's voices
into four main sections.

15. Write the present perfect progressive verb phrase in this
(9, 21) sentence: Boys' choirs have been entertaining adults for
decades.

16. Write the prepositional phrase and star the object of the
(17, 33) preposition in this sentence: During middle-school
years, boys' voices change.

17. Write the proper adjective in this sentence: The Austrian
(30) choirs are famous throughout the world.

18. Rewrite the following, adding periods as needed: Dr
(36, 40) Wayne Crabb, the choral director at St John's School,
scheduled the concert for Friday, Dec 10

19. Write the indirect object in this sentence: The composer
(25, 35) wrote me a song with my alto voice in mind.

For sentences 20 and 21, tell whether the italicized noun is in the nominative or possessive case

20. *Women* with very high voices are called sopranos.
(42)

21. The *singer's* part was alto.
(49)

22. Rewrite this sentence, adding commas as needed: Mr.
(47, 49) Yamashita the art teacher submitted pictures poems and other items of interest to the yearbook committee.

For sentences 23 and 24, tell whether the underlined verb is transitive or intransitive.

23. Danielle <u>smelled</u> the rose.
(25, 32)

24. The rose <u>smelled</u> sweet.
(22, 32)

25. Write the sentence that is more polite (a or b).
(57) (a) Jerry can go with me and him.
      (b) Jerry can go with him and me.

26. Tell whether the italicized pronouns in this sentence are
(57) used as direct objects, indirect objects, or objects of a preposition: The school office assistant gave *him* and *me* pizza for helping.

27. Tell whether the italicized pronoun in this sentence is
(60) nominative, objective, or possessive case: *Ours* is upstairs.

Diagram sentences 28–30.

28. She and Mariah sang the Mozart piece.
(38, 55)

29. Both Benjamin and Moses are tenors.
(39, 41)

30. Jo and they should have been dancing.
(23)

The Comma, Part 5: Descriptive Adjectives, Dependent Clauses

Dictation or Journal Entry

Vocabulary:

Desert and *dessert* are commonly confused. *Desert* (pronounced DEZ-rt) is an arid region, a dry, parched area lacking in vegetation and rainfall. It seldom rains in the *desert*. *Desert* (pronounced di-ZURT) means "to leave or abandon." The guard *deserted* his post. *Dessert* (pronounced di-ZURT) is the final course of a meal, usually a fruity or sweet dish such as pie, cake, or ice cream. Did you eat *dessert* after your dinner?

We remember that commas are used to indicate the natural pauses of speech. Let's look at more places where we use commas.

Descriptive Adjectives
We use a comma to separate two or more **descriptive adjectives.**

> He began working at his *neat, orderly* desk.

> A *long, warm* vacation was what he desired.

There are some exceptions. For example, if one adjective is a color, we don't use a comma to separate it from another adjective.

> The *lively yellow* canary sang cheerfully.

One way to decide whether a comma is needed is to insert the word "and" between the adjectives.

> IF YOU COULD SAY: It was a *hot and humid* day.
> YOU DO NEED A COMMA: It was a *hot, humid* day.

> YOU WOULDN'T SAY: I saw an *old and red* barn.
> SO YOU DON'T NEED A COMMA: I saw an *old red* barn.

Example 1 Insert commas where they are needed in the sentences below.

(a) Some deserts have steep rocky mountains while others are flat.

(b) Bright sparkling brown eyes attract admiration.

Solution (a) We place a comma between the two adjectives "steep" and "rocky."

> Some deserts have *steep, rocky* mountains while others are flat.

(b) We separate the adjectives "bright" and "sparkling" with a comma, but we do not place a comma before the color adjective "brown."

Bright, sparkling brown eyes attract admiration.

Dependent Clauses We remember that a **dependent clause** cannot stand alone, while an independent clause, or main clause, makes sense without the dependent clause. We use a comma after a dependent clause when it comes before the main clause.

After they ate dinner, Carol unveiled the dessert.
(DEPENDENT CLAUSE)   (INDEPENDENT/MAIN CLAUSE)

However, we do **not** use a comma when the dependent clause follows the main clause.

Carol unveiled the dessert after they ate dinner.
(INDEPENDENT/MAIN CLAUSE)   (DEPENDENT CLAUSE)

Example 2 Insert commas as needed in the sentences below.

(a) After they had visited the Mojave Desert the tourists recognized the Joshua tree.

(b) The tourists recognized the Joshua tree after they had visited the Mojave Desert.

Solution (a) We place a comma after the dependent clause "after they had visited the Mojave Desert" because it comes before the main clause.

After they had visited the Mojave Desert, the tourists recognized the Joshua tree.

(b) No comma is needed in this sentence because the dependent clause follows the main clause.

✓ Practice Rewrite sentences a and b, inserting commas to separate descriptive adjectives.

a. London often finds itself in deep dense fog.

b. I brought my biggest warmest coat to the campout, but all I really needed was my blue cotton jacket.

Rewrite sentences c–e, inserting a comma after each dependent clause.

c. When you go to the store get a few tomatoes.

d. If they look mushy buy some cantaloupe instead.

e. As soon as you get home we'll make a huge salad.

For f–i, replace each blank with *dessert* or *desert*.

f. Apple pie with ice cream was served for _____.

g. Are military people punished if they _____ their jobs?

h. The arid Death Valley is a _____ in California.

i. The last course of the meal, _____, is Christie's favorite one.

More Practice See "More Practice Lesson 63" in Student Workbook.

Review Set 63 Choose the best word to complete sentences 1–11.

1. A good teacher (teaches, learns) patiently and clearly.
(62)

2. If a coupon has expired, it is (depreciated, invalid, fractious).
(51, 55)

3. The (continuous, continual) tardiness of the employee led to dismissal.
(54)

4. Around a campfire, campers can roast marshmallows on (hangars, hangers).
(52)

5. A(n) (independent, dependent) clause cannot stand by itself and is sometimes called the subordinate clause.
(61)

6. The plural form of *boss* is (bosses, boss's).
(13, 14)

7. She (speak, spoke, spoken) the poem's lines to him.
(54)

8. The shepherd (blow, blew, blown) his horn.
(54)

9. Tom admitted that he (stealed, stole, stolen) the pie.
(54)

10. The statement "Possessive pronouns have apostrophes," is (true, false).
(60)

(62) **11.** We bathed the dog (ourself, ourselves).

12. Tell whether this word group is a fragment, run-on, or
(3) complete sentence: In poetry, related lines are grouped together in stanzas.

13. List the five common subordinating conjunctions from
(61) this list: since, nor, so that, and, than, independent, that, clause, though.

14. Tell whether this clause is dependent or
(24, 61) independent: because the coupon had expired

15. List the seven coordinating conjunctions.
(37)

16. Write the concrete noun from this list: Wednesday, June,
(8) service, calendar, holiday.

17. Rewrite this sentence, adding capital letters as
(6, 26) needed: grandpa and grandma angles grew up in scotland.

18. Write the linking verb from this sentence: Robert Frost's
(22) poem "Stopping by Woods on a Snowy Evening" sounds very informal.

Tell whether the underlined verb in sentences 19 and 20 is an action verb or a linking verb.

√ **19.** Poems <u>will</u> often <u>repeat</u> rhymes in a regular pattern.
(5, 22)

√ **20.** This <u>is</u> the poem's rhyme scheme.
(5, 22)

√ **21.** Write the prepositional phrase and star the object of the
(17, 33) preposition in this sentence: The rhyme is regular and predictable in some poems.

22. Write the predicate nominative in this sentence: A
(22, 41) special kind of stanza is a couplet.

Rewrite sentences 23 and 24, adding commas as needed.

23. Mr. Atwater please introduce us to that tall mysterious
(49, 63) gentleman in gray.

24. Stanzas give a poem a distinct interesting look.
(27, 63)

25. Replace the blank with the correct word: The word to
(51) which the pronoun refers is called the _____.

26. Write the pronoun in this sentence, and tell whether it is
(55, 58) first, second, or third person: We learned that the oldest
city in the world is Damascus in Syria.

27. Unscramble these words to make a sentence with a
(55, 58) personal pronoun as a subject:

dog   fed   her   faithful   she

28. Write the pronoun in this sentence, and tell whether it is
(57) used as a direct object, indirect object, or object of a
preposition: Darius donated it to the Salvation Army.

29. Write the pronoun in this sentence, and tell whether it is
(55, 57) nominative, objective, or possessive case: It remained in
the sun to keep warm.

30. Diagram this sentence: He, the man in the blue shorts,
(25, 48) plays professional basketball.

Compound Sentences •
Coordinating Conjunctions

Dictation or Journal Entry
Vocabulary:
The homophones *for, fore,* and *four* are pronounced the same but have different meanings. *For* is either a preposition or a conjunction meaning "because" or "directed to." I ran *for* cover *for* it was raining. *Fore* means "the front." The bow is the *fore* part of a ship. *Fore-* is also a prefix meaning "in front" or "earlier." Can you *fore*tell the future? *Four* is the number 4. A square has *four* equal sides.

Compound Sentences   Two or more simple sentences (independent clauses) joined by a connecting word such as *and, or,* or *but* form a **compound sentence**. Only sentences closely related in thought should be joined to form a compound sentence. Below, we connect two simple sentences to form a compound sentence.

TWO SIMPLE SENTENCES:

The captain's forefathers <u>were</u> soldiers.

They <u>fought</u> in the American Revolution.

ONE COMPOUND SENTENCE:

The captain's forefathers <u>were</u> soldiers, and they <u>fought</u> in the American Revolution.

Here we diagram the simple subjects and simple predicates of the compound sentence above:

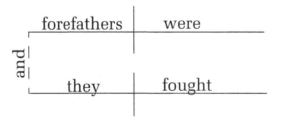

Notice that the compound sentence is made up of two independent clauses that can each stand alone and make sense. Remember that any number of independent clauses can be joined to form a compound sentence. For example, here we join four independent clauses (simple sentences) to form one compound sentence:

Nedra played the guitar, and Jerome beat the drums, but I just hummed along, and Bill didn't make a sound.

Coordinating Conjunctions

A **coordinating conjunction** can join two simple sentences to form a compound sentence. We have learned that the following are coordinating conjunctions:

and   but   or   nor   for   yet   so

Notice how coordinating conjunctions are used in the compound sentences below.

AND INDICATES ADDITIONAL INFORMATION:
The Latin Americans demanded their freedom, *and* the European countries desired their independence.

BUT SHOWS CONTRAST:
The Latin Americans wanted democracies, *but* the European countries insisted on kings and emperors.

OR SHOWS A CHOICE:
The European countries could choose a democratic government, *or* they could continue the monarchies.

Conjunctions may also connect the parts of a compound subject or predicate. Do not confuse a compound subject or a compound predicate with a compound sentence. Remember that a compound sentence has both a subject and a predicate on each side of the conjunction. A compound sentence follows this pattern:

subject <u>predicate</u>, (conjunction) *subject* <u>predicate</u>

Words <u>can hurt,</u>   (or)   *words* <u>can help</u>.
I <u>have been looking</u>,   (but)   *you* <u>have been hiding</u>.
Bryon <u>played</u> piano,   (and)   *Kerry* <u>sang</u> a song.

Example 1

Tell whether each sentence is simple or compound. If it is compound, write the coordinating conjunction that joins the two independent clauses.

(a) *France* <u>began</u> with a new monarchy in 1789, yet *she* <u>overthrew</u> that ruler.

(b) Other European *countries* <u>attempted</u> to establish democratic governments, but the *kings* successfully <u>put</u> down the revolts.

(c) In the early 1700s, most *Europeans* <u>lived</u> and <u>worked</u> in the country.

(d) In the 1800s, *people* <u>left</u> the country, and *they* <u>traveled</u> to the cities.

Solution (a) We find a subject and a predicate on each side of the conjunction: *France* <u>began</u> (conjunction), *she* <u>overthrew</u>. Therefore, the sentence is **compound**. The coordinating conjunction joining the two independent clauses is **yet**.

(b) This sentence is **compound.** It consists of two independent clauses joined by the coordinating conjunction **but**.

(c) This is a **simple** sentence. It is a single, independent clause with one subject (*Europeans*) and a compound predicate (<u>lived</u> and <u>worked</u>).

(d) This is a **compound** sentence. Two independent clauses are joined by the coordinating conjunction **and**.

Diagramming To diagram the simple subjects and simple predicates of a compound sentence, we follow these steps:

1. Diagram each simple sentence, one below the other.

2. Join the two sentences with a dotted line on the left side.

3. Write the coordinating conjunction on the dotted line.

Below, we diagram the simple subjects and simple predicates of this compound sentence:

Spats is eating, but Teddy is sleeping.

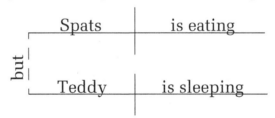

Example 2 Diagram the simple subjects and simple predicates of this compound sentence:

The steam *engine* <u>provided</u> energy for the new machines, and the *railroads* <u>were powered</u> by its energy as well.

Solution We diagram the simple subject and simple predicate of each simple sentence and place them one below the other. Then we join them with a dotted line on which we write the coordinating conjunction "and."

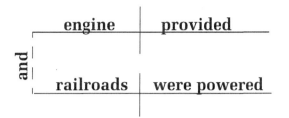

engine	provided
railroads	were powered

and

√**Practice** For a–e, tell whether each sentence is <u>simple or compound</u>. If it is compound, write the <u>coordinating conjunctions</u> that join the two or more independent clauses.

a. The *movement* of people from the country to the city <u>was</u> part of the Industrial Revolution.

b. The *Industrial Revolution* <u>began</u> in England around 1750, and *it* <u>spread</u> gradually to other European countries.

c. *Eli Whitney* <u>invented</u> the cotton gin, and *James Watt* <u>invented</u> the steam engine, but *who* <u>created</u> the first locomotive?

d. *England* <u>was</u> especially powerful in the 1800s because of the Industrial Revolution.

e. The *Industrial Revolution* <u>can be credited</u> with positive results, or *it* <u>can be blamed</u> for bad effects.

f. Diagram the simple subjects and simple predicates of this compound sentence:

English *engineers* <u>invented</u> the locomotive, and this steam *engine* on wheels <u>pulled</u> heavier loads than any horse.

For g–j, replace each blank with *for, fore,* or *four*.

g. Genealogy is the study of one's _____ fathers.

h. The number _____ comes after three.

i. The cake is _____ the party.

j. If you warn someone ahead of time, you have _____ warned them.

Review Set 64 Choose the best word to complete sentences 1–14.

1. In frustration, the athlete complained, "I have only completed a small (fraction, peace, raze) of my workout, and I'm exhausted."
(46, 51)

2. A cook can (waist, pore, substitute) vegetable oil for shortening in some recipes.
(5, 14)

3. It helps to (lay, lie) down if you feel dizzy or weak.
(10)

4. (Less, Fewer) people attended the event than did last year.
(21)

5. A(n) (independent, dependent) clause can stand by itself and is sometimes called the main clause.
(24, 61)

6. Two or more simple sentences (independent clauses) joined by a connecting word such as *and*, *or*, or *but* form a (compound, simple, longer) sentence.
(61, 64)

7. Only sentences closely related in (thought, length) should be joined to form a compound sentence.
(64)

8. A (subordinating, coordinating) conjunction can join two simple sentences to form a compound sentence.
(37, 64)

9. You (am, are, is) late for class.
(7, 15)

10. They (was, were) diligent in their work.
(7, 15)

11. That gigantic oak tree (begin, began, begun) as a tiny acorn.
(54)

12. It (growed, grew, grown) quickly and soon shaded the whole yard.
(54)

13. Is this wallet (your's, yours)?
(60)

14. He insisted on painting the model (hisself, himself).
(62)

15. Make a complete sentence from this fragment: In the school band concert.
(4)

16. Write the seven common subordinating conjunctions from this list: unless, and, until, but, when, or, whenever, nor, where, for, wherever, yet, while.
(61)

17. Tell whether this clause is independent or dependent: the
(24, 61) disease made the boy an invalid

18. Write the seven common coordinating conjunctions.
(37)

19. Write the plural of *wife*.
(13, 14)

20. Rewrite this sentence, adding capital letters as
(6, 12) needed: georgia, louisiana, and florida are located in the
south.

21. Write each adjective phrase from this sentence, and tell
(33, 34) which noun or pronoun it modifies: The story of
American civilization in the twentieth century involves
the entire world.

Rewrite 22 and 23, adding commas as needed.

22. Dear Mallory
(49, 52)   Don't forget to remind your piano teacher Mrs. Wang
that she promised to bring her famous salsa to the party.
Unless I'm mistaken everyone will want the recipe.
        Gratefully
        Heather

23. While I see your point I don't agree with you.
(56)

24. Write the clearer of the two sentences (a or b).
(51) (a) Bruce and Caleb arrived at his store.
      (b) Bruce and Caleb arrived at Bruce's store.

25. Unscramble these words to make a sentence with a
(41, 53) personal pronoun as a predicate nominative:

    she   the   best   jumper   high   was

26. Write the personal pronoun from this sentence, and tell
(53, 58) whether it is singular or plural: Move over for them.

27. Write the objective case personal pronouns.
(53, 57)

28. Write the pronoun in this sentence, and tell how it is
(55, 57) used (subject, direct object, indirect object, object of a
preposition, predicate nominative, or possession): The
coach encouraged Shelby and her.

Diagram the simple subjects and simple predicates of compound sentences 29 and 30.

✓ **29.** The railway *system* <u>made</u> it faster and cheaper to
(23, 64) transport goods, and railway *travel* <u>provided</u> cheap transportation for people.

✓ **30.** Most *people* <u>supported</u> this new form of transportation,
(23, 64) but some *people* <u>disliked</u> the noise, dirt, and potential danger.

LESSON 65

The Comma, Part 6: Compound Sentences, Direct Quotations

Dictation or Journal Entry

Vocabulary:
The common prefix *anti-* means "against." The word *antiseptic* is formed from the prefix *anti-* (against) and *septic* (infective or containing bacteria). Therefore, an *antiseptic* (noun) is a bacteria-killing substance. An a*ntiseptic* (adjective) solution fights bacteria or works against germs. The word *antisocial* is an adjective meaning "not sociable" or "hostile to society." Vandalism is an *antisocial* act.

Compound Sentences We remember that two sentences or independent clauses joined by a coordinating conjunction (*and, but, or, for*, etc.) is called a compound sentence. We place a comma between the first independent clause and the coordinating conjunction in a compound sentence.

> We might be able to add two numbers together on our fingers, but it is better to memorize our addition facts.

> Lisa passed out the math tests, and Richard gave out the pencils.

The following coordinating conjunctions signal the need for a comma in a compound sentence.

and but or nor for yet so

Example 1 Identify the coordinating conjunction in each compound sentence.

(a) He has not eaten, nor has he brushed his teeth.

(b) They can walk to the park, or they can drive their car.

(c) Donald is working, so he cannot go with us.

Solution (a) **nor**   (b) **or**   (c) **so**

Example 2 Insert a comma before the coordinating conjunction to separate the two independent clauses in the sentences below.

(a) Miguel Hidalgo gathered a group of poor farmers in Mexico and he delivered a famous challenge.

(b) Tens of thousands of people joined Hidalgo's army and they marched across Mexico.

Solution We place a comma between the first independent clause and the coordinating conjunction.

(a) Miguel Hidalgo gathered a group of poor farmers in Mexico**,** and he delivered a famous challenge.

(b) Tens of thousands of people joined Hidalgo's army**,** and they marched across Mexico.

Direct Quotations We use a comma or commas to offset the exact words of a speaker, a **direct quotation**, from the rest of the sentence.

Julie asked, "Do you know the answer to the math problem?"

"I think," said Jonathan, "that five times six equals thirty."

"You are correct," confirmed Mrs. Rivas.

Notice that the comma stays next to the word it follows. If a comma follows a direct quote, the comma goes inside the quotation marks.

YES: "Anyone can cook an omelet," said Bo.

No: "Anyone can cook an omelet", said Bo.

Example 3 Rewrite sentences a and b, inserting commas as needed to offset direct quotations from the rest of the sentence.

(a) Hidalgo cried "Will you free yourselves? We must act at once!"

(b) "The rebels could not defeat the Spaniards" explained Mrs. Sheedy.

Solution (a) We place a comma just before Hidalgo's words.

Hidalgo cried, "Will you free yourselves? We must act at once!"

(b) We place a comma after Mrs. Sheedy's words. The comma goes inside the quotation marks.

"The rebels could not defeat the Spaniards," explained Mrs. Sheedy.

Practice **a.** List the seven coordinating conjunctions.

For b–d, identify the coordinating conjunction in each sentence.

b. Stephen ran ten miles, for he felt energetic.

c. I was ready to leave, yet it was too early.

d. Freddy had already eaten, but he was still hungry.

Rewrite these compound sentences, inserting commas before the coordinating conjunctions.

e. Romeo drank the poison and he kissed Juliet for the last time.

f. Juliet slept peacefully through Romeo's kiss and she awoke to find him dead.

Rewrite sentences g and h, inserting commas to offset direct quotations.

g. Marcella said "I've always wanted to fly an airplane."

h. "I like to get the big picture" she explained.

For i–m, replace each blank with the correct vocabulary word.

i. Two germ-killing _____ are alcohol and iodine.

j. We clean wounds with a(n) _____ in order to kill the germs.

k. The prefix *anti-* means "_____."

l. An _____ act is one that is against society.

m. Robbery is an _____ act.

More Practice   See "More Practice Lesson 65" in Student Workbook.

Review Set 65   Choose the best word to complete sentences 1–12.

1. The criminal's guilty (diligence, conscientiousness,
(12, 26) conscience) prodded him to confess the crime.

2. The pants were of such (poor, pour, pore) quality that
(34) they fell apart after one washing.

3. The (sewing, sowing, soing) of new seed usually occurs
(37) in the spring.

4. Lack of funds became the (principle, principal) deterrent
(43) to the project.

5. A compound sentence has both a subject and a
(64) (predicate, object) on each side of the coordinating
conjunction.

6. Cecil Rhodes was (more, most) ambitious than many
(45, 46) British leaders.

7. The Boers (choosed, chose, chosen) to declare war on the
(54) British.

8. The British gradually (weared, wore, worn) down the
(54) Boers' strength.

9. I should have (knowed, knew, known) we'd be late.
(54)

10. Luis and (them, they) stayed for the reception.
(55, 58)

11. (Your, You're) clean car sparkles in the sunlight.
(56, 60)

12. Lung and Fong sang the song (theirselves, themselves).
(62)

13. For a–c, tell whether the clause is dependent or
(61) independent.

   (a) although Cecil Rhodes thought the British should
     conquer Africa first

   (b) the British ruled Egypt in the north and the Cape
     Colony in the south

   (c) if you have a brother or a sister

14. Write the subordinating conjunction in this
(61) sentence: The mountains are gorgeous when the snow
falls.

15. For sentences a and b, tell whether the verb is transitive
(22, 32) or intransitive.

   (a) The wind felt turbulent.

   (b) She felt the breeze.

16. Write each word that should be capitalized in this
(6, 30) sentence: the chinese elm and the liquid amber are types
of trees.

17. Write the direct object in this sentence: Cecil Rhodes
(5, 25) desired Transvaal, one of the Boer colonies.

For 18–20, tell whether the italicized noun is a direct object, an indirect object, or the object of a preposition.

18. Transvaal provided the British *people* gold.
(25, 35)

19. Some of Rhodes' followers launched a *raid* on the Transvaal.
(25, 33)

20. The attackers were easily defeated by the *Boers*.
(33, 43)

Rewrite 21 and 22, adding commas as needed.

21. Rhodes was severely criticized for attacking the Boers and he was asked to step down as prime minister.
(65)

22. Mr. Lancaster explained "The Boers were ready for the British to attack again."
(65)

23. Write the antecedent for the italicized pronoun in this sentence: The people in my town mean well, but *they* don't always recycle.
(51, 55)

24. Tell whether the italicized pronoun in this sentence is nominative, objective, or possessive case: Pass *me* the wooden spoon.
(55, 57)

25. Write each nominative case pronoun from this list: me, him, I, she, them, they, he, her, we, us.
(55)

26. Reproduce the objective case pronoun chart.
(57)

Diagram sentences 27–30.

27. The day grew cold and rainy.
(22, 44)

28. Christina baked the cake, but Tom frosted it.
(2, 64)

29. He greeted her, so she smiled.
(2, 64)

30. The author is he.
(23, 41)

LESSON 66

Relative Pronouns

> **Dictation or Journal Entry**
>
> **Vocabulary:**
> *Dilemma* (pronounced di-LEM-ma) is a "situation requiring a choice between two equally undesirable alternatives." Velma faced a *dilemma* when her car broke down in the desert: She could either walk twenty miles to the nearest town, or she could sit in the scorching heat and hope that help would arrive.

Relative Pronouns

Relative pronouns play the part of subject or object in clauses:

> Mr. and Mrs. Medrano, *who* had adopted the orphans, enjoyed their enlarged family. (subject)
>
> I thought the milk, *which* I had been drinking, was spoiled. (object)

Relative pronouns often refer to nouns that have preceded them, making the sentence more compact.

> WORDY:
> Mrs. Gonzales cared for two orphans, and the orphans were from Russia.
>
> COMPACT:
> Mrs. Gonzales cared for two orphans, *who* were from Russia.

Simple

The following are simple relative pronouns:

> *who, whom, whose, what, which, that*

WHO REFERS TO PEOPLE (AND SOMETIMES ANIMALS):

> The boy *who* lives next door mows my lawn.
>
> I have a dog *who* can jump a four-foot fence.

WHICH REFERS TO ANIMALS OR THINGS:

> The bird, *which* had already eaten, still clung to the feeder.
>
> She surveyed the room, *which* hadn't been dusted in years.

THAT REFERS TO PEOPLE, ANIMALS, OR THINGS:

> She is the kind of person *that* everyone loves.
>
> The horse *that* escaped belonged to my cousin.
>
> The noise *that* I heard last night was a mouse.

Example 1   Choose the correct relative pronoun for each sentence.

(a) The lady (*who, which*) lives on the corner has twenty llamas.

(b) The tire, (*who, which*) had been losing air for days, finally went flat.

(c) There is the teacher (*which, that*) I told you about.

Solution   (a) We choose **who** because it refers to "lady," a person. We do not use *which* for people.

(b) We choose **which** because it refers to "tire," a thing. We do not use *who* for things.

(c) We choose **that** because it refers to "teacher," a person. We do not use *which* for people.

Errors to Avoid   The relative pronoun *who* can cause problems because it changes form depending on the part it plays in the clause:

SUBJECT	OBJECT	POSSESSIVE
who	*whom*	*whose*

In the sentences below, we diagram the dependent clause to show how the pronoun is used.

SUBJECT:
Mrs. Rivas, *who* is my friend, will call today.

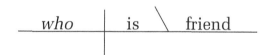

OBJECT:
Mrs. Rivas, *whom* you met, will call today.

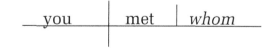

POSSESSIVE:
Mrs. Rivas, *whose* friendship I cherish, will call today.

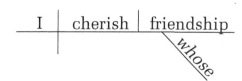

Example 2 Diagram the dependent clause to help you determine whether the pronoun is a subject or an object in the clause. Then choose the correct pronoun form.

  (a) That teacher, (*who, whom*) I admire, plans to retire soon.

  (b) Dr. Wang, (*who, whom*) lives in Oklahoma, travels frequently.

  (c) Mr. Stothers, (*who, whom*) is a musician, has two talented sons.

  (d) Only Charlie, (*who, whom*) I recognized, showed up on time.

Solution (a) That teacher, **whom** I admire, plans to retire soon. (object)

  (b) Dr. Wang, **who** lives in Oklahoma, travels frequently. (subject)

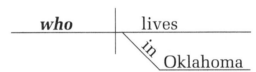

  (c) Mr. Stothers, **who** is a musician, has two talented sons. (subject)

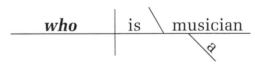

  (d) Only Charlie, **whom** I recognized, showed up on time. (object)

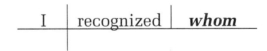

Compound The following are compound relative pronouns:

whoever, whomever, whosoever
whatever, whatsoever, whichever

He may choose *whichever* goldfish he wants.

Whatever you do, be there on time.

Notice that we carefully choose *whoever* or *whomever* depending on the part the compound relative pronoun plays in the clause.

> You may invite *whomever* you want. (object)

> *Whoever* is ready may come to dinner. (subject)

Example 3 Choose the correct compound relative pronoun for this sentence:

> (*Whoever, Whomever*) wants to go fishing should arrive by dawn.

Solution **Whoever** wants to go fishing should arrive by dawn. The pronoun is the subject, so the proper form is *who(ever)*.

Practice Choose the correct relative pronoun for sentences a–e.

a. People (*who, which*) own dogs need to train them properly.

b. The person (*who, whom*) borrowed the book must return it.

Think: $\dfrac{?\ |\ \text{borrowed}\ |\ \text{book}}{}$

c. I will gladly invite (*whoever, whomever*) you want.

Think: $\dfrac{\text{I}\ |\ \text{will invite}\ |\ ?}{}$

d. The lady (*that, which*) owns the gorilla visits often.

e. Mr. Ng, (*who, whom*) I have known for years, asked me to work for his company.

Think: $\dfrac{\text{I}\ |\ \text{have known}\ |\ ?}{}$

f. Diagram the <u>dependent</u> clause in the sentence below to show how the pronoun is used.

Juan, *who* is my best friend, helped me with the math problem.

For g and h, replace each blank with the correct vocabulary word.

    g. I faced a _____, for my alternatives were equally undesirable.

    h. A situation requiring you to choose between two equally undesirable alternatives is a _____.

More Practice

Choose the correct relative pronoun for each sentence.

1. The Vietnam Memorial commemorates all (whom, who) died in Vietnam.

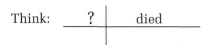

2. Richard M. Nixon, (whom, who) became president in 1968, withdrew American troops from Vietnam.

3. The Communists, (who, whom) they fought, made it illegal for the Vietnamese to leave.

Think: they | fought | ?

4. Some of the refugees (who, whom) history remembers fled to Thailand.

Think: history | remembers | ?

5. Mr. Thompson, (who, whom) you have met, fought in Vietnam.

Think: you | have met | ?

6. Those (who, whom) escaped Communism appreciate their American citizenship.

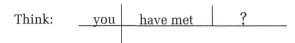

7. Mr. Ng, (who, which) lives next door, has relatives in Vietnam.

8. We will always remember those (who, which) died in Vietnam.

Review Set 66

Choose the best word to complete sentences 1–14.

1. The many-sided building was designed in the shape of a
(35, 61) (diagonal, polygon, fraction).

2. Will you (leave, let) Adeniz borrow your bicycle?
(60)

3. The triplets were identical (siblings, principles,
(43, 59) ultramoderns).

4. The rancher (rose, raised, razed) collies as a hobby.
(46)

5. We (shall, will) visit the cage of the Komodo dragon.
(9, 11)

6. The pronouns *I, me, mine, we, us,* and *ours* indicate the
(53, 58) speaker. They are (first, second, third) person.

7. The pronouns *you* and *yours* indicate the person being
(53, 58) spoken to. They are (first, second, third) person.

8. The pronouns *he, she, it, him, her, his,* and *hers* indicate
(53, 58) the person being spoken about. They are (first, second,
third) person.

9. The man (who, which) sells popcorn left early.
(66)

10. Mr. Lu, (*who, whom*) lives in Taiwan, will come to our
(66) country next month.

11. Dr. Chen, (*who, whom*) you know, will visit tomorrow.
(66)

12. Mirna and (she, her) went to lunch at noon.
(53, 55)

13. He polished the dashboard (himself, hisself).
(62)

14. The relative pronoun *who* refers to (people, animals,
(66) things).

15. Tell whether this sentence is declarative, interrogative,
(1, 3) imperative, or exclamatory: Whoa, the Komodo bit my
big toe!

16. Write the linking verb in this sentence: The Komodo
(22) dragon is the world's largest lizard.

17. Write each word that should be capitalized in this
(12, 30) sentence: would you rather have an african elephant, a siberian hamster, or a canada goose?

✓ **18.** Write the prepositional phrase and star the object of the
(33, 34) preposition in this sentence: The deadly bacteria in the Komodo's mouth will kill its prey.

19. Write each proper adjective in this sentence: Indonesian
(30) islands provide the habitat for the Komodo dragon.

20. Rewrite this sentence, adding periods as needed: The
(36, 40) last three months of the year are abbreviated Oct, Nov, and Dec

21. Write the subordinating conjunction in this
(61) sentence: Although considered harmless by zoo officials, the Komodo dragon can charge and bite.

✓ **22.** Tell whether the italicized noun in this sentence is
(28, 42) nominative or possessive case: The *Komodo's* eyes are orange.

23. Rewrite this sentence, adding commas as needed: As for
(56) me I'm going to plant geraniums not petunias this spring.

24. Replace the blank with the correct word: The noun to
(51) which a pronoun refers is called the _____.

✓ **25.** Write the clearer of these two sentences (a or b).
(51) (a) Frank called Smith before he left the office.
(b) Before Frank left the office, he called Smith.

26. Tell whether the italicized pronoun is nominative,
(55, 57) objective, or possessive case: Elise brought *her* to the barbecue.

27. Write the five singular reflexive pronouns from this
(62) list: ourselves, myself, hisself, yourself, themselves, himself, herself, itself.

28. Write the three plural reflexive pronouns from this
(62) list: myself, yourself, ourselves, himself, yourselves, theirselves, themselves.

29. Write the six simple relative pronouns from this
(66) list: who, honk, whom, if, whose, what, under, which,
and, that.

30. Diagram this sentence: The Komodo dragon has sharp,
(27, 28) sickle-shaped teeth.

Pronoun Usage

Dictation or Journal Entry

Vocabulary:

The prefix *hemi-* means "half." A *hemisphere* is a half-sphere formed by running a plane through the middle of a sphere. A globe of the world is divided into the Northern and Southern *Hemispheres*. Half a line of poetic verse is a *hemistich (pronounced HEM-i-stik)*. The student recited only a *hemistich* of the line. *Hemiplegia* is paralysis on one side of the body. The patient experienced *hemiplegia* after his stroke.

In this lesson, we will discuss areas where pronoun usage can be troublesome.

Written vs. Spoken Language

Traditionally, pronouns that follow a form of "to be" must be in the nominative case, as in the examples below.

It is *I*.

Was it *they* who called?

I knew it was *he*.

When we write, we should follow this rule. When we are speaking, however, we tend to be less formal. Our ear tells us that in casual conversation, "It is I" sounds stiff. Instead, we are more likely to say:

It is *me*.

Was it *them* who called?

I knew it was *him*.

Remember that this relaxed pronoun usage is acceptable in casual conversation, but would be unacceptable in formal speech or any form of writing.

Now we will discuss two more areas that often cause trouble in pronoun usage.

Appositions

We remember than an appositive renames a person or thing. An **apposition** is a pronoun used to rename a noun for emphasis.

Only one contestant, *you*, can enter the district spelling bee.

The principal named the winners of the essay contest, *you* and *me*.

The apposition must be in the same case form as the noun it renames. Consider the examples below.

> SUBJECT:
> *We* (NOT *us*) Southern Californians are not used to cold weather.

> OBJECT:
> They invited *us* (NOT *we*) young people.

> SUBJECT:
> Both players, Joseph and *he* (NOT *him*), are likely to score.

Example 1   Choose the correct apposition for this sentence:

> Our class sent two helpers, Onping and (*her, she*).

Solution   The apposition "Onping and her" renames "helpers," which is a direct object, so we use the objective case pronoun: Our class sent two helpers, Onping and **her.**

Comparisons   In comparison sentences, words are sometimes omitted. This usually occurs following the words *than* or *as*.

> He sings better than *I*. ("do" is omitted)

> I can jump as high as *she*. ("can" is omitted)

Notice that the pronouns in the sentences above are in the nominative case because they are used as the subjects of clauses whose verbs are understood (not stated).

The pronoun used in a comparison is important because it can change the meaning of the sentence:

> Jack loves jazz as much as *she*. ("does" is omitted)
> [MEANING: Jack loves jazz as much as she does.]

> Jack loves jazz as much as *her*. ("he loves" is omitted)
> [MEANING: Jack loves jazz as much as he loves her.]

Example 2   Choose the correct pronoun for the following sentences.
(a) We ski better than (*they, them*).

(b) I'm not as old as (*she, her*).

Solution   (a) We ski better than **they.** ("do" is omitted)

(b) I'm not as old as **she.** ("is" is omitted)

✓ Practice   Choose the correct pronoun for sentences a–e.

a. (We, Us) boys remember learning about "triangular trade."

Think: <u> ? </u> | <u>remember </u>

b. It is okay with (we, us) girls if you do a report on this topic.

Think: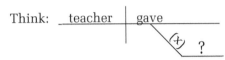

c. The teacher gave (we, us) boys the information we needed.

Think: <u> teacher </u> | <u> gave   </u>

(x) ?

d. He is better at sketching animals than (I, me). ["am" omitted]

e. They shovel snow as fast as (*we, us*). ["do" omitted]

For f–i, replace each blank with the correct vocabulary word.

f. The prefix meaning "half" is _____.

g. The stroke victim exhibited right _____.

h. The magazine quoted only a _____ of the verse of poetry.

i. The globe is divided into Eastern and Western _____.

More Practice   Choose the correct pronoun for each sentence.

1. Joseph had more integrity than (he, him). ["did" omitted]

2. (We, Us) Americans love our country.

Think: <u> ? </u> | <u>love   </u>

3. The helicopter pilot showed (we, us) passengers the glacier below.

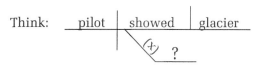

Think: pilot | showed | glacier
                        \\(+) ?

4. Lucita and (her, she) will draw the pictures.

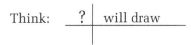

Think: ? | will draw

5. I met two new people, Jaime and (he, him).

Think: I | met | ?

6. Bob rode farther than (she, her). ["did" omitted]

7. Bill works later than (he, him). ["does" omitted]

8. I type faster than (they, them). ["do" omitted]

9. (We, Us) girls laughed together.

Think: ? | laughed

10. The burgers satisfied (we, us) students completely.

Think: burgers | satisfied | ?

Review Set 67   Choose the best word to complete sentences 1–10.

1. The dental X-ray revealed a (rite, whole, fracture) in the
(34, 51) tooth.

2. The doctor needed to (write, right, wright) legibly so the
(50) pharmacist could read the prescription.

3. The sun's (raze, rays, pores) burned the petals of the
(34, 46) rosebud.

4. Some newspaper columns offer (advise, advice) on
(45) everyday problems.

5. Debby (do, did, done) not know that some cats like to
(7, 15) swim.

6. The reflexive pronoun matches its (antecedent, verb, adjective) in person, number, and gender.
(51, 62)

7. They made the pizza (theirselves, themselves).
(62)

8. We can leave the (intensive, reflexive) pronoun out of a sentence without changing the meaning of the sentence.
(62)

9. Relative pronouns often refer to (nouns, verbs) that have preceded them, making the sentence more compact.
(66)

10. An (apposition, adjective) is a pronoun used to rename a noun for emphasis.
(67)

11. Write the simple subject in this sentence: Not all cats hate water.
(2)

12. Tell whether this group of words is a phrase or a clause: that love to swim
(24, 61)

Write each word that should be capitalized in sentences 13 and 14.

13. along the riverbanks from india to southeast asia lives a fishing cat.
(6, 12)

14. oh, cousin katrina, has your english improved?
(12, 26)

15. Write the prepositional phrase in this sentence, and star the object of the preposition: The tiger, the jaguar, and the fishing cat are examples of wild cats who love swimming.
(17, 33)

16. Rewrite this name and address, adding periods and commas as needed: Ms LeAnn J Baker PhD
(40, 47)
　　　　　　　　　　　2700 W Jenkins Ave
　　　　　　　　　　　St Paul Minnesota

17. Tell whether the sentence below is simple or compound. If it is compound, write the coordinating conjunction that joins the two independent clauses.
(64)

A fishing cat has partially-webbed feet, so it is able swim and scoop fish out of the water.

18. Tell whether the italicized nouns in this sentence are
(33, 43) direct objects, indirect objects, or objects of a
preposition: A fishing cat looks like a house cat with a
shorter *tail*, a flatter *face,* and smaller *ears.*

19. Rewrite this sentence, adding commas as
(63) needed: Janine's favorite dog is a large quiet black
poodle.

Refer to this sentence for 20 and 21: After he ate breakfast, he
brushed his teeth.

20. Write the independent clause in the sentence above.
(24, 61)

21. Write the dependent clause and underline the
(24, 61) subordinating conjunction in the sentence above.

For sentences 22 and 23, write the personal pronoun, and tell
whether it is first, second, or third person.

22. We worked hard today in the garden.
(53, 58)

23. Ming and she weeded and watered.
(53, 58)

24. List six singular pronouns.
(58)

25. List six plural pronouns.
(58)

26. Write each possessive pronoun from this list: we, us,
(60) ours, you, yours, him, it, hers.

27. Tell whether the italicized pronoun in this sentence is
(55, 57) nominative, objective, or possessive case: *They* are best
friends.

Diagram sentences 28 and 29, choosing the correct pronoun
to complete the sentence.

28. Shane and (him, he) play basketball.
(55, 58)

29. Kane wrote Monty and (I, me) a poem.
(57, 58)

30. Diagram this sentence: A fishing cat is small.
(22, 44)

LESSON 68

Interrogative Pronouns

Dictation or Journal Entry

Vocabulary:
Hear and *here* are homophones. *Hear* means "to perceive by using the ear."
We use our ears to *hear* sounds. *Here* is the opposite of "there" and means
"in or about this place." Please set that envelope right *here*.

When a relative pronoun introduces a question, it is called an
interrogative pronoun. *Who, whom, whose, what, which,*
whoever, whomever, whichever, and *whatever* are
interrogative pronouns.

Who is at the door?

What do you want?

Which shall we choose?

Whom are you calling?

Whoever would do that?

A sentence doesn't have to end with a question mark in order
to contain an interrogative pronoun. Sometimes an
interrogative pronoun introduces a question that is contained
inside a declarative sentence:

He asked *who* was at the door.

Pedro wondered *what* they wanted.

I didn't know *which* was best.

Example 1 Write each interrogative pronoun that you find in each
sentence.

(a) We couldn't guess what happened.

(b) Who won the game?

(c) I wonder which they'll find first.

(d) Whose shoes are these?

Solution (a) **what**   (b) **who**   (c) **which**   (d) **whose**

Who or Whom? In order to decide whether we should use *who* or *whom*, we
must determine what part the interrogative pronoun plays in
the sentence. If it functions as a subject or a predicate
nominative, we use *who*.

Who marched in the parade? (subject)

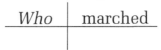

The grand marshal is *who*? (predicate nominative)

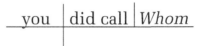

If the interrogative pronoun is an object (direct object, indirect object, or object of a preposition), we use *whom*.

Whom did you call? (direct object)

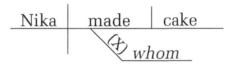

Nika made *whom* a cake? (indirect object)

To check to see that we have used *who* or *whom* correctly, we can turn the questions above into statements, substituting *he* or *she* for *who* and *him* or *her* for *whom*:

> RIGHT: You <u>did call</u> *him*.
> WRONG: You <u>did call</u> *he*.

> RIGHT: Nika <u>made</u> *her* a cake.
> WRONG: Nika <u>made</u> *she* a cake.

Errors to Avoid Do not confuse *whose* and *who's*. *Whose* is a possessive or interrogative pronoun. *Who's* is a contraction for "who is." Remember, possessive pronouns do not have apostrophes.

Who's that person? (Who is that person?)

Whose backpack is that?

Example 2 Choose the correct interrogative pronoun for each sentence.

(a) (Who, Whom) washed the dishes?

(b) (Who, Whom) did you expect?

(c) To (who, whom) are you speaking?

(d) This is mine, but (who's, whose) is that?

Solution (a) The pronoun is used as the subject, so we choose *who*.

Who washed the dishes?

(b) The pronoun is used as an object, so we choose *whom*.

Whom did you expect?

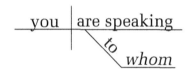

To check to see that we have used *who* or *whom* correctly, we change the question into a statement, substituting *he* or *she* for *who* and *him* or *her* for *whom*.

RIGHT: You <u>did expect</u> *him*.
WRONG: You <u>did expect</u> *he*.

(c) The pronoun is used as an object of a preposition, so we choose *whom*.

To **whom** are you speaking?

you | are speaking
to whom

(d) *Who's* is a contraction for "who is." We choose the interrogative pronoun *whose*.

This is mine, but **whose** is that?

Adjective or Pronoun? When *which, whose,* and *what* come before nouns, they are adjectives. When *which, whose,* and *what* stand alone, they are interrogative pronouns.

ADJECTIVE: *Which* shoe goes on the right foot?
PRONOUN: *Which* goes on the right foot?

ADJECTIVE: *What* lamp was broken?
PRONOUN: *What* was broken?

ADJECTIVE: *Whose* crayon is this?
PRONOUN: *Whose* is this?

Example 3 Tell whether the italicized word in each sentence is an interrogative pronoun or is used as an adjective.

(a) I wonder *whose* hat this is.

(b) *What* is your favorite color?

(c) *What* color do you like best?

(d) *Which* of the two is the correct answer?

Solution (a) *Whose* comes before the noun *hat*, so it is an **adjective.**

(b) *What* stands alone, so it is an **interrogative pronoun.**

(c) *What* precedes the noun *color*, so it is an **adjective.**

(d) *Which* stands alone. It is an **interrogative pronoun.**

√ **Practice** For a–c, write the interrogative pronoun, if any, from each sentence.

a. I could not guess what he was thinking.

b. She wondered which dress to wear.

c. Whose is that notebook?

For d–f, choose the correct interrogative pronoun for each sentence.

d. (Who, Whom) will you ask next time?

e. (Who's, Whose) is the big white dog?

f. (Who, Whom) wants more minestrone?

For g and h, tell whether the italicized word is an interrogative pronoun or is used as an adjective.

g. *What* are you doing?

h. *Which* road shall I take?

For i–l, replace each blank with *hear* or *here*.

i. We _____ sounds when vibrating air hits our eardrums.

j. There is no air on the moon, so people cannot _____.

k. _____ on Earth, there is air to carry sound waves.

l. I'd rather live _____ than on the moon.

More Practice Choose the correct word to complete each sentence.

1. (Who's, Whose) knocking on the door?

2. (Who's, Whose) voice do I hear?

3. (Who, Whom) washed the dishes?

4. To (who, whom) does this coat belong?

5. (Who, Whom) are you calling?

you | are calling | ?

6. (Who's, Whose) the man with the huge yellow hat?

7. (Who's, Whose) favorite movie is this?

8. With (who, whom) would you like to debate?

9. (Who, Whom) will win the race?

? | will win

10. (Who, Whom) did the committee choose?

committee | did choose | ?

Review Set 68 Choose the best word(s) to complete sentences 1–12.

1. The prefix *ultra-* means "(extremely, ordinarily)."
   (44)

2. The school (ultramodern, ultraconservative, principal)
   (43, 44) fully supported his teaching staff.

3. The prefix (*mal-, ultra-, dia-*) refers to something bad, ill,
   (41, 44) or wrong.

4. Over ninety percent of the people (excepted, accepted,
   (40) affected) the wedding invitation.

5. The wetlands are not the (beautifulest, more beautiful,
   (45, 46) most beautiful) part of the coastline.

6. Pronoun (case, gender) shows the job the pronoun is
   (58) performing in the sentence.

7. When a personal pronoun comes before a noun to tell (28, 60) "whose," we call it a (possessive, descriptive) adjective.

8. When a personal pronoun replaces a noun and stands (60) alone to tell "whose," we call it a (possessive, proper) pronoun.

9. (Contractions, Possessive pronouns) do not have (60) apostrophes.

10. (They're, Their) uniforms consist of navy shorts and a (38) white collared shirt.

11. The disgruntled employee complained to (himself, (62) hisself) the entire day.

12. When a relative pronoun introduces a question, it is (68) called an (interesting, interrogative) pronoun.

13. Tell whether this word group is a sentence fragment, (3) run-on sentence, or complete sentence: A cat's eyes reflect light in the dark their color is brilliant green or blue.

For 14 and 15, tell whether the underlined verb is transitive or intransitive.

14. The cat's eyes <u>glowed</u> in the headlights.
(22, 32)

15. The tapetum lucidum, a part of the eye, <u>gives</u> cats (25, 32) excellent night vision.

16. Choose the collective noun from this list: community, (8) pan, roller, cup, slope.

17. Rewrite this sentence, adding capital letters and commas (6, 47) as needed: wolfgang mozart my favorite composer was born in salzburg austria.

18. Write the prepositional phrase in this sentence, and star (17, 33) the object of the preposition: Wetlands catch dirt in runoff water.

19. Write the seven common coordinating conjunctions.
(37)

Rewrite sentences 20 and 21, adding commas as needed.

20. On Friday June 15 2001 the Los Angeles Lakers defeated
(47) the Philadelphia Seventy-Sixers to capture their second
consecutive NBA Championship.

21. The oceanographer explained "The way that plants and
(65) animals live together in a wetland community helps slow
the flow of runoff water and this keeps the coastal waters
from being flooded with dirt."

For 22 and 23, tell whether the italicized pronoun is singular
or plural.

√ **22.** The sand bucket and shovel are *theirs*.
(53, 60)

√ **23.** *He* surfs well.
(53, 55)

For 24 and 25, tell whether the italicized pronoun is
nominative, objective, or possessive case.

24. The sandy beach towel belongs to *him*.
(55, 57)

25. The lifeguard we saw posing for pictures is *he*.
(55, 57)

For 26 and 27, refer to this sentence: Although she enjoys the
ocean, Grandma did not swim today.

26. Write the independent clause in the sentence above.
(24, 61)

27. Write the dependent clause and underline the
(24, 61) subordinating conjunction in the sentence above.

28. Write the six simple relative pronouns from this
(66) list: walk, who, whom, witch, wonder, whose, what,
were, which, that.

29. Write the nine interrogative pronouns from this
(68) list: who, whopper, whom, whisper, whose, what, which,
wore, whomever, whoever, worn, whichever, whatever.

√ **30.** Diagram this compound sentence: Wetlands are useful,
(64) for they protect animals and plants.

LESSON 69

Quotation Marks, Part 1

Dictation or Journal Entry

Vocabulary:
Sometimes we can determine the meaning of a word by examining its parts. The prefix *anti-* (against) tells us that *antifreeze* means "against freezing." *Antifreeze* is a liquid of low freezing point added to engine radiators to prevent freezing in cold weather. We can also learn more about words we already know by examining their parts. Consider the word *antidote*. The dictionary tells us that *dote* comes from the Greek word for "give." An *antidote* is something that is given to counteract (work against) a poison.

Direct Quotation

A **direct quotation** gives a speaker's exact words. To indicate a direct quotation, we enclose the speaker's words in quotation marks.

> Martin Luther King, Jr., told his followers, "Don't let anyone pull you so low as to hate them."

> "We must use the weapon of love," King pleaded.

Notice that in each of the examples above, the punctuation mark following the direct quotation appears **inside** the quotation marks.

Example 1

Place quotation marks where they are needed in the sentence below.

> Jackie Robinson is a phenomenal athlete, said manager Branch Rickey.

Solution

We place quotation marks before and after Branch Rickey's words (including the comma that follows them).

> **"Jackie Robinson is a phenomenal athlete," said manager Branch Rickey.**

Direct Quotation with Explanatory Note

Sometimes a direct quotation is interrupted by an **explanatory note** such as *he said, she replied, the teacher explained*, etc. We enclose in quotation marks only the speaker's exact words, not the explanatory note. Notice that both parts of the direct quotations below are enclosed in quotation marks.

> "Unjust laws exist," said Henry David Thoreau, "and shall we be content to obey them?"

> "If a law requires you to be the agent of injustice to another," explained Thoreau, "then I say, break the law."

Example 2   Place quotation marks where they are needed in the sentence below.

> Did you know, asked the baseball coach, that Jackie Robinson played baseball, football, basketball, and track at the University of California in Los Angeles?

Solution   We place quotation marks around both parts of the coach's direct quotation, but we do not enclose the explanatory note (asked the baseball coach) in quotation marks.

> **"Did you know," asked the baseball coach, "that Jackie Robinson played baseball, football, basketball, and track at the University of California in Los Angeles?"**

Indirect Quotations   An **indirect quotation** gives the main idea of what someone said, but it does not give the speaker's exact words. We do not use quotation marks with indirect quotations.

> Martin Luther King, Jr., told others that he was influenced by Henry David Thoreau.

> Thoreau explained that disobeying unjust laws (by nonviolent actions) is sometimes necessary to achieve justice.

Example 3   Add quotation marks as needed in the sentence below.

> Jackie Robinson, first African-American to play major league baseball in the twentieth century, admitted that he hated to lose.

Solution   **No quotation marks** are necessary because this is not a direct quotation. It is an **indirect quotation.**

Practice   For a–e, rewrite correctly each sentence that needs quotation marks. If the sentence does not need quotation marks, write "none."

a. Brooklyn Dodgers general manager Branch Rickey explained that he wanted a man strong enough not to fight back against the insults that were sure to come when the first African-American entered the major leagues.

b. Jackie Robinson told Rickey that he accepted that challenge.

c. Imagine someone saying to Shaquille O'Neal, You can't play in the National Basketball Association because you are black!

d. Of course, the man went on, that's ridiculous.

e. Mr. Towner said to his class, Jackie Robinson opened the way for players of all races to succeed in professional sports.

Replace each blank with the correct vocabulary word.

f. _____ is added to the radiator to keep the fluid from freezing.

g. It keeps your car going in cold weather, but remember that _____ is poisonous.

h. In the school play, my character rushes onstage at the last minute with the _____ to the poison.

i. The prefix *anti-* means "_____."

More Practice   See "More Practice Lesson 69" in Student Workbook.

Review Set 69   Choose the best word to complete sentences 1–14.

1. The district attorney attempted to (affect, indict, advice)
(27, 39) the man for fraud.

2. The runners stop over (their, they're, there) for water and
(38) fruit.

3. To (so, sow, sew) a dress takes time and talent.
(37)

4. The police asked all storeowners to show (conscience,
(26, 36) punctuality, discretion) during the rowdy parade.

5. Last Thanksgiving, Aunt Leona made (for, fore, four)
(64) different (desserts, deserts)!

6. The plural of *dish* is (dishs, dishes).
(13, 14)

7. Of the three fish, that one has the (longer, longest) tail.
(45, 46)

8. He and (I, me) like to watch Justin as he romps in the
(55, 58) waves.

9. You brought (you, yourself) a turkey sandwich for lunch.
(62)

10. The relative pronoun (who, which) refers to people.
(66)

11. (Who, Which) refers to animals or things.
(66)

12. (Who, Which, That) refers to people, animals, or things.
(66)

13. If the interrogative pronoun is a direct object, indirect object, or object of a preposition, we use (who, whom).
(68)

14. If the interrogative pronoun functions as a subject or a predicate nominative, we use (who, whom).
(68)

15. Write the action verb in this sentence: A new presidential administration begins on January 20.
(5, 7)

16. Write the present participle, past tense, and past participle of the verb *drip*.
(7, 16)

17. Rewrite this sentence, adding capital letters as needed: my best friend, pat newmar, won a trip to honolulu, hawaii.
(6, 12)

18. Write the appositive in this sentence: The first woman nominated for president, Belva Lockwood, led the Equal Rights Party in 1884 and 1888.
(48, 49)

19. Write each objective case pronoun from this list: her, she, me, I, he, him, they, them, we, us.
(53, 57)

For 20 and 21, refer to this sentence: While he was waiting for the doctor, he read a whole novel.

20. Write the independent clause from the sentence above.
(24, 61)

21. Write the dependent clause and underline the subordinating conjunction in the sentence above.
(24, 61)

22. Write each possessive case pronoun from this list: me, she, mine, they, yours, he, his, we, hers, ours, us, theirs.
(60)

23. Write each nominative case pronoun from this list: me, him, I, she, them, they, he, her, we, us.
(53, 55)

For 24 and 25, tell whether the italicized pronoun is nominative, objective, or possessive case.

24. Wayne stepped carefully toward *her*.
(53, 57)

25. My teacher is *he* in the dark suit.
(41, 53)

For 26 and 27, tell whether the underlined verb is an action or linking verb.

✓ **26.** His voice <u>sounded</u> gentle.
(5, 22)

✓ **27.** David <u>sounded</u> the bugle at sunrise.
(5, 22)

Diagram sentences 28–30.

✓ **28.** The longest-serving individual in Congress was Joseph
(34, 41) Gurney Cannon of Illinois.

✓ **29.** My goats and sheep can share the same pasture.
(25, 38)

✓ **30.** She walked, but I ran.
(64)

LESSON
70

Quotation Marks, Part 2

Dictation or Journal Entry

Vocabulary:
Humility is "a modest sense of one's own importance." A person with *humility* (noun) is *humble* (adjective). *Arrogance*, the opposite of humility, is an offensive display of superiority or self-importance, accompanied by disrespect for others. Someone with *arrogance* (noun) is *arrogant* (adjective). An ancient Chinese proverb reads "Arrogance invites ruin; humility receives benefits."

Speaker Changes A set of quotation marks can contain the words of only one speaker. When the speaker changes, we use a new set of quotation marks. Also, when writing dialogue (conversation), we start a new paragraph every time the speaker changes.

Notice how quotation marks are used as the speaker changes in this dialogue from *Oliver Twist* by Charles Dickens:

"Do you live in London?" inquired Oliver.

"Yes. I do, when I'm at home," replied the boy. "I suppose you want some place to sleep in to-night, don't you?"

"I do, indeed," answered Oliver. "I have not slept under a roof since I left the country."

"Don't fret your eyelids on that score," said the young gentleman.

Example 1 Rewrite this dialogue from Frances Hodgson Burnett's *The Secret Garden,* inserting quotation marks as needed.

What is that? she said to the housemaid.

That's the moor, said Martha, with a good-natured grin.

Who is going to dress me? demanded Mary.

Martha stared. Can't you put on your own clothes?

Solution We know that a new paragraph means that the speaker has changed. We place quotation marks around the actual words of each speaker.

"What is that?" she said to the housemaid.

"That's the moor," said Martha, with a good-natured grin.

"Who is going to dress me?" demanded Mary.

Martha stared. "Can't you put on your own clothes?"

Titles The titles of short literary works are enclosed in quotation marks. This includes short stories, parts of books (chapters, lessons, sections, etc.), essays and sermons, one-act plays, newspaper and magazine articles, and short poems. We also enclose the titles of songs in quotation marks.

> Edgar Allan Poe's "The Tell-Tale Heart" scared the socks off Rebecca.
>
> "Father William," a poem by Lewis Carroll, amuses the reader with its silliness.
>
> Henry David Thoreau's most powerful essay, "Civil Disobedience," influenced many people.
>
> If Bob sings "Home on the Range" one more time, I'm going to scream.

We do not use quotation marks for larger works such as books, plays, movies, television programs, or operas. Instead, these titles are underlined or italicized (Our Town, *Paradise Lost*). We shall discuss this further in Lesson 73.

Example 2 Rewrite the sentences below, inserting quotation marks where they are needed.

(a) Will you sing America at the game tonight?

(b) Keats wrote a poem called Ode on a Grecian Urn.

(c) Paul dreaded the next chapter, Fun with Fractions.

Solution (a) We place quotation marks around "America" because it is a song title.

Will you sing "America" at the game tonight?

(b) We enclose "Ode on a Grecian Urn" in quotation marks because it is the name of a poem.

Keats wrote a poem called "Ode on a Grecian Urn."

(c) We enclose "Fun with Fractions" in quotation marks because it is the title of a chapter in a book.

Paul dreaded the next chapter, "Fun with Fractions."

Practice For a and b, replace each blank with the correct vocabulary word.

✓ **a.** People who do not consider themselves overly important have _____.

✓ **b.** The opposite of humility is _____.

Rewrite sentences c–e, inserting quotation marks as needed.

    c. Washington Irving's short story The Legend of Sleepy Hollow is read by students everywhere.

    d. Can you play the song America the Beautiful for me?

    e. Mark Twain's short story The Mysterious Stranger is not as well known as his novel *Tom Sawyer.*

    f. Rewrite this dialogue from Anna Sewell's *Black Beauty,* inserting quotation marks where they are needed.

> Who is your master, young man? if it be a proper question. I should judge he is a good one, from what I see.
>
> He is Squire Gordon, of Birtwick Park, the other side the Beacon Hills, said James.
>
> Ah! so, so, I have heard tell of him; fine judge of horses, ain't he? the best rider in the county.
>
> I believe he is, said James, but he rides very little now, since the poor young master was killed.

More Practice   See "More Practice Lesson 70" in Student Workbook.

Review Set 70   Choose the best word to complete sentences 1–7.

    1. The artist drew a (polygon, diagonal, dialogue) line from
    _(35, 61) one corner of the rectangle to another.

    2. The mechanic (poured, pored, poored) the antifreeze
    ₍₃₄₎ carefully into the radiator.

    3. In order to win, a rowing team must synchronize the
    ₍₃₃₎ movement of their (ores, oars, ors).

    4. The Vietnam War resulted in (postmortem, postscript,
    ₍₃₂₎ postwar) anxieties in many soldiers.

    5. Redheads, (who, which) usually have light complexions,
    ₍₆₆₎ should not go outdoors without sunscreen.

    6. That is the barn (that, who) needs a coat a paint.
    ₍₆₆₎

    ₍₆₈₎ **7.** (Who, Whom) is going to tackle the job?

8. Replace the blank with the singular present tense form of the underlined verb: They _dirty_ many dishes. Sal _____ many dishes.
_(5, 7)

9. Write the perfect tense verb phrase in this sentence: Had Sir Walter Raleigh ever come to America?
_(9, 19)

10. Write the direct object in this sentence: Sir Walter Raleigh obeyed Queen Elizabeth.
_(5, 25)

11. Write the plural of _tornado_.
_(13, 14)

12. Write the descriptive adjective in this sentence: The industrious Raleigh set out to South America to find gold.
₍₂₇₎

13. Write the four common pairs of correlative conjunctions.
₍₃₉₎

14. Write each predicate nominative from this sentence: Two Old Testament men who never die are Elijah and Enoch.
_(22, 41)

15. Rewrite this sentence, adding commas as needed: Shaquille O'Neal the Los Angeles Lakers' center received the MVP trophy for the 2001 NBA Championship.
₍₄₉₎

Replace each blank with the correct word to complete sentences 16 and 17.

16. Pronouns are _____ case when they are used as direct objects, indirect objects, or objects of a preposition.
_(53, 57)

17. Pronouns are _____ case when they are used as subjects or predicate nominatives.
_(53, 55)

18. Write the sentence that is more polite (a or b).
₍₅₇₎
(a) Aunt Peggy kissed me and her.
(b) Aunt Peggy kissed her and me.

19. Unscramble these words to make a sentence with a personal pronoun as a direct object:
_(53, 57)

won   raced   and   him   Helen

20. Unscramble these words to make a sentence with a personal pronoun as an indirect object.
_(53, 57)

Delbert   her   an   made   sandwich   avocado

For 21 and 22, tell how the italicized pronoun is used in the sentence (subject, predicate nominative, direct object, indirect object, object of a preposition, or possession).

21. The host served *us* steak and potatoes.
(42, 43)

22. Trevor thanked *them* for the gift.
(42, 43)

For 23 and 24, refer to this sentence: The fishing cat has a double layer of fur so that it doesn't get wet all the way to the skin when it is fishing.

23. Write the independent clause from the sentence above.
(24, 61)

24. Write the two dependent clauses, and underline the two subordinating conjunctions in the sentence above.
(24, 61)

25. Write the interrogative pronoun from this sentence: He wondered who might accompany him to the baseball game.
(68)

Rewrite sentences 26 and 27, adding quotation marks as needed:

26. Quan said, I once saw a twelve-foot sea snake curled up on the surface of the water.
(69)

27. To Build a Fire, a short story written by Jack London, depicts the dangers of freezing weather.
(70)

Diagram sentences 28–30.

28. Kurt invited Molly and me.
(25)

29. Both Ohio and Michigan are Midwest states.
(38)

30. Have you seen the flying snakes of India?
(34)

LESSON
71

Demonstrative Pronouns

Dictation or Journal Entry

Vocabulary:
The prefix *semi-* means "partially," "partly," or "not fully." It can mean "exactly half," as in *semicircle*, but this definition is secondary to the first one. *Semifinal* refers to a competition that precedes the final event. The team competed in the basketball *semifinals*. *Semiprecious* refers to gemstones that are rare but less valuable than precious gems like diamonds. Even though jade is rare and beautiful, it still is considered a *semiprecious* stone. *Semiconscious* means "only partly conscious." The football player appeared *semiconscious* after being hit in the head.

Pointing Pronouns   *This*, *that*, *these*, and *those* are **demonstrative pronouns.** Some people call them "pointing pronouns" because they seem to point out the person or thing being referred to, distinguishing it from others.

> *This* is a technological world.

> *That* is a printer.

> *These* are computers.

> *Those* are disks.

A demonstrative pronoun must agree in number with its antecedent (the noun that it points out).

SINGULAR:	*This* is a skateboard.
PLURAL:	*These* are skateboards.
SINGULAR:	*That* is a surfboard.
PLURAL:	*Those* are surfboards.

This, These   We use *this* and *these* to point out persons or things that are nearby in space, time, or awareness.

> *This* is a Siamese cat.

> *These* are my opinions.

> *This* has been a hectic week.

That, Those   We use *that* and *those* to point out persons or things that are farther away.

> *That* is a Burmese cat.

> *That* was a rotten plan.

> *Those* were the good old days.

Errors to Avoid   We never add "here" or "there" to a demonstrative pronoun.

> NO: This *here* is my idea.
> YES: This is my idea.

> NO: That *there* is the silliest girl.
> YES: That is the silliest girl.

We do not use "them" in place of "these" or "those."

> NO: *Them* are the good ones.
> YES: *These* are the good ones.

> NO: *Them* make me sick.
> YES: *Those* make me sick.

Adjective or Pronoun?   The demonstrative pronouns *this*, *that*, *these*, and *those* also function as demonstrative adjectives.

It is easy to tell the difference. If they stand alone, they are demonstrative pronouns. If they come before a noun, they are demonstrative adjectives.

> *These* are too small. (pronoun)

> *These* shoes are too small. (adjective)

> I wrote *this*. (pronoun)

> I wrote *this* essay. (adjective)

Example   Choose the correct demonstrative pronoun for each sentence, and write the noun that it points to.

(a) (This here, This) is a picture of the original Australians, the aborigines.

(b) Is (that, those) the reason many aborigines died?

(c) (This, These) are the aborigines that survived murder and disease.

(d) (Them, Those) are the ones responsible for taking aborigine land.

Solution   (a) **This picture**   (b) **That reason**

(c) **These aborigines**   (d) **Those ones**

Practice For a–d, replace each blank with the correct vocabulary word.

  a. The prefix _____ means "partially."

  b. The victim was only _____ after the car crash.

  c. Jewelers categorize diamonds as precious but gemstones such as jade, garnet, and amethyst as _____.

  d. The Los Angeles Lakers and the Portland Trailblazers played in the _____ game.

For e–i, choose the correct demonstrative pronoun, and write the noun it points to.

  e. (This, These) is a painting of Chinese people who resented the presence of other countries in their land.

  f. (That, Those) are the Boxers, or members of the Fists of Righteous Harmony.

  g. (This, These) is their name because they were skilled in the Chinese arts of self-defense.

  h. (These, That) are my reasons for studying the history of the Boxers.

  i. (This, This here) is the class I was waiting for.

  j. A demonstrative pronoun is sometimes called a _____ pronoun.

Review Set 71 Choose the best word(s) to complete sentences 1–9.

  1. The (morale, moral, biosphere) of the movie was that we
  (2, 23) should judge people by their inner beauty rather than by their outward appearance.

  2. The (dishonorable, compassionate, punctual) train
  (1, 22) conductor always announces departures on time.

  3. The (respectful, wasteful, prodigious) young people
  (3, 20) offered their bus seats to the elderly passengers.

  4. The prefix *homo-* means "(part, single, same)."
  (4)

  5. He built the shed (hisself, himself).
  (62)

6. A (phrase, clause) has both a subject and a predicate.
(24, 61)

7. (Them, These) are mine.
(71)

8. A relative pronoun is called an (abstract, interrogative)
(68) pronoun when it introduces a question with *who, whom, whose, what, whomever, which, whoever, whichever,* or *whatever.*

9. *This, that, these,* and *those* are (possessive,
(71) demonstrative) pronouns.

10. Tell whether this sentence is declarative, interrogative,
(1, 3) imperative, or exclamatory: Pull over to the right side of the street when you see a fire truck coming.

11. Write each action verb in this sentence: Certain frogs
(5, 7) change color so that they match their background.

12. Write the past perfect verb phrase in this sentence: The
(9, 19) tree frog had changed from nearly black to white.

Rewrite sentences 13–15, adding capital letters and periods as needed.

13. in *the voyage of the beagle,* the author describes the
(12, 20) octopus and cuttlefish as capable of changing color

14. dr samuel o mast explains how fishes known as flounder
(6, 36) can assume colors and patterns similar to their background

15. jahnelle and her mother serve dinner at st stephen's on
(12, 40) friday nights

16. Write each prepositional phrase and star each object of
(17, 33) the preposition in this sentence: Concerning color changes, most are produced by the expansion and contraction of the pigment cells.

17. Write the direct object in this sentence: Moisture, light,
(5, 25) and temperature cause color changes.

18. For sentences a and b, tell whether the underlined verb is
(22, 32) transitive or intransitive.
   (a) The blind tree frog <u>looked</u> browner.
   (b) I <u>looked</u> at the blind tree frog.

19. Write the seven common coordinating conjunctions.
(37)

Rewrite sentences 20 and 21, adding commas and quotation marks as needed.

20. Dr. Mast reported The color adaptations in flounder
(65, 69) probably resulted from stimuli received through the eyes.

21. Mast also shared that simple things like heat and light
(65, 69) will cause a color change in some animals.

Replace each blank with the correct word to complete sentences 22–26.

22. A _____ is a word that takes the place of a noun.
(51)

23. The word to which the pronoun refers is called the
(51) _____.

24. A pronoun is _____ case when used as a predicate
(53, 55) nominative.

25. A pronoun is _____ case when used as the subject
(53, 55) of the sentence.

26. A pronoun is _____ case when used as a direct
(53, 57) object, indirect object, or object of a preposition.

27. Write the nominative case pronouns from this list: I, me,
(55) we, us, he, him, she, her, they, them.

28. Write each possessive adjective in this sentence: His
(53, 60) shirt, her dress, and their hats were all made from the same fabric as my apron.

Diagram sentences 29 and 30.

29. They were watching the fireworks in the sky.
(25, 33)

30. A tree frog can turn black.
(22, 44)

LESSON
72

Indefinite Pronouns

Dictation or Journal Entry
Vocabulary:
Ware is something that is sold. The peddler sold his *wares* to the townspeople. *Ware* also refers to items of the same general kind. Would you rather give up soft*ware* or silver*ware*? *Wear* means "to have on" or "to carry on" one's body. A dentist *wears* a mask when working on a patient. *Wear* also means "to gradually erode or irritate through use." Clothes eventually *wear* out. We use the word *where* when we are asking "in what place?" or "in what situation?" *Where* did I put the keys to the car?

A pronoun that does not have a known antecedent is called an **indefinite pronoun.** It refers to a person or thing only generally.

Anybody can sign up.

Several will fit.

Something is wrong.

Singular Some indefinite pronouns refer to only one person or thing. They are singular and take singular verbs:

another	*anybody*	*anyone*
anything	*neither*	*either*
everybody	*everyone*	*everything*
each	*nobody*	*no one*
nothing	*other*	*one*
somebody	*someone*	*something*
much		

Everybody <u>wants</u> to succeed.

Each of the students <u>tries</u> hard.

Neither of us <u>is</u> going to fail.

Nothing <u>is</u> the matter with you.

Plural The following indefinite pronouns refer to more than one person or thing. They take plural verbs:

several	*both*	*few*
ones	*many*	*others*

Both <u>are</u> home sick today.

Few <u>were</u> quiet.

Many <u>are</u> agitated.

Others <u>seem</u> nervous.

Singular or Plural The following indefinite pronouns can be singular or plural depending on their use in the sentence.

all	*any*	*more*
none	*some*	*most*

They are plural when they refer to things that can be counted.

Most stores <u>close</u> on holidays.

They are singular when they refer to something that cannot be counted.

Most of the cake <u>is</u> gone.

Example 1 Write each indefinite pronoun and tell whether it is singular or plural in the sentence.

(a) *Much* has been said about college preparation.

(b) *Each* must make his or her own decisions.

(c) *Many* of the students need help with their study habits.

(d) *All* of the snow is melting.

(e) *All* are invited to the banquet.

(f) *None* of the horses were properly shod.

Solution
(a) ***Much*, singular**   (b) ***Each*, singular**

(c) ***Many*, plural**   (d) ***All*, singular**

(e) ***All*, plural**   (f) ***None*, plural**

Example 2 Choose the correct verb form (singular or plural) to match the indefinite pronoun in each sentence.

(a) *All* of you (is, are) to begin training for the sport.

(b) *Many* (need, needs) to strengthen their legs.

(c) *Few* (has, have) the discipline necessary to gain strength.

(d) (Is, Are) *anything* more fun than volleyball?

Solution (a) *All* of you **are** to begin training for the sport.

(b) *Many* **need** to strengthen their legs.

(c) *Few* **have** the discipline necessary to gain strength.

(d) **Is** *anything* more fun than volleyball?

Adjective or Pronoun? Just like demonstrative pronouns, when indefinite pronouns are placed before nouns, they function as indefinite adjectives.

Some are too expensive. (pronoun)

Some cars are too expensive. (adjective)

I gave one to *each*. (pronoun)

I gave one to *each* boy. (adjective)

Agreement with Antecedents If an indefinite pronoun is the antecedent for a personal pronoun, the personal pronoun must agree in number, person, and gender.

SINGULAR: *Everything* has *its* purpose.

(antecedent)   (personal pronoun)

PLURAL: *Both* have *their* purpose.

(antecedent)   (personal pronoun)

There is an exception. When writing, we do not use the plural *their* with the singular *everyone, everybody,* etc. When speaking, however, it has become acceptable to use *their* when *his or her* would sound awkward.

WRITTEN: *Everybody* should bring *his* or *her* own food.

SPOKEN: *Everybody* should bring *their* own food.

Example 3 Choose the correct personal pronoun to match the antecedent.
(a) *Something* left (their, its) footprints near the pond.

(b) *Neither* of the girls forgot (their, her) lunch.

(c) *Some* have paid (their, his or her) taxes already.

(a) The antecedent *something* is singular, so we choose the singular personal pronoun **its**.

> Something left **its** footprints near the pond.

(b) The antecedent *neither* is singular, so we choose the singular personal pronoun **her**.

> Neither of the girls forgot **her** lunch.

(c) The antecedent *some* refers to people (specifically taxpayers), who can be counted. We choose the plural personal pronoun **their**.

> Some have paid **their** taxes already.

√ **Practice** For sentences a and b, write the indefinite pronoun and tell whether it is singular or plural.

  a. All of us are learning to pass the volleyball accurately.

  b. Nobody serves the volleyball consistently at the beginning of the season.

For sentences c–e, choose the correct verb form to match the indefinite pronoun.

  c. *None* of those students (is, are) ready to play volleyball yet.

  d. *Some* of the players (is, are) ready to spike the ball.

  e. *Each* of us (is, are) working hard.

For f–h, choose the correct personal pronoun and verb form to match the indefinite pronoun antecedent.

  f. *Something* (have, has) left (its, their) hair on the carpet.

  g. *Many* of the world's best pianists (soaks, soak) (his, her, their) fingers in warm water before playing.

  h. *None* of my artwork (sell, sells) for what I think (it, they) (is, are) worth.

For i–l, replace each blank with *ware*, *wear*, or *where*.

  i. What are you going to _____ to school today?

j. The owner keeps very expensive _____ in his store.

k. These tourists don't know _____ they are going.

l. Calvin doesn't know what clothes to _____ because he doesn't know _____ he'll be tonight.

More Practice Tell whether each indefinite pronoun is singular, plural, or either. (S = singular; P= plural; E = either)

1. most 2. both 3. anybody 4. neither

5. either 6. some 7. everyone 8. few

9. everything 10. ones 11. each 12. many

13. something 14. nothing 15. others 16. more

17. another 18. several 19. none 20. all

Additional Practice See "Silly Story #4" in Student Workbook.

Review Set 72 Choose the best word(s) to complete sentences 1–13.

1. Two words with the same sound and spelling but
(4, 13) different meanings are (homophones, homonyms, bilingual).

2. Two words with the same sound but different spellings
(4, 13) and meanings are (homophones, homonyms, bilingual).

3. Recycling newspapers reduces the (waist, waste,
(5, 11) biosphere) of paper.

4. Parents should teach their children to (honor, dishonor,
(6, 68) here) their elders.

5. The snake's tongue is one of its (sensitivist, most
(45, 46) sensitive) organs.

6. (First, Second, Third) person pronouns include *I, me,*
(53, 58) *mine, we, us,* and *ours.* They refer to the speaker.

7. We can group pronouns into three cases: nominative,
(55, 57) objective, and (possessive, demonstrative).

8. The relative pronoun (*who, which*) refers to people.
(66)

9. The relative pronoun (*who, which*) refers to animals or
(66) things.

10. The relative pronoun (*who, that*) refers to people,
(66) animals, or things.

11. Our team sent two all-stars, Peng and (him, he).
(57, 58)

12. We use *this* and *these* to point out persons or things that
(71) are (near, far).

13. A pronoun that does not have a known antecedent is
(72) called an (indefinite, impersonal) pronoun.

For 14 and 15, refer to this sentence: Can snakes sting with
their tongues?

14. Write the simple subject.
(2, 23)

15. Write the simple predicate.
(2, 23)

16. Replace the blank with the singular present tense form of
(5, 7) the underlined verb.

Experts <u>deny</u> that snakes sting with their tongues. An
expert _____ that snakes sting with their tongues.

17. Write the past progressive verb phrase in this
(9, 21) sentence: Snakes were biting with their fangs.

18. Tell whether the underlined noun in this sentence is
(8) concrete or abstract: Biologists remain uncertain as to
why the snake's <u>tongue</u> is continually moving.

19. Rewrite this outline, adding periods and capital letters as
(20, 36) needed:

   i occupations

     a french teacher

     b biology teacher

20. Write each prepositional phrase and star the object of
(17, 33) each preposition in this sentence: The snake feels its way
over the ground with its tongue.

21. Write the possessive adjective in this sentence: His
(28, 60) tongue helps him trace scents on the ground.

22. Write the four common pairs of correlating conjunctions.
(39)

For 23–25, refer to this sentence: Even though the people in
Shakespeare's time believed that snakes could sting, we
know now that this is a falsehood.

23. Write the three dependent clauses.
(24, 61)

24. Write the independent clause.
(24, 61)

25. Write the three subordinating conjunctions.
(61)

26. Write each objective case pronoun from this list: I, me,
(57, 58) we, us, he, him, she, her, they, them.

27. Write the indefinite pronoun in this sentence and tell
(51, 72) whether it is singular or plural: Several of Brian's pet
snakes were lying in the sun.

28. Write each possessive pronoun in this sentence: This
(58, 60) cookie is his, not hers.

Diagram sentences 29 and 30.

29. The nurse gave me a tetanus shot.
(25, 35)

30. Some trees grow tall but narrow.
(23, 44)

Italics or Underline

Dictation or Journal Entry
Vocabulary:
Stationary and *stationery* are homophones. When something is not movable, it is *stationary*. In the gym, people exercise on *stationary* bicycles. Paper used for writing is *stationery*. I wrote the letter using my best *stationery*.

The word ***italics*** refers to a slightly slanted style of type that is used to indicate the titles of larger literary works or to bring special emphasis to a word or phrase in a sentence. The book title below is in italics.

The Secret Garden

When we handwrite material, or when the italic style of type is not available, we **underline** the word or words that would require italics in print.

The Secret Garden

Here are some of the main categories of words and phrases that should be italicized or underlined.

Longer Literary Works, Movies, CDs, etc.

We italicize or underline titles of books, magazines, newspapers, pamphlets, plays, book-length poems, television programs, movies, films, record albums, tapes, and CDs.

Children love watching shows such as *Mister Rogers* on television.

Have you ever read Animal Farm by George Orwell?

Paintings and Sculptures

We italicize or underline the titles of paintings, sculptures, and other works of art.

Edvard Munch painted *The Scream* to express his feelings without using his voice.

A French artist named Auguste Rodin (row-DAN) designed The Thinker, a statue that shows a man pondering a serious topic.

Ships, Planes, and Trains

We italicize or underline the names of ships, planes, and trains. (Words such as "The" and "U.S.S." are not treated as part of the vehicle's name.)

Tourists enjoy visiting the *Queen Mary*, a ship docked in Long Beach, California.

They traveled by train on the Super Chief.

Example 1   For sentences a–c, underline all the words that should be italicized or underlined.

   (a) The Spruce Goose is a famous aircraft once owned by Howard Hughes.

   (b) Paradise Lost is a long poem by John Milton.

   (c) Pablo Picasso painted Guernica to show the immense suffering of war.

Solution   (a) We underline **Spruce Goose** because it is the name of a plane. ("The" is not considered part of the name.)

   (b) **Paradise Lost** is a book-length poem.

   (c) **Guernica** is a painting.

Words as Words   We italicize or underline a word when the sentence calls attention to the word **as a word**.

   The word *clear* has many different meanings.

   His essay contained one too many *really*.

   Duck can be a verb, but *rooster* can't.

   This is also true for numerals and lowercase letters.

   Make each lowercase *b* the same height as the numeral *4*.

Foreign Words and Phrases   We italicize or underline foreign words that are not used as part of everyday English language.

   The French say *bonjour* in the morning.

   The *dramatis personae* (the characters of the play) are listed in the program.

Genus and Species Names   We italicize or underline the scientific names for a genus, species, or subspecies.

   Dogs, wolves, coyotes, and jackals are members of the genus *Canis*.

   A. harrisi and *A. leucurus* are two species of squirrels.

Example 2   For sentences a and b, underline each word that should be italicized or underlined.

   (a) The verb in this sentence is walk.

   (b) Buenos días means "good day" in Spanish.

Solution   (a) The sentence calls attention to the word **walk.**

(b) **Buenos días** is a foreign phrase.

✓Practice   For a and b, replace each blank with *stationary* or *stationery.*

a. During World War II, soldiers enjoyed receiving letters on different types of _____.

b. The _____ caboose had been there for years.

Write and underline the words that should be italicized in sentences c–g.

c. National Geographic has been a favorite magazine for decades.

d. The essay contains too many little words like is.

e. The scientific name for gum tree is eucalyptus.

f. The French people use jolie for pretty.

g. In fifth grade, students spend the night on a clipper ship called the Pilgrim.

More Practice   See "More Practice Lesson 73" in Student Workbook.

Review Set 73   Choose the best word to complete sentences 1–14.

1. One way to (honor, dishonor, sympathize) the American
(6, 22) flag is to let it touch the ground.

2. The prefix *geo-* means "(smooth, earth, not)."
(7)

3. The sociology (coarse, trail, course) included
(8) descriptions of social groups.

4. Do you have the (consideration, integrity, self-discipline)
(1, 9) to stay home and study for your math test?

5. One of the (baddest, worst) sounds I can think of is a
(45, 46) fingernail scratching a chalkboard.

6. (Italics, Elite) is a slightly slanted style of type that we
(73) use to indicate titles of larger literary works or to bring special emphasis to a word or phrase in a sentence.

7. (First, Second, Third) person is the person being spoken
(53) to—*you* or *yours*.

8. A pronoun used as a subject or predicate nominative is
(41, 55) (possessive, nominative) case.

9. The buzzard circled about Bruce and (I, me).
(53, 57)

10. Bruce and (I, me) watched the buzzard.
(53, 55)

11. Charlotte, the one for (who, whom) I voted, will be our
(66, 67) next president.

12. Animals need water as much as (we, us).
(67)

13. If the interrogative pronoun functions as a subject or a
(68) predicate nominative, we use (*who, whom*).

14. We use the demonstrative pronouns *that* and *those* to
(71) point out things that are (near, far).

15. Tell whether this word group is a sentence fragment,
(3) run-on sentence, or complete sentence: Something rotten
in Denmark or in the bottom drawer of my
refrigerator.

16. Tell whether this word group is a phrase or a clause: a
(24) short, catchy saying from William Shakespeare's *Hamlet*

17. Write the five linking verbs that are associated with the
(22) senses.

18. Write the indefinite pronoun in this sentence, and tell
(72) whether it is singular or plural: Some use this expression
without knowing its source.

19. Write each proper adjective and noun that should be
(30) capitalized in this sentence: Many europeans think the
austrian alps provide the best skiing.

√ **20.** Write the overused adjective in this sentence, and suggest
(50) one that is more descriptive: I saw a great play.

21. Write the predicate nominative in this sentence: My big
(22, 41) brother is a good speller.

22. Write the appositive from this sentence: Another
(48, 49) outstanding play, *Phantom of the Opera*, attracts viewers
from all over the country.

23. Tell whether this sentence is simple or
(2, 64) compound: Dustin plays the acoustical guitar, and Mario
accompanies him with the drums.

24. Rewrite this dialogue, adding quotation marks as needed:
(69, 70)   Howard instructed, Today, we are going to learn a
new song.
          Tina added, Listen to the soprano part.

25. Write each possessive pronoun in this sentence: That
(60) boat is yours, but the other one is hers.

26. Write the reflexive pronoun in this sentence: The team
(62) whispered among themselves.

27. Write the six plural indefinite pronouns from this
(72) list: another, few, anything, everybody, everyone,
several, ones, nobody, someone, each, both, much, many,
no one, others.

28. Write the prepositional phrase from this sentence and tell
(33, 34) what word it modifies (describes): His sense of humility
made him a likable fellow.

Diagram sentences 29 and 30.

29. The announcer on stage sounded arrogant.
(34, 44)

30. The tutor tested him and me.
(25, 57)

Irregular Verbs, Part 3

Dictation or Journal Entry

Vocabulary:
Let's look at the homophones *bear* and *bare*. The word *bear* can function as either a noun or a verb. The noun *bear* is a large, furry mammal with a short tail. The grizzly is a type of *bear*. The verb *bear* means "to carry" or "to endure patiently." The platform will *bear* the weight of the performers. The word *bare* is an adjective meaning "without clothing or covering." His *bare* arms had goose bumps from the cold wind.

We have already learned that there are no rules for forming the past tense and past participle of irregular verbs. In this lesson, we will look at some additional irregular verbs.

Remember that we must memorize the principal parts of irregular verbs. To test yourself, cover the past and past participle forms, then try to write or say the past and past participle for each verb. Make a new list of the ones you miss, and work to memorize them.

VERB	PAST	PAST PARTICIPLE
beat	beat	(has) beaten
bite	bit	(has) bitten
bring	brought	(has) brought
build	built	(has) built
burst	burst	(has) burst
buy	bought	(has) bought
catch	caught	(has) caught
come	came	(has) come
cost	cost	(has) cost
dive	dove or dived	(has) dived
draw	drew	(has) drawn
drive	drove	(has) driven
eat	ate	(has) eaten
fall	fell	(has) fallen

feel	felt	(has) felt
fight	fought	(has) fought
find	found	(has) found
flee	fled	(has) fled
fly	flew	(has) flown
forget	forgot	(has) forgotten
forgive	forgave	(has) forgiven

Example 1 Write the past and past participle forms of each verb.
(a) beat   (b) bite   (c) build   (d) burst

Solution (a) beat, **beat, (has) beaten**

(b) bite, **bit, (has) bitten**

(c) build, **built, (has) built**

(d) burst, **burst, (has) burst**

Example 2 Write the correct verb form for each sentence.
(a) Most of us (feeled, felt) that Dad's plan sounded good.

(b) We (fleed, fled) down the path with the pie.

(c) Mom suddenly (come, came) from out of nowhere.

(d) She had (catched, caught) us red-handed.

Solution (a) Most of us **felt** that Dad's plan sounded good.

(b) We **fled** down the path with the pie.

(c) Mom suddenly **came** from out of nowhere.

(d) She had **caught** us red-handed.

Errors to Avoid People sometimes treat a regular verb as if it were irregular. For example, the past tense of *drag* is *dragged*, not "drug." The past tense of *drown* is simply *drowned*, not "drownded." Avoid these errors by memorizing the irregular verbs and consulting a dictionary when in doubt. If the dictionary does not list the verb's principle parts, the verb is regular.

Practice For a–h, write the past and past participle form of each verb.

    a. catch   **b.** come   **c.** cost   **d.** dive

    e. drag   **f.** draw   **g.** drown   **h.** drive

For i–p, write the correct verb form for each sentence.

  i. After we had (ate, eaten), he told me the tale.

  j. Where did you say he (find, found) the wallet?

  k. He (drived, drove) to the police station to turn it in.

  l. Keeping the wallet would have (cost, costed) him many nights' sleep.

  m. Last night Margaret (forgave, forgived) Andy at last.

  n. Marco has (catched, caught) four trout.

  o. Jenny (flied, flew) in a helicopter yesterday!

  p. The leaves (fell, falled) because it was fall.

For q–t, replace each blank with *bear* or *bare*.

  q. The babysitter could hardly _____ the child's whining.

  r. I hope the ladder will _____ my weight.

  s. In winter, many trees have no leaves. Their branches are _____.

  t. The polar _____ is a white, furry mammal with a short tail.

More Practice See "More Practice Lesson 74" in Student Workbook.

Review Set 74 Choose the best word to complete sentences 1–12.

  1. The (biology, geology, geography) class studied igneous, sedimentary, and metamorphic rocks.
    (7, 11)

  2. The (biology, geology, geography) class studied the elevation of landforms by map.
    (7, 11)

3. The (biology, geology, geography) class studied the human circulatory system.
(7, 11)

4. Memorizing important terms in science classes requires (willpower, morale, conscience).
(9, 23)

5. The ornithologist (will, shall) explain how the owl became the symbol of wisdom.
(9, 11)

6. (First, Second, Third) person is the person being spoken about— *he, she, it, him, her, his,* and *hers.*
(53, 58)

7. The employer will give Rhonda and (I, me) a raise in hourly wage.
(25, 57)

8. It was (me, I) who thought owls were intelligent birds.
(41, 55)

9. Dr. Chen, (who, whom) you know, will visit tomorrow.
(66)

10. We use the relative pronoun (*who, whom*) for the subject of a sentence.
(66)

11. If the relative pronoun functions as an object, we use (*who, whom*).
(66)

12. (This, This here) video demonstrates the noiseless flight of the owl.
(71)

13. Make a complete sentence from this fragment: Owl the symbol of wisdom.
(4)

For sentences 14 and 15, tell whether the verb is transitive or intransitive.

14. The patient was resting after surgery.
(25, 32)

15. The carpenter sanded the wood around the doorway.
(25, 32)

16. Write the past tense and past participle of the verb *build*.
(9, 16)

17. Write the plural of the noun *authority*.
(13, 14)

18. Rewrite this sentence, adding capital letters as needed: my friend from the midwest said, "howdy, grandma, have you visited dr. noodleman yet?"
(26, 29)

19. Write the indirect object of this sentence: As we walked
(25, 35) through the dark forest, the owl gave us a fright.

Rewrite sentences 20 and 21, adding commas as needed.

20. We shall study owls falcons and hawks.
(47)

21. The owl a bird of ill omen represents death to the
(49) superstitious.

22. Rewrite this sentence, adding quotation marks as
(69, 70) needed: Mr. Parmenter said, The owl can turn its head
in almost a complete circle.

23. Write the indefinite pronoun in this sentence, and tell
(72) whether it is singular or plural: Everybody needs a
friend.

For 24 and 25, refer to this sentence: Authorities confess that
owls are not the smartest of birds.

24. Write the independent clause.
(24, 61)

25. Write the dependent clause and underline the
(61) subordinating conjunction.

26. Write the contraction in this sentence: It's afraid of its
(60) own shadow.

27. Indefinite pronouns can be either singular or plural,
(72) depending on their use in the sentence. Write the five
indefinite pronouns of this type from this list: nobody, all,
both, none, someone, many, any, some, most

Diagram sentences 28–30.

28. The owl represents Athena, a Greek deity.
(25, 48)

29. The owl has noiseless flight, and it makes mournful sounds.
(23, 64)

30. The winners are we.
(23, 41)

LESSON
75

Irregular Verbs, Part 4

Dictation or Journal Entry

Vocabulary:
Reconcile, a verb, means "to make peace," "to bring into harmony; settle," or "to bring into agreement." I hope we can *reconcile* our differences of opinion. *Reconciliation*, a noun, is a "coming together on a friendly basis after a quarrel." After their *reconciliation*, the two became friends again.

In this lesson, we will look at more irregular verbs, whose principal parts we must memorize. To test yourself, cover the past and past participle forms, then try to write or say the past and past participle for each verb. Make a new list of the ones you miss, and work to memorize them.

VERB	PAST	PAST PARTICIPLE
get	got	(has) gotten
give	gave	(has) given
go	went	(has) gone
hang (execute)	hanged	(has) hanged
hang (suspend)	hung	(has) hung
hide	hid	(has) hidden or hid
hold	held	(has) held
keep	kept	(has) kept
lay (place)	laid	(has) laid
lead	led	(has) led
lend	lent	(has) lent
lie (recline)	lay	(has) lain
lie (deceive)	lied	(has) lied
lose	lost	(has) lost
make	made	(has) made
mistake	mistook	(has) mistaken
put	put	(has) put

ride	rode	(has) ridden
rise	rose	(has) risen
run	ran	(has) run
see	saw	(has) seen
sell	sold	(has) sold

Example 1 Write the past and past participle forms of each verb.

(a) see (b) ride (c) go (d) give (e) make

Solution (a) see, **saw, (has) seen**

(b) ride, **rode, (has) ridden**

(c) go, **went, (has) gone**

(d) give, **gave, (has) given**

(e) make, **made, (has) made**

Example 2 Write the correct verb form for each sentence.

(a) Gandhi (rised, rose) up as the leader of the Congress Party in the 1920s.

(b) Oh dear, I've (losed, lost) my keys again!

(c) Abraham Lincoln (run, ran) for office several times before he was elected.

Solution (a) Gandhi **rose** up as the leader of the Congress Party in the 1920s.

(b) Oh dear, I've **lost** my keys again!

(c) Abraham Lincoln **ran** for office several times before he was elected.

Practice For a–h, write the past and past participle form of each verb.

a. hide b. hold c. lay d. lead

e. lend f. mistake g. put h. sell

For i–l, write the correct verb form for each sentence.

  i. Kurt (hided, hid) his sister's birthday present in the garage.

  j. Grandpa Steve (held, holded) baby Molly as he ate dinner.

  k. I had (laid, lain) my keys on the table.

  l. That horse has (leaded, led) the parade every year.

For m–o, replace each blank with *reconcile* or *reconciliation.*

  m. The verb _____ means "to make peace."

  n. Sometimes family members must work hard to _____ their differences.

  o. When Walt and Don shook hands, their _____ was complete.

More Practice   See "More Practice Lesson 75" in Student Workbook.

Review Set 75   Choose the best word to complete sentences 1–13.

  1. The prefix *bio-* means "(Earth, same, life)."

(1, 11)

  2. Be (punctual, considerate, conscientious) about studying for tests.

(1, 12)

  3. The (diligent, punctual, fractious) lifeguard carefully monitored the amount of chlorine in the pool.

(12, 51)

  4. Many authors enjoy writing (geologies, biographies, geographies) about famous people.

(7, 11)

  5. Did you ever (has, have) the measles when you were a child?

(7, 15)

  6. Mumps and measles (is, are) common childhood diseases.

(15, 22)

  7. Gertrude (mistake, mistook, mistaken) a stranger's suitcase for her own.

(75)

  (53, 57) **8.** The tiny bird hopped toward Dan and (him, he).

9. Snakes' tongues are more sensitive than (our's, ours).
(60, 67)

10. (Whoever, Whomever) desires to enroll in swimming
(66, 67) lessons needs to meet the lifeguard by the pool.

11. The office assistant will invite (whoever, whomever) you
(66, 67) would like.

12. (Who, Whom) did you assist on the project?
(66, 68)

13. (Those, Those there) towers can be seen for miles.
(71)

14. Tell whether this word group is a phrase or a
(24, 61) clause: mumps and measles during childhood

15. Write the plural of *woman*.
(13, 14)

16. Write each word that should be capitalized in this
(12, 31) sentence: the shuffleboard participant played the saxophone quietly while watching others play.

17. Write the predicate adjective in this sentence: Loud
(22, 44) neighbors are annoying.

18. Write the predicate nominative in this sentence: Is the
(22, 41) laughing philosopher Democritus?

Rewrite 19 and 20, adding commas as needed.

19. Dear Democritus
(52)
Why are you continually smiling?
Sincerely
Socrates

20. Democritus some believe put out his own eyes so that
(56) he might not be distracted from his thinking.

21. Rewrite this sentence, adding quotation marks as
(69, 70) necessary: When she was a young child, Ruth's favorite song was The Farmer in the Dell.

22. Write and underline the words that should be italicized
(73) in this sentence: Many people enjoy reading magazines like Newsweek and Time.

23. Write the antecedent for the pronoun in this
(51, 67) sentence: Hugo tries to run as fast as he can.

24. Write each plural pronoun from this list: I, we, us, me,
(53, 58) mine, they, you, yours, he, them, him, his, she, her,
theirs, hers, it.

For 25 and 26, tell whether the italicized pronoun is
nominative, objective, or possessive case.

25. *She* seemed uninterested in philosophers such as Plato,
(55, 57) Socrates, and Aristotle.

26. The unused philosophy book was *hers.*
(55, 57)

27. Write the intensive personal pronoun in this
(62) sentence: Bertha herself chose the furniture and window
coverings.

28. Write the indefinite pronoun in this sentence, and tell
(72) whether it is singular or plural: Much has happened
since I last saw you.

Diagram sentences 29 and 30.

29. Will you grow me some cherry tomatoes?
(25, 35)

30. The babysitter hid the scissors with sharp points.
(25, 33)

Irregular Verbs, Part 5

Dictation or Journal Entry
Vocabulary:
The noun *consequence* means "an outcome or result." The thief did not consider the *consequences* of breaking the law. The adjective *consequential* means "having important consequences; vital or influential." The most *consequential* thing that happened in Greensburg, Kansas, was the tornado.

In this lesson, we will look at one last group of irregular verbs, whose principal parts we must memorize. To test yourself, cover the past and past participle forms, then try to write or say the past and past participle for each verb. Make a new list of the ones you miss, and work to memorize them.

VERB	PAST	PAST PARTICIPLE
set	set	(has) set
shake	shook	(has) shaken
shine (light)	shone	(has) shone
shine (polish)	shined	(has) shined
shut	shut	(has) shut
sit	sat	(has) sat
slay	slew	(has) slain
sleep	slept	(has) slept
spring	sprang or sprung	(has) sprung
stand	stood	(has) stood
strive	strove	(has) striven
swim	swam	(has) swum
swing	swung	(has) swung
take	took	(has) taken
teach	taught	(has) taught

tell	told	(has) told
think	thought	(has) thought
wake	woke	(has) woken
weave	wove	(has) woven
wring	wrung	(has) wrung
write	wrote	(has) written

Example 1 Write the past and past participle forms of each verb.
(a) write   (b) think   (c) swim   (d) sleep   (e) stand

Solution (a) write, **wrote, (has) written**

(b) think, **thought, (has) thought**

(c) swim, **swam, (has) swum**

(d) sleep, **slept, (has) slept**

(e) stand, **stood, (has) stood**

Example 2 Write the correct verb form for each sentence.
(a) By the end of the wedding reception, I had (shook, shaken) hands with over one hundred people.

(b) Carolyn has (wove, woven) several wool blankets.

(c) He (swang, swung) the bat for strike three.

Solution (a) By the end of the wedding reception, I had **shaken** hands with over one hundred people.

(b) Carolyn has **woven** several wool blankets.

(c) He **swung** the bat for strike three.

Practice For a–h, write the past and past participle form of each verb.
a. take   b. set   c. teach   d. tell

e. wake   f. spring   g. strive   h. shut

For i–p, write the correct verb form for each sentence.

    i. Have you ever (wrote, written) a poem?

    j. Mr. Cabrera (sleeped, slept) during his flight across country.

    k. Freddy has (thought, thinked) about his future.

    l. Has Mr. López ever (teached, taught) French?

    m. Sal (telled, told) Sergio his secret for success.

    n. Has Dad ever (woken, woke) before the alarm?

    o. Mrs. Habib (sitted, sat) at her computer.

    p. The door had (shutted, shut).

For q and r, replace each blank with *consequence* or *consequential.*

    q. The _____ of poor nutrition is poor health.

    r. Our choice of friends is a _____ matter.

More Practice See "More Practice Lesson 76" in Student Workbook.

Review Set 76 Choose the correct word(s) to complete sentences 1–17.

    1. Granny (filt, filled) her kettles with creek water, (built, builded) a fire, (boilt, boiled) her clothes, (scrubbed, scrubs) them with homemade soap, (wrang, wrung) them out by hand, and (hanged, hung) them up to dry.
^(74, 75)

    2. We hope the two quarreling friends will soon (ware, rite, reconcile) their differences.
^(50, 75)

    3. Will that table (bare, bear, where) the weight of this bronze statue?
^(72, 74)

    4. The office assistant ordered personalized (stationary, stationery) for his employer.
⁽⁷³⁾

    5. We went to the hard (where, ware, wear) store to buy a hammer and some nails.
⁽⁷²⁾

6. A camel's hump (vary, varys, varies) in size according to
(7, 16) the physical condition of the animal.

7. The camel's hump had (shrank, shrunk) due to long
(54, 76) hours of work without nourishment.

8. Gandhi (lead, led) the strongest voice for Indian
(75, 76) independence.

9. This independence (was, were) achievable by non-violent
(7, 15) protests, or "civil disobedience."

10. (We, Us) students visited a museum of natural history.
(55, 67)

11. (Them, Those) shoes hurt my feet.
(28, 71)

12. Pronoun usage is sometimes (more, less) formal when we
(67) are speaking.

13. A relative pronoun such as *who, whom,* or *whose* is
(66, 68) called a(n) (demonstrative, interrogative) pronoun when it
introduces a question.

14. *This, that, these,* and *those* are (demonstrative,
(68, 71) interrogative), or "pointing," pronouns.

15. A demonstrative pronoun must agree in (number,
(71) spelling) with its antecedent (the noun that it points
out).

16. A(n) (direct, indirect) quotation gives a speaker's exact
(69, 70) words.

17. We use italics or (underlining, quotation marks) to
(70, 73) indicate titles of larger literary works or foreign words
and phrases.

18. Tell whether this sentence is declarative, interrogative,
(1, 3) imperative, or exclamatory: The backbone of the
single-humped camel is as straight as the backbone of a
horse.

19. Tell whether this word group is a phrase or a
(24, 61) clause: composed chiefly of fat

20. Write the verb in this sentence, and tell whether it is
(22, 32) transitive or intransitive: Do camels' spines appear straight?

21. Write each word that should be capitalized in this
(6) sentence: puerto rico is located in the caribbean sea.

22. Rewrite this outline, adding periods and capital letters as
(20, 36) needed:

    i camels
      a hump
      b spine

23. Write each prepositional phrase and star the object of
(17, 33) each preposition in this sentence: Like the camel, certain breeds of sheep store fat in their tails.

24. Write each adjective in this sentence: The gasoline
(27, 28) automobile is not the product of one single inventor.

25. Write the predicate adjective in this sentence: All things
(22, 44) are possible.

Add periods and commas as needed in sentences 26–28.

26. In 1885 a man from Munich Germany constructed a
(36, 47) tricycle driven by a crude internal combustion engine

27. In 1891 the builder of the motorized tricycle Dr Karl
(40, 47) Benz built the first gasoline-driven automobile in Germany

28. In 1885 Gottlieb Daimler also a German installed a
(47, 48) gasoline engine on a bicycle and later he patented a high-speed internal combustion engine

29. Write the six simple relative pronouns from this list:
(66) who, hose, whom, witch, whose, what, which, that.

30. Diagram this sentence: Steam-driven carriages were
(28, 41) impractical.

The Exclamation Mark
• The Question Mark • The Dash

Dictation or Journal Entry

Vocabulary:

Let us examine the homophones *cent*, *sent*, and *scent*. One one-hundredth of a dollar is a *cent*. He paid fifty *cents* for the phone call. The past tense of the verb "to send" is *sent*. I *sent* her an email. A *scent* is an odor or smell. The roses had a wonderful *scent*.

Almost every sentence ends with one of three punctuation marks. The period, the exclamation mark, and the question mark are called final, or terminal, punctuation marks.

Exclamation Mark We use an **exclamation mark** after an exclamatory sentence (a sentence showing strong emotion).

Someone gave me $100!

We can also use an exclamation mark after a word or phrase showing strong emotion. We call this an **interjection**.

Wow! Good job! Oh, no!

Careful writers try to limit their use of exclamation marks. Think of it as shouting. Sometimes shouting is appropriate, but someone who shouts all the time is soon ignored. Use exclamation marks sparingly.

Question Mark We place a **question mark** at the end of an interrogative sentence (one that asks a question).

Can you give me a ride to the skating rink?

Remember that a sentence can contain a questioning phrase without being an interrogative sentence.

I was wondering who could give me a ride.

With Quotation Marks When using exclamation marks and question marks with quotation marks, we must decide whether to place the final punctuation mark *inside* or *outside* the quotation marks. We do this by determining if the final punctuation mark punctuates the whole sentence or just the part in quotation marks.

In the sentence below, only the words in quotation marks ask a question. The question mark punctuates only the direct quotation, so it goes *inside* the quotation marks.

Everybody asked, "Where did you get that hat?"

In the next sentence, the question mark punctuates the whole sentence, so it goes *outside* the quotation marks:

Have you heard Ricky sing "Winter Wonderland"?

Example 1 Rewrite sentences a–d, inserting exclamation or question marks as needed.

(a) Is it true that weather patterns created by moist air and hot temperatures at the equator contribute to the formation of hot deserts

(b) What a surprise

(c) She looked around and asked, "Where's the elevator"

(d) My voice always cracks at the end of "The Star Spangled Banner"

Solution (a) **Is it true that weather patterns created by moist air and hot temperatures at the equator contribute to the formation of hot deserts?** (interrogative sentence)

(b) **What a surprise!** (exclamatory sentence)

(c) The question mark goes inside the quotation marks because it punctuates only the direct quotation.

She looked around and asked, "Where's the elevator?"

(d) The exclamation mark goes outside the quotation marks because it punctuates the entire sentence.

My voice always cracks at the end of "The Star Spangled Banner"!

Dash Another punctuation mark that we must use sparingly is the **dash**. The dash has specific uses, such as indicating a sudden change in thoughts, an interruption in the flow of the sentence, faltering speech, or an abrupt halt to speech.

It's too bad we— Well, it doesn't matter now.

The best man's behavior—he fell asleep at the reception—was remembered for years to come.

I saw him—at least I thought I did—at the store.

A dash can also be used to offset certain words or phrases for emphasis.

English, history, math—these subjects are difficult for me.

Call Bob—he works for Joan—if you want the facts.

Singing—that's all he ever wanted to do.

Errors to Avoid Do not use a dash in place of a period. Two complete sentences should be separated by a period, not a dash.

> INCORRECT:
> The bicycle was a gift on Edward's birthday—Edward learned quickly how to take care of it.

> CORRECT:
> The bicycle was a gift on Edward's birthday. Edward learned quickly how to take care of it.

Example 2 Rewrite sentences a–c, inserting dashes where needed.

(a) Marian's mother her name is Marian too likes tulips.

(b) "They'll never find me in the" said John, just before they found him.

(c) I finished all my homework early before three o'clock.

Solution (a) We use dashes to indicate an interruption in the flow of the sentence. **Marian's mother—her name is Marian too—likes tulips.**

(b) We use dashes to indicate an abrupt halt to speech. **"They'll never find me in the—" said John, just before they found him.**

(c) We use a dash for emphasis. **I finished all my homework early—before three o'clock.**

Practice Rewrite sentences a–d, placing exclamation marks or question marks where they are needed.

a. Whew That math test was really difficult

b. Do you understand place value

c. Who painted *The Ladies of Avignon*

d. I know It's Pablo Picasso

Rewrite sentences e–g, inserting dashes where needed.
  e. It's just what I wanted a lime green bowling ball.

  f. The party starts let's see about eight o'clock.

  g. That's all my sister dreams of horses.

For sentences h–m, replace each blank with the correct word: *scent*, *sent*, or *cent*.
  h. The _____ of the skunk reached the dog's nose quickly.

  i. Her aunt _____ the package for her birthday.

  j. The man complained, "I wouldn't give one _____ for that old lawn mower.

  k. The candy bar costs twenty-five _____s.

  l. Mrs. Cooper _____ her brothers to find the kitten.

  m. Some people identify smells, or _____s, more easily than other people.

Review Set Choose the best word(s) to complete sentences 1–15.
77 **1.** Jewelers categorize opals and amethysts as
      (54, 71) (semiprecious, fractious, continuous) stones.

    2. If one puts (hemiplegia, antifreeze, subsoil) in the car
    (67, 69) radiator, the engine should not freeze.

    3. The prefix *anti-* means "(before, after, against)."
    (65, 69)

    4. (Here, Hear) is the key to the cabinet.
    (68)

    5. (Were, Where) are you going in such a hurry?
    (72)

    6. People (who, which) exercise self-discipline can
    (66, 67) accomplish great things.

7. The boy (who, that) lives next door reads science fiction.
(66, 67)

8. Blanca Rivas, (which, who) volunteers in the cafeteria,
(66, 67) became a grandmother today.

9. We tend to use pronouns more casually in (oral, written)
(67) language.

10. Dr. Chew, (who, whom) works in Arcadia, is a skilled
(66, 67) physician.

11. (Those, Them) apples were rotten.
(71)

12. Tom ate more spinach than (she, her).
(67, 72)

13. (Direct, indirect) quotations give the main idea of what
(69, 70) someone said but do not give the speaker's exact words.

14. When we handwrite material, or when the italics style of
(73) type is not available, we (underline, capitalize) words
that require italics.

15. We use the (exclamation, question) mark after an
(1, 77) exclamatory sentence, one that shows strong emotion.

For 16 and 17, refer to this sentence:

Did Ferdinand Magellan circumnavigate the globe?

16. Write the simple subject.
(2, 23)

17. Write the simple predicate.
(2, 23)

18. Write the present participle, past tense, and past
(9, 16) participle of the verb *go*.

For sentences 19 and 20, write the verb, and tell whether it is
transitive or intransitive.

19. Ferdinand Magellan was killed in the Philippines by the
(25, 32) natives on Mactan Island on April 27, 1521.

20. Did Ferdinand Magellan complete his famous voyage?
(25, 32)

21. Write the abstract noun from this sentence: The rumor
(8) was that Ferdinand Magellan had never circumnavigated
the globe, but he had.

22. Write each word that should be capitalized in this
(20, 26) sentence: mrs. norris, our german teacher, always said, "let's try to speak as little english as possible in class."

23. Write each prepositional phrase, and star the object of
(17, 33) each preposition in this sentence: Ferdinand Magellan travelled around the world in a single voyage.

24. Write the seven most common coordinating
(37) conjunctions.

25. Tell whether the italicized pronoun in this sentence is
(55, 60) nominative or possessive case: None of *her* children survived her.

✓ **26.** Rewrite this letter, adding commas as needed:
(47, 63)

Dear Uncle Mark
   That dirty shaggy yellow dog we found last Saturday is doing fine. We fed him gave him a bath and trimmed his fur. Now he is a clean sleek yellow dog.
                    Happily
                    Betsy

27. Write the antecedent for the italicized pronoun in this
(51, 55) sentence: Before *they* took the boat out, the captain's crew checked the weather report for possible storms.

28. Write the three personal pronoun case forms.
(53, 58)

Diagram sentences 29 and 30.

✓ **29.** She was opening her umbrella, for raindrops were falling.
(59, 64)

✓ **30.** An English queen, Queen Anne, bore seventeen children.
(25, 48)

LESSON 78

Subject-Verb Agreement, Part 1

Just as a pronoun must agree with its antecedent, a verb must agree with the subject of the sentence in **person** and **number**.

Person Verbs and personal pronouns are the only parts of speech that change their form to show person (point of view).

When we learned about the irregular verbs *be, have,* and *do* in Lesson 15, we used a chart similar to the one below. Here we show two regular verbs (*work* and *wish*) and one irregular verb (*be*) in the first, second, and third person. (Most regular verbs form the third person singular by adding *-s* or *-es.* The irregular verbs must be memorized.)

	SINGULAR	PLURAL
1ST PERSON	**I** work, wish, am	**we** work, wish, are
2ND PERSON	**you** work, wish, are	**you** work, wish, are
3RD PERSON	**he** works, wishes, is	**they** work, wish, are

If the subject of a sentence is in the **first person** (I, we), the verb must also be in the first person:

I work every morning.   *We* wish every night.

I am punctual.   *We* are courteous.

If the subject of a sentence is in the **second person** (you), the verb must also be in the second person:

You work every morning.

If the subject of a sentence is in the **third person** (he, she, it, or any noun), the verb must also be in the third person:

He walks every morning.   *They* walk every morning.

Nina wishes every night.   *People* wish every night.

The *chair* is gray.   The *chairs* are gray.

Number   If the subject of a sentence is **singular**, the verb must also be singular:

> *I* <u>work</u> every morning.

> *He* <u>wishes</u> every night.

If the subject of a sentence is **plural**, the verb must also be plural:

> *We* <u>work</u> every morning.

> *They* <u>wish</u> every night.

Notice that the pronoun *you* always takes a plural verb, even when it is singular.

> *You* <u>are</u> in my way, Heather.

> *You* <u>are</u> both excellent pianists.

Compound Subjects   Sometimes it is difficult to determine if the subject of a sentence is singular or plural.

<u>Compound subjects</u> joined by *and* are considered <u>plural</u> and require a plural verb.

> *Bill* and *Steph* <u>treasure</u> their dogs.

> The *boys* and their *father* <u>repair</u> old cars.

<u>Compound subjects</u> joined by *or, nor, either/or,* or *neither/nor* can be singular or plural, depending on the subjects themselves:

<u>If both subjects are singular, we use a singular</u> verb.

> Neither *Pam* nor *Suzanne* <u>is coming</u> to visit us.

> Either *Lennie* or *Darryl* <u>teaches</u> martial arts.

<u>If both subjects are plural, we use a plural</u> verb.

> Neither the *plums* nor the *peaches* <u>look</u> edible.

> My *brothers* or *sisters* <u>know</u> my address.

If one subject is singular and the other is plural, the verb should agree with the <u>part of the subject it is closest to.</u>

> Neither the *cat* nor the *dogs* <u>are eating</u> today.

> Either the *violins* or the *piano* <u>sounds</u> out of tune.

Example Choose the correct verb form for each sentence.

(a) My sisters-in-law (is, are) elementary schoolteachers.

(b) Either Mr. Hammer or Mr. Wrench (has, have) the combination to the padlock.

(c) Neither the girls nor the boys (knows, know) who won.

(d) Bill or his sisters (picks, pick) up the mail every morning.

Solution (a) The subject "sisters-in-law" is plural, so we use the plural verb form: My sisters-in-law **are** elementary schoolteachers.

(b) When compound singular subjects are joined by *either/or*, we use the singular verb form: Either Mr. Hammer or Mr. Wrench **has** the combination to the padlock.

(c) Compound plural subjects joined by *neither/nor* require the plural verb form: Neither the girls nor the boys **know** who won.

(d) When compound subjects are joined by *or,* the verb agrees with the part of the subject it is closest to: Bill or his sisters **pick** up the mail every morning.

Practice For a–f, choose the correct verb form for each sentence.

a. In the 1800s, China (was, were) considered one of the world's oldest and most glorious civilizations.

b. The Chinese (was, were) proud of their past.

c. Margarita and she (care, cares) for children.

d. The parakeet or the finch (make, makes) a good pet.

e. Parakeets or finches (make, makes) good pets.

f. Neither the goats nor the pig (has, have) been fed.

For g–j, replace each blank with *eager* or *anxious*.

g. Even though I have studied diligently, I feel somewhat _____ about Friday's test.

h. The _____ retriever could not wait to go swimming.

i. We were _____ to begin our exciting new project.

j. The woman felt _____ about her child's fever.

More Practice

Choose the correct verb form for each sentence.

1. Neither the harmonica nor the banjos (sound, sounds) right.

2. Either the pitcher or the fielders (is, are) stalling.

3. The lory and the parrot (live, lives) in groups.

4. The sparrow and the finch (grow, grows) to about five inches long.

5. All doves (is, are) monogamous.

6. They always (stay, stays) with their mates.

7. Either a dove or a pigeon (was, were) bathing in the puddle.

8. A dove and a pigeon (was, were) pecking for seeds.

9. Either the robin or the nightingales (was, were) laying eggs.

10. Mynas and starlings (has, have) soft bills.

Review Set 78

Choose the best word to complete sentences 1–16.

1. Some cultures demonstrate (arrogance, humility, self-discipline) by bowing before another individual.
(9, 70)

2. The school nurse cleaned the child's skinned knee with (hemistich, desert, antiseptic).
(65, 67)

3. The softball pitcher will (brake, learn, rite) to pitch a "sinker."
(62)

4. The Sahara (Dessert, Desert, break) intrigues those interested in geology.
(47, 63)

5. Roberto has (run, ran) two miles each morning.
(74, 75)

6. The golden eagle has (bring, brung, brought) to its nest
(74, 75) animals weighing up to fifteen pounds.

7. Yesterday I (see, saw, seen) an orange cat with long whiskers.
(75, 76)

8. If my cat ever saw a golden eagle, she would be awfully
(75, 76) (shaked, shook, shaken) up.

9. Cats use (they're, their, there) whiskers as long levers in
(38, 60) communicating impulses to the nerve fibers.

10. The mayor, (who, which) has made tremendous
(66, 67) improvements in our city, lives next door.

11. The canary, (who, whom) sings constantly, flew in and
(66, 67) out of its cage today.

12. An (appositive, opposite) is a word or phrase that
(48, 49) immediately follows a noun to identify or give more
information about the noun.

13. We use the demonstrative pronouns *this* and *these* to
(71) point out things that are (nearby, farther away).

14. Anna or Kim (is, are) going to the store before dinner.
(9, 21)

15. We enclose (direct, indirect) quotations in quotation marks.
(69, 70)

16. We place a (question, exclamation) mark at the end of an
(1, 77) interrogative sentence.

17. Tell whether this word group is a fragment, run-on, or
(3) complete sentence: Occasionally newspapers publish
reports of a child being carried off by an eagle most of
these reports are false.

18. Write the entire verb phrase in this sentence: Have eagles
(9, 21) been carrying children away?

19. Write the plural form of each noun.
(13, 14) (a) antelope   (b) fox   (c) wolf

20. Rewrite this sentence, adding capital letters as needed:
(6, 12) milton high school's debate team meets on thursdays.

For 21 and 22, refer to this sentence:

The Spanish *padres* built missions early in California history.

21. Write the prepositional phrase, and star the object of the preposition.
(17, 33)

22. Write the two proper adjectives.
(30)

23. Write the overused adjective in this sentence, and replace it with one that is more descriptive: That cat has nice whiskers.
(27, 50)

24. Write the direct object in this sentence: Whiskers help a cat in the dark.
(5, 25)

25. Write the indirect object in this sentence: Whiskers the cat brought me his toy mouse.
(25, 35)

26. Write the intensive personal pronoun in this sentence: The whiskers themselves are not sensitive, but the root-endings are very sensitive.
(62)

27. Write the interrogative pronoun in this sentence: Eileen wondered who left the lights on.
(66, 68)

28. Rewrite this sentence, adding commas as needed: Leonardo da Vinci's most famous painting the *Mona Lisa* features a woman whose eyes seem to follow the viewer.
(48, 49)

Diagram sentences 29 and 30.

29. The whiskers around his nose looked tough and wiry.
(34, 44)

30. Teddy, Nancy's cat, appreciates food and rest, but she dislikes company.
(25, 38)

LESSON 79

Subject-Verb Agreement, Part 2

Dictation or Journal Entry

Vocabulary:

The words *infer* and *imply* both refer to meaning that is added to words or actions. To *infer* means "to draw conclusions from what one sees or hears." I *inferred* from his smile that he had won the game. To *imply* means "to express meaning indirectly" or "to suggest." His smile *implied* that he had won the game.

Problems with subject-verb agreement occur when it is difficult to identify the subject of the sentence. Until we do that, we cannot determine whether it is singular or plural.

Words Between the Subject and Verb

Words that come between the subject and the verb must not distract us. Be aware of prepositional phrases, appositives, and other words that might be mistaken for the subject of the sentence. Diagramming the simple subject and simple predicate helps us to determine which verb form to use.

The letter containing the trip details (was, were) lost in the mail.

$$\underline{\text{letter} \mid \text{was (not were)}}$$

Every one of you (knows, know) your times tables.

$$\underline{\text{one} \mid \text{knows (not know)}}$$

Sherry, my friend from the islands, (is, are) coming.

$$\underline{\text{Sherry} \mid \text{is (not are)}}$$

Example 1 Diagram the simple subject and simple predicate in order to show the correct verb form for each sentence.

(a) A box of crayons (was, were) lying on the floor.

(b) The arrival of all the relatives (pleases, please) me.

(c) The comma, like many punctuation marks, (is, are) sometimes misused.

(d) In the fall, the color of the trees (is, are) brilliant.

Solution   (a) A box of crayons **was** lying on the floor.

$$\underline{\text{box} \mid \text{was}}$$

(b) The arrival of all the relatives **pleases** me.

$$\underline{\text{arrival} \mid \text{pleases}}$$

(c) The comma, like many punctuation marks, **is** sometimes misused.

$$\underline{\text{comma} \mid \text{is}}$$

(d) In the fall, the color of the trees **is** brilliant.

$$\underline{\text{color} \mid \text{is}}$$

Reversed Subject-Verb Order   If the subject follows the verb, we can better identify the subject by diagramming:

Around the block (is, are) my best friend's house.

$$\underline{\text{house} \mid \text{is}}$$

There in the distance (was, were) the empty gold mines of many men hoping to get rich quick.

$$\underline{\text{mines} \mid \text{were}}$$

Here (comes, come) the elephants.

$$\underline{\text{elephants} \mid \text{come}}$$

There (is, are) many freckles on my nose.

$$\underline{\text{freckles} \mid \text{are}}$$

There (was, were) some fast, thrilling rides at the amusement park.

$$\underline{\text{rides} \mid \text{were}}$$

Example 2 Diagram the simple subject and simple predicate in order to show the correct verb form for each sentence.

    (a) Here (is, are) a picture of Donna Reed, the "TV Mom" of the 1960s.

    (b) Surprising everyone (was, were) the "Our Best Friend" choice for 1970—the afghan.

    (c) There (was, were) different icons in our society for each of the last few decades.

    (d) Placing first in the seventies (was, were) remote control.

Solution (a) Here **is** a picture of Donna Reed, the "TV Mom" of the 1960s.

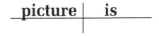

    (b) Surprising everyone **was** the "Our Best Friend" choice for the 1970—the afghan.

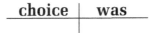

    (c) There **were** different icons in our society for each of the last few decades.

    (d) Placing first in the seventies **was** remote control.

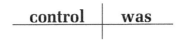

✓Practice Diagram the simple subject and simple predicate in order to determine the correct verb form for sentences a–e.

    a. In the magazine (was, were) pictures of Lassie, the favorite dog of the 1950s.

    b. At the top during the 1990s (was, were) the sport utility vehicle.

    c. Here (is, are) the car choice for the 1980s—the minivan.

d. There (is, are) favorite car choices for each decade.

e. The valued "On the Road" choice for the 1950s (was, were) the Woody Wagon.

For f–i, replace each blank with *infer* or *imply*.

f. If your words or actions express something indirectly, you _____ it.

g. If you conclude something from evidence or by reasoning, you _____ it.

h. From the dog hair all over the carpet, Mom can _____ that the dog has been in the house.

i. Owl calls _____ the presence of owls.

More Practice   Choose the correct verb form for each sentence.

1. A vase of roses (sit, sits) on her desk.

2. The bag of potatoes (was, were) heavy.

3. The carload of children (is, are) coming.

4. There (go, goes) the runners!

5. There (is, are) many varieties of birds.

6. The sound of many brass horns (blast, blasts) the silence.

7. The aroma of steaks on the barbecue (make, makes) me hungry.

8. The students in the third grade (was, were) punctual today.

Review Set 79   Choose the best word to complete sentences 1–15.

1. The soldier will not (dessert, desert, depreciate) his military assignment.
(53, 63)

2. That old dog can only (here, hear, bare) low tones.
(68)

3. The cardiologist prescribed medication (for, four, fore) the heart patient.
(64)

(65, 67) **4.** The prefix *hemi-* means "(against, half, many)."

5. She has (telled, told) us before that Ben is allergic to dairy
(75, 76) products.

6. Neither milk nor eggs (is, are) good for him.
(78)

7. I thought I had (put, putted) the cookbook back on the
(75) shelf.

8. Because of the yeast, the bread dough (rised, rose, risen)
(75) to three times its original size.

9. There (go, goes) the police cars.
(75)

10. The sight of spiders (scare, scares) me.
(79)

11. Do you think cheddar or Swiss cheese is (tastier,
(45, 46) tastiest)?

12. (We, Us) classical music enthusiasts appreciate the works
(67) of Mozart and Beethoven.

13. The leading actors are (whom, who)?
(66, 68)

14. We use the demonstrative pronouns *that* and *those* to
(71) point out persons or things that are (near, far).

15. We use a (dash, comma) to indicate an interruption in the
(77) flow of the sentence or an abrupt halt to speech.

16. Make a complete sentence from this word group: All
(3, 4) summer long on the lake.

17. Write the plural form of the noun *child*.
(13, 14)

18. Write each prepositional phrase in the sentence below.
(33, 34) Then tell which noun the phrase modifies.

The release of gases causes the holes in Swiss cheese.

19. Write the indirect object in this sentence: The local
(25, 35) producer of Swiss cheese gave us a slice of his best
product.

20. Write the appositive in this sentence: Tillamook
(48, 49) Cheddar, a cheese from Oregon, is a favorite among
many.

21. Rewrite this sentence, adding commas as needed: Well the distinct pungent odor of Swiss cheese proves distasteful to some.

^(56, 63)

22. Write the nominative case pronoun from this sentence: I made him a sandwich of Swiss cheese on rye bread.

^(53, 55)

23. Write the five compound relative pronouns from this list: whoever, his, whosoever, them, whomever, they, whichever, whatever, which.

⁽⁶⁶⁾

24. Write the five plural indefinite pronouns from this list that take a plural verb: several, no one, both, one, few, many, others, everyone.

⁽⁷²⁾

Rewrite sentences 25 and 26, adding quotation marks as needed.

25. Hazel confessed that she was responsible for the mess.

^(69, 70)

26. One of the organist's favorite songs is It Is Well with My Soul.

^(69, 70)

27. Write and underline each word that should be italicized in this sentence: Tawana played the role of Eliza Doolittle in My Fair Lady last year.

⁽⁷³⁾

28. Write the present participle, past tense, and past participle of the verb *sleep*.

^(9, 16)

Diagram sentences 29 and 30.

29. A cheese of good quality and flavor has uniform holes.

^(25, 34)

30. Swiss cheese and American cheese taste delicious.

^(38, 44)

Subject-Verb Agreement, Part 3

Indefinite Pronouns

We remember that some indefinite pronouns are singular, some are plural, and some can be either. If an indefinite pronoun is the subject of a sentence, the verb must agree with it in number. (See Lesson 72 for the complete list of indefinite pronouns.)

SINGULAR   *Nobody* <u>is</u> perfect.

PLURAL   *Few* <u>are</u> ready.

SINGULAR   *Some* <u>was</u> eaten.

PLURAL   *Some* <u>were</u> asleep.

Prepositional Phrases

Sometimes people are confused when a prepositional phrase comes between the subject and predicate. Diagramming the simple subject and simple predicate helps us to see which verb is correct.

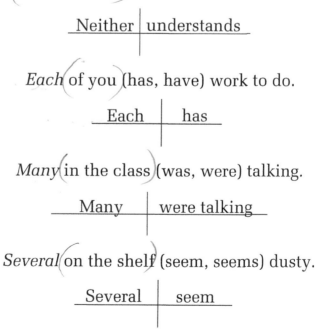

Neither of his friends (understands, understand) him.

| Neither | understands |

Each of you (has, have) work to do.

| Each | has |

Many in the class (was, were) talking.

| Many | were talking |

Several on the shelf (seem, seems) dusty.

| Several | seem |

Example 1   Choose the correct verb form for each sentence.

(a) Somebody (were, was) happy.

(b) Few (have, has) seen a sunset like that one!

(c) Everyone (in these classes) (know, knows) my name.

Solution   (a) The indefinite pronoun *somebody* is singular. It takes a singular verb: Somebody **was** happy.

(b) The indefinite pronoun *few* takes a plural verb: Few **have** seen a sunset like that one!

(c) The indefinite pronoun *everyone* takes a singular verb: Everyone in these classes **knows** my name.

Contractions   Contractions can cause us to use the wrong verb. We expand them, if necessary, to be sure the subject and verb agree.

The *dog* isn't (<u>is</u> not) in the yard.

The *dogs* aren't (<u>are</u> not) in the yard.

The *boy* wasn't (<u>was</u> not) a part of the prank.

The *boys* weren't (<u>were</u> not) a part of the prank.

She doesn't (<u>does</u> not) live in the suburbs.

They don't (<u>do</u> not) live in the suburbs.

Errors to Avoid   The contraction *there's* ("there is" or "there has") can only be used with singular subjects.

There's (there <u>is</u>) only one *girl* in line.

There's (there <u>has</u>) been a *misunderstanding*.

NO: There's two *birds* on the line.

YES: There <u>are</u> two *birds* on the line.

Also, we do not use the contraction *ain't*. It is not a word.

He isn't (NOT ain't) coming.

I haven't (NOT ain't) seen him.

Example 2   Choose the correct contraction for each sentence.

(a) (There's, There are) Rachel's sisters.

(b) Jack (don't, doesn't) need any help on the project.

(c) My shoes (hasn't, haven't) any scuffs on them yet.

(d) The man (ain't, isn't) finished with his meal.

Solution   (a) The subject, *sisters,* is a plural noun, so we use a plural verb: There **are** Rachel's sisters.

(b) *Jack* is a singular subject: Jack **doesn't** need any help on the project.

(c) *Shoes* is a plural subject, so we use a plural verb: My shoes **haven't** any scuffs on them yet.

(d) *Ain't* is not a word, so we choose *isn't*: The man **isn't** finished with his meal.

√**Practice**   For a–e, choose the correct verb form or contraction for each sentence.

a. Lindee told her friends, "You (ain't, aren't) going to believe what happened to me."

b. My favorite swing set (is, are) broken.

c. The Smiths and their neighbor (wasn't, weren't) in agreement over the height of the fence.

d. (There's, There are) only two bedrooms in my house.

e. Each of the countries (have, has) a part to play.

For f–h, replace each blank with the correct vocabulary word.

f. Pasadena, a town on the outskirts of Los Angeles, is considered a _____.

g. The "smiley face" _____ of the 1970s is still used today.

h. Traffic appears less congested in the outlying areas, or _____, of major cities.

More Practice   Choose the correct verb form for each sentence.

1. Everybody (is, are) trying to be considerate.

2. Either (is, are) fine with me.

3. Each (need, needs) attention.

4. Neither (want, wants) to admit it.

5. One of his teachers (is, are) giving him extra help.

6. Anybody in the upper grades (know, knows) the rules.

7. Nobody in the armed forces (remember, remembers) Colonel Mustard.

8. Anyone under his leadership (see, sees) his arrogance.

9. My wit (was, were) sharp.

10. My wits (was, were) about me.

11. Dad (ain't, isn't) home yet.

12. Rob (don't, doesn't) have gas money.

13. She and Mai (don't, doesn't) have any either.

14. We (ain't, aren't) finished studying.

15. They (isn't, aren't) finished either.

Review Set 80

Choose the correct verb form for sentences 1–5.

1. The ocean (is, are) the home of many mysterious things.
(78)

2. It (was, were) Great Britain who once ruled the seas.
(80)

3. An omelet with cheddar cheese and green onions (was, were) among the choices for breakfast.
(79)

4. One of those runners (deserve, deserves) a medal.
(7, 78)

5. Neither of the coaches (know, knows) who won the race.
(80)

Choose the correct contraction for sentences 6–8.

6. The nails (aren't, isn't) in the drawer.
(80)

7. (Isn't, Aren't) there a box of nails in the house?
(80)

8. (There's, There are) some in the garage.
(80)

9. People who think they are perfect are (mistake, mistook, mistaken).
(75)

10. Had people (seen, saw) the tornado coming?
(75)

11. The (good, better, best) type of protection against
(46) poisonous snakes is very stiff canvas leggings.

12. The museum curator shared with Sally and (me, I) that
(57, 67) the painting was a gift from a wealthy patron.

13. Two reasons for using the dash are an interruption in the
(77) sentence and (emphasis, quotations).

14. The skunk's (cent, sent, scent) caused the dog to rub its
(77) nose in the grass.

15. The (semiconscious, eager, prudent) man was carefully
(36, 71) placed in an ambulance.

16. Often, there are unavoidable (reconciliations,
(75, 76) consequences, substitutes) when one does something
wrong.

17. Many people in the Third World suffer from (diligence,
(12, 41) punctuality, malnutrition).

18. Write the present perfect tense verb phrase in this
(9, 19) sentence: China has called itself the *Flowery Kingdom*
because its people are polished and civilized.

19. Write the progressive tense verb phrase in this
(9, 21) sentence: The Chinese had been living in Central Asia.

Write each word that should be capitalized in sentences 20
and 21.

20. i believe that the name *flowery kingdom* originated from
(6, 12) the appreciation of flowers.

21. many birds fly south before the winter.
(12, 31)

22. Write the direct object in this sentence: The bushmaster,
(5, 25) the rattlesnake, and the Gaboon viper have long,
powerful fangs.

23. Write the correlative conjunction pair in this
(39) sentence: Neither soft leather nor soft rubber provides
protection against venomous snakes.

Rewrite sentences 24 and 25, adding periods and commas as needed.

✓ **24.** A large rounded mass of gold in its original state is called
(36, 63) a nugget

✓ **25.** The largest gold nugget was found in Victoria Australia
(36, 47) on February 5 1989

Rewrite 26 and 27, adding quotation marks as needed.

26. Holterman bragged, I extracted the biggest nugget.
(69, 70)

27. Emily said, I don't want to do the dishes tonight, Mom.
(69, 70)

I know you don't, Emily, but it is your turn, Mom insisted.

But I have loads of homework! cried Emily.

Mom pointed out, Then you should have watched less television this afternoon.

28. Write and underline each word that should be italicized
(73) in this sentence: I love it when the French teacher says merci beaucoup.

Diagram sentences 29 and 30.

✓ **29.** The old men gave LeRoy a pair of heavy boots.
(25, 35)

✓ **30.** *Flowery Kingdom* is an ancient name for China.
(22, 41)

LESSON
81

Subject-Verb Agreement, Part 4

Dictation or Journal Entry

Vocabulary:
Allegiance is loyalty and devotion, especially to one's country. We promise *allegiance* to our country when we salute the flag. A word that looks similar, *allegation*, is an assertion or statement that may or may not be true. Do you believe his *allegation* that he was not at the scene of the crime? To *allege* is to "assert" or to "offer an argument or excuse." He *alleges* his innocence.

In this lesson, we will look at nouns that can cause difficulty with subject-verb agreement.

Collective Nouns   We remember that a collective noun refers to a group or unit (a collection of people, places, animals, or things). Most of the time, these nouns take singular verbs.

If the group or unit is "acting" as one, we use a singular verb.

The *jury* <u>decides</u> the verdict.

The *audience* <u>was</u> appreciative.

A *bunch* of bananas <u>waits</u> on the counter.

However, if members of the group are "acting" individually, we use a plural verb.

The *majority* of voters <u>go</u> to the polls late in the day.

What *fraction* of the workers <u>are</u> satisfied?

A *bunch* of people <u>wait</u> in the library.

Special Nouns   Some nouns refer to a single "thing" but are still considered plural. When used as the subject of a sentence, nouns such as *pants*, *slacks*, *trousers*, *scissors*, *pliers*, *shears*, and *eyeglasses* require plural verbs.

These *scissors* <u>are</u> dull.

His *slacks* <u>were</u> too short.

However, watch for sentences like the one below. The word *pair* is the subject. *Pair* is singular and takes a singular verb.

This *pair* of pants <u>looks</u> nice.

Other nouns, especially ones that end in *-s*, appear to be plural but are considered singular. Nouns such as *measles*, *mumps*, *news*, and *lens* require singular verbs.

News <u>is</u> called "yellow journalism" if it exaggerates the facts.

Mumps <u>is</u> less common now because of vaccinations.

Some nouns have the same form whether they are singular or plural. *Corps, series, means, species,* and *gross,* as well as many animal names (*sheep, trout, bison, salmon,* etc.), are some examples. Use the meaning of the sentence to decide which verb form to use.

SINGULAR: This *series* of lectures <u>is</u> the best one in years.

PLURAL: Five new *series* <u>are</u> planned.

SINGULAR: That *deer* <u>was</u> here last winter.

PLURAL: Several *deer* <u>were</u> grazing nearby.

Finally, nouns that end in *-ics,* such as *mathematics, economics, ethics, athletics, acoustics,* and *politics,* can also be either singular or plural, depending on their meaning in the sentence. If we are referring to a body of knowledge, the noun is singular. If we are referring to a series of actions, the noun is plural:

Ethics <u>is</u> a fascinating subject.

His *ethics* <u>are</u> admirable.

Example   Choose the correct verb form for each sentence.

(a) Economics (is, are) an interesting field of study.

(b) The committee (select, selects) Carol Brady as the 1970s "TV Mom."

(c) Some species (is, are) endangered.

(d) Measles (was, were) not the best part of my childhood.

Solution   (a) "Economics" as a body of knowledge is singular. Economics **is** an interesting field of study.

(b) "Committee" is a collective noun, and its members are acting as one. The committee **selects** Carol Brady as the 1970s "TV Mom."

(c) The adjective "some" tells us that "species" is plural. Some species **are** endangered.

(d) "Measles" is singular. Measles **was** not the best part of my childhood.

√ **Practice** Choose the correct verb form for sentences a–d.

    a. The herd of sheep (was, were) waiting to be fed.

    b. In the 1990s, the most popular dog species (was, were) the Jack Russell terrier.

    c. The television staff (has, have) chosen a new set for the morning news show.

    d. The evening news (was, were) on at seven o'clock.

For e–g, replace each blank with *allegiance, allegation,* or *allege.*

    e. My parents vote in every election because of their _____ to our country.

    f. The witness made an _____ against the defendant in court.

    g. Witnesses _____ that Colonel Mustard is the murderer.

Review Set 81 Choose the best word to complete sentences 1–11.

    1. What do you think will be a(n) (icon, hemistich, hanger)
    (67, 80) for the first decade of the twenty-first century?

    2. The family was moving from the city of Chicago, Illinois,
    (71, 80) to a small (semicircle, polygon, suburb) outside of Atlanta, Georgia.

    3. I (scent, reconciled, inferred) from her blush that she was
    (75, 79) embarrassed.

    4. The little boy's upcoming surgery caused the mother
    (70, 78) (anxiety, eagerness, arrogance).

    5. As she climbed the old staircase, she (holded, hold, held)
    (75) on to the banister for dear life.

    6. This pair of pliers (is, are) too small for the job.
    (78)

7. *This, that, these,* and *those* are demonstrative (pronouns,
(71) verbs).

8. (Direct, Indirect) quotations give the speaker's exact
(69, 70) words.

9. Jon and (they, them) will arrive on time.
(55, 67)

10. We do not use quotation marks with (direct, indirect)
(69, 70) quotations.

11. Daniella, Anela, and (I, me) will be punctual.
(55, 67)

12. Tell whether this sentence is declarative, interrogative,
(1) exclamatory, or imperative: Do you know what event
triggered the beginning of World War I?

13. Write the helping verbs in this sentence: World War I
(9) probably could have been avoided.

14. Write the future perfect progressive verb phrase in this
(9, 21) sentence: By the time I graduate, I will have been
studying World War I for ten years.

15. Write the plural form of each noun. Use the dictionary if
(13, 14) you are in doubt.

(a) handful (b) scarf (c) ox

Rewrite 16–18, using correct capitalization and punctuation.

16. the first shot of world war i i am told was in june of 1914
(12, 36)

17. the high school has a chess club so why doesn't it have a
(12, 65) checkers club

18. i world war i
(20, 36)
    a countries involved
    b important dates

19. Write the proper adjective in this sentence: The Franklin
(30) stove warmed the mountain cabin.

20. Write the pair of correlative conjunctions in this
(39) sentence: Molly wanted not only hot fudge and nuts but
also a cherry on her birthday sundae.

For 21–23, refer to this sentence: Even though they were tired, the students didn't want the fascinating lecture to end.

21. Write the independent clause.
(24, 61)

22. Write the dependent clause.
(24, 61)

23. Write the subordinating conjunction.
(61)

24. Write the objective case pronoun in this sentence: The historian and she were explaining to me the many reasons for World War I.
(53, 57)

25. Write the five indefinite pronouns from this list that require a singular verb: others, other, few, one, many, nobody, anybody, several, much.
(72)

Rewrite 26 and 27, adding quotation marks as needed in these direct quotations.

26. James answered, Yes, Rob and they will be here soon.
(69, 70)

27. Each spring, Wes explained, the swallows return to Capistrano.
(69, 70)

Replace each blank with the correct word to complete sentences 28 and 29.

28. When we handwrite material, or when the italics style of type is not available, we _____ the words that require italics.
(73)

29. We use an _____ _____ after an exclamatory sentence (a sentence showing strong emotion).
(73)

30. Diagram this sentence: World War I was a four-year war, and it cost ten million lives.
(64)

Negatives • Double Negatives

Negatives Negatives are modifiers, usually adverbs, that mean "no" or "not." We will learn more about adverbs later. In this lesson, we will learn to recognize negatives and to use them correctly. Negatives are italicized in the sentences below.

I *never* buy new cars.

Philip had *nowhere* to go.

She had *scarcely* finished when the bell rang.

I could *not* hear you.

Here is a list of common negatives:

no	*not*	*never*
hardly	*scarcely*	*barely*
nowhere	*none*	*no one*
nothing	*nobody*	

Because the word *not* is a negative, the contraction *n't* is also a negative:

The class did*n't* understand decimals.

Suzy was*n't* listening.

I have*n't* enough patience.

Example 1 Write each negative that you find in these sentences.

(a) Sal could barely see the sign ahead.

(b) No one believed that Van had nothing to say.

(c) I did not invite anybody, so nobody came.

(d) Hardly anyone knew it was my birthday.

Solution   (a) **barely**   (b) **No one, nothing**

(c) **not, nobody**   (d) **Hardly**

Double   We use only one negative to express a negative idea. In the
Negatives   English language, two negatives in the same clause "cancel
each other out" and the idea becomes positive again.
Therefore, it is incorrect to use two negatives with one verb.
We call this a **double negative,** and we avoid it.

NO: Todd *never* needs *no* supervision.
YES: Todd *never* needs supervision.
YES: Todd needs *no* supervision.

NO: Brooke has*n't no* brush.
YES: Brooke has*n't* a brush.
YES: Brooke has *no* brush.

NO: *Scarcely none* are left.
YES: *Scarcely any* are left.
YES: Almost *none* are left.

Example 2   Choose the correct word to complete each sentence.

(a) The asthmatic people (could, couldn't) hardly breathe in
the smog.

(b) Jake doesn't want (no, any) cake.

(c) This computer isn't (nothing, anything) like mine.

(d) Scarcely (nobody, anybody) could figure it out.

Solution   (a) "Couldn't" and "hardly" are both negatives, so we choose
"could." The asthmatic people **could** hardly breathe in
the smog.

(b) "Doesn't" and "no" are both negatives. (To *not* want *no*
cake is to want some cake!) Jake doesn't want **any** cake.

(c) "Isn't" and "nothing" are both negatives. This computer
isn't **anything** like mine.

(d) "Scarcely" and "nobody" are both negatives. Scarcely
anybody could figure it out.

Correcting Double Negatives To correct a double negative, we can replace one of the negatives with a positive word. Look at the positive forms of the negatives below:

NEGATIVE		POSITIVE
hardly	→	almost
no	→	any, a
nobody	→	anybody
nowhere	→	anywhere
never	→	ever
neither	→	either
none	→	any
no one	→	anyone
nothing	→	anything

anything
Chris didn't do ~~nothing~~.

a
He is not ~~no~~ cheater.

either
I don't want dessert ~~neither~~.

Example 3 Rewrite this sentence, correcting the double negative:

Neither of them followed nobody.

Solution We replace the second negative, *nobody*, with a positive form—*anybody*:

Neither of them followed *anybody*.

Remember that a sentence can contain more than one negative, as long as they are not in the same clause. The sentence below is not an example of a double negative because each negative is in a different clause.

Melanie *didn't* go to the store, so she has *no* cheese.

Rare Exceptions On rare occasions, a double negative can be used for effect. Consider the following sentences:

The game was so easy, I *couldn't not* win!

Tia *barely, barely* made it on time.

In sentences such as these, the double negative is deliberate. Most double negatives, however, are unintended and incorrect. They are often heard in speech, but that is no excuse for using them.

Practice Choose the correct word to complete sentences a–e.

  a. Old Mother Hubbard (had, hadn't) scarcely any food left.

  b. Jack Sprat (could, couldn't) eat no lard.

  c. There has never been (anything, nothing) wrong with Humpty Dumpty.

  d. This hasn't (ever, never) happened to Little Bo Peep before.

  e. We're not (ever, never) going to find her sheep.

For f–j, replace each blank with *vane, vain,* or *vein.*

  f. Unfortunately, the beautiful girl was also very _____.

  g. The rooster and arrow on the roof is a weather _____, which tells the wind direction.

  h. The baseball game was rained out, so our long drive to the stadium had been in _____.

  i. The ruptured _____ appeared as a bruise.

  j. The _____ of silver caused a frenzy amongst the miners.

More Practice Choose the correct word to complete these sentences.

  1. I don't have (no, any) money, and I don't expect to have (none, any) soon.

  2. Jacob didn't want (no, any) help.

  3. Rachel doesn't want (nobody, anybody) to know her secret.

  4. Leah doesn't know (neither, either).

  5. They haven't forgotten (no one, anyone).

6. Mom hasn't gone (nowhere, anywhere).

7. Dan didn't eat (none, any) of those apples.

8. I haven't (never, ever) seen Levi.

9. Ben has hardly (no, any) time left.

10. Joseph didn't see (nothing, anything).

Review Set 82

Choose the best word to complete sentences 1–11.

1. A penny represents one (sent, scent, cent).
(77)

2. The merchandise offer (sent, scent, cent) to every home
(77) was inaccurate and misleading.

3. The young doctor's (consequential, semiprecious,
(71, 76) antisocial) decision to attend postgraduate school
delayed the start of his medical practice.

4. Hold your hips (stationery, continuous, stationary) while
(73) riding a bicycle.

5. (Its, It's) surface was wrinkled and rippled.
(60)

6. (Demonstrative, Interrogative) pronouns are sometimes
(71) called pointing pronouns.

7. In written dialog, a new (paragraph, chapter) begins every
(69, 70) time the speaker changes.

8. We enclose the actual words of each separate speaker
(69, 70) with (quotation, exclamation) marks.

9. We italicize or (underline, memorize) titles of books,
(73) magazines, newspapers, pamphlets, plays, book-length
poems, television shows, movies, films, record albums,
tapes, and CDs.

10. We use a question mark at the end of an (imperative,
(77) interrogative) sentence.

11. Negatives are modifiers, usually adverbs, that mean
(82) "(yes, no)" or "not."

For 12–18, refer to this sentence: The chemical elements in the human body would cost approximately one dollar.

12. Write the simple subject.
(2)

13. Write the simple predicate.
(2)

14. Write the prepositional phrase used as an adjective.
(33, 34)

15. Write the object of the preposition.
(17, 33)

16. Write the noun modified by the prepositional phrase.
(33, 34)

17. Write each descriptive adjective.
(27)

18. Write the number adjective.
(28)

For 19–21, refer to this sentence: Auguste Rodin designed the statue <u>The Thinker</u>.

19. Write the direct object.
(5, 25)

20. Write the appositive.
(48)

21. Diagram the sentence.
(25, 48)

For 22–25, refer to this sentence: <u>The Thinker</u> is considered realistic, for its surface is wrinkled and rippled.

22. Write the first independent clause.
(24, 61)

23. Write the second independent clause.
(24, 61)

24. Write the coordinating conjunction.
(37)

25. Diagram the sentence.
(44, 64)

26. Write the antecedent of the italicized pronoun in this
(51) sentence: The wrinkled, rippled surface of <u>The Thinker</u> gives *it* a more realistic effect.

27. Write the six indefinite pronouns from this list that
(72) require a plural verb: several, someone, ones, both, everyone, many, few, nobody, others.

Rewrite sentences 28 and 29, adding quotation marks if needed.

28. Critics said that Rodin did not finish his statue because it
(69, 70) did not have a smooth surface.

29. The docent explained, The French people began to
(69, 70) appreciate Rodin's works.

30. Write and underline the words that should be italicized
(73) in this sentence: Have you ever seen Rodin's sculpture
called The Thinker?

The Hyphen: Compound Nouns, Numbers

Dictation or Journal Entry

Vocabulary:
Already is an adverb that tells "when." The kindergarten boy reads *already*.
All ready means "completely ready." The class was *all ready* to practice the fire drill.

The **hyphen** is a punctuation mark used to connect elements of compound words and to express numbers.

Compound Nouns

We have learned that some compound nouns are hyphenated. There are no absolute rules for spelling a compound noun as one word, as two words, or hyphenated. However, certain categories of compound nouns are often hyphenated.

- Compound nouns that end in prepositional phrases:

  right-of-way   brother-in-law   stick-in-the-mud

  artist-at-large   man-about-town   attorney-at-law

- Compound nouns containing the prefix *ex-* or *self-* or the suffix *-elect*:

  ex-manager   self-discipline   mayor-elect

- Compound nouns that are units of measurement:

  board-foot   man-hour   light-year

- Compound nouns that end with the prepositions *in*, *on*, or *between*:

  drive-in   stand-in   trade-in

  add-on   goings-on   go-between

Nouns Without Nouns?

The English language is so flexible that we can create nouns from almost any part of speech. Look at the last category (compound nouns that end with prepositions) and notice that some of them don't contain an actual noun. Following are more examples of compound nouns formed from other parts of speech. We join the elements (words) with hyphens.

go-getter   show-off   has-been

get-together   look-alike   have-nots

sit-up   know-how   talking-to

The dictionary lists many of these words. But no dictionary can show every single combination of words that might make up a compound noun. If you have the need for a unique combination, use any similar words you can find in the dictionary to decide how to punctuate your compound noun.

Example 1   Write the words that should be hyphenated in sentences a–c. Be prepared to use the dictionary.

(a) When angry, one must show self restraint.

(b) The runner-up in the beauty pageant lives in Hawaii.

(c) That cup of tea was a real pick me up.

Solution   These compound words need hyphens:

(a) **Self-restraint** contains the prefix *self-* and so should be hyphenated.

(b) The dictionary tells us that **runner-up** is hyphenated.

c) **Pick-me-up** is being used as a noun but doesn't actually contain a noun. It should be hyphenated. (The dictionary confirms this by listing *pick-me-up* as an informal noun.)

Numbers   Hyphens are often used to join elements in the expression of numbers and inclusive sets or sequences.

Numbers as Words   We use a hyphen in compound numbers from twenty-one to ninety-nine:

twenty-seven   one hundred fifty-two copies

sixty-sixth day   two twenty-fifths $(\frac{2}{25})$

A Range of Numbers   A hyphen is used to indicate a range of numbers or an inclusive set or sequence.

pages 14-29   the years 1970-1980

40-50 percent   the week of April 12-19

Because the hyphen takes the place of words in pairs such as *from/through*, *from/to*, or *between/and*, we do not use one of the words and a hyphen.

INCORRECT: between 1976-1981

CORRECT: between 1976 and 1981

Example 2   Write the numbers that should be hyphenated in sentences a–c.

(a) The president of the Kiwanis Club is forty eight.

(b) The aces make up four fifty seconds of a deck of cards.

(c) Her article appears on pages 335 338.

Solution   (a) **Forty-eight** is hyphenated because it is a number between 21 and 99.

(b) The denominator **fifty-seconds** is hyphenated because it is a number between 21 and 99.

(c) The numerals **335-338** are hyphenated because they represent a sequence.

√**Practice**   For a and b, replace each blank with *already* or *all ready*.

a. We _____ learned about nouns.

b. The tourists were _____ to board their flight to Orlando, Florida.

For c–f, write each expression that should be hyphenated. Use the dictionary, if necessary.

c. Gary, a real go getter, faithfully delivers newspapers to his customers early every morning.

d. She saw the write up in the newspaper.

e. Please make good use of your remaining twenty three minutes and fifty four seconds of class.

f. *Camelot* will be performed October 15 21 in the newly refurbished theater.

More Practice   For 1–8, use words to write each number.

1. 25	**2.** 47	**3.** 76	**4.** 98
5. 21st	**6.** 32nd	**7.** 45th	**8.** 83rd

Write each expression that should be hyphenated in sentences 9–12. Use a dictionary, if necessary.

9. Self confidence is important in a job interview.

10. We must be aware of the danger of cave ins.

11. My father in law was a movie stand in.

12. Ron is such a know it all!

Review Set 83

Choose the best word to complete sentences 1–12.

1. Do you know (wear, we're, where) the nearest hospital is
(72) located?

2. The restaurant required its servers to (wear, we're, where)
(72) black pants and white shirts.

3. The chairs were arranged in a (hemisphere, coarse,
(67, 71) semicircle) around the speaker.

4. The prefix meaning *half* is (*semi-, uni-, poly-*).
(61, 71)

5. (He, Him) and I want to learn about some of the new
(55, 67) inventions introduced in the 1920s.

6. Families (sat, sitted) around their radios to hear
(76) broadcasts of news, music, and comedy shows.

7. Perhaps the people's (most, more) beloved movies were
(45, 46) those featuring Charlie Chaplin.

8. *This* and *these* are examples of demonstrative pronouns
(71) used to point out persons or things that are (nearby,
farther away).

9. Titles of short stories, essays and sermons, one-act plays,
(69, 70) newspaper and magazine articles, short poems, and songs
are enclosed in (quotation, exclamation) marks.

10. We use a (dash, italic) to indicate an interruption in the
(73, 77) flow of the sentence.

11. Ricardo hadn't seen (none, any) of Charlie Chaplin's
(82) movies.

12. We consult the dictionary if we are unsure about whether
(83) to use a (dash, hyphen) in a compound noun.

13. Tell whether this word group is a fragment, run-on sentence, or complete sentence: New inventions and technologies in American society.
(3)

14. Write the linking verb in this sentence: Americans became dependent on radios during their leisure time.
(22)

15. Write the proper noun in this sentence: During the 1920s, Americans were going to the movies.
(6)

For 16 and 17, refer to this sentence: The movies were different.

16. Write the predicate adjective.
(44)

17. Diagram the sentence.
(44)

18. Rewrite this sentence, adding capital letters as needed: on friday, my friends and i are going to see charlie chaplin's famous movie city lights.
(12, 20)

19. Write the coordinating conjunction in this compound sentence: Comedies were the most popular movies, yet viewers still enjoyed Westerns, love stories, and adventures.
(37)

For 20 and 21, refer to this sentence: "The Little Tramp," Charlie Chaplin's famous character, was a poor, shy, unlucky little man.

20. Write the predicate nominative.
(41)

21. Diagram the sentence.
(41)

22. Write each prepositional phrase, and star the object of each preposition in this sentence: People throughout the world became familiar with "The Little Tramp."
(17, 33)

23. Write the verb in this sentence, and tell whether it is transitive or intransitive: "The Little Tramp" was recognized by his square moustache, his round-topped bowler hat, his baggy pants, and his swinging cane.
(22, 32)

24. Write the reflexive pronoun in this sentence: Charlie Chaplin allowed himself to make movies that made viewers think.
(62)

25. Write the intensive pronoun in this sentence: How can
(62) the author himself write the book review?

26. Write the five indefinite pronouns from this list that can
(72) be either singular or plural: someone, all, none, several,
any, some, most.

Rewrite 27–30, adding quotation marks if needed.

✓ **27.** The cinema teacher said, He would always bounce back
(69, 70) from disaster, and he never lost his dignity or his sense of
hope.

28. The professor told us that <u>Modern Times</u> allowed Charlie
(69, 70) Chaplin to take a humorous look at the assembly line.

29. Many readers enjoy Bret Harte's short story The Outcasts
(69, 70) of Poker Flat.

30.   The movie buff asked, Have you seen Charlie
(69, 70) Chaplin's <u>City Lights</u>?
    No, the companion replied, but I have seen
<u>Modern Times</u>.

Adverbs That Tell "How"

Adverbs are descriptive words that modify or add information to verbs, adjectives, and other adverbs. They answer the questions "how," "when," "where," "why," and "how much" (or "to what extent"). The italicized adverbs below modify the verb *ran*:

> HOW: Juan ran *beautifully.*
>
> WHEN: He ran *early.*
>
> WHERE: He ran *there.*
>
> WHY: He ran *because.*
>
> HOW MUCH: He ran *more.*

"How" An adverb that tells "how" usually modifies a verb or verb phrase and often ends in the suffix *-ly*. For example, let's think about how Brent skis:

> Brent skis *recklessly.*

Brent might also ski *cautiously, hastily, gleefully, clumsily,* or *slowly.* These adverbs all answer the question "how."

Example 1 Write the adverbs that tell "how" from this sentence:

> The emcee spoke quickly and loudly.

Solution The adverbs **quickly** and **loudly** tell "how" the emcee spoke.

Suffix *-ly* We remember that descriptive adjectives often end with suffixes such as *-able*, *-ful*, *-ive*, or *-ous*. Below are the adjective and adverb forms of some nouns. Notice that the adverb is formed by adding *-ly* to the adjective.

NOUN	ADJECTIVE	ADVERB
fear	*fearless*	*fearlessly*
nature	*natural*	*naturally*
grace	*graceful*	*gracefully*
danger	*dangerous*	*dangerously*
sense	*sensible*	*sensibly*

Of course, not every word that ends in *-ly* is an adverb. *Lovely, friendly, orderly,* and *lonely* are all adjectives.

Adjective or Adverb? Some words, such as *hard, fast, right, early,* and *long,* have the same form whether they are used as adjectives or adverbs. However, we can always tell how the word is being used because an adjective modifies a noun or pronoun, and an adverb modifies a verb, adjective, or other adverb.

ADJECTIVE: That test was *hard.* (modifies the noun "test")
ADVERB: Jim worked *hard.* (modifies the verb "worked")

ADJECTIVE: It was a *fast* race. (modifies the noun "race")
ADVERB: Juanita ran *fast.* (modifies the verb "ran")

ADJECTIVE: Make a *right* turn at the corner.
ADVERB: Please turn *right* at the corner.

We must learn to see the difference between an adverb and a predicate adjective. Look at the following sentence:

The new student felt lonely.

It might seem that *lonely* tells "how" the student felt. But we remember that we can identify a predicate adjective by replacing a possible linking verb (felt) with a "to be" verb:

The new student *was* lonely. (lonely student)

The word *lonely* describes the student, not the act of feeling. It is an adjective. Compare this to a sentence containing an action verb:

The fox moves silently.

If we replace an action verb with a "to be" verb, the sentence no longer makes sense:

The fox *is* silently? (silently fox?)

Silently does not describe the fox. It describes the act of moving. It is an adverb.

Example 2 Tell whether the italicized word in each sentence is an adjective or adverb. Also, tell which word it modifies.

(a) Lorene pedaled *hard* through the rain.

(b) Her cold, *hard* ride was not in vain.

(c) The two children grew *friendly.*

Solution (a) The word *hard* is an **adverb. It modifies the verb "pedaled."** *Hard* tells "how" Lorene pedaled.

(b) The word *hard* is an **adjective. It modifies the noun "ride."** *Hard* tells "what kind" of ride.

(c) The word *friendly* is an **adjective. It modifies the noun "children."** *Friendly* tells "what kind" of children.

Practice For sentences a–c, write each adverb that tells "how" and tell what word or phrase it modifies.

a. The flock of mallards settled peacefully on the pond.

b. Fast, powerful cars and trucks can burn fuel rapidly.

c. Hector completed the assignment quickly and easily.

For d–g, tell whether the italicized word is an adjective or an adverb, and tell what word or phrase it modifies.

d. The principal sounds *tired*.

e. Did the politician speak *truthfully*?

f. She has been *truthful*.

g. The choir was singing *joyfully*.

For h and i, replace each blank with *heel* or *heal*.

h. Valerie's swollen _____ made her shoes uncomfortable.

i. A wound may take several days to _____.

Review Set 84 Choose the best word to complete sentences 1–12.

1. The earth is divided into the Northern and Southern
(61, 67) (polygons, brakes, Hemispheres).

2. The stroke victim suffered from (hemiplegia, hemistich,
(61, 67) polytheism).

3. "Little Miss Muffet sat on a tuffet..." is an example of a
(43, 67) (principle, rite, hemistich).

4. Everybody in the second and third grades (is, are) going
(15, 78) on a field trip.

5. Ilbea and Jerry (was, were) looking forward to the
(15, 78) wedding.

6. Either the custodian or the students (know, knows)
(54, 78) where the vacuum cleaner is located.

7. The Model T, (who, which) wasn't very pretty, came in
(66) black only.

8. The winner, (he, him), may drive the Model T to the
(67) formal ball.

9. These burritos are pretty good, but (those, them) tacos are
(71) delicious.

10. The cows don't have (no, any) hay to eat.
(82)

11. Two reasons we use the dash are interruptions and
(77) (interest, emphasis).

12. This Model T isn't (nothing, anything) like my old
(82) Studebaker.

13. Make a complete sentence from this fragment: Both
(4) horses and mules capable of pulling plows.

For 14 and 15, write the verb, and tell whether it is transitive
or intransitive.

14. In the 1920s, most Americans spent more money on new
(25, 32) products.

15. By then, most American homes were equipped with
(25, 32) electricity.

16. Write the collective noun in this sentence: Americans
(8) enjoyed an assortment of new inventions—vacuum
cleaners, washing machines, refrigerators, etc.

17. Tell whether this word group is a phrase or a
(24) clause: before the introduction of refrigerators

For 18–20, refer to this sentence: Henry Ford gave Americans their first affordable automobile.

18. Write the direct object.
(5, 25)

19. Write the indirect object.
(25, 35)

20. Diagram the sentence.
(25, 35)

Rewrite sentences 21–24, adding commas as needed.

21. Electric lights electric heat and the Model T Ford
(47) changed American life.

22. In 1908 Henry Ford an American businessman
(47, 49) manufactured a car called a Model T.

23. Look in the encyclopedia under "Ford Henry" to find
(52) information on the Model T.

24. The Model T they say was well built and inexpensive.
(56)

25. Write the indefinite pronoun in this sentence, and tell
(72) whether it is singular or plural: Most of us have seen a Model T.

26. Rewrite this sentence, adding quotation marks as
(69, 70) needed: London Bridge is a song many of us learn as children.

27. Write and underline each word that should be italicized
(73) in this sentence: The Canterbury Tales is a long literary work in medieval English.

28. Write and hyphenate words that should be hyphenated in
(83) this sentence: Dave's great grandfather was considered a real do gooder.

Replace each blank with the correct word to complete sentences 29 and 30.

29. _____ are descriptive words that modify or add
(84) information to verbs, adjectives, and other adverbs.

30. Adverbs answer the questions "_____," "when,"
(84) "where," "why," and "how much" (or "to what extent").

Using the Adverb *Well*

Dictation or Journal Entry

Vocabulary:

The words *metal* and *mettle* are homophones. *A metal* is an element such as copper or iron. The *metal* used for pennies is copper. *Mettle* refers to the quality of one's character, especially one's courage and fortitude.

Another pair of similar homophones is *meddle* and *medal*. The word *meddle* means "to interfere." The mother *meddled* with her grown son's plans. *Medal* is an award. Each runner received a participation *medal*.

Good The words *good* and *well* are difficult parts of speech. *Good* is a descriptive adjective or a predicate adjective. It modifies a noun or pronoun, as in these sentences:

Mrs. McWhirter is a *good* teacher.
(descriptive adjective modifying "teacher")

She praised her students for their *good* behavior.
(descriptive adjective modifying "behavior")

The pie tastes *good*.
(predicate adjective describing "pie")

Well The word *well* is usually an adverb. It modifies an action verb and explains "how" someone does something.

The soprano sings *well*.

Magic Johnson plays basketball *well*.

How *well* can you play?

We do not use the word *good* as an adverb.

NO: Freddy dances *good*.
YES: Freddy dances *well*.

NO: This gadget works *good*.
YES: This gadget works *well*.

Example 1 Replace each blank with *well* or *good*.

(a) Last night I slept _____.

(b) Did you have a _____ time at the picnic?

(c) Elizabeth cooks _____.

(d) She is a _____ cook.

Solution (a) Last night I slept **well**. *Well* is an adverb that modifies the verb *slept*. It tells "how" I slept.

(b) Did you have a **good** time at the picnic? *Good* is an adjective that modifies the noun *time.*

(c) Elizabeth cooks **well.** *Well* is an adverb that modifies the verb *cooks.* It tells "how" Elizabeth cooks.

(d) She is a **good** cook. *Good* is an adjective that modifies the noun *cook.*

Feeling Well? The word *well* is used as an adjective when referring to the state of one's health. You feel *good* about passing a test, for example, but when you wish to state that you are in good health, it is preferable to say that you are *well.*

I feel *well* today.

Is she *well,* or is she sick?

Example 2 Choose either *well* or *good* to complete each sentence.
(a) You don't look as if you feel (good, well).

(b) Glen felt (well, good) about winning the cup.

Solution (a) You don't look as if you feel **well.** We use *well* when when referring to one's health.

(b) Glen felt **good** about winning the cup. We do not use *well* because we are not referring to the state of Glen's health.

✓**Practice** Choose the correct descriptive word for sentences a–e.
a. The students worked (good, well) together and finished the project.

b. Kevin did a (good, well) job painting the fence.

c. Most people can carry a tune fairly (good, well).

d. Alex is a (good, well) guitarist.

e. This old teapot still serves me (good, well).

Replace each blank with *metal, mettle, meddle,* or *medal.*
f. Copper, iron, gold, and silver are _____s.

g. The five-day marathon really tested her _____.

h. A first place _____ was awarded to the fastest runner.

i. Please do not _____ in my affairs.

More Practice Choose the correct descriptive word for each sentence.

1. Ferns grow (good, well) in the forest.

2. How (good, well) did you study last night?

3. Robert cooks (good, well).

4. He is a (good, well) cook.

5. The pancake tasted (good, well).

6. Frank feels (good, well) when he gets As.

7. Christopher and Emily paint (well, good).

8. They've done some (good, well) paintings.

9. Waverly slept (good, well).

10. Judy had a (good, well) sleep too.

Review Set 85 Choose the best word to complete sentences 1–11.

1. Please add (for, fore, four) eggs to the pancake batter.
(64)

2. This pancake is (for, fore, four) you.
(64)

3. The prefix *poly-* means "(one, same, many)."
(13, 61)

4. In many cultures, a child's entrance into adulthood involves some kind of (right, write, rite).
(50)

5. The seedling (grew, growed, grown) into a large tomato plant.
(54, 74)

6. Whining is the (little, less, least) effective way of getting what you want.
(46)

7. (This, This here) is my sister.
(71)

8. A pronoun that does not have a known antecedent is called an (indefinite, unknown) pronoun.
(72)

9. An adverb that tells "how" usually modifies the verb or
(84) verb phrase and often ends in (-*ly, -ing, -ed*).

10. Sledding enthusiasts think cold weather is (good, well).
(85)

11. Aidan knows (good, well) that dinner is at six o'clock.
(85)

12. Write the four principal parts (present tense, present
(9, 16) participle, past tense, and past participle) of the verb
rebel.

13. Diagram the simple subject and simple predicate of this
(2, 23) sentence: The 1920s, a decade of fast-paced and exciting
times, was one long party for some young Americans.

14. Write the possessive noun in this sentence: The young
(10, 28) people's desire was to enjoy life rather than to work hard.

For 15 and 16, write each prepositional phrase and star the
object of each preposition.

15. Despite my work on the fence, the rabbits still got in.
(17, 33)

16. At the deli on the corner, I ordered a corned beef
(17, 33) sandwich on rye with mustard.

17. Write each word that should be capitalized in this
(6, 12) sentence: last september, xana and haldor went all the
way to thessaloniki, greece, to be married.

For 18–20, refer to this sentence: Snowball and Snicker
stalked and attacked my bare feet.

✓ **18.** Write the compound subject.
(2, 38)

✓ **19.** Write the compound predicate.
(2, 38)

✓ **20.** Diagram the sentence.
(38)

✓ **21.** Rewrite this sentence, adding commas as needed: The
(63) noisy crowded flea market was full of bargains.

✓ **22.** Write the antecedent of the italicized pronoun in this
(51) sentence: The bicyclists could have taken the paved
road, but *they* chose the dirt path instead.

23. Write the verb in this sentence, and tell whether it is
(25, 32) transitive or intransitive: Gilda, a gifted painter of portraits, frequented the museum.

Write the interrogative pronoun in sentences 24 and 25.

24. What did you find in the closet?
(68)

25. I wondered who would find that.
(68)

26. Write five adverbs that end in -*ly*.
(84)

27. Write five words that have the same form whether they
(84) are used as adjectives or adverbs.

For 28–30, tell whether the italicized word is used as an adjective or an adverb.

28. The children played *rambunctiously*.
(84)

29. The children were *noisy*.
(84)

30. The *noisy* children drew frowns of disapproval.
(84)

The Hyphen: Compound Adjectives

We have seen how hyphens are used in compound nouns and with numbers. In this lesson we will learn more uses for hyphens.

Compound Adjectives

Just as we combine words to form compound nouns, we can combine words to form **compound adjectives**. A compound adjective is a group of words that works *as a unit* to modify a noun with a single thought. It is not a list of adjectives, each modifying a noun in its own way.

COMPOUND ADJECTIVE:	*night-blooming* jasmine
TWO ADJECTIVES:	*shiny yellow* buttercups
COMPOUND ADJECTIVE:	*bookkeeping* office
TWO ADJECTIVES:	*dark, dusty* room
COMPOUND ADJECTIVE:	*black-and-white* dress
THREE ADJECTIVES:	*baggy green corduroy* pants

As shown above, compound adjectives can be spelled as one word, left as separate words, or hyphenated. How they appear is sometimes a matter of rule but is often a matter of custom or style. The following guidelines will help you form many compound adjectives confidently.

Clarity

Our goal is to make our meaning as clear as possible to the reader. When we use hyphens to join two or more words, it helps the reader understand that the words are to be read as a single unit. This prevents confusion. Consider this sentence:

Snow covered New York at Christmas is a beautiful sight.

The reader, seeing a subject (snow), a verb (covered), and a direct object (New York), is likely to misread the sentence. So we hyphenate the compound adjective for greater clarity:

Snow-covered New York at Christmas is a beautiful sight.

Borrowed Phrases and Clauses   One of the ways we modify nouns is by borrowing descriptive phrases and clauses and using them as compound adjectives. Hyphens help join words that work as a unit to modify a noun.

Prepositional Phrases   When we use a prepositional phrase to modify a noun, it is functioning as a compound adjective. If it comes *before* the noun, it should be hyphenated.

An *out-of-date* report is unacceptable.
(The report was *out of date*.)

After-dinner mints come in pastel colors.
(We had mints *after dinner*.)

Words Out of Order   When we borrow a descriptive phrase or clause and place it before a noun, we often eliminate or rearrange some of the words. To help them express a single thought, words that are out of their normal order can be held together by hyphens.

Don't put on those *grass-stained* socks.
(Those socks are *stained with grass*.)

Let's feed that *hungry-looking* lion.
(That lion *looks hungry*.)

An Exception   We *do not* use a hyphen in a compound adjective that begins with an adverb ending in *-ly*.

some *nicely kept* homes, a *securely fastened* gate

the *newly married* man, my *painfully swollen* ankle

Number + Unit of Measure   We use a hyphen when joining a number to a unit of measure to form a compound adjective.

24-foot rope, *nine-mile* walk, *fifteen-year* loan

We *do not* use a hyphen when the number alone modifies the noun:

24 feet, nine miles, fifteen years

Fractions   We use a hyphen in a fraction that functions as an adjective.

Jean won the election by a *two-thirds* majority.

The tank was *four-fifths* full.

If the numerator or the denominator of a fraction is already hyphenated, *do not* use another hyphen:

A *five twenty-fifths* increase equals a *one-fifth* increase.

We *do not* use a hyphen if the fraction functions as a noun.

Three tenths of the birds were fox sparrows.

Example 1 Write the words that should be hyphenated in sentences a–e.

(a) The strawberry filled dessert had us licking our lips.

(b) She earned above average grades.

(c) That was a foul tasting cough syrup.

(d) Marc drew a four inch line on his paper.

(e) Four fifths of the girls wanted to take gymnastics.

Solution (a) We hyphenate **strawberry-filled** because the words work as a unit to modify the noun *dessert* with a single thought: filled with strawberries.

(b) We hyphenate **above-average** because it is a prepositional phrase that comes before and modifies the noun *grades*.

(c) We hyphenate **foul-tasting** to help it retain its meaning (something that tastes foul).

(d) We hyphenate **four-inch** because it is a compound adjective formed by a number and a unit of measure.

(e) **None.** We do not hyphenate the fraction four fifths because it is functioning as a noun.

Dictionary Clues Remember, dictionaries cannot contain all the compound words we can create. If you are faced with an unfamiliar compound, you can search the dictionary for similar compounds and use them as clues.

Other Uses for Hyphens We use hyphens to avoid confusion or awkward spelling, and to join unusual elements.

With Prefixes and Suffixes If you add a prefix or suffix to a word, and the resulting word is misleading or awkward, use a hyphen for clarity.

Will you *re-cover* (not *recover*) the chair with new fabric?

It had a hard, *shell-like* (not *shelllike*) surface.

Also, use a hyphen to join a prefix to any proper noun.

pro-American, mid-July, post-World War II

Letter + Word,
Number + Number   Hyphens are used to combine unusual elements into single expressions.

When a letter (or group of letters) modifies a word in a compound noun or adjective, a hyphen is often used.

A-frame, L-shaped, PG-rated, U-turn, T-shirt

We can also use a hyphen to join numbers in expressions such as the following:

The score at halftime was *27-43*.

You've got a *fifty-fifty* chance of flipping tails.

Example 2   Write the words, if any, that should be hyphenated in sentences a–d. Be prepared to use the dictionary.

(a) Claire must research the house for her glasses.

(b) Why do you say that you are antiShakespeare?

(c) If your brother is a photographer, he knows about f stops.

(d) We agreed to split the bill sixty forty.

Solution   (a) We hyphenate **re-search** to avoid misleading the reader.

(b) We hyphenate **anti-Shakespeare** because we are joining a prefix and a proper noun.

(c) We consult the dictionary and find that **f-stops** is a hyphenated term.

(d) We use a hyphen to form the expression **sixty-forty**.

Practice   Write the words, if any, that should be hyphenated in sentences a–e.

a. The movie may have been G rated, but it still made my uncle jump once or twice.

b. The rapidly approaching storm made the horses nervous.

c. Next week, let's repair all the dancers.

d. We'll need a forty meter length of twine.

e. Kurt's rain soaked shoes left a trail of puddles on the gray tile floor.

For f and g, replace each blank with *creek* or *creak*.

f. Sometimes the limbs of old trees will squeak or _____ when the wind blows.

g. Frogs and polliwogs often live in a _____.

Review Set 86

Choose the best word to complete sentences 1–12.

1. Ores like gold and silver are precious (mettles, medals, metals).
(85)

2. The physician predicted that the fractured femur would take about six weeks to (heal, heel).
(84)

3. A person of (metal, medal, mettle, meddle) approaches life's challenges with determination.
(85)

4. Since Rich was late, Harold had (already, all ready) left for school.
(83)

5. Why has Shelly (throwed, threw, thrown) tulip bulbs all over the back yard?
(54)

6. Well, everyone (know, knows) that you simply plant them where they fall.
(72, 80)

7. Shelly's cat chases (mouses, mice) in the potting shed.
(13, 14)

8. The equator is (warm, warmer, warmest) than the South Pole.
(45)

9. We use a (comma, hyphen) to combine the parts of a compound word.
(83, 86)

10. We sometimes use a (dash, hyphen) to join a letter to a word, as in *L-shaped*.
(83, 86)

11. (Adjectives, Adverbs) are descriptive words that modify or add information to verbs, adjectives, and other adverbs.
(84)

12. Adverbs answer the questions "how," "when," "why" "how much" and "(where, who)."
(84)

13. Tell whether this sentence is declarative, interrogative,
(1, 77) imperative, or exclamatory: The scientist cried,
"Eureka!"

14. Write the action verb in this sentence, and tell whether it
(5, 32) is transitive or intransitive: Who put bells on my shoes?

15. Write the past perfect verb phrase in this sentence: My
(9, 19) own sister had confessed to the joke.

16. Rewrite the following, adding commas, periods, and
(29, 52) capital letters as needed:

dear lenora

　　when you visit mother and me in
tennessee this spring don't forget to
bring your journal

　　　　love

　　　　james

17. Write each descriptive adjective in this sentence: The
(27) principal reason for colder winters and warmer summers
is the angle at which the rays of the sun strike the earth.

18. Write the correlative conjunctions in this
(39) sentence: Neither Tarzan nor Jane desired to leave the
jungle.

For 19–23, refer to this sentence: Roosevelt was admired but
Hitler was feared.

19. Write the first independent clause.
(24, 61)

20. Write the second independent clause.
(24, 61)

21. Write the coordinating conjunction.
(37, 64)

22. Rewrite the compound sentence, adding commas as
(64, 65) needed.

23. Diagram the sentence.
(64)

24. Write the personal pronoun from this sentence, and tell
(53, 55) whether it is nominative or objective case: He didn't
believe the old man's ghost story, but Smith avoided the
abandoned house anyway.

For 25–28, write the questions answered by the italicized adverb. Problem 25 is completed for you.

25. They danced *gracefully*.   <u>   How?   </u>
(84)

26. They danced *later*.   <u>   </u>
(84)

27. They danced *there*.   <u>   </u>
(84)

28. They danced *more*.   <u>   </u>
(84)

Diagram sentences 29 and 30.

29. Mrs. Perkins offered Daniel some help.
(25, 35)

30. Adolf Hitler, the absolute dictator of Germany, declared a
(34, 48) new era of German history, the Third Reich.

LESSON 87

Adverbs That Tell "Where"

Dictation or Journal Entry

Vocabulary:

The homophones *miner* and *minor* may confuse us. A *miner* is one who digs in the ground for valuable ore. The *miner* spent many hours searching for gold in the mine. The noun *minor* refers to a person who is not legally an adult. In the United States, a person is a *minor* until the age of eighteen. The adjective *minor* means "of less size, amount, or importance." It was only a *minor* inconvenience to do without a curling iron.

We have learned to identify adverbs that tell "how." In this lesson, we will learn to identify adverbs that tell "where." Again, let's think about how Brent skis:

Brent skis *recklessly.*

"Where" Now, let's think about **where** Brent skis:

Brent skis *everywhere.*

He might also ski *far, downhill, home, outside,* or *anywhere.*

Here are some common adverbs that tell "where:"

near	*anywhere*	*up*	*in*
far	*everywhere*	*here*	*out*
down	*nowhere*	*there*	*home*
above	*somewhere*	*away*	*inside*
under	*around*	*ahead*	*outside*

We remember that words like *in, out,* and *down* can also be prepositions. But in order to function as a preposition, a word must have an object. When a word like *in, out,* or *down* does not have an object, it is an adverb.

PREPOSITION: The dog ran *out* the door. (object "door")

ADVERB: The dog ran *out.* (no object)

Example 1 For sentences a–d, write each adverb that tells "where," and give the verb or verb phrase that it modifies.

(a) The children ran ahead.

(b) Cheryl fell here.

(c) The boys looked everywhere for their dog.

(d) The spectators were sitting down to watch the parade.

Solution (a) The word **ahead** tells "where" the children **ran.**

(b) The word **here** modifies the verb **fell.** It tells "where" Cheryl fell.

(c) The word **everywhere** modifies the verb **looked.** It tells "where" the boys looked.

(d) The word **down** modifies the verb phrase **were sitting.** It tells "where" they were sitting.

Diagramming Adverbs We diagram adverbs just as we do adjectives. We write the adverb on a slanted line under the word it modifies. Here we diagram this sentence:

Brent skis *outside*.

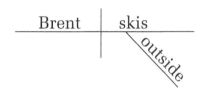

Example 2 Diagram this sentence: He walked home.

Solution The adverb *home* tells "where" he walked, so we diagram the sentence like this:

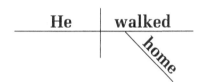

Practice For sentences a–d, write each adverb that tells "where," and give the verb or verb phrase that it modifies.

a. Joel was hiding somewhere.

b. Caylee had come home.

c. Emma might have been staying inside.

d. Paige jumped around.

Diagram sentences e and f.

e. Edna and George went downtown.

f. I left my keys somewhere.

For g–i, replace each blank with *miner* or *minor*.

  g. Marianne's stuffy nose was a _____ annoyance.

  h. Peter may not vote because he is still a _____.

  i. In 1849, thousands of would-be gold_____s flooded California.

Review Set 87

Choose the best word to complete sentences 1–12.

  1. The entire cross-country team received (mettles,
  (85) meddles, metals, medals) for having the best team score at the meet.

  2. A nosy person tries to (mettle, meddle, metal, medal) in
  (85) other people's business.

  3. The campers were (all ready, already) to load the bus and
  (83) be on their way.

  4. The (vein, vane, vain) celebrity assumed that everybody
  (82) adored him.

  5. Yesterday Benito (drawn, drew) a picture of a giraffe.
  (74)

  6. The committee (suggest, suggests) planting marigolds
  (81) along Main Street.

  7. The right-fielder we want is (he, him).
  (53, 55)

  8. We use a hyphen in compound numbers from (twenty-
  (83, 86) one, forty-one) to ninety-nine.

  9. We use a (hyphen, period) when we form new words
  (83, 86) with the prefixes *ex-* or *self-* or the suffix *-elect*.

  10. An adverb that tells ("how," "where") usually modifies
  (84, 87) the verb or verb phrase and often ends in *-ly*.

  11. (Good, Well) is usually an adverb that modifies an action
  (85) verb and tells "how."

  12. (Good, Well) is a descriptive adjective or predicate
  (85) adjective that describes a noun or pronoun.

For 13 and 14, refer to this sentence: No full moon occurs in a moonless month.

13. Write the simple subject.
(2)

14. Write the simple predicate.
(2)

15. Write the present progressive verb phrase in this
(9, 21) sentence: For centuries, astronomers have been studying the monthly lunar phases.

16. Write the indirect object in this sentence: Eight times
(25, 35) between 1809 and 1999, astronomers assigned February no full moon.

17. Write each word that should be capitalized in this
(12) sentence: the man in the poem sat by the fire during the winter.

18. Write the overused adjective in this sentence: A good
(50) painting hung on the wall above the fireplace.

Rewrite sentences 19 and 20, adding capital letters, periods, and commas as needed.

19. on july 20 1969 three astronauts were orbiting the moon
(6, 47)

20. when the waiter in the starched white shirt asks if we
(26, 63) want bleu cheese thousand island or french dressing on our salads tell him i want vinegar and oil

For 21–24, refer to this sentence: When the 1969 moon landing was successful President Kennedy's goal was achieved.

21. Write the independent clause.
(24, 61)

22. Write the dependent clause.
(24, 61)

23. Write the subordinating conjunction.
(61)

24. Rewrite the sentence, adding commas as needed.
(63)

25. Write the personal pronoun and its antecedent in this
(51, 53) sentence: If people want to rename the great space base in Florida, let them do it.

26. Write the nominative case pronoun in this sentence: He
(53, 55) told me that the *Eagle*, a much smaller spacecraft,
actually landed on the moon.

27. Write the adjective and adverb forms of each noun.
(84) (a) peace   (b) harm

28. Write the five words from this list that can be either
(84) adjectives or adverbs: slowly, hard, quickly, fast, right,
neatly, long, early.

29. Write the five adverbs from this list that tell
(87) "where": outside, fast, ahead, slowly, around, quietly,
away, there.

30. Diagram this sentence: The astronauts of Apollo 11 were
(38, 41) Michael Collins, Buzz Aldrin, and Neil Armstrong.

Word Division

Dictation or Journal Entry
Vocabulary:
The homophones *past* and *passed* are different parts of speech. *Past* can be a noun (history teaches us about the *past*); an adjective (we learn from *past* mistakes); an adverb that tells "where" (he walked *past*); and a preposition (go *past* the store). *Passed* is always the past tense of the verb *pass*. Geese *passed* overhead as the sun slipped *past* the horizon.

When writing, we use a hyphen to divide a word if we run out of room at the end of a line. It is important to know *where* (or *whether*) to divide a word.

Note: Using a computer does not free us from this responsibility. Many "automatic" word divisions are unacceptable in good writing.

Observe the following guidelines when dividing a word.

Between Syllables Words can be divided only between syllables. We check the dictionary if we are in doubt about how a word is divided. The hyphen always appears with the first half of the word.

> cen- tral   na- tive   nar- row   tar- get

One-Letter Syllables A one-letter syllable should not be divided from the rest of the word.

> uten- sil (not u- tensil)

> avi- ary (not a- viary or aviar- y)

Because of this, two-syllable words such as the following are never divided:

> amaze   lucky   evolve   icon

When a word contains a one-letter syllable, we divide the word *after* that syllable.

> presi- dent (not pres- ident)

> nega- tive (not neg- ative)

> experi- ence (not exper- ience)

Compound Words Divide a compound word between its elements. If the word is already hyphenated, divide it *after* the hyphen.

> silver- ware (not sil- verware)

> super- market (not supermar- ket)

> mass- produce (not mass -produce or mass-pro- duce)

Prefixes and Suffixes Divide a word after a prefix or before a suffix.

> pre-determine (not predeter-mine or prede-termine)

> power-less (not pow-erless)

Longer Words Some longer words contain more than one possible dividing place. We divide them as needed to fit the line.

> car- nivore *or* carni-vore

> fan- tanstic *or* fantas- tic

Do Not Divide Some words and expressions are never divided.

One-Syllable Words One-syllable words cannot be divided, no matter how many letters they contain. Remember that even when you add -*ed*, some words are still one syllable.

> breathe   feigned   mouthed   straight

Short Words Words with four letters should not be divided even if they are more than one syllable.

> buoy   liar   pity   very

Also, we do not divide contractions or abbreviations.

Example Use hyphens to divide each of the words. Remember that not all words should be divided. Use the dictionary if necessary.

(a) partner   (b) erupt   (c) episode

(d) cavernous   (e) countertenor   (f) walked

Solution (a) We divide between syllables: **part- ner**

(b) We do not divide a one-letter syllable from the rest of the word. **Erupt** cannot be divided.

(c) We divide a word *after* a single-letter syllable: **epi- sode**

(d) We divide a word *before* a suffix: **cavern- ous**

(e) We divide a compound word between its elements: **counter- tenor**

(f) We do not divide one-syllable words. **Walked** cannot be divided.

Practice Use a hyphen to divide words a–f. Remember that not all words should be divided. Use the dictionary if necessary.

a. adapt   **b.** absence   **c.** chocolate

d. fury   **e.** haven't   **f.** twenty-seven

For g and h, replace each blank with *past* or *passed*.

g. *Passed* is the _____ tense of *pass*.

h. Yesterday I _____ your house on my way to the library.

More Practice Divide each word correctly.

1. through	**2.** diameter
3. epitaph	**4.** able
5. circular	**6.** antifreeze
7. can't	**8.** necessary
9. prudence	**10.** semicircle
11. abrupt	**12.** fracture
13. hangar	**14.** polygon
15. postwar	**16.** shouldn't
17. massive	**18.** shopped
19. hemisphere	**20.** antiseptic

Review Set 88 Choose the best word to complete sentences 1–13.

1. The weather (vane, vein, vain) was splintered as a result
(82) of the tornado.

2. The (allegiance, allegation, allege) against the accountant
(81) was mishandling of funds.

3. Heidi's (allegiance, allegation, allege) to her friends
(81) blinded her to their faults.

4. Sadly, some historical buildings were (raised, razed, rays) *(46)* in order to build the new freeway.

5. Martin and Leroy (lead, leaded, led) the troop. *(75)*

6. It was (her, she) who said it couldn't be done. *(53, 55)*

7. Grandpa and (them, they) are already in the car. *(53, 55)*

8. I loaned the history book to (she, her) and Grandma. *(53, 57)*

9. (All, Some) adverbs end in *-ly*. *(84)*

10. Jalana skated (good, well). *(85)*

11. Jalana is a (good, well) skater. *(85)*

12. When words such as *in, out,* and *down* have objects, they *(87)* are (adverbs, prepositions).

13. When words such as *in, out,* and *down* do not have *(87)* objects, they are (adverbs, prepositions).

For 14 and 15, refer to this group of words: grandma and grandpa always attend the town's memorial day parade one year grandpa and uncle roy rode on a float

14. Tell whether the word group is a sentence fragment, run- *(3)* on sentence, or complete sentence.

15. Rewrite the group of words, adding capital letters and *(6, 12)* periods where they are needed.

16. Write the linking verb in this sentence: Maureen quickly *(22)* grew tired of the practical jokes.

17. Write each proper noun in this sentence: Germany, *(6)* France, and Austria are on the continent of Europe.

18. Write the direct object of this sentence: Many people put *(5, 25)* sugar in their iced tea.

19. Write each prepositional phrase and star the object of *(17, 33)* each preposition in this sentence: After the storm had passed, a rainbow appeared on the horizon.

20. Write each adjective in this sentence: America's flag flies
(27, 28) in big cities, small towns, and front yards everywhere.

21. Rewrite this outline, adding periods and capital letters as
(20, 36) needed.
    i breeds of dogs
      a working breeds
      b sporting breeds

22. Write the appositive in this sentence: My second cousin,
(48, 49) Juliet, gets mad if you call her Julie.

23. Rewrite this sentence, adding commas as needed: If
(63) you're brave take the long dark road through the forest.

24. Write the objective case personal pronoun in this
(53, 57) sentence: It was a surprise to him that everyone knew the
plan.

25. Write the possessive pronoun in this sentence: She told
(60) me that the llama with the black tail is theirs.

26. Write the intensive pronoun in this sentence: Mary and
(62) Debby were determined to dig the hole themselves.

Choose the correct word to complete sentences 27 and 28.

27. We use a _____ in a fraction that functions as an
(83, 88) adjective.

28. We can use a _____ to form a compound adjective,
(83, 88) a group of words that work as a unit to modify a noun.

Diagram sentences 29 and 30.

29. We studied European history.
(23, 25)

30. My uncle showed me his medal of valor.
(25, 35)

Adverbs That Tell "When"

We have learned to identify adverbs that tell "how" and "where." In this lesson, we will learn about adverbs that modify a verb to tell "when." Again, let's think about how and where Brent skis:

HOW: Brent skis *recklessly*.

WHERE: Brent skis *everywhere*.

"When" Now we will think about **when** Brent skis:

Brent skis *daily*.

He might also ski *nightly*, *hourly*, *monthly*, or *today*.

Here are some common adverbs that tell "when."

after	*always*	*before*	*constantly*
currently	*daily*	*early*	*ever*
hourly	*late*	*monthly*	*never*
nightly	*now*	*someday*	*soon*
then	*tomorrow*	*tonight*	*weekly*
yearly	*yesterday*		

Adverb Position An adverb usually appears near the verb it modifies.

We will *soon* leave for the airport.

We will leave *soon* for the airport.

But an adverb can appear almost anywhere in a sentence.

Soon we will leave for the airport.

We will leave for the airport *soon*.

Even though the adverb *soon* modifies the verb *leave* in each of the sentences above, it is not necessarily placed near the verb. Since the placement of the adverb can vary, we must learn to identify adverbs even when they are separated from the verbs they modify.

Example 1 For each sentence, write the adverb that tells "when" and the verb or verb phrase it modifies.

(a) Tomorrow he will learn the answer.

(b) Perkins always sleeps late on weekends.

(c) Why did Jeremy leave the performance early?

Solution (a) The adverb **tomorrow** tells "when" he **will learn**. *Tomorrow* modifies the verb phrase *will learn.*

(b) The adverb **always** modifies the verb **sleeps**.

(c) The adverb **early** modifies the verb phrase **did leave**.

Example 2 Diagram this sentence: My grandparents exercise daily.

Solution We place the adverb *daily* under the verb *exercise*:

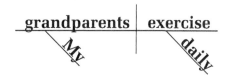

Practice For sentences a–d, write the adverb that tells "when" and the verb or verb phrase it modifies.

a. Tonight you and Tony and I will study our grammar.

b. Tony will come to your house early.

c. Yearly, each homeowner in the state of California pays a property tax.

d. The dentist will fill the cavity in Jill's tooth tomorrow.

Diagram sentences e and f.

e. Marion buys special treats daily.

f. My cousin will soon marry.

For g–i, replace each blank with *lose, loose,* or *loss.*

g. Did you win or _____ the badminton game?

h. The _____ of that game cost the team the championship.

i. The second grader said, "Look at my _____ tooth!"

Review Set 89

Choose the best word(s) to complete sentences 1–10.

1. The prefix meaning "extreme" is (*ultra-, post-, in-*).
(32, 44)

2. The prefix meaning "not" is (*ultra-, post-, in-*).
(29, 32)

3. The prefix meaning "through, across, or between" is (13, 35) (*mono-, uni-, dia-*).

4. The prefix meaning "under" is (*ultra-, mal-, sub-*).
(14, 41)

5. When Charles Lindbergh arrived in Paris, he had not (75, 76) (sleep, sleeped, slept) for thirty-three hours.

6. It was (her, she) who won the role of Desdemona.
(58, 67)

7. (Who, Whom) disappeared in a cloud of dust?
(66, 68)

8. The lawn was green and (well-watered, well watered).
(83, 86)

9. The (well-watered, well watered) lawn was green.
(83, 86)

10. Becky has a cold and doesn't feel (*good, well*) enough to (27, 45) attend the soccer match.

11. Write whether this word group is a phrase or a (24, 61) clause: Since the days of Wilbur and Orville Wright

12. Write the verb in this sentence and tell whether it is (7, 16) present or past tense: Courageous people flew the small, fragile planes of the 1920s.

13. Write the helping verb in this sentence: People were (9, 15) flying these delicate planes long distances.

14. Write the direct object of this sentence: Charles (5, 25) Lindbergh astonished the world with his flight from New York City to Paris.

15. Write the abstract noun in this sentence: Charles (8, 10) Lindbergh's fortitude amazed everyone.

16. Write each word that should be capitalized in this
(6, 12) sentence: charles lindbergh had to fly thousands of miles over the stormy atlantic ocean.

17. Write each prepositional phrase and star the object of
(17, 33) each preposition in this sentence: After thirty-three hours in the air, Charles Lindbergh was so sleepy that he pulled his eyelids open with his fingers.

18. Write the proper adjective in this sentence: Charles
(6, 30) Lindbergh became an American hero.

19. Rewrite the following sentence, adding capital letters,
(40, 73) underlining, and periods as needed: the name of c lindbergh's plane was the spirit of st louis

20. Rewrite this sentence, adding commas as needed: For
(56, 63) your information as his little plane shook in the wind Charles Lindbergh flew through deep dense fog clouds and thunderstorms before he landed in Paris France.

21. Write the relative pronoun in this sentence: Charles
(66, 67) Lindbergh, who was nicknamed "Lucky Lindy," had courage and endurance.

22. Write the apposition (pronoun) in this sentence: We
(51, 67) aviators understand how significant the flights of Charles Lindbergh and Amelia Earhart were to air travel.

23. Write the indefinite pronoun in this sentence: Nobody
(51, 72) knows why Amelia Earhart's plane crashed.

24. Write the demonstrative pronoun in this sentence: This
(51, 71) is why some people are afraid to fly.

25. Write the word that should be hyphenated in this
(83, 86) sentence: The one way streets in big cities confuse unfamiliar drivers.

26. Write whether this sentence is true or false: We may
(83, 88) divide a word only between its syllables.

27. Write each adverb in this sentence: Yesterday Ben hiked
(84, 89) slowly and cautiously uphill.

For 28 and 29, write whether the italicized word is a preposition or an adverb.

28. The rabbit ran *around* the yard.
(33, 87)

29. The rabbit ran *around*.
(33, 87)

30. Diagram this sentence: Amelia Earhart, a courageous
(25, 28) pilot, carefully planned her solo flight.

LESSON 90

Adverbs That Tell "How Much"

Dictation or Journal Entry

Vocabulary:
Let us examine the homophones *aloud* and *allowed*. *Aloud*, an adverb, means "loudly" or "audibly." The teacher instructed the student to read the passage *aloud*. *Allowed* is the past tense of the verb *allow*. It means "to permit." The baby-sitter *allowed* her charges to go to the park. *Allowed* can also mean "conceded" or "admitted." The professor *allowed* that there are many theories about the creation of the earth. Finally, *allowed* can mean "made provision for." I've *allowed* ten dollars a week for dog food this year.

"How Much" or "To What Extent" Some adverbs tell "how much" or "to what extent." These adverbs are sometimes called **intensifiers** because they add intensity (either positive or negative) to the words they modify.

Notice how the adverbs in the sentences below add intensity to the words they modify:

The rabbit was *terribly* frightened.

She worked *awfully* hard on her essay.

He was *too* excited to sleep.

You have been *most* generous.

Brent skis *quite* skillfully.

We *just* got here.

Some adverbs that tell "how much" or "to what extent" are easy to identify because they end in *-ly*. However, many others do not. Here are some common intensifiers:

absolutely	*almost*	*altogether*
awfully	*barely*	*completely*
especially	*even*	*extremely*
fully	*hardly*	*highly*
incredibly	*just*	*least*
less	*most*	*not*
partly	*quite*	*rather*
really	*so*	*somewhat*
terribly	*thoroughly*	*too*
totally	*vastly*	*very*

An adverb that tells "how much" or "to what extent" usually modifies an adjective or another adverb. However, it occasionally modifies a verb.

MODIFYING AN ADJECTIVE

The hikers were *absolutely* exhausted.

The adverb *absolutely* modifies the adjective *exhausted* and tells "how exhausted" the hikers were.

MODIFYING ANOTHER ADVERB

The teenager drove *rather* carelessly.

The adverb *rather* modifies the adverb *carelessly* and tells "how carelessly" the teenager drove.

MODIFYING A VERB

The waiter *highly* recommends the pasta.

The adverb *highly* modifies the verb *recommends* and tells "to what extent" the pasta is recommended.

Example 1 For each sentence, write the adverb that tells "how much" or "to what extent" and give the word it modifies.

(a) People change the environment rather quickly.

(b) It may be too difficult for animals and plants to adjust.

(c) Whole species have vanished completely.

(d) Very special animals like dolphins, whales, and gorillas are endangered.

Solution (a) The adverb **rather** modifies **quickly**, another adverb.

(b) The adverb **too** modifies the predicate adjective **difficult**.

(c) The adverb **completely** modifies the verb phrase **have vanished**.

(d) The adverb **very** modifies the adjective **special**.

Diagramming Adverbs That Modify Adjectives or Other Adverbs

We have learned to diagram adverbs that modify verbs. Now we will diagram adverbs that modify adjectives or other adverbs. As shown in the examples below, we place the adverb on a line underneath the adjective or adverb that is being modified:

People are cutting the rain forests quite rapidly.

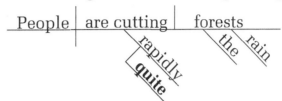

Look at the sentence below. The adverb *rather* modifies the adjective *risky,* which modifies the direct object *deal.*

The executive made a rather risky deal.

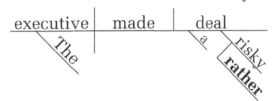

Example 2 Diagram this sentence:

Extremely endangered animals include eagles.

Solution We place the adverb *extremely* underneath the adjective it modifies, *endangered,* which describes "animals."

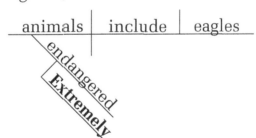

not Since the word *not* is an adverb, contractions like *couldn't* contain the adverb *not.* When we diagram contractions, we diagram *n't* as an adverb:

I couldn't find it.

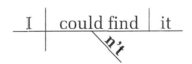

Example 3   Diagram this sentence:

People don't easily change their habits.

Solution   We place the adverbs *not* (*n't*) and *easily* under the verb phrase *do change*.

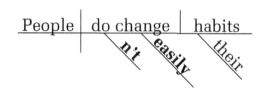

Practice   For sentences a–e, write each adverb that tells "how much" or "to what extent" and the word it modifies.

a. Americans need to become very serious about protecting the Florida manatee, the bald eagle, the peregrine falcon, and the California condor.

b. These animals are extremely endangered.

c. Some populations disappeared quite rapidly.

d. It is so necessary to protect them!

e. Some people don't know this.

For f–h, replace each blank with *allowed* or *aloud*.

f. Smoking is not _____ on airplanes.

g. The young boy read _____ to himself.

h. Fred's mother _____ that his excuse for tardiness was a good one.

Diagram sentences i and j.

i. Tropical rain forests are vastly important.

j. We must very diligently protect our environment.

More Practice   See "More Practice Lesson 90" in Student Workbook.

Review Set 90   Choose the best word to complete sentences 1–7.

1. An income-tax reduction will (affect, effect) almost (27) everyone in the country.

2. The (faints, feints) of the military provided the distraction needed to rescue the prisoners of war.
(28)

3. The word *prepositional* is (polysyllabic, polychromatic, diligent).
(12, 61)

4. After a week of camping, the family had a (prodigious, persevering, prudent) pile of dirty laundry.
(16, 20)

5. Ingrid says that she feels (good, well) about the test.
(27, 85)

6. In the early 1920s, many African Americans (were, was) influenced by the ideas of Marcus Garvey.
(7, 15)

7. At that time, much of Africa (were, was) ruled by European colonizers.
(7, 15)

8. Write the future tense verb phrase in this sentence: Perhaps you will study Marcus Garvey.
(9, 11)

For 9 and 10, write the simple predicate of the sentence, and tell whether the verb is transitive or intransitive.

9. Marcus Garvey encouraged black people to take pride in their race and their roots.
(5, 32)

10. After the storm, we played in the water.
(5, 32)

11. Write the collective noun in this sentence: Our house is just about the right size for our family.
(8, 10)

12. Rewrite the following, adding capital letters as needed: you can go east and you can go west, but you probably have to go north to get to south dakota.
(12, 29)

13. Write the object of the preposition in this sentence: Mom said that dish should bake for thirty-five minutes.
(17, 33)

14. Write the coordinating conjunction in this sentence: It doesn't seem fair that sometimes we can try our best but still fail.
(37)

15. Rewrite this sentence, adding commas as needed: Mrs. Polley the new librarian asked "Children how many Mother Goose poems do you know?"
(49, 65)

Rewrite 16 and 17, adding quotation marks as needed.

16. Do you know, asked the historian, what flag has
(69, 70) endured the longest without change?

17. Let's look it up! cried an interested visitor.
(69, 70)
The Danish flag is the oldest unchanged flag in existence, said the historian.

18. Write and underline the word that should be italicized in
(73) this sentence: Dannebrog is the name of the banner adopted in 1218 as the standard of the Danes.

19. Write the punctuation mark needed at the end of this
(1, 77) sentence: Who knows what country has a flag with a large white cross on a red background

20. Rewrite this sentence, adding a dash where it is
(77) needed: This flag represents a Scandinavian nation Denmark.

21. Write the part of this sentence that should be
(83, 88) hyphenated: The antiques in this store are 100 200 years older than we are!

22. Replace the blank with the correct word to complete this
(83, 88) sentence: To find out if a compound word needs a hyphen, we look up the word in a _____.

23. Indicate which is *not* a correct statement about using a
(88) hyphen to divide a word. Write *A, B, C, D,* or *E.*

A. One-syllable words are always divided.

B. We do not divide words containing four letters or less even if they are more than one syllable.

C. We do not divide a one-letter syllable from the rest of the word.

D. We divide a compound word between its elements.

E. When a word contains a single-vowel syllable (for example, di-a-mond), we divide the word after that syllable (dia-mond).

24. Write the five adjectives from this list: lovely, quickly,
(27, 84) lively, slowly, friendly, patiently, cautiously, orderly, lonely.

Write each adverb in sentences 25–27.

25. The teacher looked everywhere for her book.
(84, 87)

26. The accountant figures income taxes for his clients
(84, 89) yearly.

27. I was totally surprised to find that my sleeping bag was
(84, 90) completely full of extremely heavy rocks, and I highly
suspect that you are partly responsible for this.

Diagram sentences 28–30.

28. The young woman appeared stern.
(28, 44)

29. Have you memorized that rhyme?
(25, 28)

30. These crackers taste rather stale.
(44, 90)

LESSON
91

Comparison Adverbs

> **Dictation or Journal Entry**
> **Vocabulary:**
> Know the difference between *weather* and *whether*. The *weather* is the condition of the atmosphere. Dr. George, a meteorologist, predicts the *weather*. The word *whether* introduces an alternative or possibility. Ray doesn't know *whether* he'll be able to attend the event.

Like adjectives, some adverbs can express the three degrees of comparison: positive, comparative, and superlative. Below are examples of the positive, comparative, and superlative forms of some adverbs:

POSITIVE	COMPARATIVE	SUPERLATIVE
soon	sooner	soonest
near	nearer	nearest
sweetly	more sweetly	most sweetly
early	earlier	earliest

Positive   The positive form describes an action without comparing it to anything.

Jill will arrive *soon.*

Comparative   The comparative form compares the action of **two** people, places, or things.

Jill will arrive *sooner* than Jack.

Superlative   The superlative form compares the action of **three or more** people, places, or things.

Of the three, Jill will arrive *soonest.*

Example 1   Choose the correct adverb form for each sentence.
(a) Of the two boys, Brent can ski (faster, fastest).

(b) Of our many adverb lessons, this one is (harder, hardest).

Solution   (a) Of the two boys, Brent can ski **faster.**

(b) Of our many adverb lessons, this one is **hardest.**

Forming Comparison Adverbs We form comparison adverbs the same way we form comparison adjectives. How we create the comparative and superlative forms of an adverb depends on how the adverb appears in its positive form. There are two main categories to remember.

One-Syllable Adverbs We create the comparative form of most one-syllable adverbs by adding *er* to the end of the word. The superlative form is created by adding *est*.

POSITIVE	COMPARATIVE	SUPERLATIVE
long	longer	longest
soon	sooner	soonest
tall	taller	tallest

Two-Syllable Adverbs Most adverbs with two or more syllables don't have comparative or superlative forms. Instead, we put the word "more" (or "less") in front of the adverb to form the comparative, and the word "most" (or "least") to form the superlative.

POSITIVE	COMPARATIVE	SUPERLATIVE
often	more often	most often
carefully	more carefully	most carefully
happily	less happily	least happily

Since most adverbs are formed by adding the suffix *-ly* to an adjective, the rule above applies to most adverbs.

Irregular Comparison Adverbs Some adverbs have irregular comparative and superlative forms. We must learn these if we haven't already.

POSITIVE	COMPARATIVE	SUPERLATIVE
little	less	least
good, well	better	best
badly	worse	worst
far	farther	farthest
much	more	most

We check the dictionary if we are unsure how to create the comparative or superlative form of any adverb.

Example 2 Complete the comparison chart by adding the comparative and superlative forms of each adverb.

POSITIVE	COMPARATIVE	SUPERLATIVE
(a) far	_____	_____
(b) well	_____	_____
(c) sadly	_____	_____
(d) quietly	_____	_____

Solution

POSITIVE	COMPARATIVE	SUPERLATIVE
(a) far	**farther**	**farthest**
(b) well	**better**	**best**
(c) sadly	**more sadly**	**most sadly**
(d) quietly	**more quietly**	**most quietly**

Practice Write the correct adverb form for sentences a–e.

a. Dale laughs (more loudly, most loudly) than his sister.

b. In our family, Isabel calculates math problems (more quickly, most quickly).

c. The judges liked this dance routine (better, best) than the other one.

d. Of the four batters, Nathan hit the ball (harder, hardest).

e. I ski (worse, worst) than you, but Waldo skis (worse, worst) of all.

For f–h, replace each blank with *weather* or *whether*.

f. What is the _____ prediction for the weekend?

g. The professor doesn't know _____ he can add any more students to his class.

h. Mr. Slick needs to decide _____ he likes AnnieMae or Priscilla.

More Practice

Write the correct adverb for each sentence.

1. Alison swims (weller, better) than I.

2. She is the (better, best) on her team.

3. She swam (farther, farthest) than he.

4. He practiced (less, least) than she.

5. Of the three swimmers, he practiced (less, least).

6. Of the two, he swims (slower, slowest).

7. She practices (longer, longest) than I.

8. He swam (harder, hardest) than I.

Review Set 91

Choose the best word to complete sentences 1–11.

1. The jogger ran (passed, past) the snack bar to the drinking fountain.
(88)

2. Did you (loose, lose, loss) your passport in the airport?
(89)

3. The Gold Rush of 1849 brought many hopeful (minors, miners) to California in search of gold.
(87)

4. Each step (creaked, creeked) as the family dog attempted to sneak up the stairway.
(86)

5. Little Jack Horner (eat, ate, eaten) a Christmas pie.
(74, 75)

6. The people of the United States, Britain, and France (remembers, remember) the casualties of World War I.
(7, 16)

7. (Adjectives, Adverbs, Conjunctions) are descriptive words that "modify" or add information to verbs, adjectives, and other adverbs.
(64, 84)

8. (*Good, Well*) is usually an adverb. It modifies an action verb and explains "how" someone does something.
(27, 85)

9. (Good, Well) is a descriptive adjective or a predicate adjective. It describes a noun or pronoun.
(27, 85)

10. Adverbs have three degrees of comparison—positive, comparative, and (nominative, superlative).
(42, 91)

11. The (positive, superlative) adverb form describes an action without comparing it to anything.
(91)

12. Write whether this sentence is declarative, interrogative, imperative, or exclamatory: Little Jack Horner cried, "What a good boy am I!"
(1, 77)

13. Write whether this word group is a sentence fragment, a run-on sentence, or a complete sentence: Sat in a corner.
(2, 3)

14. Write the verb phrase in this sentence, and underline the helping verb: Little Jack Horner was eating a Christmas pie.
(9, 16)

15. Write the future tense verb phrase in this sentence, and tell whether the verb is transitive or intransitive: Little Jack Horner will put his thumb into the pie.
(11, 32)

16. Rewrite this outline, adding capital letters as needed:
(6, 20)
    i. little jack horner
      a. sat in a corner
      b. ate a christmas pie

17. Write each adjective in this sentence: The Christmas pie contained a round, ripe, juicy plum.
(27, 28)

18. Rewrite this sentence, adding periods as needed: We can write 75¢ in decimal form as $075
(36, 40)

19. Write the antecedent for the italicized pronoun in this sentence: Mr. Wilson convinced Amy that *she* must help other unfortunate women.
(51, 55)

20. Write the nominative case pronoun from this sentence: The cook was she who started all the gossip.
(53, 55)

21. Write the relative pronoun in this sentence: The pastry chef, who had studied in Paris, thought his desserts were too good for them.
(66, 68)

Write each word pair that should be hyphenated in sentences 22 and 23.

22. The basketball player wore number thirty two on his
(83, 88) jersey.

23. The caramel filled candy bar melted all over the sofa.
(83, 86)

Write each adverb in sentences 24 and 25.

24. Meredith often dreams of a place where there isn't any
(84, 90) homework.

25. Because of the lightning, the boaters got off the lake
(84, 89) immediately.

For 26–28, write the word from each pair that is divided correctly. Remember that some words are never divided. Use the dictionary, if necessary.

26. shouldn't, should-n't
(86, 88)

27. break-fast, bre-akfast
(86, 88)

28. seld-om, sel-dom
(86, 88)

Diagram sentences 29 and 30.

29. The cat with the rings on her tail is a valuable purebred.
(34, 44)

30. The swimmer trained hard, and her reward was a gold
(28, 38) medal.

LESSON
92

The Semicolon

The **semicolon** (;) is sometimes called a "mild period." It is used as a connector. It indicates a pause longer than a comma but shorter than a colon. In this lesson, we will learn how to use the semicolon correctly.

Related Thoughts In a compound sentence, we can use a semicolon instead of a coordinating conjunction (*and, but, or, for, nor, yet, so*) between the two independent clauses. However, these clauses must contain related thoughts.

> YES: The restaurant opened three months ago; it is already a neighborhood favorite. (related thoughts)

> NO: The restaurant opened three months ago; I like grapes. (not related thoughts)

Example 1 Use a semicolon instead of the coordinating conjunction in this sentence:

> The day started with sunshine, but it ended with rain.

Solution We replace the comma and conjunction with a semicolon:

> The day started with sunshine; it ended with rain.

Conjunctive Adverbs An adverb used as a conjunction is called a **conjunctive adverb**. Words such as *also, besides, still, however, therefore, consequently, otherwise, moreover, furthermore,* and *nevertheless* are examples of conjunctive adverbs. We place a semicolon before a conjunctive adverb.

> YES: Fruits and vegetables do not arrive by magic to our supermarkets; however, most of us don't think about the process of getting fresh produce to market.

Using a comma where a semicolon is needed results in a run-on sentence:

> NO: Fruits and vegetables do not arrive by magic to our supermarkets, however, most of us don't think about the process of getting fresh produce to market.

Example 2   Place a semicolon where it is needed in this sentence:

We have learned many pairs of homophones, still, there are many more we need to introduce.

Solution   We place a semicolon before the conjunctive adverb *still*:

We have learned many pairs of homophones; still, there are many more we need to introduce.

With Other Commas   If an independent clause contains commas, we can use a semicolon to show where one independent clause ends and another one begins.

UNCLEAR: Laura enjoys reading, art, and cooking, and soccer, softball, and music are Jeanie's pastimes.

CLEAR: Laura enjoys reading, art, and cooking; and soccer, softball, and music are Jeanie's pastimes.

Semicolons can also be used to separate phrases or dependent clauses that contain commas.

The United States has many large cities, including Los Angeles, California; Chicago, Illinois; and New York City, New York.

He vowed to study harder in math, English, and history; do his homework and chores on time; and be courteous to his sister, brother, and parents.

Example 3   Place semicolons where they are needed in sentences a and b.

(a) We plan to visit Boston, Massachusetts, Providence, Rhode Island, and Trenton, New Jersey.

(b) John plays the guitar, the organ, and the piano, and Bryon plays the drums, the saxophone, and the trumpet.

Solution   (a) We separate each "city, state" pair of words with a semicolon for clarity:

We plan to visit Boston, Massachusetts; Providence, Rhode Island; and Trenton, New Jersey.

(b) Because the independent clauses in this sentence already contain commas, we separate the two clauses with a semicolon:

John plays the guitar, the organ, and the piano; and Bryon plays the drums, the saxophone, and the trumpet.

Practice Rewrite sentences a–c, replacing commas with semicolons where they are needed.

  a. Homophone pairs include *coarse, course, stationary, stationery*, and *waste, waist.*

  b. Tomatoes, lettuce, and grapes are planted on large farms, the crops are picked when they are ripe.

  c. Many people don't eat enough fruits and vegetables, moreover, they eat too much fat.

  For d–g, replace each blank with *blew* or *blue.*

  d. Red, yellow, and _____ are primary colors.

  e. When one is sad or discouraged, one feels _____.

  f. The winds of the hurricane _____ at 100 miles per hour.

  g. The clown _____ up balloons to give to his audience.

More Practice See "More Practice Lesson 92" in Student Workbook.

Review Set 92 Choose the best word to complete sentences 1–11.

  1. No talking is (allowed, aloud) during a standardized
  (90) exam.

  2. The (loose, lose, loss) of buses forced people to find
  (89) alternative transportation.

  3. The volunteer (past, passed) out brochures explaining the
  (88) blood donation drive.

  4. A sign that reads "No (Miners, Minors) Allowed" means
  (87) that no one under the age of 21 may enter.

  5. The Knave of Hearts (runned, ran) away with the tarts.
  (75, 76)

  6. There (is, are) many poems by Langston Hughes that
  (15) imitate the rhythm of popular African-American forms of music.

7. (Adjectives, Adverbs) answer the questions "how,"
(27, 84) "when," "where," and "how much."

8. Langston Hughes writes (good, well).
(27, 85)

9. The poetry of Hughes's friend Countee Cullen is very
(27, 85) (good, well).

10. The (comparative, superlative) adverb form compares the
(91) action of two people, places, or things.

11. The (comparative, superlative) adverb form compares the
(91) action of three or more people, places, or things.

For 12–14, refer to this sentence: The Queen of Hearts had
made some tarts.

12. Write the simple subject.
(2, 23)

13. Write the simple predicate.
(2, 23)

14. Diagram the sentence.
(25, 28)

15. Write the present participle of the verb *call*.
(7, 16)

16. Write the past participle of the verb *grow*.
(16, 54)

17. Write each word that should be capitalized in this
(12, 6) sentence: hey, queen of hearts, do you realize your tarts
have been stolen?

18. Write each limiting adjective in this sentence: Her knave
(27, 28) stole the tarts.

19. Write the positive, comparative, and superlative forms of
(45, 46) the adjective *hot*.

20. Write the direct object of this sentence: The Knave of
(5, 25) Hearts brought back the tarts.

21. Rewrite this letter, adding commas as needed:
(52, 56) Dear King

   The Knave of Hearts has promised not to steal
tarts ever again. Therefore you needn't punish
him any more.

Gratefully
The Queen of Hearts

22. Choose the sentence that is more polite. Write *A* or *B*.
(53, 57) A. The Queen of Hearts gave me and him a tart.
B. The Queen of Hearts gave him and me a tart.

23. Write the apposition in this sentence: Nobody was
(67) surprised when we tourists became lost.

24. Rewrite this sentence, adding quotation marks as
(69, 70) needed: I remind people to make a note of where the bus
is parked, the tour guide said, but they always think
they can remember.

25. Write the word pair, if any, that should be hyphenated in
(83, 86) the following sentence. (Write "none" if the answer is
none.)
The street musician was well dressed.

26. Write the word from this list that is divided correctly:
(86, 88) u-tensil, uten-sil, ut-ensil.

Write each adverb in sentences 27 and 28.

27. The student spoke confidently and enthusiastically.
(84)

28. My most recent book report was on *Black Beauty,* a story
(90) about a horse's life in England.

Diagram sentences 29 and 30.

29. The King of Hearts really wanted those tarts.
(25, 90)

30. Aunt Janine traveled north and attended college.
(38, 87)

LESSON 93

Descriptive Adverbs • Adverb Usage

Improving Our Writing

Without adverbs, our sentences would be dull. This sentence has no adverbs:

Brent skis.

We want to express ourselves in a vivid and colorful manner. One way is to use **descriptive adverbs.** The sentence above is more interesting when we use adverbs to describe how Brent skis:

Brent skis *wildly.*

Brent might also ski *frantically, gracefully, clumsily, athletically,* or *effortlessly.*

Example 1 Replace each blank with at least one adverb to make the sentence more descriptive.

(a) Lorna _____ painted the fence.

(b) Admiral Peacock rowed _____.

Solution Our answers will vary. Here are some examples.

(a) Lorna **carefully, sloppily, wearily, lazily, diligently, energetically, quickly, grudgingly** painted the fence.

(b) Admiral Peacock rowed **frantically, courageously, far, more, fast, steadily, clumsily, sporadically, skillfully.**

***Sure* or *Surely*?**

The word *sure* is an adjective and not an adverb. *Sure* should not take the place of the adverbs *surely, certainly,* or *really.*

NO: Dad is *sure* working.
YES: Dad is *surely* working. (modifies verb "is working")

NO: I'm *sure* hungry.
YES: I'm *really* hungry. (modifies predicate adjective "hungry")

NO: You are *sure* welcome to visit.
YES: You are *certainly* welcome to visit. (modifies predicate adjective "welcome")

We remember that *sure* is an adjective, and we use it only as an adjective or predicate adjective, as in the sentences below:

Helen is *sure* of the answer. (predicate adjective)

That's a *sure* sign of success. (adjective modifying the noun "sign")

I was *sure* the door was locked. (predicate adjective)

Example 2   Replace each blank with *sure* or *surely*.
(a) Most people (sure, surely) hope they do not become ill.

(b) Are you (sure, surely) you can attend the concert?

Solution   (a) Most people **surely** hope they do not become ill. (*Surely* is an adverb. It modifies the verb "hope.")

(b) Are you **sure** you can attend the concert? (*Sure* is a predicate adjective. It describes the pronoun "you.")

Real or **Really?**   Like *sure*, the word *real* is an adjective and should not take the place of the adverb *really*. *Real* modifies a noun or pronoun, while *really* modifies a verb, adjective, or adverb.

NO: I'm *real* glad you came.
YES: I'm *really* glad you came. (modifies predicate adjective "glad")

NO: That's a *real* big sandwich.
YES: That's a *really* big sandwich. (modifies adjective "big")

NO: Jerry played *real* well.
YES: Jerry played *really* well. (modifies adverb "well")

We remember that *real* is an adjective, and we use it only as an adjective or predicate adjective, as in the sentences below:

The man in the frightening costume looked like a *real* gorilla. (adjective modifying the noun "gorilla")

Are these flowers *real* or fake? (predicate adjective)

Example 3   Replace each blank with *real* or *really*.
(a) Coach tossed the ball (real, really) far.

(b) That stuffed animal looks (real, really).

Solution   (a) Coach tossed the ball **really** far. (*Really* is an adverb. It modifies another adverb, "far.")

(b) That stuffed animal looks **real.** (*Real* is a predicate adjective. It describes the noun "animal.")

Bad or Badly? The word *bad* is an adjective. It describes a noun or pronoun, and often follows linking verbs like *feel, look, seem, taste, smell,* and *is.* The word *badly* is an adverb that tells "how." We do not use *bad* as an adverb.

> NO: I did *bad* on the test.
> YES: I did *badly* on the test. (adverb that tells "how")

> NO: Brent skis *bad.*
> YES: Brent skis *badly.* (adverb that tells "how")

> NO: Today Jerry played *bad.*
> YES: Today Jerry played *badly.* (adverb that tells "how")

We remember that *bad* is an adjective, and we use it only as an adjective or predicate adjective, as in these sentences:

> Kari felt *bad* today. (predicate adjective)

> The outcome of the game looks *bad.* (predicate adjective)

> I earned a *bad* grade on the test. (adjective modifying the noun "grade")

Example 4 Replace each blank with *bad* or *badly.*

(a) Sometimes I sing very (bad, badly).

(b) The stale bread tasted (bad, badly).

Solution (a) Sometimes I sing very **badly.** (*Badly* is an adverb that tells "how" I sing.)

(b) The stale bread tasted **bad.** (*Bad* is a predicate adjective. It describes the noun "bread.")

Practice For a–c, replace each blank with *deer* or *dear.*

a. We open our letters with the word _____ in order to express our love and concern for the recipient.

b. Like cows, _____ are cud-chewers.

c. The lock of her child's hair was _____ to Olivia.

For d and e, replace each blank with at least one adverb to make the sentence more descriptive.

    d. Corey skated through the park _____.

    e. Amanda _____ drove to work.

Choose the correct word to complete sentences f–j.

    f. Aunt Sukey was (sure, surely) happy to see you.

    g. Uncle George laughed (real, really) hard at the joke.

    h. It was (real, really) funny.

    i. Did your broken arm hurt (bad, badly)?

    j. Yesterday I played basketball very (bad, badly).

More Practice

Choose the correct word to complete each sentence.

    1. You (sure, surely) sang well today.

    2. I'm (sure, really) tired.

    3. They (sure, certainly) tried hard.

    4. Boomer is (real, really) hungry.

    5. He's behaving (real, really) well.

    6. I skinned my knee (bad, badly).

    7. It was a (bad, badly) wound.

    8. My throat hurt (bad, badly).

    9. Our dress rehearsal went (well, bad).

    10. It was a (bad, badly) day.

Additional Practice

See "Silly Story #5" in Student Workbook.

Review Set 93

Choose the best word to complete sentences 1–9.

    1. The instructor asked each student to read a piece of (90) poetry (allowed, aloud).

2. A (lose, loose, loss) bolt caused the wheel to fall off the
(89) cart.

3. The children enjoyed watching polliwogs in the nearby
(86) (creak, creek).

4. The physician pulled the (mettle, medal, meddle, metal)
(85) sliver out of the hapless hiker's foot.

5. They have (telled, told) the baker to mark the cake with a *B*.
(75, 76)

6. The baker's muffins were the (good, better, best) in town.
(45, 46)

7. (Who, Whom) are you taking to the Golden Gate Bridge?
(66, 68)

8. Neither of Teddy's friends (has, have) seen the Golden
(15, 80) Gate Bridge.

9. She was disappointed when she discovered she didn't
(82) have (any, no) money.

10. Tell whether this word group is a phrase or a clause: as
(24, 61) fast as you can swim

For 11–14, refer to this sentence: Joyce baked me a cake.

11. Write the action verb.
(5, 7)

12. Write the direct object.
(5, 25)

13. Write the indirect object.
(25, 35)

14. Diagram the sentence.
(25, 35)

15. Write each word that should be capitalized in this
(12, 29) sentence: in the south, one would not bake a cake or
casserole on a hot summer day.

16. Write the proper adjective in this sentence: The baker
(30) had promised us a sample of his Mississippi mud pie.

17. Write the seven most common coordinating
(37) conjunctions.

Rewrite sentences 18 and 19, adding commas as needed.

18. I wanted to see Yosemite National Park Jeff hoped to visit
(47, 49) Yellowstone but we're going to Mount Rushmore.

19. The Golden Gate Bridge I understand is considered one
(56, 63) of the most remarkable engineering achievements of the
twentieth century.

20. Write the verb in this sentence, and tell whether it is
(5, 32) transitive or intransitive: Mansel and Maxine visited this
bridge in San Francisco.

21. Rewrite the following dialog, adding quotation marks as
(69, 70) needed.

    What type of bridge is the Golden Gate? asked the
curious tourist.

    The guide responded, It is a suspension bridge.

22. For a–d, write the question that each adverb answers
(84, 87) ("how," "where," "when," "how much," or "to what
extent").

  (a) Glenda sang extensively.   (b) Glenda sang there.

  (c) Glenda sang sweetly.   (d) Glenda sang late.

23. Tell whether the italicized word in this sentence is an
(27, 85) adjective or an adverb: The fresh coat of green paint
looks *good*.

24. Write the word pair that should be hyphenated in this
(83, 86) sentence: The all knowing chief engineer described the
Golden Gate Bridge as "a mighty door, swinging wide
into a world of wonder."

For 25–27, tell whether the italicized adverb modifies
another adverb, an adjective, or a verb.

25. The chief engineer spoke *rather* vainly.
(84, 90)

26. The bridge was *extremely* long.
(84, 90)

27. The chief engineer *highly* recommended a jaunt across
(84, 90) the Golden Gate Bridge.

Replace each blank with the correct response to complete sentences 28 and 29.

28. We make most one-syllable adverbs comparative by
(91)   adding _____ to the ending; we make them
superlative by adding _____ to the ending.

29. Adverbs with two or more syllables usually form their
(91)   comparative degree by adding the word _____ or
less; they form their superlative degree by adding the
word *most* or _____.

30. Rewrite this sentence, placing a semicolon where it is
(92)   needed: Orange trees require a warm climate however,
grapes can be grown almost anywhere.

LESSON 94

The Colon

The **colon** (:) signals to the reader that more information is to come. In this lesson we will learn to use the colon correctly.

Between Independent Clauses
We have learned that a semicolon can join two independent clauses that contain related thoughts. A colon can join two independent clauses when the first clause introduces the second or the second clause illustrates the first.

> Before I can write in my journal, I must do two things: I must complete my homework and help with the dishes.

> The kitchen was a mess: dirty pans filled the sink, the refrigerator was standing open, and the floor was covered with flour.

Example 1 Insert colons where they are needed in these sentences.

(a) There is one sure way to pass the test do the homework.

(b) The horse's bloodlines were impressive both of his parents were champions.

Solution (a) The first independent clause introduces the second, so we place a colon between them:

There is one sure way to pass the test: do the homework.

(b) The second independent clause illustrates the first. We place a colon between them:

The horse's bloodlines were impressive: both of his parents were champions.

Introducing a List
We use a colon to introduce a list.

This is my grocery list: butter, eggs, bread, and milk.

He always wanted to visit other countries: Scotland, Denmark, Norway, and Sweden.

All of my dogs learn three commands: sit, stay, and come.

We do not use a colon if the sentence is grammatically correct without it.

No: You should bring: a pencil, a book, and an eraser.

Yes: You should bring these things: a pencil, a book and an eraser.

The Following, As Follows We use a colon with the words *the following* or *as follows* when they introduce a list. Sometimes the list will begin on a separate line.

Please study *the following* parts of speech: nouns, verbs, and pronouns.

The ingredients are *as follows*:
2 eggs
1/4 cup milk
1 teaspoon sugar

Example 2 Insert colons where they are needed in these sentences.

(a) At camp you will need the following a sleeping bag, a comb, soap, and a towel.

(b) In the back of the truck are shovels, rakes, and brooms.

Solution (a) We use a colon after the words *the following* when they introduce a list:

At camp you will need the following: a sleeping bag, a comb, soap, and a towel.

(b) We do not use a colon if the sentence is grammatically correct without it. No colon is needed in (b).

Salutation of a Business Letter We use a colon after a salutation in a business letter.

Gentleman:

Dear Mrs. Espresso:

Time When we write the time of day with digits, we use a colon to separate the hours and minutes.

Class begins at 9:15 a.m.

Example 3 Insert colons where they are needed in these sentences.

(a) Dinner will be served at 630 p.m.

(b) Dear Sir
I am interested in applying for a job...

Solution (a) We place a colon between the hours and minutes when we write the time of day. We write **6:30** p.m.

(b) We use a colon after the salutation in a business letter, so we write **Dear Sir:**

Quotations We can use a colon to introduce a quotation.

The beginning of Lincoln's Gettysburg address is familiar to us:

> Four score and seven years ago our fathers brought forth on this continent a new nation...

Mother's letter went on: "It rained again last night..."

Example 4 Insert colons where they are needed in these sentences.

(a) Monica's speech began "Thank you all for having me."

(b) Please tell me who said these words "Give me liberty, or give me death."

Solution (a) We can use a colon to introduce a quotation, so we write:

Monica's speech began: "Thank you all for having me."

(b) Please tell me who said these words: "Give me liberty, or give me death."

Practice Rewrite a–d, inserting colons where they are needed

a. Please wake me up at 700 a.m.

b. Students in the sixth grade study the following subjects English, math, history, science, and P.E.

c. Dear Madam

I wish to inquire about your new waffle turner...

d. Martin Luther King, Jr., spoke these famous words "I have a dream!"

For e–g, replace each blank with the *pare, pair,* or *pear.*

e. Do you need a _____ of volunteers for the game?

f. That _____ looks yellow, juicy, and delicious.

g. When you _____ an onion, your eyes might sting.

Review Set 94 Choose the best word to complete sentences 1–12.

1. The Achilles' tendon attaches at the (heal, heel) of the foot.
(84)

2. (Already, All ready) you have sold your merchandise quota for the month.
(83)

3. The miners discovered a (vane, vain, vein) of silver in the hillside.
(82)

4. Unfortunately, the novice computer user erased all of the (stationary, icons, allegations) on the desktop.
(80, 81)

5. Mary (has, have) a little lamb.
(15)

6. The lamb didn't have (anything, nothing) to do.
(82)

7. That lamb doesn't have (no, any) homework.
(82)

8. Because they add intensity to the words they modify, adverbs that tell "how much" or "to what extent" are sometimes called (intensifiers, humidifiers).
(90)

9. The word *not* is an (adverb, adjective).
(90)

10. Therefore, *n't* is also an (adverb, adjective).
(90)

11. The word *sure* is an (adverb, adjective), and *surely* is an adverb.
(93)

12. A child is (sure, surely) hungry in the morning!
(93)

13. Write the four principal parts (present tense, present participle, past tense, and past participle) of the verb *follow*.
(16)

14. Write the past perfect verb phrase in this sentence: Mary's lamb had followed her to school.
(16, 19)

15. Write the past perfect progressive verb phrase in this sentence: The school had been enforcing the rule against animals at school.
(19, 21)

16. Write the linking verb in this sentence: With her lamb at school, Mary appeared disobedient.
(22)

Write each word that should be capitalized in sentences 17 and 18.

17. some children sing a song titled "mary had a little lamb."
(12, 20)

18. i believe mary had a lamb, not a hippopotamus.
(12, 6)

19. Write the predicate adjective in this sentence: The lamb's fleece was white.
(22, 44)

20. Write the appositive in this sentence: Mary's pet, a little white lamb, followed her everywhere.
(48, 49)

21. Rewrite this sentence, adding commas as needed: The energetic imaginative Franklin Delano Roosevelt was the only man to be elected president four times.
(63)

22. Rewrite this sentence, adding a dash where it is needed: Franklin D. Roosevelt, famous for his fireside chats, was elected president four times 1932, 1936, 1940, and 1944.
(77)

23. Write the demonstrative pronoun in this sentence: These were informal radio talks with the American people.
(51, 71)

24. Write the adverb from this list: faith, faithful, faithfully.
(84, 91)

25. Write the 6 adverbs from this list that tell "how much" or "to what extent": not, quite, fleece, very, brown, rather, somewhat, skipping, too.
(84, 90)

26. Rewrite this sentence, placing a semicolon where it is needed: Eleanor Roosevelt was a remarkable woman she showed a special concern for the problems of women and African Americans.
(92)

27. Write the descriptive adverb in this sentence: Eleanor Roosevelt spoke courageously to women's groups across the country.
(93)

28. Rewrite this sentence, adding a colon where it is needed: The mail carrier began his route at 800 a.m. daily.
(94)

Diagram sentences 29 and 30.

29. Mary and her lamb ran and played.
(38)

30. Franklin Roosevelt gave the American people a sense of
(35, 33) hope.

The Prepositional Phrase as an Adverb • Diagramming

Dictation or Journal Entry

Vocabulary:
Let's look at the homophones *site*, *cite*, and *sight*. A *site* is a location or position. The worker arrived at the construction *site*. *Cite* means "to quote or refer to." The writer *cited* research from related studies. *Sight* is "the act of seeing." Eye surgery restored the elderly man's *sight*.

Adverb Phrases

We have learned that a prepositional phrase can function as an adjective by modifying a noun or a pronoun. A prepositional phrase can also function as an adverb. A prepositional phrase that modifies a verb, an adjective, or another adverb is called an **adverb phrase**. It answers the question "how," "when," "where," "why," or "to what extent." The italicized adverb phrases below modify the verb "skied."

HOW
Brent skied *like a lunatic.*

WHEN
Brent skied *after lunch.*

WHERE
Brent skied *in Switzerland.*

WHY
Brent skied *for fun and exercise.*

TO WHAT EXTENT
Brent skied *throughout the day.*

Most adverb phrases modify verbs. However, an adverb phrase can also modify an adjective or another adverb, as in the examples below.

Brent is ready *for the ski trip.* (modifies predicate adjective "ready")

Brent skied far *from the ski lodge.* (modifies adverb "far")

Example 1

Write the adverb phrase, and tell which word it modifies.

(a) Smoking can lead to lung disease.

(b) Fresh air is good for one's health.

(c) Please wait here in the library.

Solution

(a) The adverb phrase **to lung disease** modifies the verb **can lead**. It tells "where."

(b) The adverb phrase **for one's health** modifies the predicate adjective **good**.

(c) The adverb phrase **in the library** modifies the adverb **here**.

Diagramming We diagram a prepositional phrase under the verb, adjective, or adverb it modifies. For example:

Brent skied down the mountain.

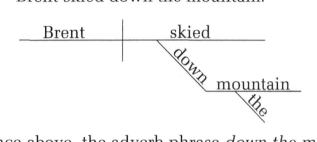

In the sentence above, the adverb phrase *down the mountain* modifies the verb *skied*. It tells where Brent skied.

Example 2 Diagram the three sentences from Example 1.

Solution (a) Smoking can lead to lung disease.

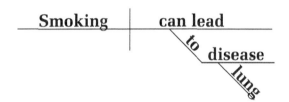

(b) Fresh air is good for one's health.

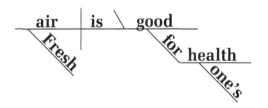

(c) Wait here in the library.

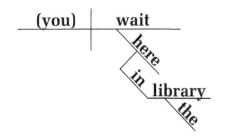

Practice For a–e, write each adverb phrase and tell which word it modifies.

   a. Success develops through hard work.

   b. Fido was born on a small farm.

   c. Vitamin D comes with sunshine.

   d. We were not aware of your plans.

   e. Are you wise concerning nutrition?

Diagram sentences f and g.

   f. Celebration galloped behind Lady.

   g. Lady led Celebration around the corral.

For h–j, replace each blank with *site*, *cite*, or *sight*.

   h. Glaucoma can cause the loss of eye _____.

   i. If you write a research paper, you must _____ your references.

   j. The _____ of the new library has been chosen.

More Practice Diagram sentences 1–3.

   1. She trotted down the street.

   2. Are you knowledgeable about your health?

   3. I wonder about the mysteries of outer space.

Write each adverb phrase from sentences 4 and 5, and star the object of each preposition.

   4. The grandiose architecture was reduced to a heap of rubble.

   5. She sat on the lawn in a dress of green silk.

Review Set 95 Choose the best word to complete sentences 1–10.

   1. The (eager, anxious, punctual) mother relaxed at the news that her lost child had been found.
   (1, 78)

2. The (sent, cent, scent) of strong perfume filled the room.
(77)

3. As a (consequential, consequence, allegation) of repeated
(76, 81) tardiness, one must spend time after school picking up
playground trash.

4. David killed the (prodigious, consequential, respectful)
(20, 76) giant, Goliath.

5. The crew of the *Columbia* (has, have) become famous
(15) since the moon mission.

6. Of all the astronauts, who walked the (more, most)
(91) gracefully on the moon?

7. *Real* is an (adverb, adjective).
(91, 93)

8. *Really* is an (adverb, adjective).
(91, 93)

9. The basketball player performed (real, really) well.
(91, 93)

10. Joy jumped rope (bad, badly) today.
(91)

Write the verb in sentences 11 and 12, and tell whether it is
transitive or intransitive.

11. The cow jumped over the moon.
(22, 32)

12. The little dog, the cat, the fiddle, and the spoon watched
(5, 32) the cow.

13. Write the collective noun in this sentence: *Mother Goose*
(8) is a collection of nursery rhymes.

14. Write the possessive noun in this sentence: The dog's
(10) laugh caused the dish to run away with the spoon.

15. Write the plural of *dish.*
(13, 15)

16. Write the plural of *echo.*
(13, 14)

For sentences 17–19, write the prepositional phrase, and star
the object of each preposition.

17. The cow jumped over the moon.
(17, 33)

18. The dish ran away with the spoon.
(17, 33)

19. The *Eagle*, a smaller spacecraft, was detached from the *Columbia*.
_(17, 33)

20. Write the correlative conjunctions in this sentence: Neither Aldrin nor Armstrong claimed the moon for the United States.
₍₃₉₎

21. Rewrite this sentence, adding commas as needed: "When learning to waltz" the dance instructor said "count 1-2-3 in your head."
₍₆₅₎

22. Write the possessive pronoun in this sentence: Yours will last longer if you take care of it.
_(51, 60)

23. Write the indefinite pronoun in this sentence: Butter is one of the ingredients in shortbread.
₍₇₂₎

24. Write and underline each word that should be italicized in this sentence: The Eagle was detached from the Columbia.
₍₇₃₎

25. Write the five adverbs from this list: lonely, happy, here, still, almost, lovely, now, quite.
₍₈₄₎

26. Rewrite this sentence, adding semicolons where they are needed: Gerardo hoped to visit Paris, France London, England and Dublin, Ireland.
₍₉₂₎

27. Rewrite this letter, adding a colon where it is needed:
₍₉₄₎

Gentlemen

    Are you interested in obtaining car insurance?

For 28 and 29, refer to this sentence: Celly galloped over the bridge.

28. Write the prepositional phrase used as an adverb, and tell which word it modifies.
_(33, 95)

29. Diagram the sentence.
_(33, 95)

30. Diagram this sentence: Astronauts train quite extensively for space travel.
_(87, 95)

Preposition or Adverb?
• Preposition Usage

Dictation or Journal Entry

Vocabulary:
Four words that refer to the frequency of an event are *annual, biannual, semiannual,* and *perennial. Annual* means "once a year." The *annual* company company party is in July. *Biannual* and *semiannual* both mean "twice a year." The *biannual* (or *semiannual*) newsletter contains a financial report. *Perennial* means "all year long" or "year after year." The bickering between the neighbors is *perennial.*

Preposition or Adverb? Most prepositions can also be used as adverbs. We remember that an adverb stands alone, but a preposition always has an object.

ADVERB: Brent skied *up.*

PREPOSITION: Brent skied *up the *hill.*

ADVERB: Brent skied *past.*

PREPOSITION: Brent skied *past *me.*

ADVERB: Brent skied *off.*

PREPOSITION: Brent skied *off the *cliff.*

Diagramming can help us determine whether a word is being used as an adverb or a preposition. Look at the word "down" in these two sentences:

ADVERB: Lady kicked *down* the fence.

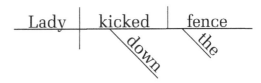

We can see that "fence" is a direct object telling what Lady kicked. It is not an object of a preposition.

PREPOSITION: Then she trotted *down the street.*

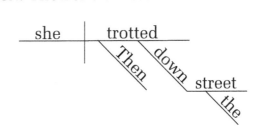

In this sentence, "street" is the object of the preposition "down."

Example 1   Tell whether the italicized word in each sentence is an adverb or a preposition.

   (a) Humphrey went *outside.*

   (b) My coat is *inside* the classroom.

   (c) Steve is jogging *around* the field.

   (d) The doctor is rushing *over.*

Solution   (a) *Outside* is an **adverb** that tells where Humphrey "went."

   (b) *Inside* is a **preposition.** Its object is "classroom."

   (c) *Around* is a **preposition.** Its object is "field."

   (d) *Over* is an **adverb** that tells where the doctor "is rushing."

Preposition Usage   Certain pairs of prepositions are frequently misused. In this lesson, we will learn to use these prepositions correctly:

in and *into*

between and *among*

beside and *besides*

***In* or *into*?**   The preposition *in* refers to position but not movement.

I am *in* the classroom.

She was *in* the car.

The preposition *into* refers to moving from the outside to the inside.

I went *into* the classroom.

She stepped *into* the car.

***Between* or *Among*?**   We use *between* when referring to two people, places, or things.

The sister and brother divided the inheritance *between* themselves.

There is not much difference *between* you and me.

We use *among* when referring to three or more people, places, or things.

> The soprano was one *among* many who desired the part.

> John is *among* the greatest musicians of all time.

Beside or Besides? The preposition *beside* means "at the side of."

> The woman stood *beside* her husband.

> She parked the car *beside* the house.

Besides means "in addition to" or "as well as."

> *Besides* the students, the parents are invited.

> Who *besides* me wants ice cream?

Example 2 Choose the correct preposition for each sentence.

(a) Please enter (in, into) the exhibit.

(b) Nancy wanted Remington to walk (beside, besides) her.

(c) Joel was (among, between) the five tallest players on the basketball team.

Solution (a) Please enter **into** the exhibit.

(b) Nancy wanted Remington to walk **beside** her.

(c) Joel was **among** the five tallest players on the basketball team.

Practice For sentences a–d, tell whether the italicized word is an adverb or a preposition.

a. The fugitive ran *by.*

b. The pirate came *aboard* the ship.

c. Dalia hurried *across* the street before the light changed.

d. Please come *across* with me.

For e–g, choose the correct preposition.

e. Rachel found her homework (in, into) the trash can.

f. (Among, Between) his freshman year and his senior year, the teenager had grown twelve inches!

g. Would anyone (beside, besides) James like to go with me?

For sentences h–j, replace each blank with *annual, biannual, semiannual,* or *perennial.*

h. Plants that bloom year after year are labeled _____.

i. *Biannual* and _____ both mean "twice a year."

j. Holidays such as Independence Day and Memorial Day are _____ events.

Review Set 96

Choose the best word to complete sentences 1–10.

1. Writers must (site, cite, sight) their references.
(95)

2. The fruit basket contains apples, oranges, and (pairs, pares, pears).
(94)

3. The (deer, dear) elderly woman came through the neighborhood to deliver her freshly-baked loaves of bread.
(93)

4. The policewoman (blue, blew) her whistle loudly at the pedestrian.
(92)

5. The four types of sentences are declarative, interrogative, imperative, and (transitive, exclamatory).
(1)

6. A verb must be (active, passive, linking) to have a direct object.
(5, 25)

7. Everyone (was, were) frustrated with Georgie Porgie.
(15)

8. I haven't seen (no, any) fish in the creek.
(82)

9. I believe that fishing pole is (ours, our's).
(51, 60)

10. Little Red Riding Hood's grandmother was not feeling (good, well).
(85)

11. Tell whether this word group is a sentence fragment, a run-on sentence, or a complete sentence: Kissed the girls and made them cry.
(3)

12. Unscramble these words to make an interrogative sentence:

(1, 77)

    seen   you   have   Georgie Porgie

For 13–15, refer to this sentence: Whenever Georgie Porgie kissed the girls, they cried.

13. Write the independent clause.
(24, 61)

14. Write the dependent clause.
(24, 61)

15. Write the subordinating conjunction.
(61)

For 16–18, refer to this sentence: Has Georgie Porgie been kissing the girls again?

16. Write the entire verb phrase.
(9, 21)

17. Write the direct object.
(5, 25)

18. Diagram the sentence.
(23, 25)

19. Write the four principal parts (present tense, present participle, past tense, and past participle) of the verb *kiss*.
(16)

20. Write the abstract noun in this sentence: The audacity of Georgie Porgie infuriated the school children.
(8)

Rewrite 21 and 22, adding commas and capital letters as needed.

21. the playground supervisor cautioned georgie porgie "you must stop kissing the girls."
(20, 65)

22. sister maria taught mathematics chinese and music at st. mark's catholic school.
(12, 47)

23. Write each word that should be capitalized in this letter:
(12, 29)

dear brother phillip,

    i am enjoying my visit to the pacific northwest. tomorrow we plan to take a ferry across puget sound.

    i hope the sun comes out before i leave because i want to see mount rainier.

              warmly,
              stefania

24. Write each adjective in this sentence: Hard-working,
(27, 28) tireless John Collier helped many Native Americans.

25. Write the verb phrase from this sentence, and tell
(25, 32) whether it is transitive or intransitive: Could Native
American tribes and individuals purchase land?

26. Write whether the italicized pronoun in this sentence is
(57, 55) nominative, objective, or possessive case: Did Congress
help *them*?

27. Write the antecedent for the italicized pronoun in this
(51) sentence: Although Collier hoped to help preserve the
distinct customs and traditions of different Native
American peoples, *he* was unsuccessful in his attempts to
persuade Congress to approve such programs.

28. Rewrite this sentence, adding quotation marks as
(69, 70) needed: Little Red Riding Hood is a fairy tale about a
young girl visiting her grandmother.

29. Write the adverb that tells "how much" in this
(90) sentence: The big, bad wolf was rather clever when he
dressed in the grandmother's clothing.

30. Tell whether the italicized word in this sentence is a
(17, 96) preposition or an adverb: The big, bad wolf jumped *up*
and chased Little Red Riding Hood.

LESSON 97

The Apostrophe: Possessives

We use the apostrophe to show possession.

Singular Possessive Nouns   To give a singular noun ownership, we add an apostrophe and an *s* (*'s*). The noun then becomes a **singular possessive noun**, as in the examples below.

SINGULAR NOUN	SINGULAR POSSESSIVE NOUN
artist	artist's paints
horse	horse's hooves
boss	boss's rule
tree	tree's leaves
fox	fox's path
Ms. James	Ms. James's goal

In a compound noun, possession is formed by adding *'s* to the last word.

sister-in-law	sister-in-law's idea
high school	high school's mascot
bridesmaid	bridesmaid's duties

Shared or Separate Possession   When more than one noun shares possession of something, we add *'s* to the last noun.

Sara, Lauren, and Erika's soccer game

When the nouns each possess something separately, we add *'s* to each noun.

Mary's and Bob's signatures

Example 1   Use *'s* to make each singular noun possessive.

(a) buddy   (b) Harris

(c) commander-in-chief   (d) box

(e) Julia and Jake (daughter)

Solution	(a) **buddy's**	(b) **Harris's**
	(c) **commander-in-chief's**	(d) **box's**
	(e) **Julia and Jake's** daughter	

Plural Possessive Nouns

To give a regular plural noun ownership, we add only an apostrophe. The noun then becomes a **plural possessive noun**, as in the examples below.

PLURAL NOUN	PLURAL POSSESSIVE NOUN
skateboards	skateboards' wheels
daughters	daughters' bedroom
the Williamses	the Williamses' yard

In a plural compound noun, possession is formed by adding *'s* to the last word.

attorneys general's opinions

brothers-in-law's business

Irregular Plurals

To give an irregular plural noun ownership, add *'s*.

children	children's stories
men	men's clothing
geese	geese's migration
oxen	oxen's yoke

Many people make errors when forming plural possessive nouns. To avoid this, form the plural noun first. Then apply the guidelines above to make it possessive.

Example 2

Use the apostrophe to form a plural possessive noun from each plural noun.

(a) cattle   (b) mice

(c) friends   (d) doctors

(e) mothers-in-law

Solution	(a) **cattle's**	(b) **mice's**
	(c) **friends'**	(d) **doctors'**
	(e) **mothers-in-law's**	

Practice   For a and b, replace each blank with the correct vocabulary word.

    a. A _____ is a geometric figure with three sides and three angles.

    b. A three-legged stand, or _____, displayed the artist's canvas.

For c–h, write each word that requires an apostrophe to show possession.

    c. The two mothers-in-laws dresses were the same color for the wedding.

    d. Paula, Erin, and Megans job was to pick up trash on campus.

    e. All three horses appetites were healthy.

    f. Joan played with her two friends dogs.

    g. Owning a scooter was every childs dream.

    h. A nail punctured the buss tire.

More Practice   For 1–8, make each singular noun possessive.

    1. unicycle   **2.** principal   **3.** desert   **4.** suburb

    5. sibling   **6.** hemisphere   **7.** story   **8.** metal

For 9–16, make each plural noun possessive.

    9. deer   **10.** rays   **11.** miners   **12.** fish

    13. boys   **14.** sheep   **15.** ladies   **16.** men

Review Set 97   Choose the best word to complete sentences 1–12.

    1. The (whether, weather) forecast is for rain and snow.
    (91)

    2. Does your pen have (blew, blue) ink?
    (92)

    3. Thirsty (dear, deer) wandered the park looking for water.
    (93)

    4. The experienced traveler packed a (pare, pear, pair) of comfortable shoes for the trip.
    (94)

5. (Do, Does) you know anyone who can eat no fat?
(15)

6. We remember that a transitive verb (does, doesn't) have a
(25, 32) direct object.

7. We remember that an intransitive verb (does, doesn't)
(25, 32) have a direct object.

8. Economics (was, were) not the reason that Jack ate the
(15) lean.

9. As far as we know, the Sprats ate no (berrys, berries).
(13, 14)

10. Jack did not have two (wifes, wives).
(13, 14)

11. Farmers were some of the (harder, hardest) hit by the
(45, 46) Great Depression.

12. The Curtises have misplaced (they're, there, their)
(28, 38) volleyball.

For 13–16, refer to this sentence: Jack Sprat could eat no fat.

13. Write the simple subject.
(2, 23)

14. Write the simple predicate.
(2, 23)

15. Write the helping verb.
(9)

16. Diagram the sentence.
(23, 25)

17. Write the four principal parts (present tense, present
(16) participle, past tense, past participle) of the verb *break*.

18. Write the linking verb in this sentence: Jack Sprat and
(22) his wife seem content and happy.

For 19 and 20, refer to this sentence: Jack Sprat gave his wife
the fat.

19. Write the indirect object.
(25, 35)

20. Diagram the sentence.
(25, 35)

21. Write each word that should be capitalized in this nursery rhyme:
(6, 12)

jack sprat could eat no fat,
his wife could eat no lean;
and so between them both, you see,
they licked the platter clean.

22. Rewrite this sentence, adding commas and capital letters as needed: the title i believe is "jack sprat."
(20, 56)

23. Add periods and capital letters to this outline:
(20, 36)

i jack sprat
    a jack—lean
    b wife—fat

24. Write the proper adjective in this sentence: The unfortunate farmers from the Dust Bowl region were called "Okies."
(6, 30)

25. Diagram the sentence above.
(33, 41)

26. Write the direct object of this sentence:
(5, 25) In 1934 and 1935, a terrible drought struck the farms of the Great Plains.

27. Tell whether the italicized pronoun in this sentence is nominative, objective, or possessive case: The Dust Bowl received its name because the drought caused the soil to dry so that *it* blew away on the wind.
(55, 57)

28. Write the intensive pronoun in this sentence: The soil itself turned the sky dark as night in the middle of the day.
(62)

29. Write the demonstrative pronoun in this sentence: This is why thousands of farm families left their homes in the Great Plains and fled westward.
(71)

30. Write the word modified by the italicized adverb in this sentence: The once self-sufficient farmers lived *pitifully,* like the serfs in the Middle Ages.
(84)

The Apostrophe: Contractions, Omitting Digits and Letters

Dictation or Journal Entry

Vocabulary:
We recall that the prefix *uni-* means "one." A *unicorn* is a mythical animal that resembles a horse with one horn on its forehead. The *unicorn* defends itself with its horn. *Unify* is a verb meaning "to cause to be as one." Sometimes hardships can *unify* the people of a community. *Unique* is an adjective meaning "one of a kind." The archeologist found a *unique* fossil specimen.

Contractions   When we combine two words and shorten one of them, we form a **contraction.** We insert an apostrophe to take the place of the letter or letters taken out.

Sometimes a verb is shortened, as in the examples below.

I have	⟶	I've
we are	⟶	we're
he will	⟶	he'll
she would	⟶	she'd
it is	⟶	it's

Other times we combine the verb and the word *not.* We shorten the word *not,* and insert an apostrophe where the letter *o* is missing.

do not	⟶	don't
is not	⟶	isn't
are not	⟶	aren't
were not	⟶	weren't
could not	⟶	couldn't

Note: the contraction *won't* (will not) is spelled irregularly.

Example 1   Use an apostrophe to write the contractions of a–d.

(a) you are   (b) they are

(c) would not   (d) did not

Solution   (a) **you're**   (b) **they're**

(c) **wouldn't**   (d) **didn't**

Omitted Digits We use an apostrophe when the first two digits are omitted from the year.

$$2000 \longrightarrow \text{'}00$$
$$1976 \longrightarrow \text{'}76$$
$$1920 \longrightarrow \text{'}20$$

Omitted Letters We use an apostrophe to show that we have taken letters out of a word. In informal writing, we can leave out letters to indicate the way we imagine the words being spoken.

good morning $\longrightarrow$	good mornin'
best of luck $\longrightarrow$	best o' luck
until then $\longrightarrow$	'til then
let them go $\longrightarrow$	let 'em go

Plurals of Letters, Numbers, and Words We use an apostrophe and an *s* (*'s*) to form the plurals of lowercase letters, numbers, signs, and words used as words. Notice that the letters, numbers, or words may be italicized or underlined.

The teacher gave five *A*'s in the class.

There were too many <u>me</u>'s in the paragraph.

How many +'s did you receive on your report card?

This is one of the few times when an apostrophe is used to form a plural. Be especially careful not to form regular plurals with apostrophes.

Example 2 Rewrite sentences a–c, inserting apostrophes where they are needed.

(a) We held a presidential election in the year 00.

(b) The farmer yelled, "Good mornin, Hank."

(c) The English teacher asked me to remove some of the *is*s, *are*s, and *was*s from my essay.

Solution (a) **We held a presidential election in the year '00.**

(b) **The farmer yelled, "Good mornin', Hank."**

(c) **The English teacher asked me to remove some of the *is*'s, *are*'s, and *was*'s from my essay.**

Practice For sentences a–d, write each word that needs an apostrophe.

  a. As the Industrial Revolution spread, conditions in the factories werent good.

  b. Langston Hughes writes, "So since Im still here livin, ... But for livin I was born."

  c. Until 74, no rain had been reported in some parts of the Atacama desert for 400 years!

  d. Three more 7s are needed to complete the pattern.

Make contractions of e and f.

  e. should not   **f.** they would

For g–k, replace the blanks with the correct word.

  g. The numerical meaning of *uni-* is _____.

  h. If something is one of a kind, it is _____.

  i. A mythical, horse-like animal with a horn on its forehead is a _____.

  j. *Tri-, uni-, poly-, in-,* and *anti-* are all _____.

  k. The word _____ means "to cause to be as one."

More Practice See "More Practice Lesson 98" in Student Workbook.

Review Set 98 Choose the best word to complete sentences 1–9.

  1. The plantation owner explained that his land had been
  (95) the (sight, site, cite) of a Civil War battle.

  2. Are you students (already, all ready) for your field trip?
  (83)

  3. A proud person might also be (vane, vain, vein).
  (82)

  4. That wound will need two weeks to (heel, heal).
  (84)

  5. What (do, does) your iguana eat?
  (15)

  6. Because he had no knife, Tommy Tucker (teared, tore,
  (54, 74) torn) the bread with his hands.

7. A predicate (adjective, nominative) is a noun that follows
(41, 44) a linking verb and renames the subject of the sentence.

8. The workers are (them, they) who benefit from the Social
(53, 58) Security Act.

9. Americans (who, which, whom) had lost their jobs could
(66, 68) accept Social Security money without shame because
they had worked to earn this benefit.

10. Write whether this word group is a phrase or a
(24, 61) clause: Although he sings for his supper.

11. Make a complete sentence from the word group above.
(3)

12. Write the future perfect tense verb phrase in this
(9, 19) sentence: As soon as he eats his bread and butter,
Tommy Tucker will have solved his hunger problem.

13. Write the future progressive tense verb phrase in this
(9, 21) sentence: This June, Tommy will have been searching for
a wife for seven years.

Write the verb from sentences 14 and 15, and tell whether it
is transitive or intransitive.

14. Little Tommy Tucker ate bread and butter.
(25, 32)

15. Little Tommy Tucker sang for his supper.
(22, 32)

16. Rewrite this sentence, correcting the double
(82) negative: Little Tommy Tucker hasn't no wife.

For 17 and 18, refer to this sentence: Little Tommy Tucker
was a singer.

17. Write the predicate nominative.
(22, 41)

18. Diagram the sentence.
(23, 41)

Write each prepositional phrase, and star the object of each
preposition in sentences 19 and 20.

19. Despite Roosevelt's successes, some people were still
(17, 33) critical of his new agencies and labeled them "alphabet
soup."

20. Under Roosevelt, America cared for the poor.
(17, 33)

For 21 and 22, refer to this sentence: Social Security was the most important of the New Deal programs.

21. Write whether the sentence is simple or compound.
(2, 64)

22. Diagram the sentence.
(33, 44)

For 23 and 24, refer to this sentence: Was the purpose of the Social Security Act achieved?

23. Write the prepositional phrase that modifies a noun.
(33, 34)

24. Write the noun that is modified by the prepositional
(33, 34) phrase.

25. Rewrite this sentence, adding commas as needed: Before
(47, 56) the Social Security Act many Americans worried that job loss old age or illness might leave them in poverty.

26. Write each indefinite pronoun in this sentence: No one
(72) wants to accept something for nothing.

27. Write the words that should be hyphenated in this
(83, 86) sentence: The Social Security Act helped increase workers' self confidence.

28. Rewrite this sentence, adding a semicolon where it is
(92) needed: The average person's left hand does most of the typing it does 56%.

29. Write the word that needs an apostrophe in this
(97, 98) sentence: Of the 293 ways to make change for a dollar, Ive only figured out 273.

30. Diagram this sentence: Tommy Tucker sang for his
(33, 64) supper, and he asked for bread and butter.

The Complex Sentence • The Compound-Complex Sentence

Dictation or Journal Entry

Vocabulary:

The prefix *re-* means "back" or "again." *Remember, renew,* and *report* reflect the prefix *re-* in their definitions. To *remember* is to bring something back to memory. Grandpa *remembers* when he was a young boy. The word *renew* means "to bring something back to new." People *renew* their wedding vows on special anniversaries. The word *report* means "to carry back a message." A journalist *reports* the news to the public.

We have learned how to join two simple sentences, or independent clauses, with a coordinating conjunction to form a compound sentence.

<u>Lisa plays the piano well</u>, **and** <u>she practices every day</u>.

independent clause | coordinating conjunction | independent clause

In a compound sentence, each of the independent clauses can stand alone. They are equal grammatical parts.

Lisa plays the piano well. = She practices every day.

Subordinate Clauses

Not all sentences are composed of equal parts. Sometimes a dependent clause is connected to an independent clause. We remember that we can turn an independent clause into a dependent clause, or **subordinate clause**, by adding a subordinating conjunction such as *after, although, because, even though, if, since, unless,* or *when.*

<u>Lisa plays the piano well</u> ***because*** <u>she practices every day</u>.

independent clause | subordinating conjunction | dependent clause

The subordinate clause "because she practices every day" cannot stand alone; it is dependent on the main clause, "Lisa plays the piano well."

Complex Sentence

A **complex sentence** contains one independent clause and one or more dependent, or subordinate, clauses. In the sentences below, we have underlined the independent (main) clause and italicized the subordinating conjunction that introduces the dependent clause.

<u>Ice cream feels good on the throat</u> *after* a tonsillectomy is performed.

When it rains, <u>the creek floods</u>.

Compound-Complex Sentence A **compound-complex sentence** contains two or more independent clauses and one or more dependent clauses. In the compound-complex sentence below, we have underlined the two independent clauses and italicized the subordinating conjunction that introduces the dependent clause.

> *Whenever* I catch the flu, <u>my stomach hurts</u>, and <u>my body aches</u>.

> <u>We can get in the pool</u>, or <u>we can join the volleyball game</u>, *as long as* we put on sunscreen.

Example For a–d, tell whether each sentence is simple, compound, complex, or compound-complex.

  (a) A pig rolled in the mud.

  (b) Before I eat dinner, I wash my hands.

  (c) The dog wags his tail, and he sniffs his food before he gobbles it up ravenously.

  (d) The little girl stroked her kitten, and it purred loudly.

Solution (a) This is a **simple** sentence. It is one independent clause.

  (b) This sentence is **complex.** It has one independent clause ("I wash my hands") and one dependent clause ("Before I eat dinner").

  (c) This is a **compound-complex** sentence. It has two independent clauses ("The dog wags his tail" and "he sniffs his food") and one dependent clause ("before he gobbles it up ravenously").

  (d) This is a **compound** sentence—two independent clauses joined by the coordinating conjunction "and."

Practice For a–d, tell whether each sentence is simple, compound, complex, or compound-complex.

  a. The small green frog hopped into the water.

  b. Before we leave our mountain cabin, we vacuum the floors, and we change the sheets on the beds.

  c. The snow becomes slushy and soft as the warm rays of the sun peek through the clouds.

d. The dentist gave specific instructions for tooth care, and the boy followed them.

For e–h, replace each blank with the correct vocabulary word.

e. Do you _____ the list of helping verbs?

f. The nurse will _____ the complaints of her patients to the doctor.

g. The leather conditioner claimed to _____ the car seats to their original condition.

h. We must _____ our driver's licenses every few years.

More Practice Tell whether the sentence is simple, compound, complex, or compound-complex.

1. The pronoun patrol apprehended me because I used the word "hisself."

2. Brenda used the word "ain't," so the contraction council indicted her.

3. Adventurous, energetic Granny rode a camel throughout the land of Israel.

4. As the curtain fell, cheers rose, and people stood to applaud.

Review Set 99 Choose the best word(s) to complete sentences 1–12.

1. With his binoculars, the ranger (cited, sited, sighted) the
(95) lost hiker in the distance.

2. Military personnel receive (metals, mettles, medals) for
(85) acts of bravery.

3. The weather (vein, vane, vain) indicated that the wind
(82) was coming from the north.

4. The prosecuting attorney (alleged, aloud, reconciled) that
(75, 81) the defendant committed the offense.

5. Two simple sentences or independent clauses joined
(64) with a (preposition, adverb, coordinating conjunction) form a compound sentence.

6. Dependent clauses are sometimes called (independent,
(64, 99) subordinate) clauses.

7. A (compound, simple, complex) sentence contains one
(64, 99) independent clause and one or more dependent or
subordinate clauses.

8. A (compound, compound-complex, complex) sentence
(64, 99) contains two or more independent clauses and one or
more dependent or subordinate clauses.

9. Wee Willie Winkie (ran, runned) through the town to
(74, 75) make sure all of the children were in bed.

10. (Them, Those) aggressive young boys are going to need
(28, 60) guidance.

11. It was (I, me) who answered the question correctly about
(55, 67) World War II.

12. The end of the softball tournament was (real, really)
(84, 93) intense.

13. Write the seven common coordinating conjunctions.
(37)

14. Write the coordinating conjunction in this sentence: Wee
(37) Willie Winkie runs upstairs and downstairs.

15. Write five subordinating conjunctions from this
(61, 99) list: while, as, group, even though, sleep, before, hungry,
though.

For 16 and 17, tell whether the sentence is simple,
compound, complex, or compound-complex.

16. While I was waiting in line at the market, I saw my
(64, 99) brother ahead of me, and he paid for my groceries.

17. My helpful neighbor, Isabel, fed my cat, watered the
(64, 99) lawn, and brought in my mail and newspapers.

18. Write each proper noun in this sentence: Did Willie
(6) Winkie run up and down the streets of Miami, Florida?

19. Write the common noun in the sentence above.
(6)

20. Write each predicate adjective in this sentence: Willie
(22, 44) Winkie was energetic and loud.

21. Diagram the sentence above, sentence 20.
(22, 44)

22. Write the comparison adjective in this sentence: Two
(45, 46) heads are better than one.

23. Write the superlative adjective in this sentence: Cyndel
(45, 46) has the biggest treehouse I've ever seen.

24. Write the appositive in this sentence: Do you ever
(48, 49) wonder how many books Mr. Kennedy, our school
librarian, has read?

25. Write the possessive form of each noun.
(28, 97) (a) mouse   (b) bees   (c) children

26. Rewrite this sentence, adding comas as needed: My
(47, 49) favorite dish spaghetti is made with tomatoes onions and
garlic.

27. Write and underline each word that should be italicized
(73) or underlined in this sentence: Ivanhoe, a book by Sir
Walter Scott, takes place in thirteenth-century England.

28. Write the adverb phrase that tells "where" in this
(84, 87) sentence: We all jumped into the pool.

Diagram sentences 29 and 30.

29. David bought and repaired a very old radio.
(38)

30. The sparrow fluttered away.
(23, 87)

Active or Passive Voice

Dictation or Journal Entry
Vocabulary:
Verity, veritable, and *verify* come from the Latin word *veritas,* which means "truth." *Verity,* a noun, is a "fact, truth, or reality." We must check for the *verity* of things we read in books. *Veritable,* an adjective, means "real" or "genuine." My dad is a *veritable* genius. *Verify,* a verb, means "to prove the truth of." Scientists *verify* their theories with experiments.

A transitive verb can be either **active** or **passive**. When the subject acts, the verb is **active.**

> The *van* <u>hit</u> the garbage can.

When the subject is acted upon, the verb is **passive.**

> The *garbage can* <u>was hit</u> by the van.

Passive verbs contain a form of "to be." Often the sentence contains a prepositional phrase beginning with "by." The subject *receives* the action; it does not *do* the action.

> PASSIVE: The mother <u>was followed</u> by the stray dog.

> ACTIVE: The stray dog <u>followed</u> the mother.

Active Voice

Writing is more exciting and powerful in the active voice. We try to use the active voice as much as possible.

> WEAK PASSIVE:
> The *research* <u>had been completed</u> by Jaime Placencia.

> STRONG ACTIVE:
> *Jaime Placencia* <u>had completed</u> the research.

> WORDY PASSIVE:
> The *tourists* <u>were led</u> through the Statue of Liberty by the guide.

> CONCISE ACTIVE:
> The *guide* <u>led</u> the tourists through the Statue of Liberty.

> INDIRECT PASSIVE:
> The *groceries* <u>were delivered</u> by Joe to the invalid.

> DIRECT ACTIVE:
> *Joe* <u>delivered</u> the groceries to the invalid.

Passive Voice

We see that the passive voice can be wordy and indirect. It can confuse the reader and tends to be dull. However, the passive voice does have a purpose. We use the passive voice in order to leave something unsaid. When the doer is unimportant or unknown, or when we want to emphasize the receiver of the action, we use the passive voice.

The *class* <u>was</u> totally <u>confused</u>.

All the *crops* <u>were destroyed</u> during the drought.

The *research* <u>had been completed</u>.

Example Tell whether the verb in each sentence is active or passive voice.

(a) The young woman drove the taxi cab.

(b) The taxi cab was driven by the young woman.

(c) The endangered condor was sighted by the bird watcher.

(d) The bird watcher sighted the endangered condor.

Solution (a) The verb is **active.** The subject (woman) acts.

(b) The verb is **passive.** The subject (cab) is acted upon.

(c) The verb is **passive.** The subject (condor) is acted upon.

(d) The verb is **active.** The subject (bird watcher) acts.

Practice Tell whether each verb in sentences a–d is active or passive voice.

a. The hungry cats were fed by the compassionate girl.

b. The compassionate girl fed the hungry cats.

c. The player was hit by the broken bat.

d. The broken bat hit the player.

For e–g, replace each blank with *verity, verify,* or *veritable.*

e. The witness will _____ that I am telling the truth.

f. The lawyer questioned the _____ of my statement.

g. Our plan of action has been a _____ success.

Choose the best word to complete sentences 1–13.

1. A man of (medal, meddle, metal, mettle) does his best to
(85) protect his family from harm.

2. (Mettling, Meddling, Metaling, Medaling) neighbors do
(85) not mind their own business.

3. Citizens pledge their (compassion, reconciliation,
(75, 81) allegiance) to their country.

4. Most big cities are surrounded by smaller neighborhoods
(80, 81) known as (suburbs, icons, allegiances).

5. In a compound sentence, each of the two simple
(64, 37) sentences can stand alone, for they are (equal, unequal)
parts.

6. Jack (losed, losted, lost) his balance and fell.
(74, 75)

7. After the fall, Jack (shaked, shaken, shook) himself off
(75, 76) and went to get help.

8. Jack and Jill (fetch, fetches) a pail of water.
(7, 16)

9. Verbs are either active or (passive, lazy).
(5, 100)

10. (Passive, Active) voice verbs contain a form of "to be."
(15, 100)

11. The subject receives the action of the (passive, active)
(5, 100) verb.

12. When the subject acts, the verb is (active, passive) voice.
(5, 100)

13. We try to use (passive, active) voice whenever possible.
(5, 100)

14. Write the four common pairs of correlative conjunctions.
(39)

For 15 and 16, refer to this sentence: Either Jack or Jill will
fetch a pail of water.

15. Write the correlative conjunctions.
(39)

16. Diagram the sentence.
(38, 39)

17. Write five common subordinating conjunctions from this
(61) list: swimmer, after, while, in order that, watch,
whenever, as if, dolphin.

18. Tell whether this sentence is simple, compound, complex, or compound-complex: If you place an apostrophe in a possessive pronoun, the apostrophe posse may issue you a citation.
(64, 99)

For 19 and 20, refer to this sentence: The pair, Jack and Jill, went up the hill.

19. Write the appositive.
(48, 49)

20. Diagram the sentence.
(34, 48)

For 21 and 22, tell whether the verb is active or passive voice.

21. Jack was injured by his fall.
(5, 100)

22. Jack had injured his head.
(5, 100)

23. Rewrite this sentence, adding periods as needed: When Mr Parsons moved to St Petersburg, he became interested in architecture
(36, 40)

24. Rewrite this letter, adding commas as needed:
(52, 56)

Dear Tom and Christina

Unless you have other plans please join us for dinner at 7:00. We're having tamales your favorite.

Warmly
Mom

25. Tell whether the italicized pronoun in this sentence is nominative, objective, or possessive case: Whatever they claim, the fault was *theirs*.
(55, 57)

26. Write the interrogative pronoun in this sentence: Who invented meatloaf?
(66, 68)

27. Rewrite this sentence, adding the needed punctuation marks: You're not serious are you
(56, 77)

28. For a–c, use a hyphen to divide each word that may be divided at the end of a line.
(83, 88)

(a) antifreeze   (b) clockwise   (c) thought

29. Rewrite this sentence, adding a colon where it is
(94) needed: Before the United States entered World War II,
Germany invaded the following countries Austria,
Czechoslovakia, Poland, Denmark, Norway, Belgium,
The Netherlands, and France.

30. Diagram this sentence: Down the stairway scurried the
(85, 87) cat.

LESSON 101

Parentheses • Brackets

Dictation or Journal Entry

Vocabulary:

The word *antihistamine* contains two parts: *anti-* (against) and *histamine*, (a compound that causes allergic reactions). An *antihistamine* acts against an allergic reaction. After the bee stung me, I took an *antihistamine*. If we know that a toxin is a poison, then we know that an *antitoxin* will work "against" a poison.

Parentheses

We use **parentheses** to enclose a thought only loosely related to the main idea of the sentence. Parentheses can enclose additional or explanatory information, personal commentary, figures, or examples that are not essential to the sentence and are not intended to be a part of it grammatically. A single word or figure, a phrase, or an entire sentence can be enclosed in parentheses. (The singular form of *parentheses* is *parenthesis*. Remember, however, that parentheses are always used in pairs.)

Additional Information

In the sentences below, the information enclosed in parentheses is additional, but nonessential, information.

> Mrs. Sims (she lives next door) bakes the best biscuits.

> I work twelve hours a day (except for holidays), but I like my job.

Clarifying Meaning or Figures

We use parentheses around words or figures that are included to explain or clarify meaning.

> Movement along the San Andreas Fault (California) results in numerous earthquakes.

> They earned ten dollars ($10) painting signs.

> Libby's favorites have always been the Baroque composers (Bach, Handel, Vivaldi, etc.).

Personal Commentary

In informal writing, we can use parentheses around words that express our personal thoughts about something in the sentence.

> Jill's little brother Nick (I've always liked him) was the life of the party!

> Frank finally turned off the television (can you believe it?) and took out the garbage.

All of the *sentence's* punctuation marks are placed outside the parentheses.

> YES: This belongs to Lois (Bobby's friend).

> NO: This belongs to Lois (Bobby's friend.)

If the *words in parentheses* require a question mark or exclamation mark, we place it inside the parentheses. However, we never include a period if the parentheses are within a sentence.

> YES: The new concert hall (it's gorgeous!) is finally open.

> NO: Mike (you'll remember him from last summer.) is performing there.

If parentheses are inserted into a sentence where a comma, colon, or semicolon would normally occur, the punctuation is placed after the parentheses.

> YES: As far as Latrisa is concerned (you can trust her), it's a good idea.

> YES: Please reply by tomorrow (Friday); Saturday will be too late.

Example 1 Rewrite sentences a–c below, adding parentheses where they are needed.

(a) We lost two trees both elms in the storm.

(b) The baby-sitter charged five dollars $5 per hour to watch the children.

(c) If you've seen Stan's latest project he's always got one going, you know it's wackier than ever.

Solution (a) The words "both elms" provide additional but nonessential information. We enclose them in parentheses.

We lost two trees **(both elms)** in the storm.

(b) We enclose $5 in parentheses to confirm the number.

The baby-sitter charged five dollars **($5)** per hour to watch the children.

(c) We enclose the personal commentary in parentheses. The comma goes after the parentheses.

If you've seen Stan's latest project **(he's always got one going),** you know it's wackier than ever.

Brackets We use **brackets** to insert our own words (additions, explanations, comments, etc.) into quoted material.

> "The courthouse," said the tour guide, "was constructed the same year the town was founded [1855]."

> John F. Kennedy said, "Ask not what your country [the United States of America] can do for you; ask what you can do for your country."

> "You can say this about him [Bob]: he's punctual."

Example 2 In the sentence below, use brackets to enclose words that are not a part of the direct quotation.

> Rudyard Kipling's The Jungle Book reads: "His mother did not call him Lungri the Lame One for nothing," said Mother Wolf quietly.

Solution We enclose in brackets words that were inserted to clarify what *Lungri* means.

> Rudyard Kipling's The Jungle Book reads: "His mother did not call him Lungri **[the Lame One]** for nothing," said Mother Wolf quietly.

Practice For sentences a–d, insert parentheses or brackets as needed.

> **a.** "We know," the lecturer began, "that she Anne Frank was a German Jewish girl and a victim of the Holocaust."

> **b.** The wood for the fence cost two hundred dollars $200.

> **c.** Please bring something a book to read or a puzzle to pass the time.

> **d.** Mariel enjoyed summer camp we hoped she would, and she plans to go back next year.

For e–g, replace each blank with the correct vocabulary word.

> **e.** The doctor gave the patient an _____ to work against the effects of the poison.

> **f.** The prefix _____ means "against."

g. _____ reduce the effects of histamines, which cause allergic reactions.

Choose the best word to complete sentences 1–12.

1. The (annual, biannual, perennial) fall celebration
(96) included a pie-eating contest, a hayride, and a square dance.

2. Published in February and August, the (annual,
(96) semiannual, perennial) magazine appealed to skateboarding enthusiasts.

3. Alexis (alleged, amazed, implied) that she would attend
(79, 81) the class picnic.

4. The (pear, minor, eager) dog quivered with excitement as
(78, 94) his master picked up the leash and prepared for their evening walk.

5. They (ain't, hasn't, haven't) heard of the Golden Rule of
(15, 82) Life.

6. Everyone (agree, agrees) that the Golden Rule of Life is a
(7, 16) good rule to live by.

7. Isaac Watts (use, using, used) the word *golden* to express
(7, 16) quality or great value.

8. (Your, You're) a good example of someone who follows
(60, 98) the Golden Rule of Life.

9. Negatives are modifiers, usually (nouns, adjectives,
(82) adverbs), that mean "no" or "not."

10. I studied (good, well) for the test.
(85)

11. To give a regular plural noun ownership, we add a(n)
(97, 98) (apostrophe, comma, period).

12. We use (quotation marks, italics, parentheses) to enclose
(73, 101) a thought not pertaining to the main idea of the sentence.

13. Write the verb in this sentence, and tell whether it is
(5, 32) transitive or intransitive: Sometimes hardship can unify
people.

14. Tell whether this sentence is declarative, imperative,
(1, 36) exclamatory, or interrogative: Whether you walk or run,
you'll still get there.

15. Write the plural of each singular noun.
(13, 14)
(a) baby   (b) child   (c) boy

16. Write each prepositional phrase in this sentence, and star
(17, 33) the object of each preposition: In the 1800s, the *London
Encyclopedia* named Isaac Watts, the British theologian
and hymn writer, as the first user of the phrase "The
Golden Rule."

17. Rewrite this sentence, adding periods as needed: I believe
(36, 40) Dr Foster went to Gloucester at 9 am

18. Write and underline each word that should be italicized
(73) in this sentence: "Doctor Foster" is a nursery rhyme from
a book called Mother Goose.

19. Form an (a) adjective and (b) adverb from the noun *faith*.
(27, 84)

Write each adverb in sentences 20–24.

20. Dr. Foster will not go that far again.
(84, 90)

21. Dr. Foster stepped in a puddle today.
(84, 87)

22. In the future, Dr. Foster will step more carefully.
(84, 90)

23. Dr. Foster stepped clumsily into the water.
(84)

24. Dr. Foster was partly responsible for the mistake.
(84, 90)

25. Write the prepositional phrase used as an adverb in this
(90, 95) sentence, and tell which word it modifies: The water
rose to his middle.

26. Write whether the italicized word in this sentence is a
(17, 96) preposition or an adverb: The doctor did not fall *down*.

27. Rewrite this sentence, adding a semicolon where it is
(92) needed: Darryl examined the five-dollar bill he noticed
that the names of states are listed across the top of the
Lincoln Memorial.

28. Rewrite this sentence, adding a colon where it is
(94) needed: The four words in the English language that
end in *dous* are as follows tremendous, horrendous,
stupendous, and hazardous.

29. Write the possessive form of each plural noun.
(28, 97) (a) sons   (b) daughters   (c) brothers

30. Diagram this sentence: Both LeAnn and Margaret
(25, 38) recommend the broiled scallops.

Interjections

Interjections A word or short phrase used to show strong emotion is called an **interjection.** An interjection is one of the eight parts of speech. It can express excitement, happiness, joy, rage, surprise, pain, or relief. Interjections are italicized below.

Ah! Now I remember.

Ouch! I burned my finger on the hot iron.

Oh dear, I forgot my lunch money again.

Oh, excuse me. I didn't mean to interrupt.

An interjection is not a sentence and has no relationship with the words around it. For this reason, it is usually set apart from the rest of the sentence by some sort of punctuation. Generally, an exclamation point follows an interjection, but if the emotion is not very intense, a comma follows the interjection.

INTENSE: *Wow!* Did you see that aircraft?

NOT INTENSE: *Okay*, I understand now.

Below is a list of common interjections. Notice that sounds can be interjections too.

ah	*oh dear*	*ugh*	*man*
aha	*oh my*	*uh oh*	*drat*
bam	*oh yes*	*well*	*oops*
boy	*far out*	*yippee*	*bravo*
oh no	*whee*	*good grief*	*okay*
whoops	*goodness*	*ouch*	*wow*
hey	*ow*	*yikes*	*hooray*
phew	*yuck*	*hurrah*	*pow*
boo	*oh*	*shh*	*whew*

We must not overuse interjections. They lose their effectiveness when used too frequently.

Example 1   Write each interjection that you find in a–d.
(a) Goodness! You frightened me.

(b) Phew! That was a close call.

(c) Oh my, you were right after all.

(d) Hooray! Vacation is finally here.

Solution   (a) **Goodness**   (b) **Phew**

(c) **Oh my**   (d) **Hooray**

Diagramming   We diagram an interjection by placing it on a line apart from the rest of the sentence.

Good grief! You cut your hair.

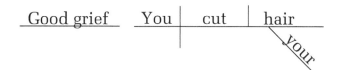

Example 2   Diagram this sentence:

Ugh, this assignment is difficult.

Solution   We place the interjection on a line apart from the rest of the sentence.

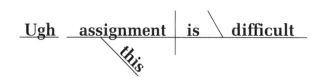

Practice   Write the interjection that you find in a–d.
a. Okay, Jim can go with us to the movies.

b. Hey, wait for me!

c. Bam! Pow! Take that!

d. Yuck! A skunk just sprayed our dog.

Diagram e and f.
e. Yippee! We won the game.

f. Oops, I made a mistake.

For g–j, replace each blank with *sometime, some time,* or *sometimes.*

g. _____ little brothers and sisters can be annoying.

h. I would like to visit Hawaii _____.

i. It might take _____ to solve the problem.

j. Drop by _____. I'd love to see you.

Review Set 102

Choose the best word to complete sentences 1–8.

1. A mythical horse with one horn on its head is known as a
(93, 98) (deer, unicorn, hare).

2. The gymnast balanced on three parts of his body—his
(35, 97) head and his hands—in a position known as a (tripod, diagonal, feign).

3. The thirsty runner didn't have (nothing, anything) to
(82) drink.

4. An event that takes place twice per year is called a(n)
(96) (annual, biannual) event.

5. (*Good, Well*) is a descriptive adjective or a predicate
(85) adjective that describes a noun or a pronoun.

6. When we combine two words and shorten one of them,
(98, 82) we form a(n) (appositive, conjunction, contraction).

7. We may use (parentheses, prepositions) to add unrelated
(17, 101) information to a sentence.

8. A word or short phrase used to show strong emotion is
(31, 102) called an (interjection, antihistamine, injustice).

For 9–12, refer to this sentence: Do elephants really fear mice?

9. Write the simple subject.
(2, 8)

10. Write the simple predicate.
(2, 9)

11. Write the direct object.
(5, 25)

12. Diagram the sentence.
(23, 87)

13. Write the predicate nominative in this sentence: Is
(22, 41) Raymond L. Ditmars the curator of mammals at the New York Zoological Park?

14. Write each prepositional phrase in this sentence, and star
(17, 33) the object of each preposition: At a park in Washington, the director claims that elephants pay no attention to the numerous mice in their barns.

15. Write the limiting adjectives in this sentence: Elephants
(27, 28) pay no attention to the rats and mice in the hay during circuses.

16. Write (a) the coordinating conjunction and (b) the
(37, 61) subordinating conjunction in this sentence: One writer claims that dogs and human beings cause elephants the greatest fear.

For 17–19, refer to this sentence: Some people still believe that elephants are afraid of mice.

17. Tell whether the sentence is simple, compound,
(64, 99) complex, or compound-complex.

18. Write the independent clause.
(61, 99)

19. Write the dependent clause and circle the subordinating
(61, 99) conjunction.

20. Write the intensive pronoun in this sentence: Sitting on
(51, 62) the tuffet was Little Miss Muffet herself.

21. Write the reflexive pronoun in this sentence: Did the
(51, 62) spider chase Little Miss Muffet by itself?

22. Rewrite this sentence, adding punctuation marks as
(69, 77) needed: Little Miss Muffet screamed Theres a spider

Write each adverb in sentences 23–25.

23. Afterward, Miss Muffet ate more cautiously.
(84, 89)

24. Miss Muffet was terribly frightened by the spider.
(84, 90)

25. Yesterday a spider frightened Miss Muffet away.
(87, 89)

26. Write whether the italicized word in this sentence is an
(17, 96) adverb or a preposition: Little Miss Muffet sat *on* a tuffet.

27. Rewrite this sentence, adding a semicolon where it is
(92) needed: Almonds are nuts they are members of the peach family.

28. Rewrite this sentence, adding a colon where it is
(94) needed: In most clock advertisements, the time displayed is 1010 a.m. or p.m.

29. Write the possessive form of each plural noun.
(97, 98) (a) teachers   (b) nurses   (c) presidents-elect

30. Diagram this sentence: The spider sat down beside Miss
(34, 87) Muffet.

Spelling Rules: Silent Letters
k, g, w, t, d, and *c*

Dictation or Journal Entry

Vocabulary:
Fidelity and *faith* come from the Latin root word *fides,* meaning "faith." *Fidelity* is steadfast loyalty; faithfulness to duties, obligations, or promises. The elderly couple's *fidelity* to one another was obvious when they celebrated their sixtieth wedding anniversary. *Faith* is belief not based on proof. Sara had *faith* that her sister was telling the truth.

Why Are Some Letters Silent? The English language contains many words that are spelled differently than they are pronounced. There are several reasons for this.

As the language changed and grew through the centuries, the way people pronounced a word often changed, yet the way the word was spelled remained the same.

Some early scholars insisted on applying Latin rules of spelling to English words. (Since English borrowed the Latin alphabet, this idea wasn't illogical.)

More words were borrowed from other languages, and their foreign spellings were kept.

In the midst of this, the printing press appeared. It helped to "freeze" the spelling of all these words, no matter how irregular. Most English words are spelled today just as they were in the 1500s. As a result, there are many words that contain letters we no longer (or never did) pronounce.

The Letter *k* A silent *k* at the beginning of a word is always followed by an *n*.

> *k*now   *k*nock   *k*neel   *k*nife

The Letter *g* A silent *g* may also be followed by an *n* at the beginning or the end of a word.

> *g*nat   *g*naw   fei*g*n   rei*g*n   campai*g*n

The Letter *w* A silent *w* can come before the letter *r*.

> *w*rinkle   *w*ritten   *w*rench   *w*reath

Sometimes the silent *w* comes before the letter *h*.

> *w*hole   *w*ho   *w*hose

Other silent *w*'s appear in the words *answer, sword,* and *two.*

The Letter t A silent *t* can follow the letter *s*.

cas*t*le rus*t*le lis*t*en has*t*en

A silent *t* can also come before the letters *ch*.

Sco*t*ch ma*t*ch ske*t*ch pi*t*ch

Not all words that end with the "ch" sound have a silent *t* (much, rich, attach, such, sandwich, etc.). When in doubt, check the dictionary.

Other silent *t*'s appear in words borrowed from the French, such as *ballet*, *depot*, *debut*, *gourmet*, and *mortgage*.

The Letter d The letters *ge* usually follow a silent *d*.

fu*d*ge e*d*ge bri*d*ge do*d*ge ba*d*ge

We also find silent *d*'s in these words:

a*d*jective a*d*just We*d*nesday han*d*some

The Letter c A silent *c* can follow the letter *s*.

s*c*issors s*c*ene s*c*ience s*c*ent

Example Rewrite these words and underline each silent letter.

(a) kneel (b) answer (c) wrong

(d) badger (e) gnarl (f) itch

Solution (a) **_k_neel** (b) **ans_w_er** (c) **_w_rong**

(d) **ba_d_ger** (e) **_g_narl** (f) **i_t_ch**

Practice Rewrite words a–h, and underline each silent letter.

a. wrestle **b.** whose **c.** gnashing **d.** knife

e. knot **f.** knees **g.** scenery **h.** thistle

For i and j, replace each blank with *fidelity* or *faith*.

i. Annie has _____ that her essay will receive a high grade.

j. Jorge demonstrated his _____ to his family by helping to pay the bills.

Review Set 103 Choose the best word to complete sentences 1–13.

1. The traveler (renewed, remembered, verified) his identity by showing his driver's license.
(99, 100)

2. Motorists must (unify, renew, sight) their automobile
(98, 99) insurance regularly.

3. Miss Harper's attempts to (cite, pair, unify) the
(95, 98) neighborhood were warmly received.

4. A (rectangle, square, triangle) has three sides and three
(97) angles.

5. The pronoun *it* is (first, second, third) person.
(53, 58)

6. The pronoun *you* is (first, second, third) person.
(53, 58)

7. When we (begin, began, begun) using the Gregorian
(54, 74) calendar, the longest day of the year was either June 21 or
June 22.

8. Jaime won't do (anything, nothing) unkind to his younger
(82) brother.

9. (*Good*, *Well*) is usually an adverb that modifies an action
(85) verb and explains "how" someone does something.

10. He thought she was the (more, most) gentle and
(90, 91) compassionate of the two sisters.

11. (Beside, Besides) rings and bells, the fine lady will have
(17, 96) music wherever she goes.

12. We usually place punctuation marks (before, after)
(101) parentheses.

13. An interjection is one of the (three, eight, twelve) parts of
(102) speech.

14. Tell whether this word group is a sentence fragment, a
(3, 4) run-on sentence, or a complete sentence: June 21 is
considered the longest day of the year however, that is
not always the case.

15. Write each prepositional phrase in this sentence, and star
(17, 33) the object of each preposition: In the year before each
leap year, the longest day of the year is June 22.

16. Write the predicate adjective in this sentence: In every
(22, 44) year but a leap year, December 22 is the shortest.

17. Write the pair of correlative conjunctions in this
(39) sentence: Not only the longest day of the year but also the shortest day is called a *solstice.*

18. Tell whether this sentence is simple, compound,
(64, 99) complex, or compound-complex: The solstices are the times of the year when the sun is at its greatest distance from the Equator.

19. Write the relative pronoun in this sentence: The man who
(51, 66) rode a horse to Banbury Cross went to visit a fine lady.

20. Tell whether this word group is a phrase or a clause: with
(24, 61) rings on her fingers and bells on her toes

Write each adverb in sentences 21–23.

21. The lady will be beautifully dressed.
(84)

22. Did he visit her daily?
(84, 89)

23. The nursery rhyme is too vague about the relationship
(84, 90) between the rider and the lady.

24. Write the prepositional phrase used as an adverb in this
(33, 95) sentence, and tell which word it modifies: The gentleman rides like a gallant knight.

25. Rewrite this sentence, adding a semicolon where it is
(92) needed: Red apples taste delicious however, green ones are better for cooking.

26. Rewrite this sentence, adding a colon where it is needed:
(94) There are three things I do every Saturday brush the dog, write in my journal, and visit Aunt Trudy.

27. Write the possessive form of each noun.
(97, 98)
    (a) shark   (b) Mr. Jones   (c) Benito

28. Write the contraction for the words *do* and *not.*
(97, 98)

29. Write the word *whistle* and underline the silent letters.
(103)

30. Diagram this sentence: Usually, June 21 is the longest
(34, 87) day of the year.

LESSON 104

Spelling Rules: Silent Letters *p*, *b*, *l*, *u*, *h*, *n*, and *gh*

> **Dictation or Journal Entry**
>
> **Vocabulary:**
> *Patience* and *forbearance* are similar traits found in a person of strong character. *Patience* (from the Latin root *patiens,* meaning "suffering") is the ability to wait calmly and to endure annoyance, hardship, or difficulty without complaining. We must have *patience* until our turn comes. *Forbearance* is self-control and restraint. He showed great *forbearance* during the long illness.

The Letter *p*   The Greek language is a source of many words that contain a silent *p*. The silent *p* occurs only before the letters *n*, *s*, and *t*.

    pneumonia   **p**salm   **p**sychology   **p**terodactyl

Other words with a silent *p* include *recei**p**t, cu**p**board,* and *cor**p**s.*

The Letter *b*   Many words contain the letter *m* followed by a silent *b*.

    plum**b**   com**b**   succum**b**   clim**b**   lam**b**

Other silent *b*'s are found in the words *de**b**t, dou**b**t,* and *su**b**tle.*

The Letter *l*   Many words that contain a silent *l* follow a similar pattern: an *l* followed by a consonant that makes the *l* difficult to pronounce.

    cha**l**k   ta**l**k   wa**l**k   yo**l**k   fo**l**k

    pa**l**m   ca**l**m   wou**l**d   cou**l**d   shou**l**d

    ca**l**f (calves)   ha**l**f (halves)

Other silent *l*'s are found in the words *co**l**onel* and *sa**l**mon.*

The Letter *u*   A silent *u* usually follows the letter *g*. It reminds us to pronounce the *g* with a "hard" sound (g) rather than a "soft" sound (j), at either the beginning or the end of the word.

    g**u**ardian   g**u**ess   g**u**ide   plag**u**e   vag**u**e

The Letter *h*   A silent *h* usually follows *c*, *r*, or *g*, as in these words:

    sc**h**eme   ac**h**e   r**h**ombus

    ag**h**ast   g**h**ost   r**h**eumatism

An initial *h* can also be silent, as in the words ***h**onor,* ***h**our,* and ***h**eir.*

The Letters gh The letter combination *gh* is always silent when it comes before the letter *t*.

light   daughter   freight   bought

bright   taught   straight   thought

A *gh* at the end of a word can be silent as well:

weigh   thorough   though   sigh

sleigh   dough   bough   high

The Letter n Sometimes the letter *m* is followed by a silent *n*, as in these words:

column   condemn   hymn   solemn

Example Rewrite these words and underline the silent letters *p, b, l, u, h, n,* and *gh.*

(a) dough   (b) should   (c) walk   (d) crumb

(e) ache   (f) limb   (g) through   (h) hymn

(i) would   (j) subtle   (k) psalm   (l) guard

Solution (a) **dough**   (b) **should**   (c) **walk**   (d) **crumb**

(e) **ache**   (f) **limb**   (g) **through**   (h) **hymn**

(i) **would**   (j) **subtle**   (k) **psalm**   (l) **guard**

Practice Rewrite words a–l, and underline the silent letters *p, b, l, u, h, n,* and *gh.*

a. guess   **b.** although   **c.** chorus   **d.** rhyme

e. could   **f.** calf   **g.** scepter   **h.** corps

i. pneumonia **j.** debt   **k.** tomb   **l.** yolk

For m and n, replace each blank with *patience* or *forbearance.*

m. During the argument, Jake felt angry, but he exercised _____ and maintained his self-control.

n. Karen had _____ while teaching her youngest sister how to use the computer program.

Choose the best word to complete sentences 1–10.

1. Leslie demonstrated her usual (humility, renewal,
(70, 104) forbearance) when the excited puppy muddied her new
white T-shirt.

2. The art expert pronounced the old oil painting a
(98, 100) (veritable, perennial, unified) masterpiece.

3. Do you (pare, remember, site) what year George
(95, 99) Washington was born?

4. The (annual, principle, unique) watercolor won
(96, 98) recognition for its realistic depiction of the artist's own
studio.

5. A (phrase, clause) may contain nouns and verbs, but it
(24, 63) does not have both a subject and a predicate.

6. Chop suey isn't (no, a) typical Chinese dish.
(82)

7. While in New York, Li Hung-chang, the great Chinese
(74, 75) statesman, (bring, brung, brought) his American friends
to a Chinese restaurant.

8. Li Hung-chang was (he, him) who motivated restaurant
(53, 55) proprietors in New York to serve chop suey.

9. My friend Mr. Cheung cooks very (good, well).
(84, 85)

10. The two gentlemen divided the black hen's eggs
(17) (between, among) themselves.

11. Write the verb phrase in this sentence, and tell whether it
(9, 100) is active or passive: Chop suey was popularized in 1896.

12. Write the prepositional phrase used as an adjective in
(33, 34) this sentence, and tell which word it modifies: The
meaning of *chop suey* is "miscellaneous pieces or bits."

13. Write the proper adjective in this sentence: *Chop suey* is
(22, 30) a Chinese word, although it is not applied to any
particular dish in Asia.

Rewrite sentences 14 and 15, adding commas as needed.

14. Pork beef chicken celery onions noodles and sprouts
(47, 52) are some of the ingredients found in chop suey.

15. Mr. Wu did you know that this special dish chop
(49, 56) suey is practically unknown in China?

16. Write and hyphenate the words that should be
(83, 88) hyphenated in this sentence: By Friday afternoon, Shane
was almost three fourths completed with the shed's new
roof.

17. Write each adverb in this sentence: The gentlemen
(87, 89) checked everywhere to see if Hickety Pickety had
recently laid any eggs.

For 18–20, refer to this sentence: When they checked the
nest, they found a dozen eggs.

18. Write the independent clause.
(61, 99)

19. Write the dependent clause.
(63, 99)

20. Write the subordinating conjunction.
(61, 99)

21. Write the indirect object in this sentence: Will you
(25, 35) please fry me three eggs?

22. Rewrite this sentence, adding a semicolon where it is
(92) needed: A cat has many muscles it has 32 in its ears.

23. Rewrite the following, adding a colon where it is
(94) needed: I need these items for school notebook, paper,
pencil, pen, and eraser.

24. Write the possessive form of a–c.
(28, 97) (a) Bob and Chris (their house) (b) hens (c) gentlemen

25. Write the contraction for the words *she* and *would*.
(97, 98)

26. Rewrite this sentence, adding parentheses where they are
(101) needed: A dime has one hundred eighteen 118 ridges
around it.

27. Rewrite words a–c, and underline each silent letter.
(103, 104) (a) gnat   (b) guard   (c) limb

Diagram sentences 28–30.

28. Ugh, goodbyes are so difficult!
(23, 102)

29. Wow, Hickety Pickety was laying eggs everywhere!
(23, 102)

30. The chef served Li's American friends chop suey.
(25, 35)

Spelling Rules: Suffixes, Part 1

> **Dictation or Journal Entry**
> **Vocabulary:**
> *Frugal* is an adjective meaning "avoiding waste." Rather than throw away the leftover vegetables, the *frugal* woman put them in her soup. *Frugally* is an adverb. She *frugally* saved her money. *Frugality* is a noun. He demonstrated *frugality* by fixing his old bike instead of buying a new one.

When we used the suffixes *-er* and *-est* to form comparison adjectives and adverbs, we learned some of the spelling rules for adding suffixes. In this lesson, we will examine more rules for adding suffixes. As always, we check the dictionary if we are not sure how a word is spelled.

Words Ending in *y*

A final *y* usually changes to *i* when suffixes (except for the suffix *-ing*) are added:

rely + able = reliable

modify + er = modifier

amplify + ed = amplified

pity + ful = pitiful

cry + s = cries

worry + some = worrisome

steady + ly = steadily

dry + est = driest

glory + ous = glorious

cloudy + ness = cloudiness

sunny + er = sunnier

beauty + ful = beautiful

but: relying, modifying, applying, pitying, crying, worrying, steadying, drying, glorying

When preceded by a vowel, the final *y* does not change to *i* when a suffix is added.

enjoy + able = enjoyable

play + ed = played

employ + er = employer

gray + est = grayest

buy + ing = buying

Exceptions   Important exceptions include the following:

$$lay + ed = laid$$
$$pay + ed = paid$$
$$say + ed = said$$
$$day + ly = daily$$

Example 1   Add suffixes to these words ending in *y*.

(a) display + ed = _____

(b) rainy + er = _____

(c) tardy + ness = _____

(d) penny + less = _____

(e) merry + ly = _____

Solution   (a) display + ed = **displayed** (The *y* is preceded by a vowel, so it does not change to an *i*.)

(b) rainy + er = **rainier** (The final *y* usually changes to *i* when suffixes are added.)

(c) tardy + ness = **tardiness**

(d) penny + less = **penniless**

(e) merry + ly = **merrily**

Words Ending in a Silent *e*   We usually drop the silent *e* before adding a suffix beginning with a vowel (including the suffix -*y*).

$$fame + ous = famous$$
$$nose + y = nosy$$
$$scare + y = scary$$
$$come + ing = coming$$
$$explore + ation = exploration$$
$$live + able = livable$$
$$blue + ish = bluish$$
$$sense + ible = sensible$$

However, we keep the final *e* when we add a suffix beginning with a consonant.

$$\text{arrange} + \text{ment} = \text{arrangement}$$
$$\text{like} + \text{ness} = \text{likeness}$$
$$\text{time} + \text{less} = \text{timeless}$$
$$\text{sincere} + \text{ly} = \text{sincerely}$$
$$\text{peace} + \text{ful} = \text{peaceful}$$

Exceptions Exceptions to the rules above include the following words:

$$\text{judge} + \text{ment} = \text{judgment}$$
$$\text{argue} + \text{ment} = \text{argument}$$
$$\text{wise} + \text{dom} = \text{wisdom}$$
$$\text{gentle} + \text{ly} = \text{gently}$$
$$\text{true} + \text{ly} = \text{truly}$$

Also, when adding *-ous* or *-able* to a word ending in *ge* or *ce*, we keep the final *e* to indicate the soft sound of the *c* (as in *celery*) or *g* (as in *giant*).

$$\text{manage} + \text{able} = \text{manageable}$$
$$\text{trace} + \text{able} = \text{traceable}$$
$$\text{change} + \text{able} = \text{changeable}$$
$$\text{outrage} + \text{ous} = \text{outrageous}$$
$$\text{courage} + \text{ous} = \text{courageous}$$

Example 2 Add suffixes to these words ending in a silent *e*.

(a) believe + able = _____

(b) live + ing = _____

(c) explore + ing = _____

(d) love + ly = _____

(e) late + ly = _____

(f) change + able = _____

(g) true + ly = _____

Solution (a) believe + able = **believable** (We usually drop the silent *e* when the suffix begins with a vowel.)

(b) live + ing = **living**

(c) explore + ing = **exploring**

(d) love + ly = **lovely** (We usually keep the final *e* when the suffix begins with a consonant.)

(e) late + ly = **lately**

(f) change + able = **changeable** (We keep the silent *e* after the *g* to retain the soft *g* sound.)

(g) true + ly = **truly** (This is an exception to the rule.)

Practice Add suffixes to words a–k.

a. plenty + ful = _____

b. drowsy + ness = _____

c. dreary + est = _____

d. happy + ly = _____

e. care + ful = _____

f. move + ing = _____

g. like + ly = _____

h. time + er = _____

i. knowledge + able = _____

j. write + ing = _____

k. blame + less = _____

For l–n, replace each blank with *frugal, frugally,* or *frugality.*

l. The _____ student did not waste paper.

m. He _____ saved newspaper and recycled it.

n. She showed _____ when she shopped for the lowest prices.

Review Set
105

Choose the best word to complete sentences 1–8.

1. We must check the (morale, verity, mettle) of any
(85, 100) information we gain from the Internet.

2. The prefix *re-* means "(two, again, under)."
(99)

3. The prefix *uni-* means "(same, three, one)."
(98)

4. I admired the girl's (reconciliation, patience, allegation)
(81, 104) as she waited for her turn on the swing.

5. (Who, Whom) first manufactured ice cream?
(66, 68)

6. Mistress Mary (sure, surely) is growing magnificent
(93) flowers.

7. She walked (in, into) her house after gardening.
(17, 96)

8. Have you been (studiing, studying) the spelling rules?
(9, 21)

For 9–11, refer to this sentence: Although we can guess, we cannot know for certain the date of the invention of ice cream.

9. Write the independent clause.
(24, 61)

10. Write the dependent or subordinate clause.
(61, 63)

11. Write the subordinating conjunction.
(61, 99)

12. Write and capitalize the proper noun in this
(6, 29) sentence: There is reason to believe that ice cream originated in italy.

13. Write the indirect object in this sentence: In 1769, Mrs.
(25, 35) Elizabeth Raffald gave us the recipe for ice cream.

14. Write the comparative adjective in this sentence: I ate
(45, 46) more ice cream than he.

Rewrite 15 and 16, adding commas where they are needed.

15. Dear Cory
(52, 56)   In America ice cream was first advertised by a man named Hall on June 8 1786.
                    Sincerely
                    Amanda

16. There is I believe a record of Mrs. Johnson serving ice
(47, 56) cream at a ball in New York on December 12 1789.

17. Write and hyphenate words that should be hyphenated in
(83, 86) this sentence: Mistress Mary tended her well kept
garden.

Write each adverb in sentences 18–20.

18. Flowers called "pretty maids" grow here.
(84, 87)

19. The flowers grow best under Miss Mary's care.
(84)

20. Silver bells and cockle shells grow beautifully in her
(84) garden.

21. Write each prepositional phrase in this sentence and tell
(33, 95) which word it modifies: Mistress Mary worked in her
garden for fun.

22. Rewrite this sentence, adding a semicolon where it is
(92) needed: Los Angeles is in California it is north of San
Diego and south of San Francisco.

23. Rewrite this sentence, adding a colon where it is
(94) needed: I want one thing for my birthday a parakeet.

24. Write the possessive form of a–c.
(97, 98)
(a) bass   (b) alto and tenor (parts)   (c) choir directors

25. Write the contraction of the year 2001.
(97, 98)

26. Rewrite this sentence, adding parentheses where they are
(101) needed: The *Architeuthis* giant squid has the largest
eyes of any beast.

27. For a–c, write each word, and underline each silent letter.
(103, 104)
(a) written   (b) knot   (c) plumber

28. Write the letter that comes before a silent *b*.
(103, 104)

Diagram sentences 29 and 30.

29. Yes, I will buy you some ice cream.
(25, 35)

30. During the sixteenth century, Catherine de Medici took
(34, 95) ice cream from Italy to France.

LESSON 106

Spelling Rules: Suffixes, Part 2

> **Dictation or Journal Entry**
>
> **Vocabulary:**
> *Generous* is an adjective meaning "willing to give or share freely; unselfish."
> My *generous* friend gave me one of his favorite books. *Generously* is an
> adverb. He *generously* distributed food to the needy. *Generosity* is a noun.
> My unselfish friend is known for his *generosity*.

Doubling Final Consonants When a one-syllable word ends with a single consonant preceded by a single vowel, we double the final consonant before adding a suffix that begins with a vowel.

$$\text{mop} + \text{ed} = \text{mopped}$$

$$\text{win} + \text{er} = \text{winner}$$

$$\text{drop} + \text{ing} = \text{dropping}$$

$$\text{big} + \text{est} = \text{biggest}$$

$$\text{fun} + \text{y} = \text{funny}$$

Exceptions include the words *bus* (bused), *sew* (sewing), *bow* (bowed), and *tax* (taxing).

When a word of two or more syllables ends with a single consonant preceded by a single vowel, we double the final consonant if the word is accented (stressed) on the last syllable.

$$\text{begin} + \text{ing} = \text{beginning}$$

$$\text{prefer} + \text{ed} = \text{preferred}$$

$$\text{commit} + \text{ed} = \text{committed}$$

Do Not Double We **do not** double the final consonant of any of the words described above (words ending with a single consonant preceded by a single vowel) when adding a suffix that begins with a consonant.

$$\text{glad} + \text{ly} = \text{gladly}$$

$$\text{hat} + \text{less} = \text{hatless}$$

$$\text{sad} + \text{ness} = \text{sadness}$$

We **do not** double the final consonant if it is preceded by two vowels or another consonant:

$$\text{rain} + \text{ed} = \text{rained}$$

$$\text{broad} + \text{ly} = \text{broadly}$$

$$\text{warm} + \text{est} = \text{warmest}$$

$$\text{wish} + \text{ful} = \text{wishful}$$

Example   Add suffixes to these words.

(a) hop + ing = _____

(b) admit + ed = _____

(c) mad + ly = _____

(d) cloud + less = _____

(e) chalk + y = _____

Solution   (a) hop + ing = **hopping** (We double the final consonant when we add a suffix beginning with a vowel.)

(b) admit + ed = **admitted** (When a two-syllable word is accented on the final syllable, we double the final consonant if it is preceded by a single vowel.)

(c) mad + ly = **madly** (When the suffix begins with a consonant, we do not double the final consonant before adding the suffix.)

(d) cloud + less = **cloudless** (A final consonant preceded by two vowels is not doubled.)

(e) chalk + y = **chalky** (A final consonant preceded by another consonant is not doubled.)

Practice   Add suffixes to words a–e.

a. snap + ed = _____

b. top + ing = _____

c. sad + ly = _____

d. befit + ed = _____

e. glad + ness = _____

For f–h, replace each blank with *generous*, *generously*, or *generosity*.

f. One who is willing to share is _____.

g. Another word for *unselfishness* is _____.

h. The older students _____ gave extra help to the younger students.

Choose the best word to complete sentences 1–8.

1. The husband's (fidelity, perseverance, diligence) to his
   (16, 103) wife was evidence of their strong marriage.

2. I hope I will conquer the fear of flying (sometime, some
   (102) time, sometimes).

3. (Sometime, Some time, Sometimes) people's fears are
   (102) irrational.

4. After the loss of a loved one, (sometime, sometimes, some
   (102) time) must pass before our sorrow diminishes.

5. The zoo visitors were (told, telled, tell) that elephants do
   (75, 76) not grow as tall as generally supposed.

6. Humpty Dumpty didn't feel (good, well) after his fall off
   (85) the wall.

7. He was (really, real) glad that the King's horses and men
   (93) came to help him.

8. Within a quotation, we use (brackets, semicolons) to
   (92, 101) insert our own explanations or comments.

9. Write the first person personal pronoun in this
   (53, 58) sentence: She told me that elephants grow to
   approximately eleven or twelve feet in height.

10. Write the perfect tense verb phrase in this sentence: We
    (9, 19) have overestimated the elephant's size.

11. Write the collective noun in this sentence: The adult
    (8) males of the African species are the largest elephants.

12. Write each word that should be capitalized in this
    (12, 30) sentence: the tallest elephants on record lived in east
    africa and measured eleven feet four inches.

13. Write whether this word group is a phrase or a
    (24, 61) clause: the most accurate estimate of a large elephant's
    weight

Rewrite sentences 14 and 15, adding commas where they are needed.

14. Remember I spotted the elusive reclusive short-eared
(47, 56) owl on March 4 2002.

15. The veterinarian asked "Have you fed washed weighed
(56, 65) and measured your elephant?"

16. Rewrite this sentence, adding quotation marks if
(69, 70) needed: Wally replied, No, I haven't had time to do all
that.

Write each adverb in sentences 17 and 18.

17. Humpty Dumpty sat precariously on the wall.
(84)

18. Suddenly, he fell down.
(84, 89)

19. Write the prepositional phrase used as an adverb in this
(33, 95) sentence, and tell which word it modifies: Throughout
the day, the King's men glued together pieces of Mr.
Dumpty.

20. Write whether the italicized word in this sentence is a
(17, 96) preposition or an adverb: Humpty fell *off* the wall.

21. Rewrite this sentence, adding a semicolon where it is
(92) needed: Tigers have striped fur they also have striped
skin.

22. Rewrite this sentence, adding a colon where it is needed:
(94) The following quote is from *David Copperfield* "The
influence of the Murdstones upon me [David] was like
the fascination of two snakes on a wretched young bird."

23. Write the possessive form of each plural noun.
(97, 98) (a) spiders   (b) sheep   (c) cattle

24. Write the contraction for the words *they* and *are*.
(97, 98)

25. Write the interjection in this sentence: Oops, I forgot
(1, 102) your birthday.

26. Rewrite words a–c, and underline each silent letter.
(103, 104) (a) lamb   (b) knee   (c) patch

27. Write the silent letter that you see in these words: chalk,
(103, 104) talk, folk, palm, should

28. Write the past tense of each verb.
(7, 16)
(a) say   (b) pay   (c) lay

29. Add suffix *-ed* to the word *drop*.
(105, 106)

30. Diagram this sentence: Jumbo, Marsha's pony, easily
(25, 34) won the prize for the longest tail.

LESSON
107

Spelling Rules: *ie* or *ei*

> **Dictation or Journal Entry**
> **Vocabulary:**
> *Procrastinate* is a verb meaning "to put off doing something until a future time." We *procrastinate* if we postpone or delay doing our work. *Procrastination* and *procrastinator* are nouns. *Procrastination* is a bad habit. A *procrastinator* often misses deadlines.

To determine whether to use *ie* or *ei* to make the long *e* sound in a word, we recall this rhyme:

Use *i* before *e*

Except *after* c

Or when sounded like *ay*

As in *neighbor* and *weigh*.

USE *i* BEFORE *e*:

bel*ie*ve	y*ie*ld	sh*ie*ld	br*ie*f	v*ie*w
ch*ie*f	pr*ie*st	n*ie*ce	rel*ie*ve	ach*ie*ve

EXCEPT AFTER *c*:

c*ei*ling	rec*ei*ve	conc*ei*t
dec*ei*ve	conc*ei*ve	perc*ei*ve

OR WHEN SOUNDED LIKE *ay*:

n*ei*ghbor	w*ei*gh	fr*ei*ght	r*ei*gn

Exceptions The following words are exceptions to the rule. We must memorize them.

either	neither	leisure	seize
ancient	height	forfeit	weird

Example Write the words that are spelled correctly.

(a) yeild, yield (b) beleive, believe

(c) cieling, ceiling (d) receipt, reciept

(e) nieghbor, neighbor (f) wiegh, weigh

Solution (a) **yield** (Use *i* before *e*.) (b) **believe**

(c) **ceiling** (Except after *c*.)   (d) **receipt**

(e) **neighbor** (Or when sounded as *ay*.)

(f) **weigh**

Practice For a–f, write the words that are spelled correctly.

    a. preist, priest   **b.** neice, niece

    c. decieve, deceive   **d.** percieve, perceive

    e. freight, frieght   **f.** riegn, reign

For g–i, replace each blank with *procrastinate, procrastinator,* or *procrastination.*

    g. I will do it now; I will not _____.

    h. He used to be a _____, but now he does his work immediately.

    i. Debby's _____ resulted in poor productivity.

Review Set
107

Choose the best word to complete sentences 1–9.

    1. Waiting until the night before a big exam to study is one
(106, 107) example of (willpower, perseverance, procrastination).

    2. A (punctual, unique, generous) person gives away money
(1, 106) and possessions to those in need.

    3. Mending one's socks rather than buying a new pair is an
(23, 105) example of (frugality, compassion, morale).

    4. Having belief in something that one cannot see is an
(1, 103) example of (compassion, faith, punctuality).

    5. Neither the *Sequoia washingtoniana* nor the *Sequoia*
(80, 81) *sempervirens* (is, are) as large as the giant eucalyptus or peppermint tree of Australia.

    6. Did the iguana eat (good, well) while we were away?
(84, 85)

    7. Ms. Perrin bakes (gooder, best, better) bread than the
(84, 91) bakery can.

(84, 93)   **8.** I think we sang (real, really) well on that song!

9. The cashier handed me a (receipt, reciept).
(107)

10. Write the past tense of the verb *grip*.
(105, 106)

11. Write the present perfect progressive verb phrase in this
(9, 21) sentence: Baron von Mueller has been recording heights of more than four hundred feet for the Australian eucalyptus tree.

12. Tell whether this word group is a phrase or a clause: the
(24, 61) tall trees of California's coast

Write each word that should be capitalized in sentences 13 and 14.

13. miss myrtus declared, "the united states forest service
(12, 20) has found specimens four hundred eighty feet tall."

14. i believe uncle bill visited the california redwoods last
(12, 6) may.

15. Rewrite this sentence, adding commas where they are
(47, 52) needed: Firs poplars and cottonwoods grow very tall.

16. Write the antecedent for the italicized pronoun in this
(51, 53) sentence: Valentine, will *you* be mine?

17. Rewrite this sentence, adding quotation marks where
(69, 70) they are needed: Curly Locks is the name of a nursery rhyme I learned years ago.

18. Write the prepositional phrase used as an adverb in this
(33, 95) sentence, and tell which word it modifies: Boldly, Betsy went through the door.

19. Write whether the italicized word in this sentence is an
(17, 96) adverb or a preposition: Barney was afraid to look *down*.

20. Rewrite this sentence, adding a semicolon where it is
(92) needed: I am taller than Jane regardless, she always beats me at basketball.

21. Rewrite this sentence, adding a colon where it is needed:
(94) You have two choices either go or stay.

22. Write the plural possessive form of each singular noun.
(97, 98) (a) man   (b) woman   (c) child

23. Rewrite this sentence, adding apostrophes where they are
(97, 98) needed: Johns professor gives *As* only to outstanding
students.

24. Rewrite this sentence, adding brackets where they are
(101) needed: In the novel, the main character said, "I think
she meaning Mrs. Wu ate the last muffin."

25. Write whether this sentence is true or false: When we
(102) write, we should use as many interjections as we possibly
can.

26. Rewrite words a–c, and underline each silent letter.
(103, 104) (a) thumb   (b) talk   (c) writing

27. Write the silent letter that usually follows the letter *g* and
(103, 104) reminds us to pronounce the "hard" *g*.

28. Add the suffix *-ly* to the word *true*.
(105, 106)

29. Add the suffix *-ful* to the word *plate*.
(105, 106)

30. Diagram this sentence: Neither you nor I can quit yet.
(38, 39)

Appendix

Dictations

Week 1
In the 1830s, England sent her poor and helpless to workhouses. These unfortunate people worked long hours for ragged clothes and little food. Charles Dickens expressed his concern for this practice in his book <u>Oliver Twist</u>. The main character, Oliver, spends his childhood in a workhouse. He and the other orphans nearly starve to death.

Week 2
People of all ages enjoy the book <u>The Secret Garden</u> by Frances Hodgson Burnett. The main character, Mary Lennox, is an orphan like Oliver Twist. Mary's parents die during a plague of cholera in India, leaving her to live with a bizarre uncle in England. The secret garden provides a place of escape for an extremely unhappy and lonely girl. The gardener, Ben Weatherstaff, helps Mary overcome her struggles and shows her the value of nature and love.

Week 3
William Shakespeare authored one of the most famous love stories of all time. Written in 1597, <u>Romeo and Juliet</u> contains beautiful poetic lines that people still quote today. Although some readers find the poetry difficult to understand, they still appreciate the dramatic and remarkable language. Romeo belongs to the Montague family, and Juliet is a member of the Capulet family. For a very long time, a feud has raged between these two noble families. This feud makes Romeo and Juliet's marriage impossible, and ultimately leads to their deaths.

Week 4   George Orwell wrote the book <u>Animal Farm</u> in defiance of totalitarianism, the belief that an all-powerful government should rule over every area of people's lives. George Orwell, a political writer, urged people to rise up against power-hungry leaders like Adolf Hitler. In <u>Animal Farm</u>, animal characters reveal how people behave when they have too much power. Old Major, a boar, incites the animals to fight against the humans.

Week 5   <u>The Diary of Anne Frank</u> contains the written entries of a girl named Anne Frank. Anne Frank, a German Jewish girl, was a victim of the Holocaust. The Holocaust refers to the German Nazis' attempt to exterminate the Jews. Anne Frank hid from the German Nazis for two years in Amsterdam. The Frank family and some friends lived in a secret apartment in a warehouse. Anne Frank died in a concentration camp at the age of sixteen.

Week 6   "I Have a Dream" is a famous speech delivered by Martin Luther King, Jr., on August 28, 1963. Martin Luther King was a Southern Baptist minister who dreamed of a country that overcomes its divisions and learns to live together in love. Dr. King is considered the most influential civil rights leader of all time. Always believing the best, he encouraged nonviolent means to bring about change.

Week 7   John F. Kennedy was elected president of the United States in 1961, at forty-two years of age. He was the youngest person ever elected to the presidency. John F. Kennedy delivered a powerful inaugural address. He identified a new, younger generation of Americans who would now lead our country. He described a new generation that would guide the United States and the world into freedom, cooperation, and democracy.

Week 8 Many students enjoy reading <u>The Adventures of Huckleberry Finn</u>, the story of a young boy named Huckleberry Finn. Huck tries to escape the restrictions of society by running away from his guardian, Widow Douglas, and his dad, Pap. He joins a runaway slave named Jim on Jackson's Island. Huck and Jim experience different life events while floating down the Mississippi River on a raft. Huck and Jim attempt to go to the North to obtain Jim's freedom.

Week 9 Robert Louis Stevenson, born in Scotland in 1850, contributed much to classical literature. His novel <u>Treasure Island</u> tells the story of Jim Hawkins, a thirteen-year-old boy. Like many boys his age, Jim finds maps and hidden treasure fascinating. He and a friend, an old pirate named Long John Silver, discover hidden treasure. Unfortunately, Long John Silver is also a killer. Besides magnificent riches, Jim Hawkins encounters a dangerous adventure.

Week 10 We find the inaugural oath of the President of the United States in Article II, Section 1, of the Constitution of the United States of America. It reads: "I do solemnly swear (or affirm) that I will faithfully execute the Office of President of the United States, and will to the best of my ability, preserve, protect, and defend the Constitution of the United States." At his inauguration in 1789, George Washington completed the oath by uttering the words "So help me, God." Every subsequent president has followed Washington's example and added this phrase at the end of his oath.

Week 11   A preamble is an introductory statement to a document. The Preamble to the Constitution was written in 1787. It reads as follows: We, the people of the United States, in order to form a more perfect Union, establish justice, insure domestic tranquility, provide for the common defense, promote the general welfare, and secure the blessings of liberty to ourselves and our posterity, do ordain and establish this Constitution for the United States of America.

Week 12   On November 19, 1863, in Gettysburg, Pennsylvania, President Lincoln delivered a speech of three short paragraphs. This speech is often referred to as the Gettysburg Address. Here are the first few lines: Fourscore and seven years ago our fathers brought forth on this continent a new nation, conceived in liberty, and dedicated to the proposition that all men are created equal. Now we are engaged in a great civil war, testing whether that nation, or any nation so conceived and so dedicated, can long endure.

Week 13   Abraham Lincoln continued the Gettysburg Address: We are met on a great battlefield of that war. We have come to dedicate a portion of that field, as a final resting place for those who here gave their lives that that nation might live. It is altogether fitting and proper that we should do this. But, in a larger sense, we can not dedicate—we can not consecrate—we can not hallow—this ground.

Week 14   The Gettysburg Address continues with these lines: The brave men, living and dead, who struggled here, have consecrated it, far above our poor power to add or detract. The world will little note, nor long remember what we say here, but it can never forget what they did here. It is for us the living, rather, to be dedicated here to the unfinished work which they who fought here have thus far so nobly advanced.

Week 15　　Abraham Lincoln concluded his Gettysburg Address with these lines: It is rather for us to be here dedicated to the great task remaining before us—that from these honored dead we take increased devotion to that cause for which they gave the last full measure of devotion—that we here highly resolve that these dead shall not have died in vain—that this nation, under God, shall have a new birth of freedom—and that government of the people, by the people, for the people, shall not perish from the earth.

Week 16　　At Plymouth Rock, on December 22, 1820, the famous orator Daniel Webster delivered a speech that summarized the significance of the Pilgrims for all Americans. In this speech, now known as "The Plymouth Oration," he honored the Pilgrim Fathers for their sufferings, labors, virtues, piety, and principles of civil and religious liberty. "Whatever makes men good Christians, makes them good citizens," he said.

Week 17　　In 1636, sixteen years after landing on the shores of North America, the English Puritans of Massachusetts Bay founded Harvard College, the first institution of higher learning in North America. This school was located in Cambridge, a town near Boston. Here, students would study Greek, Latin, and the Hebrew Bible. To enter Harvard, a student had to first be able to read and speak Latin, be familiar with the classics, and know Greek grammar.

Week 18　　Francis Scott Key was an American lawyer and poet born in Maryland in 1779. During the War of 1812, he witnessed the British bombardment of Fort McHenry in Baltimore Harbor. The sight of the American flag still flying over the fort at daybreak inspired him to write the poem "The Star-Spangled Banner," which became the national anthem of the United States. We often sing this song at major sporting events, including the Olympics.

Week 19   The Star-Spangled Banner

O say, can you see, by the dawn's early light,
What so proudly we hailed at the twilight's last gleaming,
Whose broad stripes and bright stars, thro' the perilous fight,
O'er the ramparts we watched, were so gallantly streaming?
And the rockets' red glare, the bombs bursting in air,
Gave proof thro' the night that our flag was still there.
O say, does that star-spangled banner yet wave
O'er the land of the free and the home of the brave?

Week 20   Ogden Nash (1902-1971), a popular American writer of light verse, became famous for his satirical poetry with far-fetched rhyme and silly puns. Many of his poems appeared in the Saturday Evening Post. In 1931, Ogden Nash dedicated to his mother a collection of poems called Many Long Years Ago, which includes "The Panther":

The panther is like a leopard,
Except it hasn't been peppered.
Should you behold a panther crouch,
Prepare to say Ouch.
Better yet, if called by a panther,
Don't anther.*

*Ogden Nash. *Many Long Years Ago.* Little, Brown and Company. Boston, 1945.

Week 21   In order to be the best person that one can be, one must cultivate certain character traits. Self-discipline, a desirable character trait, refers to one's ability to teach, train, or discipline oneself. In order to control appetites, tempers, passions, or impulses, one must possess self-discipline. Musicians, artists, athletes, and students all exercise self-discipline as they practice and learn new skills. People use self-discipline to improve their quality of life.

Week 22   Another character trait we should cultivate is compassion, a sympathetic attitude that prompts us to stand with another person who is experiencing difficulty.

Compassion stirs our desire to help others. A caring person does not callously disregard anyone. Compassion allows us to see our neighbor as ourself. If we have prejudice, we cannot exhibit compassion. The world will be a better place when we learn to have compassion for all people and treat them as we would like to be treated.

Week 23   We add respectfulness to compassion and self-discipline as desirable attributes. We try to be respectful of other people and things. Citizens of the United States show respect for their flag by keeping it from ever touching the ground and by shining a light on it at night. Sometimes men show respect for women by standing up when a woman enters the room. Youths show respect for adults by addressing them as Mr. or Mrs. We demonstrate respect for our peers by treating them the way we would like to be treated ourselves.

Week 24   Quality people are responsible. Responsible people accept the blame when they make a mistake. They try to make wise choices regarding the use of their time and money. They complete their chores and homework, and they arrive on time to school or work. Responsibility is a sign of maturity. Employers and friends know they can depend on someone who is responsible. Therefore, responsible people earn other people's trust and admiration.

Week 25   The Declaration of Independence
In Congress, July 4, 1776
(first paragraph)

When, in the Course of human events, it becomes necessary for one people to dissolve the political bands which have connected them with another, and to assume, among the powers of the earth, the separate and equal station to which the laws of nature and of nature's God entitle them, a decent respect to the opinions of mankind requires that they should declare the causes which impel them to the separation.

Week 26 The Declaration of Independence
(continued)

We hold these truths to be self-evident: that all men are created equal; that they are endowed by their Creator with certain unalienable rights; that among these are Life, Liberty, and the pursuit of Happiness; that, to secure these rights, governments are instituted among men, deriving their just powers from the consent of the governed....

Week 27 If I Can Stop One Heart from Breaking
by Emily Dickinson (1830–1886)

If I can stop one heart from breaking,

I shall not live in vain;

If I can ease one life the aching,

Or cool one pain,

Or help one fainting robin

Unto his nest again,

I shall not live in vain.

Week 28 Possibly the most famous boundary in America is the Mason-Dixon line, which divides Pennsylvania and Maryland. The Mason-Dixon line received its name from Englishmen Jeremiah Mason, an astronomer, and Charles Dixon, a surveyor. The pair surveyed the region between 1763 and 1767, but the Mason-Dixon line didn't become nationally known until the Civil War, when all the states north of it had abolished slavery, and none of those to the south had taken such action. Some of the stone markers set by Mason and Dixon are still in place.

Week 29 The Underground Railroad began about one hundred fifty years ago. It was a secret network of routes with guides, safe houses, and supporters used by Africans and their descendants to escape from slavery in this country. African Americans living in Delaware or Virginia usually headed north. Those living in the deep South traveled toward Mexico. On their way to freedom, they hid in the homes, churches, and schoolhouses of those who supported them.

Week 30   Through the Underground Railroad, tens of thousands of people escaped slavery with the help of more than three thousand guides, or "conductors." Harriet Tubman, a famous black conductor, had served as a field hand and house servant on a Maryland plantation before escaping to the North before the Civil War. In her nineteen trips south, Harriet Tubman rescued more than three hundred slaves, including her own parents. She personally guided these people to freedom in Canada and became known as "the Moses of her people."

Journal Topics

1. Describe your family pet or one you'd like to have.

2. Describe your favorite sport.

3. Have you been to the doctor or dentist? Tell about your experience.

4. What is your favorite season of the year? Why?

5. Describe your favorite food.

6. Explain why it is important to be punctual.

7. Write an example of a story with a moral. For instance, you might write:

   The tortoise and the hare ran a race. The hare knew that he was much faster than the tortoise, so he decided to take a nap and play around. The tortoise won the race because he stayed focused on the task in front of him. The moral of the story is to give every situation your best effort.

8. Describe a place where you might find natural rocks.

9. Describe an invention of the twentieth century.

10. What future event are you anticipating? Why?

11. Write about a natural disaster (fire, earthquake, storm, etc.).

12. Discuss the steps in planning a party.

13. Describe a train.

14. How do you celebrate Independence Day on July 4th?

15. How do you decide what clothes to wear each day?

16. Have you ever experienced a cold, the flu, or allergies? Describe your discomfort.

17. Write about your favorite color or colors. Where do you see these colors?

18. Write about a feminine noun of your choice.

19. Everyone has experienced a disagreement with another person. Tell about an argument you have had, and explain how you solved it.

20. Describe your favorite teacher and his or her special characteristics.

21. Describe your favorite meal.

22. If you could visit anywhere in the world, where would you go?

23. Describe ice cream.

24. Have you visited a capital city in the United States? Give some details about a capital city.

25. Which president of the United States do you most admire? Why?

26. Do you know someone who would make a good president of the United States? What makes you think so?

27. Using many descriptive adjectives, tell about a beautiful day.

28. Give an example of someone showing compassion.

29. Presidents need courage to lead the United States. Tell about a time when one of our presidents demonstrated courage.

30. How can we show sympathy for someone who has lost a loved one?

31. What is your favorite movie or video? Why?

32. Give some examples of courteous behavior.

33. How do we show respect for the flag of the United States of America?

34. Choose a game show on which you would like to be a contestant. Give some reasons why you would be a good contestant.

35. Tell about your favorite type of music.

36. Describe your favorite athlete.

37. Do you have a favorite song? Describe the person or group that sings it, or describe the song.

38. Tell about a professional or college sports team, or tell about a sports team you know.

39. Describe the perfect vacation.

40. Tell how you can demonstrate responsible behavior.

41. Describe a conscientious person that you know. How does this person show that he or she is conscientious?

42. How can friends demonstrate loyalty to one another?

43. To what do you pledge your allegiance? Why?

44. How can you show respect for your family?

45. Tell about a time when you displayed the virtue of integrity.

46. Share one of your most embarrassing moments.

47. If you could live anywhere in the world, where would you choose to live? Why?

48. Describe a career that you consider worthwhile.

49. How should you treat your best friend?

50. Think of a literary or TV character that resembles you. Describe him or her.

51. Describe a desert.

52. What is your favorite dessert? Name its ingredients and describe how it looks and tastes.

53. Your friends demonstrate some positive character traits. Tell about those traits.

54. What do you like most about your family?

55. Describe how you study for a test.

56. Describe one of your siblings. If you are an only child, describe a friend or relative.

57. Tell about a time when you practiced generosity.

58. What do you like best about yourself?

59. Have you ever shown courage? Describe the incident.

60. Sometimes people have very vivid dreams. Tell about a dream you've had.

61. We admire generous people. Describe a generous person you know.

62. Sometimes it is difficult to be patient. Tell about a time when you exercised patience.

63. Tell about a time when someone had patience with you.

64. Describe a person you know who has a good sense of humor.

65. Sometimes small children do and say funny things. Describe something that you did or said when you were small, or describe something you saw a small child do or say.

66. Some people like snakes and lizards. Others don't. How do you feel about them?

67. If you were to fix a meal for a friend, what would you make? Explain how you would do it.

68. Explain how or why self-discipline is important in your life.

69. Describe a humble person that you know.

70. Sometimes it is difficult to forgive. Tell about a time when you forgave someone.

71. Tell about a time when someone forgave you.

72. Explain why people need to have prudence.

73. Describe an injustice in the world.

74. What new skill would you like to learn someday? Why?

75. If you were a teacher, what grade and subjects would you like to teach? Why?

76. Why is it important to use discretion in choosing our friends?

77. Describe your conscience.

78. What is the most beautiful thing you have ever seen?

79. What is your favorite smell? Why?

80. Describe the sounds you hear at night.

81. What is your least favorite time of day? Why?

82. Tell about your favorite vacation.

83. If you could visit any place, where would it be?

84. What makes someone brave?

85. What will your life be like ten years from now?

86. If you could choose someone famous to meet, whom would you choose?

87. If you had been born one hundred years ago, how would your life be different?

88. Describe what you think your mother was like when she was your age.

89. Describe what you think your father was like when he was your age.

90. If you could get into a time machine and travel back to any time in history, what time would you choose? Why?

91. What is your favorite holiday? Why?

92. Who would you most like to see walk into the room where you are right now? Why?

93. If you could change one thing about yourself, what would it be?

94. Would you rather be too hot or too cold? Why?

95. If you could visit another planet, which one would you choose? Why?

Index

B

Bad or *Badly*, 501
Bare, 392
Be, 68–69
Bear, 392
Between, 78
Bi-, 58
Biannual, 517
Bicycle, 58
Bilingual, 58
Bio-, 48
Biography, 48
Biology, 48
Biosphere, 48
Blew, 494
Blue, 494
Borrow, 293
Both—and (correlative conjunction), 192
Brackets, 545
Brake, 234
But (conjunction), 182–183

C

Can, 240
Capital, 146
Capitalization, 24–25, 53, 94–95, 126,
    141–142, 151–152
  abbreviations and initials, 126
  areas of country, 141
  family words, 126
  first word in line of poetry, 53
  first word of direct quotation, 95
  first word of sentence, 53
  greetings and closings, 142
  hyphenated words, 152
  I, 53
  literary and music titles, 94
  outlines, 95
  proper adjectives 146, 151
  proper nouns, 24–25
  religions, Bible, deity, 141
  rules for, 24–25, 53, 94–95, 126, 141–142,
    151–152
  school subjects, 126
  seasons of the year, 152
  titles of persons (family words), 126
Capitol, 146
Case, 207–208, 211–212, 281–283, 293–295,
    300–302
  nominative, 207–208
  nominative pronoun, 281–283
  objective, 211–212
  objective pronoun 293–295
  personal pronoun 300–302
  possessive, 207–208
Cent, 407
Cite, 512
Clarity, 459
Clause, 116–117, 182, 315–316, 533–534
  dependent, 116–117, 315–316, 533–534
  independent 116–117, 315–316, 533–534
  subordinate, 315–316, 533–534
Coarse, 34
Collective noun, 35, 431
Colon, 506–508
Comma, 234–235, 245–247, 263–264,
    287–289, 327–328, 332–334,
    339–340, 494–495
  after dependent clauses, 328
  after introductory words, 287–288
  before conjunction 332–334, 339
  in compound sentence, 332–334, 339
  in dates, 234
  in direct address, 245
  in direct quotation, 340
  in letter, 263–264
  in series, 235, 495
  in titles or academic degrees, 245
  reversed names, 263–264
  separating descriptive adjectives,
    327–328
  with appositives, 246
  with interjections, 549–550
  words out of natural order, 287–288
Common noun, 24–25
Comparative degree, 221–224, 228–229,
    488–490
Comparison adjectives, 221–224, 228–229
Comparison adverbs, 488–490
Comparisons using pronouns, 353
Compassion, 105
Complete sentence, 9, 14
Complex sentence, 533–534
Compound adjective, 459
Compound forms, hyphen in, 43–44, 443
Compound nouns, forming plurals, 64
Compound parts of sentence, 187–188,
    533–535
  diagramming, 187–188
  subject and verbs, 187

Exclamation point or mark, 1, 407–408, 549–550
Exclamatory sentence, 1, 407–408

F

Faint, 135
Family words, 126
Feint, 135
Fewer, 99, 228
Fidelity, 554
For, 182–183, 332
Forbearance, 558
Fore-, 332
Foreign words and phrases, 388
Four, 332
Frac-, 257
Fraction, 257
Fractions, hyphens in, 460
Fractious, 257
Fracture, 257
Fragment, sentence, 9, 14
    defined, 9
    correcting, 14
Frugal, 563
Frugality, 563
Frugally, 563
Future perfect progressive tense, 100–101
Future perfect tense, 89–90
Future progressive tense, 100–101
Future tense, 48–49

G

Generosity, 569
Generous, 569
Generously, 569
Geo-, 28
Geography, 28
Geology, 28
Good or *well*, 454–455
Greeting, in a letter, 142, 263

H

Hangar, 263
Hanger, 263
Heal, 449
Hear, 358
Heel, 449
Helping verb(s), 39
Hemi-, 352
Hemiplegia, 352
Hemisphere, 352
Hemistich, 352
Here, 358

Hole, 116
Homo-, 14
Homonyms, 14
Homophones, 14
Honor, 24
Humility, 370
Hyphen(s), 443–445, 471–472
    in compound nouns, 443
    in fractions, 460–461
    in numbers, 444
    in word division, 471–472

I

I, me, 53, 268, 281–283, 293–295, 300–302
Icon, 425
Imperative Sentence, 1
Improving our writing, 20, 131, 240
Imply, 419
In-, 141
Incapacitate, 141
Incredible, 141
Indefinite adjective, 136
Indefinite pronoun, 380–383, 425
Independence, 151
Independent clause, 315, 533–534
Indict, 192
Indirect object 172–173, 211, 294–295
    defined, 172
    diagramming, 173–174
    recognizing, 172–173
Indirect quotation, 366
Infer, 419
Initials, 126
Injustice, 151
Integrity, 24
Intensive pronoun, 322
Interjection, 549–550
Interrogative pronoun, 358–359
Interrogative sentence, 1
Interrupting elements, 408–409
Interruptions (dash), 408–409
Intransitive verb, 156–157
Introductory elements, 287
Invalid, 281
Irregular plural noun(s), 58–59, 62–64
    defined, 58
    forms, 58–59, 62–64
    rules for forming, 58–59, 62–64
Irregular verbs, 68–69, 275–276, 392–393, 397–398, 402–403
    be, have, do, 68–69, 538
    defined, 68

as an object, 270, 293–295, 300–302, 344, 352–353
case, 269–270, 300–302
compound personal, 295
contractions, distinguishing between, 311, 360
demonstrative, 375–376
diagramming, 306–307, 321
I, 53
indefinite, 380–381, 425
intensive, 322
interrogative, 358–359
modifiers, 310–311
nominative case, 269, 281–283, 300–302
number, 269, 382, 414–415
objective case, 270, 293–295, 300–302
person, 268–269, 300–302, 413–415
personal, 268–269, 300–302
possessive, 270, 300–301, 310–311, 345
reflexive, 321
relative, 344–345
use of *who* and *whom*, 346–347, 358–359
Proper adjective, 146, 151
capitalization of, 146, 151
Proper noun(s), 24–25, 34–35
abstract, 34–35
capitalization of, 24–25
Prudence, 178
Punctual, 1
Punctuation
apostrophe, 44, 523–524, 528–529
brackets, 543–544
colon, 506–508
comma, 234–235, 245–247, 263–264, 287–289, 327–328, 339–340, 533–534, 549–550
dash, 408–409
exclamation mark, 407–408, 549–550
hyphen, 152, 443–445, 459–462, 471–472
italics or underline, 387–389
parentheses, 543–544
period, 1, 178–179, 196–198
of appositives, 246–247
of dialogue, 95, 340, 365, 370
of letters, 142
of outlines, 95, 178–179
of sentence, 178–179
of titles, 94, 371, 387
question mark, 1, 407–408
quotation mark, 95, 340, 365, 370–371, 407–408

semicolon, 494–495
underline or italics, 387–389

Q
Question mark, 1, 407–408
Quotation, direct, 95–96, 340, 365–366, 370–371, 407–408
Quotation, indirect, 366
Quotation marks, 365–366, 370–371, 407–408

R
Raise, 228, 300
Rays, 228
Raze, 228
Re-, 533
Real or *really*, 500–501
Reconcile, 397
Reconciliation, 397
Reflexive pronoun, 321–322
Regular verb, 28–31, 74–75, 89–90, 99–101
Relative pronoun, 344–347
Reliable, 9
Religions, capitalization of, 141–142
Remember, 533
Renames the subject, 201–203
Renew, 533
Report, 533
Respectful, 9
Right, 252
Rise, 300
Rite, 252
Run-on sentence, 10–11, 14
correcting, 14

S
Salutation of letter (colon after), 507–508
Scent, 407
Seasons of the year, 152
Self-discipline, 39
Semi-, 375
Semiannual, 517
Semicircle, 375
Semicolon, 494–495
Semiconscious, 375
Semiprecious, 375
Sent, 407
Sentence, defined, 1, 9–10, 178
capitalization of first word of, 53
combining, 240–241, 332–333
complex, 533–534
compound, 332–333, 339, 533–534

declarative, 1
diagramming, 112–113, 332–334
exclamatory, 1, 407
fragment, 9–11, 14
imperative, 1
improving, 14, 240–241, 332–333
interrogative, 1, 407
punctuation of, 1, 178–179, 407, 494–495
run-on, 9–11, 14, 494
simple, 9–11, 112–113
Series, commas in, 235–236, 495
Set, 207
Sew, 182
Sibling, 306
Sight, 512
Silent letters, 554–555, 558–559
Simple predicate, 5, 112–113
Simple preposition, 78–80, 84
Simple sentence, 5, 112–113
Simple subject, 5, 112–113
Singular, 28–29, 43, 58–59, 62–64, 281–282, 380–381
Sit, 207
Site, 512
So, 182
Some time, 549
Sometime, 549
Sometimes, 549
Sow, 182
Spelling
adding suffixes, 130–131
to words ending in consonants, 569–570
to words ending in silent *e*, 564–565
to words ending in *y*, 563–564
adjectives and adverbs, 449–450
guidelines, 554–555, 558–559, 563–564, 569–570, 574–575
plural forms, 58–59, 62–64
possessives, 523–524
words with awkward prefixes, 461
words with *ie* and *ei*, 574–575
words with silent letters, 554–555, 558–559
Split predicate, 7, 419–421
Stationary, 387
Stationery, 387
Sub-, 62
Subject of a sentence, 207
agreement with verb, 28–29, 68–69
complete, 112–113

compound, 28–29, 187, 414
diagramming, 112–113
of imperative and interrogative sentences, 9, 358–359
pronoun as, 281–282, 307, 425
simple, 5, 112–113
understood, 9
Subject-verb agreement, 28–29, 68–69, 413–415, 419, 425–427, 431
Submarine, 62
Subordinating conjunction, 316–317, 533–534
Subsoil, 62
Substitute, 62
Suburb, 425
Suffixes, 130–131, 481–482
Superlative degree, 221–224, 228–230, 488–490
Sure and *surely*, 499–500
Sympathy, 105

T
Teach, 321
Tense of a verb, 28–31, 48–49, 68–69, 74–75, 89–90, 99–101, 392–393, 397–398, 402
Their, 187
There, 187, 426
They're, 187
Time of day, 196, 507
Titles, 94, 126–127, 196–197, 371, 387
To, 84
Too, 84
Transitive verb, 156, 538–539
Tri-, 58
Triangle, 523
Tricycle, 58
Tripod, 523
Troublesome verbs, 68–69, 275–276, 392–393, 397–398, 402–403
Two, 84

U
Underline or italics, 387–388
Ultra-, 216
Ultraconservative, 216
Ultraviolet, 216
Uni-, 58
Unicorn, 528
Unicycle, 58
Unify, 528
Unique, 528

V

Vain, 436
Vane, 436
Vein, 436
Verb(s), defined, 19
    action, 19–20, 28
    active voice, 538–539
    agreement with subject, 413–415,
        419–421, 425–427, 431–432
    being, 105–106
    compound, 187–188
    diagramming, 112–113
    helping (auxiliary), 39
      list of, 39
    in contractions 426
    irregular, 68–69, 275–276, 392–393,
        397–398, 402–403
    linking, 105–106
    passive voice, 538–539
    principal parts of, 74–75
    regular, 28–31, 48–49
    tense, 28–31, 48–49, 89–90, 99–101
    transitive, 156–157
Verify, 538
Veritable, 538
Verity, 538
Vivid words, 20, 131, 252

W

Waist, 19
Ware, 380
Waste, 19
Weather, 488
Wear, 380
Well and *good*, 454–455
Where, 380
Whether, 488
Who and *whom*, 345–346, 358–360
Who's, 89, 359
Whole, 116
Whose, 89, 359
Willpower, 39
Wright, 252
Write, 252

Y

Yes and *no*, comma after, 287–289
You understood, 9
You're and *Your*, 287